The Early History of Economics in the United States

Since the latter half of the 20th century, the economics departments of American universities were internationally renowned for providing competitive and advanced levels of education. However, from the 1870s up until the beginning of WWI, German universities held international supremacy when it came to the quality of teaching, the enrollment of foreign students, and scholarly publications. This book examines the role of the German Historical School of Economics (GHSE) in the development of the discipline of economics in the US during this period.

The chapters explain that, prior to the influence of the GHSE, political economy was in a dismal state in the US, both as a profession and an academic discipline. As a result, many Americans elected to go to Germany in pursuit of an advanced education in political economy, having been inspired by the unmatched international reputations of theorists of the GHSE. After they returned home, these German-trained Americans challenged the dominant status of classical orthodoxy and revolutionized the discipline of economics in the US by importing the ideas, methods, and approaches of the GHSE. In doing so, they established the first dedicated political economy departments, graduate programs, and chairs at American universities and colleges. Although the precise magnitude and value of the influence of the GHSE is impossible to quantify, there is no doubt that Americans are deeply indebted to this school of thought for its contributions to the early development of the discipline of economics in the US. The chapters also examine what has been lost since: the current mainstream in economics has eliminated many of the features that were once so important to the discipline that it has effectively limited contemporary economics to a small fraction of the complex organism defined by the German Historical School. This situation has facilitated the poverty of the leading economic school of thought, as well as the discipline of economics in general.

This book represents a significant contribution to the literature on the history of economic thought and economic education in the US. It will be of particular interest to students and scholars of economics, political science, sociology, and the philosophy of economics.

Birsen Filip holds a PhD in philosophy and master's degrees in economics and philosophy. She has published numerous articles and chapters on a range of topics, including political philosophy, geopolitics, and the history of economic thought, with a focus on the Austrian School of Economics and the German Historical School of Economics.

Routledge Studies in the History of Economics

Theology, Morality and Adam Smith
Edited by Jordan J. Ballor and Cornelis van der Kooi

Classical Economics, Keynes and Money
Edited by John Eatwell, Pasquale Commendatore and Neri Salvadori

Global Commerce in the Age of Enlightenment
Theories, Practices, and Institutions in the Eighteenth Century
Jesús Bohorquez

Metaphors in the History of Economic Thought
Crises, Business Cycles and Equilibrium
Edited by Roberto Baranzini and Daniele Besomi

Liberalism and the Philosophy of Economics
Tsutomu Hashimoto

An Economic Philosophy of Production, Work and Consumption
A Transhistorical Framework
Rodney Edvinsson

The Early History of Economics in the United States
The Influence of the German Historical School of Economics on Teaching and Theory
Birsen Filip

For more information about this series, please visit: www.routledge.com/series/SE0341

The Early History of Economics in the United States

The Influence of the German Historical School of Economics on Teaching and Theory

Birsen Filip

Routledge
Taylor & Francis Group
LONDON AND NEW YORK

First published 2023
by Routledge
4 Park Square, Milton Park, Abingdon, Oxon OX14 4RN

and by Routledge
605 Third Avenue, New York, NY 10158

Routledge is an imprint of the Taylor & Francis Group, an informa business

British Library Cataloguing-in-Publication Data
A catalogue record for this book is available from the British Library

Library of Congress Cataloging-in-Publication Data
Names: Filip, Birsen, author.
Title: The early history of economics in the United States : the influence of the German Historical School of Economics on teaching and theory / Birsen Filip.
Description: Abingdon, Oxon ; New York, NY : Routledge, 2023. | Series: Routledge studies in the history of economics | Includes bibliographical references and index.
Identifiers: LCCN 2022019572 (print) | LCCN 2022019573 (ebook) | ISBN 9781032162409 (hbk) | ISBN 9781032162454 (pbk) | ISBN 9781003247715 (ebk)
Subjects: LCSH: Economics—United States—History.
Classification: LCC HB119.A2 F55 2023 (print) | LCC HB119.A2 (ebook) | DDC 330.0973—dc23/eng/20220429
LC record available at https://lccn.loc.gov/2022019572
LC ebook record available at https://lccn.loc.gov/2022019573

ISBN: 978-1-032-16240-9 (hbk)
ISBN: 978-1-032-16245-4 (pbk)
ISBN: 978-1-003-24771-5 (ebk)

DOI: 10.4324/9781003247715

Typeset in Bembo
by codeMantra

To Rene, Zoe, and Bombidi

Contents

1 Introduction

The US emerged from WWI as the sole economic and political power in the west, rivaled only by the Soviet Union in the east. During the Cold War Era (1947–1991), American universities were well on their way to becoming the primary models of higher education that would be followed and emulated by their counterparts worldwide. For most of this period, the economics departments of American universities were internationally renowned for providing competitive and advanced levels of education. Then, with the rise of neoliberalism during the Reagan-Thatcher Era, American economists and universities started to become leaders of the discipline and profession of economics around the globe. However, it was not until after the collapse of the Soviet Union that the US officially became an unrivaled world power, which allowed American economists and universities to dominate the discipline of economics on a global scale without a competing school of economic thought. Since then, economics has become increasingly oriented toward abstract mathematical modeling, more so than at any time in the past. In fact, according to neoliberals, the main criterion for being accepted as a respectable and competent economist is to demonstrate a high level of skill in mathematics. Conversely, an inability to master mathematical economics has come to be viewed as a sign of incompetence and ineptness within the discipline.

Neoliberals have proceeded to extensively apply the methods, language, and presentations of mathematics to economics. However, they have been unable to effectively relate their sophisticated mathematical models to real-world issues and problems. That is to say, neoliberals have largely ignored the fact that mathematical expression has limits in economics, as all human preferences, choices, and actions cannot be accurately represented through mathematical equations, presentations, and languages. Instead of trying to understand the true nature of human beings and the motivations behind their choices and actions, neoliberals have elected to oversimplify human nature by promoting the notion that everybody is self-interest oriented, rational, utilitarian, and individualistic, in order to allow them to use their advanced mathematical modeling techniques. This oversimplification of human nature has enabled economists to focus on the purely calculable aspects of life that are mainly associated with material and monetary gain, while

DOI: 10.4324/9781003247715-1

ignoring and escaping from incalculable features that shape the diverse preferences, choices, and actions of human beings, such as culture, traditions, customs, moral and ethical values, and the particular historical development of a society, in addition to countless other factors.

Over the years, neoliberalism has shown itself to have many flaws, errors, and failures. Nonetheless, its leading economists believe that since neoliberalism is the latest program of research, it is the best one to have ever existed, which means it should lead the discipline of economics. In other words, neoliberals did not consider their economic program of research to be a phase in a continuous historical evolution; instead, they defended neoliberalism as being absolutely valid and universal. On this basis, mainstream economists were able to falsely convince themselves that, along with a majority of the economists around the world, neoliberal economics was the only legitimate economic program of research that could lead and shape the discipline and profession of economics and achieve positive outcomes. Consequently, notable theorists and practitioners from the leading school of economic thought (i.e., neoliberalism) have been largely unconcerned with the history of economics and the history of economic thought, because they believed that learning and understanding previously existing economic programs of research was of no benefit for students or economics in general.

In the 1970s, the discipline of economics underwent a series of important changes at American universities, including the official abandonment of the history of economic thought as a mandatory class in most graduate programs, after it had already been neglected for decades. Subsequently, many economics departments around the world followed suit. As a result, the study of the history of economic thought came to be viewed as little more than a mere hobby and a useless endeavor that did not make any important contributions to the progress of the discipline of economics (Filip 2020). In fact, studying, working, and conducting research in the history of economic thought not only became largely irrelevant to the discipline of economics, they were openly unwelcome. These circumstances caused economics students to lose interest in the history of economics and the history of economic thought, which led to the emergence of generations of economists that were, and continue to be, unfamiliar with the origins and historical development of their own discipline. Meanwhile, scholars of the history of economic thought often encountered difficulties when trying to publish their works in leading mainstream economic journals, apply for positions at universities and other institutions, and obtain support for their research (Filip 2020).

The abandonment of the history of economic thought as a mandatory class not only led to students and economists largely forgetting the history of their discipline, it has also inhibited the development of critical and creative thinking. Learning about the goals, failures, concerns, inconsistencies, achievements, successes, and crises of previous schools of economic thought, as well as the work of their adherents, can help avoid similar mistakes, understand current problems, and find effective solutions to them. Doing so could also play a significant role in critiquing and potentially discrediting the neoliberal economic program of research, thereby engendering the emergence of alternative approaches to teaching, studying, and practicing economics. In other words, the rigorous study of the history of economic thought at universities around the world could have brought the dominant status of neoliberalism into question by simply exposing students and economists to alternative views, ideas, methodologies, policies, presentations, and goals that have existed across history.

This book focuses on explaining the instrumental role that the German Historical School of Economics (GHSE) played in the development of the discipline of economics in the US from the late 19th century up until the onset of WWI, particularly the creation of economics departments, graduate schools, and economic chairs at American universities. However, this book will not discuss the important role of Alfred Marshall (1842–1924) in the development of the discipline of economics, even though he extensively studied history and political economy and had a thorough understanding of the GHSE. It will also refrain from exploring the crucial contributions of John Maynard Keynes (1883–1946), though it is important to mention that the rise of Keynesianism, and later neoliberalism, resulted in economists neglecting the important role of the GHSE in the development of their discipline. Ultimately, Keynesian, neoclassical, neoliberal, and heterodox economists were all complicit in the abandonment or erasure of the heritage of the GHSE.

Even though adherents of the GHSE produced some of the most productive and valuable works in the history of economics and economic thought, their role in the development of the discipline of economics is essentially absent from the classrooms and textbooks of modern academia. In fact, only a handful of contemporary scholars are even aware that the GHSE had any involvement in the development of economics in the US. Moreover, the GHSE has also been 'pretty much forgotten in its home country,' as 'most German economists do not know much more about it than their American colleagues' (Richter 1996, 568). Unfortunately, by turning their backs on the history of economic thought, modern economists have inhibited the progress of their own discipline by obstructing diversity in views, methods, theories, models, solutions, etc. They have also created a generation of economists that are completely disconnected from the realities of social and economic life, as well as the history of their own discipline.

This book is intended to serve as a reminder that, from the 1840s until the beginning of WWI, Germany was credited with being the only country in the world to offer systematic academic training in economics. This period was accepted as the golden years of German universities, as the country was internationally recognized as the center of higher education, not only for political economy, but many other disciplines as well. During that time, Germany set the standards for scholarly education and publications in political economy, even though it was not an economic, political, or military power. A key contributing factor to this international prestige was the GHSE occupying the status of the world's leading school of economic thought. Its professors were renowned for providing a high-quality education in political economy and successfully discrediting many of the principles and methods of orthodox classical economics. Furthermore, international journals that were published in many different languages often referred to the views and ideas of the theorists of the GHSE, because they were considered reliable and respectable authorities and sources in their discipline. In fact, mastering the concepts, principles, methods, and views of the GHSE was widely accepted as an academic requirement for serious scholars around the world, as opposed to being a choice or preference. Therefore, it was necessary for international students and academics to gain a proficiency in German in order to become respected political economists, because it was considered to be the language of the academic world, particularly when it came to publications, international conferences, and congresses.

The impeccable reputations acquired by German universities and their professors in the second half of the 19th century resulted in dramatic increases in enrolment on the part of international students seeking to advance their education in political economy, to the point where Germany surpassed both Britain and France in terms of the number of applications received from abroad. Subsequently, once these international students and academics returned to their home countries after completing their education, they brought their German experiences with them. This is primarily how the GHSE was able to shape the development of political economy in the US.

For most of the 19th century, the discipline of political economy in the US was shaped by classical economics, which found its origins in the works of Adam Smith (1723–1790), David Ricardo (1772–1823), Jean-Baptiste Say (1767–1832), and John Stuart Mill (1806–1873). During that period, before German influence became widespread, American colleges and universities did not have dedicated political economy departments. Instead, political economy classes were occasionally offered (e.g., once per year) by the social science or moral philosophy departments. There were also no graduate programs for political economy in the US, and a graduate degree was not a criterion for obtaining a professorship at most colleges and universities. This minimal level of commitment to the subject of political economy on the part of American universities and colleges also meant that professors teaching these courses were not expected to make new discoveries, nor were they called upon to contribute to the progress of knowledge in their discipline. As a result, students who were genuinely interested in political economy were neither motivated nor afforded the opportunity to advance their knowledge and education in the US. In response, a considerable number of American students went abroad to study in the political economy departments of German universities.

Germany was not just the preferred destination for American students seeking to further their education abroad, it was almost the exclusive choice for a number of reasons. Foremost among them was the prominent status of

German undergraduate and graduate programs when it came to providing an advanced level of education, due in large part to the unparalleled international reputations of the theorists of the GHSE. Over the course of their studies and training in Germany, many students and economists from the US enrolled in classes on historical and statistical investigation, as did many of their peers from various other international locations. In particular, young American students took advantage of the opportunity to study under some of the most prominent adherents of the GHSE, including Wilhelm Georg Friedrich Roscher (1817–1894), Karl Knies (1821–1898), Johannes Conrad (1839–1915), Gustav von Schmoller (1838–1917), Lujo Brentano (1844–1931), and Adolf Wagner (1835–1917), among others.

While in Germany, American students were exposed to fundamentally novel ideas, approaches, and viewpoints in terms of how a program of higher education in political economy could be organized. They were very impressed with, and ultimately influenced by, the high quality of teachings conducted by the GHSE, as well as the research methods, ideas, and aspirations of some of its well-known contributors. Subsequently, these American students brought their German experiences with them after they returned to the US, where many of their newly acquired views, concepts, methods, and ideas were fully embraced by their peers. Studying at German universities boosted their prestige, and many of them ended up becoming leading academics at universities across the US, where they contributed to the gradual establishment of economic departments and graduate schools. In doing so, they attempted to emulate the ones that they experienced at German universities by integrating the topics, issues, methods, and techniques that were being studied and developed by the GHSE into their newly created American economic departments and graduate schools. More broadly, their efforts launched a series of significant changes that altered the direction of the discipline of economics in the US. By the early 20th century, American universities had elevated their standards and earned reputations for providing a high-quality education in the discipline of economics. Additionally, many German-trained Americans ended up achieving prominence in the discipline of economics at the national and international levels by writing books and articles on various economic subjects that were very well received.

This book explains the direct influence of the GHSE on the early development of the discipline of economics and economic departments at American universities from last quarter of the 19th century until the outbreak of WWI. To do so, it is divided into nine chapters. The introduction is followed by a chapter that highlights a number of important features of the GHSE that were deeply influenced by cameralism and the Historical School of Jurisprudence, including the collectivist approach, the use of statistics, the development of public finance and public administration, support for institutional progress, the idea of ethical and historical economics, and the concept of a national economy. Understanding the intellectual sources of the GHSE could provide insights into why the development of the discipline of economics in the US during the 20th century created a disconnect between modern economics and its origins.

Chapter 3 identifies some of the well-known contributors to the GHSE, though it does not attempt to provide a comprehensive picture of their work. It then describes some of the fundamental features of the GHSE, including the inductive historical method, the collectivist approach, statistics, and the national economy. It also discusses how theorists of the GHSE attributed an important role to ethics in the discipline of economics. Furthermore, this chapter explains that the fundamental features of the GHSE were essential when it came to responding to the prevailing social and economic inequality, misery, and poverty of the time in Germany, which were largely attributed to urbanization and industrialization, among other factors. The GHSE basically defended positive state actions in the form of social and economic reforms and policies designed to overcome such issues and problems, which had become widespread throughout the country. However, they were adamant that these types of state actions were only justified if they played a role in the achievement of common welfare. Understanding fundamental principles, ideas, approaches, and methods of the GHSE is crucial to recognizing the similarities between this school of thought and its American disciples who revolutionized the development of the discipline and profession of economics in the US during the last few decades of the 19th century.

Chapter 4 provides brief biographical information about some of the distinguished American economists who went to Germany to obtain an advanced education in political economy under the guidance of theorists of the GHSE from the 1870s until the onset of WWI. By conducting an analysis of the writings of various German-trained American political economists, it also explains why they were not satisfied with the classical orthodoxy or the quality of the education and teachings being offered in the area of political economy at their domestic universities. As a result, they challenged many aspects of the discipline of economics that were previously considered settled by classical economists. This chapter also discusses some of the striking similarities between the methods, approaches, policies, reforms, goals, values, and ideas defended by these returning American economists and those advocated by the GHSE. However, this chapter is not intended to provide a comprehensive list of all the contributions that these German-trained American political economists made to the discipline of economics. It is important to understand the intellectual sources that contributed to the development of the discipline and profession of economics from the 1870s to WWI, because it could provide insights into why such a disconnect emerged between modern economics and its origins following the 20th century.

Chapter 5 concentrates on the early establishment of political economy departments at American universities, which integrated many of the features that returning American students experienced at German universities under the leadership of the GHSE. In doing so, it presents some of the American political economists who played major roles in their development. It then describes a number of the features of the newly established economics departments, including some of the classes being offered, the adoption of the seminary method, the teaching of statistics, and the provision of adequate university library resources, all of which were believed to be indispensable when it came to the training of freethinking scholars by the GHSE. This chapter also highlights that students at both the undergraduate and graduate levels had to demonstrate a proficiency in the German language if they were to pass their exams at American universities. This was attributed to the fact that German was the language of the international scientific community during the dominance of the GHSE.

To illustrate the influence of the GHSE on the development of the discipline of economics in the US, Chapter 6 explains the roles of German-trained American political economists in the foundation and evolution of various economic associations and a number of prominent economic journals. Their objectives were to provide platforms and environments that allowed for the free exchange of academic ideas and professional discussions between political economists, and to encourage and support advanced scholarly training and research in the US. Many of these journals and associations were actually inspired by ones that already existed in Germany.

Chapter 7 demonstrates that efforts to protect the environment and natural resources are not strictly recent developments. In the 19th century, courses about the protection of the environment and the conservation of natural resources were already being offered by the adherents of the GHSE in Germany. Consequently, German-trained American political economists in the US were concerned about the destructive use and exploitation of natural resources and sought remedies to help preserve them. These American economists believed that any efforts aimed at effectively protecting the environment were directly opposed to some of the fundamental features of classical economics, including methodological individualism, free trade and the laissez-faire approach. To the contrary, they were of the view that humanity could not always advance by exploiting the natural environment so as to satisfy the selfish wants and desires of the economic man of classical economics. Accordingly, they supported positive state actions to protect the environment and advocated for the provision of an ethical education, so that people would understand the importance of conservation efforts.

Chapter 8 looks into possible explanations as to why the GHSE declined as it did. It begins by highlighting the role of the Battle of Methods (*Methodenstreit*) between Schmoller and Carl Menger (1840–1921) in damaging the reputation of the GHSE. It then focuses on accusations that the GHSE was the original intellectual source of the destructive consequences of WWI and the rise of socialist nationalism in Germany. However, this chapter counters those accusations by explaining that, in reality, adherents of the GHSE were of the view that state interventions should only be used to achieve common welfare and not to constrain or coerce people in any way. They did not support despotic state authority, because they regarded the state as an ethical institution, which they considered to be an indispensable condition of human progress. Nevertheless, accusations that the GHSE supported the policies of Nazi Germany significantly diminished the prestigious status that it had previously occupied. After WWII had concluded, the German education system and its scholars were unable to regain the international standing and respect that they had formerly enjoyed. At the same time, the reputations of American economists and universities started to gain unprecedented traction around the world. Chapter 8 also argues that the leading theorists of neoclassical and neoliberal economics in the US have turned their discipline into an ahistorical and value-free science, while also intensifying the mathematization and formalization of economics, in order to make it into a branch of the natural sciences. The book is concluded in Chapter 9.

This book aims to contribute to the restoration of the lost memory of the GHSE by demonstrating its important role in the early development of the discipline of economics at American universities. It is intended to serve as a reminder of what has been lost, as economics has significantly diverged from its original raison d'être. That said, this book does not attempt to provide a complete summary of the goals, ends, and concerns of the GHSE and its American disciples, nor does it seek to explain all of the contributions made by these theorists to the field of economics. Rather, it aims to show that studying the role of the GHSE in the development of economics, as well as the goals, conflicts, ideas, agreements, failures, and successes of this school of thought, could provide insights that could help redefine the priorities, goals, and principles of modern economics, which is currently experiencing significant anomalies and an identity crisis. Furthermore, investigating the GHSE and the Americans that trained under it also reveals that the current preoccupation that many prominent economists seem to have with inequality, environmental disasters, social justice, and the integration of the common good and moral and ethical reasoning into economics is not a new phenomenon.

Bibliography

Filip, Birsen. 2020. *The Rise of Neo-liberalism and Decline of Freedom*. Cham: Palgrave MacMillan.

Richter, Rudolf. 1996. 'Bridging Old and New Institutional Economics: Gustav Schmoller, the Leader of the Younger German Historical School, Seen with Neo-institutionalists' Eyes.' *Journal of Institutional and Theoretical Economics*. Vol. 152, No. 4: 567–592. URL: http://www.jstor.org/stable/40751932

2 The German Historical School of Economics and Its Intellectual Sources

Cameralism and the Historical School of Jurisprudence

Introduction

The German Historical School of Economics (GHSE) was known by many names, including the Realistic School, *die historische Schule der Nationalökonomie* (the Historical School of Economics), *Geschichtliche Methode der Nationalökonomie* (Historical Method of Economics), *Neupreussische Nationalökonomie* (Neo-Prussian School of Economics), and the Historical-Ethical School of Economics (Cunningham 1894, Jevons 1876, Schmoller 1902, St. Marc 1892). It was the dominant school of economic thought from the 1840s up until the onset of WWI. During that period, the majority of German economics professors, officials, and government bureaucrats were trained under the disciples of the GHSE at universities in Heidelberg, Berlin, Bonn, Breslau, Halle, Leipzig, and Strasbourg. Some of the topics and subjects that these individuals studied in the disciplines of political economy at those universities were very distinct from those offered at institutions of higher learning in other European countries. For example, adherents of the GHSE focused on the historical inductive method, the collectivist approach, ethical economics, statistics, and theoretical national economy (*Nationalökonomie*). Meanwhile, they mistrusted the classical orthodoxy and attributed many of the destructive outcomes of industrialization and urbanization to the abstract, ahistorical, rational, individualist, materialist, and egoistic universal man defended by classical economists. They also argued against the laissez-faire system defended by classical orthodoxy, while contending that state reforms, regulations, and the social and economic institutions of the state played vital roles in the progress and development of economics. Additionally, they maintained that political economy was not a value-free discipline, arguing instead that the development and progress of economics was strongly related to the moral and ethical development and practices of society. All of these distinct features of the GHSE were strongly related on its two unique intellectual sources: cameralism and the Historical School of Jurisprudence (HSJ). That means, even though 1843 is widely accepted as the year that the GHSE came into existence with the publication of Wilhelm Georg Friedrich Roscher's (1817–1894) *Outline for Lectures of Political Economy*, its development

DOI: 10.4324/9781003247715-2

actually dates back further than that. In order to properly understand the development and progress of the GHSE, which influenced various aspects of the discipline and profession of economics in the US from the 1870s until the onset of WWI, both directly and indirectly, it is necessary to not only take account of its activities during its dominant years in Germany, but also its formative years when cameralism and the HSJ played crucial roles in the formation of some of its original ideas, goals, approaches, and principles.

This chapter begins by discussing cameralism during its formative years in order to provide some insight into the original intellectual sources of the GHSE, as well as the reasons why classical theory was undermined in Germany during the dominance of the GHSE. In doing so, it occasionally presents some of the main contributors to cameralism. It also explains two fundamental components of cameralist science: police science, or public administration, and economic science. Next, cameralist views on the role of the state, economics, the development of statistics, and the role of moral and ethical values in the achievement of the common good are explored, so as to demonstrate the origins of some of the fundamental features of the GHSE. This chapter also briefly identifies and describes some of the theorists of the GHSE who were influenced by cameralism. However, it does not concentrate on the divergent views held by cameralists, as its contributors and adherents were not unanimous about the exact contents and components of cameralism and cameralist science; rather, it attempts to identify and explain some of the common ideas that they defended. With respect to the role of the HSJ in the development of the fundamental ideas and methods of the GHSE, this chapter mainly focuses on the influence of Friedrich Carl von Savigny (1779–1861), even though the original development of the GHSE was also influenced by the works of other members of the HSJ, including Karl Friedrich Eichhorn (1781–1854), Johann Friedrich Gößchen (1778–1837), and Leopold von Ranke (1795–1886).

A Brief History of Cameralism, Its Features, and Goals

Cameralism, which was 'the German Mercantilism,' emerged in the German-speaking regions of Europe in the 16th century and subsequently vanished by the middle of the 19th century (Haney 1915, 113). During that time, it had a significant influence on the development of philosophical, social, political, and administrative thinking. In fact, it could be said that cameralism contained the 'germs of all the subsequent social science and governmental practice in Germany' (Small 1923A, 159). However, most of its development as an economic science (*Wirtschaftswissenschaft*) was achieved in the 18th century (Raeff 1975, 1232). This was strongly related to the fact that German territories witnessed the existence of 'some 300 German-speaking kingdoms, duchies, free cities, and tiny principalities' (Balabkins 1988, 13). Since their survival was dependent on the strength of their neighbors, these small states focused on establishing 'strong bureaucracies, run by officials' who obtained their degrees in *Kameralwissenschaft* (ibid.).

The term cameralism was derived from the Latin word 'camera' (*Kammer*), which refers to 'the royal treasure chamber' (Neff 1950, 62). Initially, the chamber was actually the place where 'the royal income was stored' (Haney 1915, 113). Over time, its meaning and purpose were progressively modified to make the term less literal, and the chamber eventually became 'synonymous with finance' (Roscher 1878, 95). At the end of the Middle Ages, 'most German countries' possessed 'an institution called the Council (Kammer) whose province it was to administer the public domain, and to watch over regal rights' (ibid.: 96). Then, in the 17th century, the chamber referred to 'a distinct group' of people who thought and 'wrote from the point of view of Ministers of State' (Cannan 1929, 13, Wakefield 2009, 17). It managed 'the intimate affairs of princes, dukes, kings, and emperors' (Wakefield 2009, 17). The King would have meetings with the presidents of these territorial chambers 'to discuss with them common measures for the promotion of the commerce and industry of the realm' (Dorn 1932A, 84). They would also prepare 'annual reports' about the territories for the King, who, in turn, used this data and information to create important social and economic policies (ibid.: 92). Broadly speaking, the territorial chamber supported the strengthening of the financial and political independence of the ruler (i.e., the king, prince, or emperor) and the improvement of productive forces (ibid.: 83).

Other tasks performed by the territorial chambers included attending to 'the local treasuries' and collecting 'the taxes and the income from the royal domains' (Dorn 1932A, 84). That is to say, they were 'generally responsible for the prompt and accurate collection of the budgetary income' (ibid.). Territorial chambers also observed:

> the movements of commerce, kept in constant touch with local merchants, superintended the fairs in the larger cities, informed themselves on the needs of consumers at home and in the neighboring states, and went out in search of markets for Prussian manufacture.
>
> (ibid.)

Essentially, these chambers served as the administrative cores of the German principalities, as they were responsible for managing public affairs and public finances, designing economic policies, and safeguarding the legal rights of the people. Ultimately, people started to call members of the territorial chamber cameralists, which resulted in their 'political, juristic, technical and economic' ideas becoming known as cameralism (Haney 1915, 114). Territorial chambers became vital centers of the 'bureaucratic mechanism' of cameralism (Dorn 1932A, 83).

Cameralists were essentially trying to find ways to improve the economy, which was in severe distress due to the fact that the German territories served as the theater for catastrophic battles, sieges, and military occupations during the Thirty Years War (1618–1648), the Swedish-Polish War (1655–1660), and a Swedish invasion (1674–1679). The resulting destruction of cities, villages, roads, populations, farmland, commerce centers, factories, and workshops led to unprecedented hardships for the people of the region for more than a century. In particular, the destruction of roads interrupted domestic and foreign trade, while also raising prices for land, houses, food, manufactured products, and imported goods. Furthermore, the significant loss of population during the many wars brought about severe labor shortages in the region. Consequently, economic stagnation was persistent, as not enough people were available to work in the production of goods or in the agriculture sector, which brought some villages to the brink of famine.

The destructive outcomes brought by the Thirty Years War and other conflicts continued to be felt in the German territories in the 18th century, which led cameralists to respond by developing social and economic policies to address these deficiencies. They specifically advocated for positive actions in the social and economic lives of people on the part of the ruler aimed at preventing the further impoverishment of the country during peacetime. Their main objective was to come up with strategies that would improve the economic and social conditions of people, while simultaneously accounting for the poor and limited economic resources of the German territories, which lacked colonies, foreign trade, and fertile soil. As such, they focused their efforts on finding ways to increase the revenues of the state, which were directly related to improving the capacities and skills of human capital and better managing natural resources and domestic industries.

In the 17th century and early decades of the 18th century, cameralist officials did not receive any formal training on how to improve the economic and social conditions of people, because cameralism was originally a field of jurisprudence, while the cameralists themselves were jurists. Consequently, they were not particularly skilled in other disciplines of the social and natural sciences. This state of affairs led to Friedrich Wilhelm I (1688–1740), who was the King of Prussia from 1713 to 1740, being unsatisfied with 'incompetent cameral officials' in the areas of economy, finance, and trade (Wakefield 2005, 311). In order to reorganize society in a way that advanced the science of the state, or the science of governing (*Staatswissenschaften*), and achieve economic prosperity and the general or collective welfare (also referred to as the ultimate ends of the state, the common good, or the general or common happiness of society), the king thought that it was necessary for current and future cameralist officials to become familiar with important details about the territories that comprised the kingdom, in addition to other relevant information in the areas of economy, finance, and trade.

Friedrich Wilhelm I played a major role in the expansion of intellectual life in Prussian cities, which 'marked the beginning of the academic development of cameralism and Polizei as sciences to be taught to future state officials' (Tribe 1984, 263). That is to say, it was during his reign that cameralism became a new and independent discipline that was taught at Prussian universities known as cameralist science (*Kameralwissenschaften*) (Small 1923A, 160). For instance, he took 'the important step of founding, at Halle and Frankfurt on the Oder, special chairs of economy and cameralistic science' (Roscher 1878, 96). Specifically, in 1727, Friedrich Wilhelm I established professorial chairs for *Oeconomie, Policey und Kammer-Sachen* at the University of Halle,[1] which became the leading center of cameralism (Tribe 1984, 263). That same year, professorial chairs for *Oeconomie, Policey und Kammer-Sachen* were also established at Frankfurt University. By the end of the 18th century, almost every German and Austrian university offered lectures on *Cameralia, Oeconomica*, and *Polizeisachen* in order to help the chambers respond to the needs of the German territories.

Cameralist science was created as a new academic discipline with the intention of providing future state officials or cameral officials (*Kammerbedienten*) with solid foundations in public administration, finance, economics, commerce, statistics, technology, and politics (Parry 1963). Additionally, students at the universities were expected to master 'mineralogy, applied mathematics, technical chemistry and other sciences,' so as to acquire the necessary knowledge and training that would allow them to manage the various natural resources of the state, including fisheries, mines, agricultural lands, and forests (Wakefield 2005, 313). By teaching cameralist science to university students, 'future ambassadors and ministers' would not be complete 'strangers in any part of the housekeeping of the state' (Small 2001, 253–254). Instead, these important state officials would understand that 'all affairs of state have an inseparable influence upon one another and an interconnection with one another' (ibid.: 254).

In the second half of the 18th century, the principal purpose of Prussian universities became to 'train future civil servants in Cameralism' (Dorn 1932B, 270). In fact, a majority of 'civil servants had studied at one or more of the Prussian universities' by the end of that century (ibid.). After graduating, they integrated themselves into some of the leading classes of Prussian society (ibid.: 270–273). More precisely, these cameralists played a major role in the Prussian bureaucracy, which was for 'many decades the most creative force in Prussian history … this bureaucracy not merely reformed itself but adapted the Prussian state to the conditions of modern life' (Dorn 1931, 404).

Despite the fact that cameralists were not in full agreement on all issues, they played a major role in developing the science of economic policy and finding remedies for 'economic evils' (Haney 1915, 114). They systemized public administration to better serve the king in his pursuit of common welfare (i.e., common happiness) (Jackson 2005, 1294). Ultimately, they ended up developing rules and regulations that were 'political, juristic, technical, and economic' (Neff 1950, 62). In fact, their work was widely accepted as 'a blueprint for governance in early modern Germany' (Wakefield 2009, 2, 4). The following sections discuss some of the main contributors to the cameral sciences and the role of the state and moral norms in cameralism. They also explain two fundamental components of the cameralist science: police science, or public administration (*Polizeiwissenschaft*), and economic science (*Wirtschaftswissenschaft*).

The Main Contributors to Cameralism

The original ideas of cameralism can be 'traced in the thought of Lutherand of Ossa (1506–1556),' George Obrecht (1547–1612), 'Bornitz and Klock (1583–1655),' and Veit Ludwig von Seckendorff (1626–1692), all of whom highly valued 'money and a dense population, and placed great confidence in government regulation' (Haney 1915, 115). However, Seckendorff, who studied philosophy, jurisprudence, and history at the University of Strasburg, was the most well known among these early cameralists. In fact, his two books, *Der Teutsche Fürsten Staat* (1655) and *Der Christen Staat* (1685), played significant roles in the development of cameralistic practices and thinking (Small 2001, 61). Seckendorff accepted the state as a moral entity that had an obligation to achieve the common good by promoting the development of the agricultural sector, supporting small businesses, and prohibiting monopolies.

Philipp Wilhelm von Hörnigk (1638–1712), who studied law, was also among the important early contributors to cameralism (Haney 1915, 118). In fact, his *Österreich über alles wenn es nur will* (1684), which mainly focused on cameralist policies, was 'one of the best known of the Kameralistic writings' (Haney 1915, 118). It was first published 'anonymously in Gottingen in 1684, and reached a total of 16 editions but no translations, and … the book essentially remained in print for 100 years' (Reinert and Reinert 2009, 21). Hörnigk defended the autonomy of the nation. As such, he attributed a great deal of importance to the development of the agriculture sector for the purpose of achieving self-sufficiency in food production. He also advocated for the proper care and cautious use of natural resources, so as to improve the economic situation of the German territories. In general, he argued that:

> the inhabitants of the country should make every effort to get along with their domestic products, to confine their luxury to these alone, and to do without foreign products so far as possible (except where great need leaves no alternative, or if not need, widespread, unavoidable abuse, of which Indian spices are an example).
>
> (Neff 1950, 84)

Christian Wolff (1679–1754) was also accepted as one of the most important contributors to cameralism. In fact, it was believed that Wolff's *Law of Nations* played a key role in the development of cameralism (Backhaus 2009B, 5). Theorists of the GHSE also recognized the significant part that he played in the development of political economy in Germany. In his work, Wolff emphasized the importance of perfection while also highlighting the role of the paternalistic state in ensuring and maintaining the conditions of perfection. He also underscored the importance of the formation of society and the state in the achievement of perfection. Wolff (1750, 3) believed that people came together 'to form a society, with no other view but to be in a condition with joint powers to promote a common good, and to defend themselves against any assaults of an enemy.'

Johann Heinrich Gottlob Justi (1717–1771), one of the leading German political economists[2] of his time, was also known as a major contributor to cameralism. He was also widely recognized as 'the most prolific writer of all economists in any language, publishing a total of 67 books of which 8 works were translated into five languages' (Reinert 2009, 33). Justi studied 'law and cameral sciences in Wittenberg and Jena' (Backhaus 2009A, XI). In '1750 he was called to a chair "Cameral Sciences and Rhetorics" at the new Theresian Academy of Knights in Vienna,' which was established in 1746 (ibid.). The Theresian Academy was intended to be 'the institution where knights, typically destitute nobility, were supposed to be trained' in public administration (ibid.: 4). Subsequently, Justi ended up becoming an eminent professor of cameral science at Austrian and German universities. Outside of academia, Justi also became:

> an economic advisor to governments, a publisher and organizer of translations (*Übersetzungsunternehmer*), a personal national research council in several fields, a manager of government investments, a prospector of mines, and an entrepreneur of last resort on behalf of the State.
>
> (Reinert 2009, 34)

In these various roles, he had a major influence in 'shaping economic and particularly industrial policies of the Habsburg monarchy in the second half of the 18th century' (Chaloupek 2009, 149).

Justi's book *Staatswirthschaft* (1755), which contained his main work on cameralistic sciences, focused on 'political and economic management,' as well as 'provisions for the good order of social life' (Tribe 2018, 48). This book was influenced by works of Christian Wolff as were a number of his other publications. In fact, Justi and Wolff shared many similar views on various subjects, including the role of the state, moral and ethical judgments, and common/general happiness (*gemeinschaftliche Glückseligkeit*). However, many regarded Justi as 'the greatest of the German Cameralists,' given that he laid the foundation of modern economic policy, public finance, public administration, and business management (Monroe 1951, 378, Neff 1950, 65). He essentially perfected cameralistic science, meaning that he systematized the science of economic policy, public finance, and public administration, thereby helping to solidify the scientific status of cameralism (Neff 1950, 65).

The development of cameralism continued with the lectures and textbooks of Joseph von Sonnenfels (1732–1817), an Austrian jurist who was 'appointed in 1763 to the newly founded chair of police and cameralistic sciences at the University of Vienna,' where he taught *Policey und Kameralwissenschaft* (Tribe 2018, 48). In those classes, Sonnenfels relied on 'Justi's *Staatswirtschaft* (1755) as a textbook until he published his own "*Grundsätze der Polizey, Handlung und Finanz*" [*Principles of Police, Commercial and Financial Science*] (3 vol., 1765–1776),' which contained his main work on cameralism (Chaloupek 2009, 149).

Other contributors to the development of cameralism included Johann Joachim Becher (1635–1682), Theodor Ludwig Lau (1670–1740), Julius Albert von Rohr (1688–1742), Wilhelm Freyherr von Schröder (1640–1688), Justus Christoph Dithmar (1677–1737), Georg Heinrich Zincke (1692–1768), Johann Peter Süssmilch (1707–1767), Jakob Friedrich Freiherr von Bielfeld (1717–177), Joachim Georg Darjes (1714–1791), and Christian Daniel Voss (1761–1821). Despite some differences between their respective views, all of them supported a strong state and the implementation policies and program that promoted the industrial and economic advancement of German-speaking territories. Many of the ideas and policies put forth by these thinkers played instrumental roles in overcoming various economic problems, thereby improving the social and economic conditions of the people and contributing to the achievement of common welfare. Furthermore, all of them ended up playing crucial roles in the early development of political economy.

Cameralism and the Role of the State

According to cameralists, human beings could not live in isolation; they needed to reside in a community, which made the existence of the state a necessity (Rath 1940, 85). They regarded the state as a unification of all members of a big family, where the interests of each family member had to be reconciled with those of the state. In particular, Justi (1951, 379) explained that the state was 'a society of men who occupy a considerable portion of the surface of our earth' that were 'united with a view to their common welfare' and 'placed a supreme authority over themselves for this purpose.' Similarly, Wolff (1750, 3) emphasized that 'men came to form a society' that was unified under the supreme power of the state in order to achieve a 'common Good' or common happiness, which 'comprises the highest good.' Since common happiness was desired by both the rulers and the ruled, the latter chose to co-operate with each other, while also allowing themselves to be guided by the state, in order to achieve it. According to Wolff, common happiness required the attainment of physical, material, intellectual, and spiritual perfection. Generally speaking, cameralists believed that the concept of happiness included but was not limited to elements like justice, fairness, the improvement of living standards, the practice of ethical values, pride in one's work, training, and education.

In order to understand the types of public policies and programs that could make people happy, cameralists studied the meaning of happiness for both individuals and the community based on the views of different civilizations and empires. Justi argued that there were many rulers across history that did not care about the achievement of common happiness. In some of those instances, 'instead of being used for the common happiness, state's revenues' were 'often wasted,' 'used with short sighted niggardliness,' 'applied at the wrong point for the best results,' or 'unsystematically administered' (Small 2001, 329). Cameralists were of the opinion that understanding historical developments 'served as thinking devices with the ambition of improving existing state practice in fields such as education, state administration, poor relief, elder care, military training and road building,' for the purpose of achieving common happiness (Miller 2020, 130).

According to cameralists, happiness was not an individualistic or egoistic concept. To the contrary, they believed that the happiness of any segment of the population was dependent upon the happiness of the whole population and vice versa (Rath 1940, 94). In other words, achieving common happiness requires the unity of all parts of the whole, referring to the unity of multiple individual wills. Given that each human being aims to achieve his own happiness, when:

> many human beings combine their wills, and resign to this combined will the use of their energy, i.e., when they set over themselves a supreme power, and subordinate their particular will to it, there can be no other intent than that each identifies his own happiness with the happiness of the whole society.
>
> (Small 2001, 344)

That essentially means achieving common happiness necessitates that the interests, wills, and ends of individuals are reconciled with the common interest, will, and ends of society. Even though cameralists defended the unity of will, they were not advocating for the elimination of free will. They recognized the importance of free will in achieving one's own perfection, which is also known as the highest development of individuality.

The semantics of common happiness, which was a very comprehensive concept of welfare, played a central part in defining the role of the cameralist state. For cameralists, it was the duty of the state to contribute to the achievement of common happiness by directing society toward the unity of multiple individual wills (Rath 1940, 88). They were of the view that the state must prudently and constantly improve the welfare of people through the legal framework, economic policies, and the establishment of adequate institutions of society. In fact, all cameralists stressed that the state can be the only entity to possess the supreme authority to regulate and implement policies if common happiness was to be achieved. In particular, Sonnenfels was of the opinion that the achievement of 'general happiness' through good governance was 'the object of all states'; in fact, he thought that this should be 'their perpetual aim' (Small 2001, 419). Justi (1951) also believed that achieving common happiness in a civil society necessitated a role for the state. With that in mind, he identified some of the specific sources of evil and unhappiness in a society, which included a lack of good education for the youth, 'the scarcity of food in the country, or the defective impulse to perform remunerative work, the oppression of the land under heavy taxation and other wrongs of government' (Small 2001, 284). In fact, Justi (1951, 396) maintained that all 'organizations, and institutions of the state' had to derive their goals and objectives (i.e., raison d'être) from the great purpose of all civil societies, which is to safeguard the welfare of the people, in part through the elimination of sources of evil and unhappiness. Accordingly, he regarded any state with 'any institution or organization that conflicts with this great purpose' as being 'monstrous in form and structure' (ibid.).

Wolff (1750, 3) believed that the achievement of happiness, which would lead people toward 'greater Degrees of Perfection,' including material, moral, physical, and intellectual perfection, required the state to manage and administer all of the natural and human resources available to the nation. In order to properly manage human resources, Wolff and other cameralists advocated for state investments in programs that would develop and perfect the capacities, talents, and skills of its inhabitants. Nobody would be excluded from these types of state programs that provided people with opportunities to realize the development of their individualities. According to cameralists, as the development of individuality increases, free will would guide people to perfection, which, in turn, would bring common happiness.

The achievement of common happiness required the ruler to be familiar with many of the specific features of the ruled and his country. That would include possessing precise knowledge about the size, natural resources, key industries, and other geographic features of his country, as well as the history, customs, cultural and religious practices, education, skills, and talents of his people. With this information, the ruler 'must devote all his effort to put his land and people in a constantly more flourishing condition of gaining the means of livelihood, and must thus secure for them increasing prosperity' (Small 2001, 212). More specifically, the constant involvement of the state in the lives of its subjects with the aim of helping them achieve their perfection, which was 'an avowed and prominent part' of the cameralistic program, was accepted as a condition for attaining the common happiness of the entire society (ibid.: 50). For example, the state could regulate all wealth, businesses, natural resources, and different aspects of civil society, provided that those measures contributed to advancing common happiness. Cameralists believed that the government control and regulation of economic and social life for the purpose of achieving common/general happiness/welfare was justified, because without bringing happiness to his subjects, 'the ruler could not become powerful, while without power the ruler was not in a position to secure the welfare of his subjects' (Tribe 2018, 44). Basically, if the ruler wanted to increase and stabilize his power, he had to look after 'nothing except welfare' and happiness for his subjects (Cannan 1929, 14). That means the interests of the ruler and those of his subjects were intertwined (Justi 1760, 43–44). Consequently, harming the interests of the ruler was also detrimental to his subjects and vice versa. For example, if the inhabitants of a particular nation were economically well off, then so too would be the economy of the entire country on an aggregate level. Conversely, if the subjects are poor, then the whole country would endure hardship because the ruler cannot extract 'money from them,' much like one cannot 'squeeze water out of a dry sponge'

(Small 2001, 174). Therefore, any factor that negatively impacts people in terms of their well-being, work, health, income, education, and living conditions, hindered the achievement of the common good.

According to cameralists, it was up to the ruler to remove any obstacles to the achievement of common happiness, and that required state regulations and investments. As such, cameralists advocated public spending on 'the salaries and pensions of all civil servants,' 'police, and justice bureaus,' which could play important roles in the achievement of 'good order' in society (ibid.: 331). They also defended for public spending on 'governmental buildings,' 'the ecclesiastical and school systems,' and 'the comfort and adornment of the country' (Small 1923A, 164, 2001, 331). They also defended state interventions to facilitate an 'adequate ordering of all means of making the land yield support,' giving 'special attention to those goods which are most generally necessary, i.e., the products of the field, of grazing, of forestry, of the iron, spinning, weaving, and wool trades' (Small 2001, 82). Based on the cameralist view, the state was also responsible for the 'marking of time by bells, and by night watchmen, inns and other places of refreshment, market-places, public conveyances, aesthetic regulations, parks and pleasure gardens, amusements, etc.' (ibid.: 372). Furthermore, some cameralists even believed that it fell under the purview of the state to promote the provision of 'joyful entertainment such as comedies, operas, ballets and other popular plays, in order to make countries delightful to live' (Kanamori 2009, 112).

The important role that cameralists attributed to the state when it came to facilitating the conditions of common happiness led to them being criticized for elevating the government to the rank of an end in itself. As a result, they were perceived as servants of authoritarian and absolutist states that were opposed to political and economic liberalism. It was even claimed that they contributed to the emergence of 'a centralized and sophisticated apparatus of public administration designed to serve the absolutist monarchs of Germany and Austria' (Spicer 1998, 149). Many also regarded the cameralist ruler as a 'benevolent despot' (Wagner 2012, 132). As such, many of the reforms and policies proposed by cameralists were perceived as raising 'the standards which a benevolent despot should adopt' (Small 2001, 71).

In reality, cameralists were arguing that the ruler did not have natural freedom, meaning that he was not free to simply act as he pleased. They supported placing restrictions on the authority of the ruler, recognizing that his interests would differ or conflict with those of his subjects. In order to prevent the ruler from misusing his power for the purpose of advancing his personal preferences and caprices, cameralists advocated for his actions to be limited by the rule of law. In other words, common happiness could not be achieved by the individual ruling of the king; it required an institutional structure in the form of public laws that the ruler had to strictly obey. These laws could not be changed by the ruler. For example, a ruler could not drastically increase taxes in order to improve his own standard of living, because this would end up impoverishing the country in the long run. Furthermore, subjects were 'entitled to oppose the system of government if there is clear evidence that the state fails to fulfil its ultimate purpose' (Schmidt am Busch 2009, 420). Justi (1951, 385) raised concerns about corruption and the abuse of state power and authority when he stated:

> Men are seldom prudent managers of their own property; they are either spendthrifts or misers, and the difference is simply a question of more or less. How can we feel assured, therefore, that they will be good and prudent managers of property not their own, namely, the property of the state? How can we expect that they will restrain their natural tendencies to extravagance or avarice when managing the property of a stranger, when they never hold these tendencies within bounds in the case of their own property, although they easily foresee that these tendencies will always be accompanied by inconveniences and harmful consequences for themselves?

Justi believed that achieving common happiness required a good ruler whose will has been 'moderated' 'through the guidance of reason' (Small 2001, 364). The personal wants and desires of the ruler should not influence the requirements of the common good. Even if the ruler is 'convinced that his personal will is a good will, a wise ruler will not try to make it his governmental will; e.g., he will not try to impose his religion upon his subjects' (ibid.). In the event of a conflict between the interests of the ruler and the common interests of the ruled, the ruler must subordinate to the latter, as his responsibility is to make his subjects happy and unite them in the achievement of common happiness (Justi 1760, 45, 46).

The cameralist concept of happiness prioritized freedom, the rights and needs of individuals, and the protection of property rights. According to Justi, 'freedom, safety of property rights, and prosperous industry' were absolutely necessary in order to have common happiness, and it was the main task of the ruler to ensure that the state possessed 'the means to assure' those characteristics (Neff 1950, 65). However, freedom also required that people subject themselves to the laws of the state (Justi 1760, 47, 48). That is to say, individuals were free as long as they obeyed the legal framework. For Sonnenfels, the freedom of the ruled came from 'their complete identification with the objectives of welfare, security and the common good' (Tribe 1984, 276). In other words, the freedom of the individuals was 'subordinated to the dictates of the common good' (ibid.).

Cameralists believed that people accepted the premise of living under the protection of a ruler in order to enjoy external and internal security, public safety, and the good order of civil life, all of which were necessary for the achievement of common happiness. Meanwhile, any ruler who deprives his:

> subjects of the necessaries of life by contributions, and compels them to trench upon their capital, acts directly contrary to the purpose of civil

> societies; it overturns civil societies at their foundation, and it ceases, therefore, to be a legitimate supreme authority, and becomes tyranny.
> (Justi 1951, 389)

In fact, Justi (ibid.: 396) argued that any state that impairs the freedom of its citizens has 'slight chance of developing a flourishing working class.' He believed that 'freedom is certainly included in the welfare and happiness of the citizens; and without it we cannot imagine them happy. To disregard this liberty is likewise prejudicial to the welfare of the state' (ibid.). Justi maintained that 'men would have been the most insane fools if they had been willing deliberately to exchange their most precious possession, freedom, for a government under which they would be slaves' (Small 2001, 340).

Cameralists sought to prevent the emergence of an abusive ruler. For example, Wolff (1750) maintained that it was necessary for the ruler to be a 'Philosopher King,' who governed wisely and in accordance with virtues, so as to preclude him from abusing his power and infringing upon the freedom and common happiness of his subjects. He specifically stated that 'either a King must be a philosopher, or a Philosopher King' to make his subjects happy (Wolff 1750, 9–10). Wolff (1750, 27, 43) believed that philosophy was an absolute necessity for a ruler if 'civil happiness' was to be achieved and 'public security and peace' were to be preserved. In fact, he was convinced that the affairs of a good government could not be 'managed without philosophy' (ibid.: 83). Conversely, he argued that rulers who 'reason unphilosophically' came up with 'the very worst' decisions, actions, and policies (ibid.: 43–44). Similarly, other cameralists had complete faith in a wise ruler who relied on moral values and rational thinking to temper his ambitions and adopt measures that would achieve the conditions of common happiness.

The Police Science (Polizeiwissenschaft)

Polizeiwissenschaft (i.e., police science), derived from the word *Polizei*, which in turn finds its origins in the Greek term *polis*, was accepted as the foundation of cameralism in the Prussian territories during the 18th century. It dealt with the conduct of people by relying on public institutions and measures that define and ensure the conditions of external and internal security, public safety, and the 'good order' of civil life, all of which were necessary for the achievement of common happiness (Tribe 1984, 274). Police science focused on the elimination of crimes, violence, and poverty in order to ensure public and private security and safety. The state could utilize police science to govern, control, manage, and regulate all available resources (i.e., human and natural) on its territories so as to remove any obstacles to the achievement of safety, security, and good order, which would contribute to economic development and improve living standards. It is important to emphasize that the laws of police science 'must not contradict moral laws; they must only determine how morally-permissible things can be directed to increase the wealth of the state' (Haney 1915, 123).

Justi and Sonnenfel played major roles in the 'systematization' of police science (Tribe 1984, 275). However, other cameralists also contributed to establishing the rules and norms of police science 'to the smallest detail,' so that it could effectively achieve good order, security, and public safety (ibid.: 274). In the end, their efforts led to the establishment of a police science that was like 'a well-intentioned genius who carefully levels the way for those committed to his care,' as it:

> secures the villages and holdings in which they dwell, and the streets along which they walk; protects the fields that they cultivate, secures their homes against fire and flood, and they themselves against illness, poverty, ignorance, superstition and immorality; who, even if he cannot prevent all accidents, seeks however to diminish and ease their consequences, and offers refuge in time of need to every pauper, casualty or person in need. Its watchful eye is ubiquitous; its helping hand is ever-ready, and we are invisibly surrounded by its unceasing care.
>
> (ibid.)

Since police science aimed to achieve safety and security for society as a whole, cameralists supported universal access to public health care services, because having a healthy population was an important aspect of societal safety and security. To ensure societal health, the state could care for the sick at hospitals or in their own homes by providing various medical services, including surgeries, midwifery, regular checkups, and treatments for specific illnesses or injuries. It could also facilitate the conditions of proper public hygiene and ensure that the streets, 'water supply,' and 'the air' that people breathed were sufficiently clean (ibid.). Police science was also involved in regulating the quality of food as a condition of safety and security in society. Additionally, it was also responsible for safeguarding the safety of 'gates, harbors,' 'roads, streets, postal systems, bridges, fountains, reservoirs, water-mains,' and 'paving' (Small 2001, 372).

Providing security went beyond protecting people's lives and ensuring their safety; it also involved safeguarding their private properties. Cameralists believed that guaranteeing the security of private property would contribute to the general welfare of the population. At the same time, however, they were worried that the accumulation of excessive amounts of private property and wealth in the hands of a few individuals could threaten good order and the welfare of the population. In his critique of wealthy individuals, Justi maintained that some of these people did not become rich through hard and honest work, but rather via corruption and manipulation. He further argued that these types of people were 'the source of all disorders' and had the potential to destroy the state (ibid.: 390). Justi also believed that corruption, gambling, and fraudulent bankruptcies could endanger safety, security, and the good order of society, as did a number of other cameralists. However, while police science involved itself in many aspects of social and economic life, it did not directly intervene in the private spheres of individuals by targeting the choices and decisions that they made in their 'households' (Tribe 1988, 72).

Cameralism and Economics

In the 18th century, each nation was accepted as 'a unit, and the interest of each was supposed to be opposed to that of all the rest, as the great object of each of them was to get as much gold and silver as possible at the expense of the others' (Cannan 1929, 11). At that time, 'trade between nations was looked on very much as some barbarians are said to have regarded trade in general, not as a method of co-operation but as a sort of tolerated robbery' (ibid.). In fact, the most important goal of 'a statesman seemed to be the making of ingenious arrangements for cheating the foreigner out of some of his gold and silver' (ibid.). It was during this period of robbery and cheating that cameralism emerged as a science of economic policy that sought to achieve economic development and prosperity.

Cameralism was accepted as a form of 'mercantilism' that was 'organized as a predecessor of a scientific economics' (Tribe 1984, 265). This is mainly due to the fact that cameralism was inspired by the same sources that nurtured mercantilism. However, cameralism and mercantilism also had many diverging characteristics on account of the fact that the former was developed according to the particular social, economic, and historical conditions of the Prussian territories, whereas the latter gained prominence among some of the key players on the international scene from the 16th to the 18th centuries, including the English, French, Spanish, and Dutch. Mercantilists considered 'wealth and money identical' and believed that 'the great object of a community so to conduct its dealings with other nations as to attract to itself the largest possible share of the precious metals' (Ingram 1888, 34). That is to say, mercantilism focused purely on increasing 'the quantity of the precious metals possessed by the nation, either through the agency of mining at home, or by means of foreign trade' (Roscher 1878, 169). In fact, an emphasis on a positive trade balance meant that international trade was 'placed at the top of the list of economic activities and agriculture at the bottom' (Neff 1950, 53). However, it was argued that this 'view stands and falls with the altogether too limited idea of national wealth,' as mercantilists neglected the role of developing 'the agriculture, and to the finer kinds of industry' (Roscher 1878, 169). Adam Smith (1979, 450) explained that based on mercantilism:

> wealth consisted in gold and silver, and that those metals could be brought into a country which had no mines only by the balance of trade, or by exporting to a greater value than it imported; it necessarily became the great object of political economy to diminish as much as possible the importation of foreign goods for home-consumption, and to increase as much as possible the exportation of the produce of domestic industry.

Accordingly, mercantilist governments imposed various restrictions on importation and encouraged exportation in order to ensure a positive balance of trade. For example, they sought to limit imports by advocating for the imposition of high duties and the prohibition of certain types of foreign merchandise being brought into the country. Furthermore, each nation focused on exporting the largest possible quantity of domestic goods, while imposing restrictions on the exportation of precious metals.

Although cameralism and mercantilism shared some similarities, the two systems were far from identical. For instance, cameralists questioned the focus on the accumulation of precious metals as sources of wealth that characterized the mercantile system. To the contrary, they regarded precious metals as only one part of national wealth. Accordingly, cameralists argued that wealth and state power did not have to be dependent on the acquisition of precious metals. Therefore, it was not necessary to conquest territories in distant lands in order to generate wealth, as 'the key to wealth was right at home, in local fields, forests, mines and manufactories' (Wakefield 2005, 319).

Cameralists had little interest in foreign markets and exportation. As such, Prussian territories did not play a prominent role in international trade compared to the British, French, Spanish, and Dutch. Part of the reason why cameralists did not focus on international commercial expansion to the same extent as mercantilists was because they prized the development of domestic industry more than 'their English and French prototypes' (Neff 1950, 62). They were also concerned that trade with distant territories was fragile, because it could be disrupted by various events like war and harsh weather conditions. Cameralists also believed that the importation of foreign goods that could be produced by the domestic economy resulted in 'the destruction of the community' and the weakening of the economy, because it drives money out of the country (Small 2001, 112). Accordingly, they sought to limit the consumption of imported goods. That said, they believed that any decisions pertaining to the possible imposition of trade restrictions had to take the necessity of the goods into consideration. For example, restrictions could be placed on the exportation of necessary goods for the purpose of preventing future famines.

Cameralists were particularly opposed to the importation of 'unnecessary foreign articles of luxury,' including silk products, coffee, sugar, alcohol, and tobacco, because that would worsen the balance of payment and increase their dependency on other countries (ibid.: 451). Consequently, they advocated for the importation of luxury goods to be limited through the imposition of heavy import duties. Furthermore, instead of supporting the enrichment of a handful of people through international trade, cameralists essentially called for them to be treated as though they were 'the meanest criminals' (ibid.: 112). Instead of importing luxury goods, cameralists encouraged the domestic production of such products, even if the Prussian equivalents were of lower quality than the originals. For example, cameralists supported the cultivation of tobacco plants in Silesia and the Ukermark despite their lower quality in order to save the money spent on buying American tobacco. Similarly, they also supported the development of silk and porcelain industries in Berlin. This is not surprising, given that cameralists believed that 'it would be better to pay for an article two dollars which remain in the country than only one which goes out' (Neff 1950, 64).

Since Prussia did not possess colonies, valuable goods to export, or fertile soil, cameralists focused on the development and discovery of new sources of revenue. They also supported the careful management and development of domestic economic activities, given that domestic industry was accepted as being more reliable and easier to protect. In fact, they advocated the application of the methodology of the natural sciences to properly manage domestic resources and domestic economic activities, thereby generating great amounts of revenue. That is why it is claimed that cameralism was 'intimately and ineluctably tied' to the natural sciences (Wakefield 2005, 319, 2009, 20, 17). In particular, cameralists had complete faith in the ability of natural science to improve the administration and management of the natural resources of the country. For example, the natural sciences were applied to better manage and conserve the soil, mined metals and minerals, water resources, forests, gardens, plants, and livestock.

Cameralists especially prioritized the careful management of natural resources and the agriculture sector. This included efforts to increase the quality and variety of domestically produced agricultural goods. For instance, the government could implement measures to encourage the better cultivation of arable land with the intention of limiting the 'sterilization of the soil, declining value of the revenues of the state, and diminishing population'[3] (Small 2001, 462). Moreover, if the production of a specific agriculture product was deemed to be more important for the welfare of the nation than others, then the state could establish incentives to stimulate its production such as tax breaks for farmers that cultivate the desired crops.

In the agriculture sector, cameralists also supported 'rules of rotation of crops and other regulations, like the wages of laborers'; the 'adoption of special standards for particular products, kinds of seed to be used'; and the 'enactment of ordinances to protect growing crops from thieves' (ibid.: 375). They also advocated for an active state role in providing farming materials, as well as inputs to production if the individual proprietors were in need of assistance. The state provision of veterinary services was also highly supported by cameralists. For example, Sonnefels stressed the point that the 'direct and indirect consequences of cattle diseases are among the important objects of public attention' (ibid.: 462). Consequently, he called for measures to help avoid outbreaks of diseases among cattle, including state funding for veterinary schools and the investigation of such ailments (ibid.). Sonnenfels also argued that the state must help farmers in the event of natural disasters or other misfortunes that caused crops to fail.

Cameralists also prioritized the development of manufacturing industries. They trusted that domestic factories would eventually find ways to improve the quality of their products and lower the cost of production. Some of the measures that they advocated in order to encourage the consumption and production of domestic products included state support for infant industries that fabricated luxury goods and waiving taxes on purchases of domestically produced goods. Cameralists also believed that in order to protect small and medium-sized business owners, 'the state must take measures to prevent exorbitant or oppressive terms in case of loans by individuals' (ibid.). This is due in part to the fact that when 'an individual proprietor is too poor properly to cultivate his tract, the state is in danger of suffering loss of a portion of its dues' (ibid.). Accordingly, cameralists called for the prevention of 'excessive debt by setting a limit to the amount which may be borrowed' (ibid.: 463). They also supported the prevention and removal of monopolies. The objective of these types of state actions was to avoid the deterioration of living conditions for poor and weak business owners. That means state interference in the affairs of private enterprises was justified, provided that the policies were designed to achieve common happiness. In other words, cameralists did not regard all economic actions performed by individuals as purely private matters, because every one of them had the potential to affect the overall economy of the nation, as well as common happiness.

Cameralists were also opposed to any economic activities that damaged or overexploited national resources, including the pollution of soil and water sources, overfishing, deforestation, and excessive mining. This is because they were of the view that activities that overexploited and neglected natural resources ultimately diminished the wealth of the state, which, in turn, inhibited the achievement of common happiness. For example, Justi underlined that:

> forests have long remained in common use and common ownership, and even if forests have over time been transferred into private hands, they remain under the supervision and direction of the state, because they require "special oversight", or more literally, "special precaution" ("besondere Vorsorge").
>
> (Hölzl 2020, 154)

That means cameralists believed that natural resources belonged to society even if they were privately owned. As a result, they supported state regulations designed to prevent deforestation and encourage the 'conservation of forests' (ibid.). In fact, cameralists relied heavily on state regulations to protect natural resources and maintain ecological equilibrium, as they believed that the state and its population would benefit from the best use, conservation, and protection of nature.

In addition to better managing natural resources, cameralists also focused on taxes as a means of creating revenue for the state. However, they were of the view that taxes occupied a secondary position when it came to being a source of state revenue, behind the funds generated from the careful management of natural resources, mining, manufacturing, and the agricultural sector. They also believed that taxation should be guided by a desire to achieve equality, justice, and general happiness as opposed to the greedy ambitions of the ruler. According to Justi (1951, 396), 'the general welfare of the state and of the subjects is the great purpose of all civil societies,' and as such, the level of taxation needed to be reasonable so as to ensure that 'the welfare of the state and of the subjects and civil freedom suffer no harm.' He argued that since all inhabitants of a nation have 'an equal share in the purpose of civil societies, the general welfare, and since they all enjoy equal protection,' they must all contribute to paying for state expenses (ibid.: 390). However, he was critical of the system of contribution in many states, whereby 'the richest subjects always contribute least to the expenses of the state; and since nothing can be collected from the poor all the burden of contributions falls upon the middle class' (ibid.: 391). Justi (1951, 389) was adamant that inhabitants of the state should only be expected to contribute to state revenues if they are 'in a position to be able to pay them.' That meant those citizens with more properties and larger incomes should be expected to make a greater contribution to state revenues. In other words, 'a tax should be levied in proportion to property, that it should be certain and not arbitrary, that it should be convenient to pay, and that it should be economical to administer' (Wagner 2012, 130).

Justi (1951, 389) argued taxes could become 'tyrannical exactions and a violent theft of the property of the subjects' if they exceeded certain limits. He believed that 'profit (Gewinnst) should be taxed' in 'a way that an agreeable life is still possible and that the substance of income and wealth will not be reduced' (Peukert 2006, 489). Furthermore, he argued that 'subjects should not be asked to make contributions except in an amount to balance the inadequateness of the state's income from other sources to meet necessary expenses' (Neff 1950, 65). Justi thought that the rate of taxation should account for the economic situations of subjects, the growth of the population, and living standards. Additionally, he believed that the rate of taxation should account for the particular development of industries. Accordingly, cameralists advocated for state credit and tax exemptions for infant industries.

Justi (1951, 389) warned that since rulers are ultimately just human beings, they can be 'very ingenious in thinking up new needs, when they have such an easy prospect of obtaining what they want.' The natural outcome of rulers resorting to eliciting contributions from the ruled in the form of taxes is destined to be that these taxes are progressively increased, to the extent that they eventually become an 'intolerable burden to the subjects, resulting in the ruin of both the subjects and the state itself' (ibid.: 385). However, cameralists were confident that a virtuous ruler would not impose oppressive taxes in order to increase state expenditures. In fact, they claimed that it was immoral and unjust to impose a very high level of taxation that constituted a heavy burden on people and businesses. As such, they maintained that the state should only obtain contributions from its citizens for the purpose of funding necessary expenditures.

Cameralists were always looking for new avenues to generate additional state revenues, including attempts to guide private consumption in a way that would benefit economic growth. However, they were against the imposition of taxes on food and other essential goods, as the negative impacts of such an action would be felt mostly by low-income families. Instead, they strongly advocated for the high taxation of luxury goods, such as coffee, sugar, alcohol, and tobacco, as they considered the consumption of such products to be wasteful and immoral. Cameralists were of the view that the creation of luxurious goods resulted in the creation of new 'wants of citizens, and thereby perhaps makes it harder for some to support themselves' (Small 2001, 451). They did not regard the taxation of imported luxury goods as an oppressive measure, because deciding between the consumption of necessary and luxury goods was a personal matter. Furthermore, cameralists believed that raising taxes on luxury goods would likely shift the tax burden toward wealthier consumers, because people with better economic situations would be more willing to pay a premium to satisfy their expensive tastes.

The cameralist economy was a mixed economy that included both public and private properties and enterprises. The state used its own properties and enterprises to generate the revenues required to finance the expenses associated with its activities, including the construction of infrastructure, the provision of health care and education services, ensuring 'enough employees in each profession,' safeguarding domestic security, and more (Backhous 2009b, 2). According to cameralists:

> the prices of goods bought and sold should be regulated; wages should likewise be controlled; the cheapest possible food, drink and clothing should be available, commensurate with the social standing of the person concerned; poorhouses should be made available to the unemployed, and begging outlawed.
>
> (Tribe 2018, 46)

It is important to understand that cameralists were not attempting to achieve a perfectly equal society through a highly regulated economic system. Justi (1951, 394) recognized that the ideal of achieving an egalitarian society where 'all subjects have perfectly equal property, and in which equality of contributions therefore presents no difficulty,' is 'proper for noble and sympathetic souls who see the great majority of men living an exceedingly hard and miserable life, and are touched by the sight.' He further pointed out that there have been many cases in:

> ancient and modern times, and in various republics of antiquity has caused great disturbances and unrest, when the poor citizens demanded that the rich and property-owning classes should consent to a new and equal distribution of all immoveable property. The demands of these

> poor citizens are completely justified in the eyes of anyone who considers the matter without prejudice.
>
> (ibid.: 395)

At the same time, he was conscious that the 'complete equality of property among all the members of a civil society may be in itself, it is impossible in all states where the use of money and full property rights have been introduced' (ibid.). He explained that 'since families neither have the same diligence and skill nor make the same expenditures, there would always be families who accumulated money, and others in need, who would have to sell their property' (ibid.). Accordingly, any efforts aimed at achieving a perfectly equal society were doomed to fail. Instead, cameralists believed that the key to common happiness was ensuring good order, security, and safety. Thus, they focused on financing, regulating, and administering various public services and programs that were designed to achieve those objectives, but also required significant expenditures. More precisely:

> the establishments and institutions for the protection of the state, as well as those for the common advantage and convenience of all citizens, which are ordinarily called police (Policey) establishments, likewise require large outlays; and the maintenance of relations and intercourse with other states similarly cannot go on without expenditures.
>
> (ibid.: 379)

In order to finance public expenditures aimed at achieving good order, security, and safety, cameralists focused on improving the national economy, as well as properly administering the human and natural resources of the country.

Cameralism on Moral Values

The views of Wolff and Justi on the subject of moral and ethical values were influenced by their studies on ideal communities in ancient civilizations, including the Spartans and the Peruvian Empire. Those ancient civilizations defended 'egalitarian' principles and an 'ethical and virtuous communal life' (Peukert 2006, 484). According to Justi, the populations of these two particular civilizations:

> lived happily and contented, and nobody felt the burning passion of ambition and avarice which cause so much evil in the world … None was poor or wretched else … because the main source of all vice, money, did not exist.
>
> (Peukert 2006, 484 ff.24)

Given that the social and economic conditions observed in the 18th-century Prussian territories were radically different from those that prevailed in Sparta and the Peruvian Empire, Wolff and Justi believed that common happiness, which required economic development, prosperity, order, safety, security, and the perfection of individuality, could be achieved via the moral perfection of the ruler and his subjects.

Cameralists believed that common happiness was highly dependent on the virtuous behavior of both the ruled and the ruler. That said, they suggested that common happiness ultimately had to be guided by a virtuous ruler. Basically, the ruler had to acquire and practice virtues, including justice, honesty, and prudence, if common happiness was to be achieved. That means the ruler had to be a student of moral philosophy before assuming power. To be more precise, the ruler needed to acquire an appropriated education, as well as solid intellectual and spiritual foundations, early in his life, so that he could go on to make morally and ethically sound decisions after coming to power. Justi (1760, 26–27) believed that a wise and virtuous ruler would always seek to unite his will and happiness with those of his subjects; he would simultaneously prevent his will and happiness from getting into conflicts with those of his subjects. Such a ruler would also ensure that his subjects lived their lives in accordance with moral and ethical values, which would help achieve common happiness.

In order to have a society that is guided by moral and ethical values, cameralists emphasized the importance of education. They supported a public education system that was accessible to everyone regardless of the economic and social status of their family (Small 2001, 432). According to Justi, teachers at:

> public schools should be chosen from the most educated, witty, and intelligent men. Every village school master should be a true teacher of morals and good conduct when the general welfare of the people and of each state is concerned.
>
> (Peukert 2006, 481)

After graduating, students were supposed to have acquired the necessary education and development to ensure that all of their decisions and actions would be guided by moral and ethical values.

Cameralism and the German Historical School of Economics

While political economy found 'its origin chiefly in the study of questions of finance and foreign commerce' in England and Italy, it developed out of the science of law and the cameralistic sciences in Germany (Roscher 1878, 97). That is to say, the development of a separate and independent discipline of political economy began during the 17th century in Germany with the emergence of cameralism. The first chair in political economy was established at Frankfurt University in 1727, nearly a century ahead of Britain, which did not do so until 1826 at Oxford University (Backhaus 2009B, 5,

Tribe 1984, 263). Since the discipline of economics arose out of cameralism, the establishment of the first chair in political economy in Germany essentially marked the beginning of modern economics. Subsequently, in the early 19th century, cameralists faced 'heavy criticism from a competing system of political and economic theory; and by the 1820s cameralism at least had all but disappeared' (Tribe 1984, 277). At that time, classical economics started to garner some attention in Germany. However, since cameralism was already being taught at German universities since 1727 and cameralistic public administration and finance were successfully being practiced, German political economists did not really have a reason to turn to classical economics. For them, the fundamental principles, ideas, and policies of classical economics, including individualism, the laissez-faire approach, competitiveness, the overexploitation of natural resources, and the destruction of the natural environment for purely economic gains, were all foreign concepts that were unfit for the German spirit and way of thinking, both of which were highly influenced by cameralism. Despite the fading role of cameralism in the 19th century, universities in Germany and Austria continued to teach cameralist science, which played a significant role in the initial development of public administration, political economy, finance, statistics, bureaucratic organization, and political practices and thinking in those two countries.

Karl Heinrich Rau (1792–1870), a German political economist who was a very influential professor at the University of Heidelberg, where he lectured for nearly five decades, had a crucial role in the development of cameralism and mathematical economics in the 19th century (Neff 1950, 191). Rau's textbook *Lehrbuch der politischen Ökonomie* (1826) 'dominated instruction in economics in German universities for almost 50 years' (Mitchell 1969, 531). In fact, it was widely considered to be an encyclopedia of economic knowledge in the 19th century, when it became the main textbook of cameralism in Germany and was frequently used to train public servants. Many of the ideas and methods that it presented were similar to those put forth by other cameralistic writers, as he discussed *Nationalokonomie* and *Staatswirthschaft* at length. However, the ideas presented by Rau in *Lehrbuch der politischen Ökonomie* (1826) were also 'modern, and distinct from an eighteenth century cameralistic tradition where the discussion of economic activity was irrevocably linked to the work of economic administration; but although it incorporated elements of Smithian political economy' (Tribe 2002, 5). Rau argued that while cameralism could not remain the same as it had been in the previous century, it might be possible to 'rejuvenate it' (Tribe 1988, 193). Accordingly, he combined cameralistic ideas with the classical economics of Adam Smith (Neff 1950, 217). In doing so, he emphasized the importance of reforming the discipline of economics, while supporting the historical method and statistical observations.

Rau's *Lehrbuch der politischen Ökonomie* was very influential in the development and formation of the economic thoughts, ideas, and approaches of some of the prominent theorists of the GHSE, mainly Wilhelm Georg

Friedrich Roscher (1817–1894) and Bruno Hildebrand (1812–1878). Even though cameralism lost its leading status in the early decades of the 19th century, adherents of the GHSE were generally familiar with it, because *polizeiwissenschaft* and *staatswirthschaft* were still being taught at German universities and considered important components of the discipline of political economy under the leadership of the GHSE (St. Marc 1892, 85–86). These courses dealt with the essence of the state, including its constitution, goals, justice, security, public safety, public administration, and the good order of civil life, all of which were necessary for the achievement of the common good (ibid.: 85). Roscher (1878, 98), who is accepted as the founder of the GHSE, due in large part to the publication of his *Outline for Lectures of Political Economy* in 1843, pointed out that political economists were required to possess 'knowledge of the natural side of the cameralistic sciences' in the 19th century. According to him, such knowledge was 'indispensable to every detailed and living theory, and especially to the application of economic science to practice' (Roscher 1878, 98).

Roscher actually attended Rau's lectures in Heidelberg. As a result, he was strongly influenced by Rau's views and ideas in his own work *System der Volkswirtschaft* (1854). In fact, the 'descriptive features' of Rau's works inspired Roscher to 'adapt theoretical principles to historical circumstances' (Tribe 1988, 206). This led Roscher to undertake significant efforts to 'modernize' cameralism, which involved applying certain 'aspects' of political theory and history to political economy (ibid.: 203, 206). In his *Geschichte der National-Oekonomik in Deutschland* (1874), Roscher basically 'trimmed cameralism to its bare economic essentials, discarding most of the extraneous garbage about technology, agriculture, forestry and the rest' (Wakefield 2005, 313–314). He also eliminated some of the fundamental policies of cameralism. For instance, he did not believe that population growth would necessarily lead to increases in state revenue and wealth, which was one of the main tenets of cameralists. Additionally, Roscher did not support the idea of a ruler that planned and designed all minuscule aspects of economic activity in society in order to advance the development of the national economy. He also opposed extremely protective trade measures. Meanwhile, some of the features of cameralism that were supported by Roscher (1878, 91) included an emphasis on 'the close connection between politics and Political Economy, in the case of the science of finance, or of the science of governmental house-keeping, otherwise the administration of public affairs.' He also used the term police in the same sense as cameralists, referring to the power of the state and its institutions to prevent 'all disturbances of external order among the people' (Roscher 1878, 92). Like the cameralists, he argued that the police could 'extend its action into all the domains of national life' whenever the domestic peace, security, and order were endangered (ibid.).

In addition to Roscher, other theorists of the GHSE were also influenced by cameralism. In fact, many of them worked to further develop, 'refine and extend' Roscher's views on cameralism (Wakefield 2005, 314). During the leadership of the GHSE, cameralist principles, goals, and policies became important parts of the national economy (*Nationalökonomie*). Furthermore, university classes under the GHSE focused on the development and progress of the national economy, as was the case when cameralism was dominant. Another similarity between the cameralists and adherents of the GHSE was that both considered multidisciplinary research and the study of ancient civilizations to be important. More specifically, both schools of thought believed that political economy required other social sciences and historical investigation in order to achieve economic progress and development. Moreover, adherents of the GHSE and cameralism placed a high value to the historical approach because they thought it allowed them to gain a better understanding of the development and advancement of institutions of society. To be more precise, they thought that it was important to properly comprehend the historical evolution of the industries, customs, and cultural practices of societies in order to determine what factors facilitated or inhibited their progress. In fact, adherents of both cameralism and the GHSE relied on historical enquiry to provide the basis for any great institutional decisions made by the ruler.

The treatment of ethical values was another point of convergence between cameralism and the GHSE. Basically, theorists of the GHSE tried to integrate ethical standards into economics. To be more precise, they declared that moral and ethical judgments played a central role in the decisions and actions of both states and individuals. Gustav von Schmoller (1838–1917) produced the most extensive work on the importance of ethics in social and economic life and making economics into an ethical discipline. He argued that the most advanced civilizations placed a high value on the ethical and moral practices of individuals, as well as those of social and economic institutions. According to him, there would be no progress in economics or the institutions of society in the absence of moral and ethical practices.

Without the existence of cameralism, the GHSE would likely have turned out very differently, given the many parallels that existed between these two schools of thought. That is to say, the GHSE could not have reached the level of success it achieved without the significant contributions that cameralism made to its fundamental ideas and principles.

The Historical School of Jurisprudence

In the 19th century, the historical approach, which aimed to reveal the laws and patterns of historical changes, deeply influenced all social sciences, including political economy in the German territories. It was mainly developed and supported by the HSJ early in that same century. Friedrich Carl von Savigny (1779–1861) and Gustav Hugo (1764–1844) were accepted as two of the main founders of the HSJ. Hugo was a law professor at the University of Göttingen, who focused on civil law. Meanwhile, Savigny taught criminal law, Roman law, and its history at the University of Berlin from 1810 to 1842, before being appointed chancellor of Prussia by Fredrich William IV in 1842 (Kantorowicz 1937, 332). In the 19th century, the 'concept of legal science' (*Rechtswissenschaft*) originated in his work (Reimann 1990, 840).

Karl Friedrich Eichhorn (1781–1854), Johann Friedrich Gößchen (1778–1837), and Leopold von Ranke (1795–1886) also played major roles in the development and spread of the HSJ. All three were professors in the faculty of law at the University of Berlin. It was actually the publication of 'the first volume' of the *Zeitschrift für geschichtliche Rechtswissenschaft* (*Journal of Historical Jurisprudence*) by Savigny, Eichorn, and Göschen in 1815 that marked 'the official beginning' of the HSJ (Beiser 2011, 214). Additionally, Savigny's book *Vom Beruf unserer Zeit für Gesetzgebung und Rechtswissenschaft* (*Of the Vocation of Our Age for Legislation and Jurisprudence*), which was published in 1814, was accepted as one of the most important books among adherents of the HSJ.

The views, principles, goals, and methods of the HSJ were not accepted by all legal theorists in the German territories. Most notably, a famous debate began between the HSJ and the Philosophical School of Jurisprudence (PSJ) in 1814 centered on a disagreement about the codification of law. In fact, one could argue that this debate pertained to the development of legal thought in the German territories since the 15th century. To fully understand the debate between the HSJ and PSJ, it is important to remember that German legal thought experienced periods of considerable change at the end of the 18th century. There was also significant diversity in 'the legal organization of the Germanic territories' prior to the first codification by the Prussian government that took place in 1794 (Becchi 2009, 195). At that time, it was not uncommon for different German territories to employ various combinations of Prussian, Austrian, and Napoleonic codes, along with different territorial, Roman, and natural laws (ibid.: 195). The Roman legal system, which was regarded as the common law of Europe up until the 19th century, actually predates the 15th century, while the origins of natural law can be traced back to the 17th century (Ziolkowski 2004, 102). Roman law maintained that 'the authority is nature itself,' whereas natural law advocated for the universality and authority of 'human reason' (ibid.). Ultimately, the development of German legal thought that occurred at the end of the 18th century was a direct outcome of the reaction against natural law theory. To be more precise, intellectuals ended up discrediting 'natural law' in the final decade of the 18th century, which contributed to codification in 1794 (ibid.: 103).

Despite the codification in 1794, prominent German legal thinkers became preoccupied with finding a suitable structure for the country's civil laws following the victory of the German resistance movement over the Napoleonic occupation. Subsequently, in 1814, an intellectual dispute pertaining to the introduction of a new code for all German territories arose between Anton Friedrich Justus Thibaut (1772–1840), a professor of law at Heidelberg who adhered to the PSJ, and Savigny of the historical school. The Thibaut-Savigny debate over codification marked one of the most important chapters in the development of German legal thought in the 19th century.

Thibaut and Savigny publicly expressed their respective views on how laws should be reorganized in Germany in the post-Napoleonic era. In 1838, Thibaut published *Über die sogenannte historische und nichthistorische Rechtsschule*, in which he defended a unified legal code for all German states. More specifically, he supported the notion of establishing a new standardized code of law for all of Germany by unifying the different systems of law that were already in effect in its various territories, namely Roman law, the Prussian code, the Austrian code, and the Napoleonic code. According to him, 'the law is the arbitrary result of the will of the legislator, independent of anterior law, and accommodated to the demands and uses of the moment' (Small 1923B, 732). In other words, the main goal of the PSJ was to establish a rational system of law based on the powers of reason.

In his books, *Of the Vocation of Our Age for Legislation and Jurisprudence* (1814) and *On the Purpose of the Journal for Historical Jurisprudence* (1815), Savigny provided a powerful critique of legal codification based on his rejection of the rationalist aspects of the system of law, and explained why he believed that codification represented an obstacle to the organic progress of laws. He argued that human reason was limited, while emphasizing the importance of history in the development of each generation and their legal systems. In his opposition to Thibaut's defense of reason as an important element of legal science, Savigny insisted that each society had its own particular law, which reflected its unique characteristics and changed organically over time. According to Savigny's theory, 'the law is a spontaneous growth of the entire life of the nation, the real character of which can be revealed only by historical and comparative studies' (Neff 1950, 356). He further believed that historical studies could help law students, academics, lawyers, and judges comprehend the meaning of prevailing laws and rules, given that law develops according to the history of each nation. More precisely, he explained that 'in the earliest times to which authentic history extends, the law will be found to have already attained a fixed character, peculiar to the people, like their language, manners and constitution' (Savigny 1831, 27). In particular, he underscored the parallels between the development of law and language, as both are connected to 'the being and character of the people' and 'manifested in the progress of the times' (Savigny 1831, 27). Savigny (1831, 27) specifically stated that:

> For law, as for language, there is no moment of absolute cessation; it is subject to the same movement and development as every other popular tendency; and this very development remains under the same law of inward necessity, as in its earliest stages. Law grows with the growth, and strengthens with the strength of the people, and finally dies away as the nation loses its nationality.

That means, according to Savigny, the content of the law is not 'something imposed on a community from above or from without, but is an inherent part of its ongoing life, an emanation of the spirit of the people' (Rodes 2004, 165). Contrary to Thibaut's defense of the rational construction of law, Savigny maintained that laws were outcomes of the national spirit (*Volksgeist*). Therefore, laws developed according to organic changes in the national spirit, which are experienced by the people that make up a particular society. In other words, the laws of any state originally emerged from the specific historical experiences, cultures, popular beliefs, languages, traditions, moral and ethical values, and customs of its own people. Hence, law was not originally developed via legislative arbitrariness based on the powers of reason.

Savigny believed that since the national spirit is an organic historical development that manifests itself in the laws of the people, the law must also be an organic historical development. In other words, he believed that the law was a purely historical discipline, and as such, historical studies could help trace the common element of law. He further claimed that since 'each age of a nation' was 'the continuation and development of all past ages,' historical studies allow us to 'appropriate to ourselves the whole intellectual wealth' of the past (Savigny 1831, 132, Small 1923B, 730). Savigny focused on the influence of the past on the present, because he was of the view that the past did not completely disappear; rather, it continued to influence the present in various ways. To be more precise, he believed that historical study was the only way to understand people's moral judgments, practices, habits, manners, beliefs, and unique spiritual qualities, all of which are shaped by their history.

Ultimately, Savigny was of the view that neither human beings nor the development of societies and their institutions could be understood without connecting them with their pasts. This is because antecedent developments are displayed in the essential features and characteristics of people and the institutions of their societies. In defending the importance of historical study, Savigny (1831, 136) stated that:

> history, even in the infancy of a people, is ever a noble instructress, but in ages such as ours she has yet another and holier duty to perform. For only through her can a lively connection with the primitive state of the people be kept up; and the loss of this connection must take away from every people the best part of its spiritual life.

For Savigny and the adherents of the HSJ, even if 'the present is purposely opposed to the past,' the submissiveness of the present to the past will always exist (Rodes 2004, 167). It is only when people understand that they are part of an ongoing historical process that there can be an improvement of the law. In his defense of historical study, Savigny stressed that when the significance of 'the national and historical elements in human existence' are not properly understood, then 'the conception of life appears sterile and unreal' in the works of social theorists (Liedke 1958, 377). Savigny was able to reconcile 'historical truth with logical order' by 'presenting law as a phenomenon that was rooted in the organic whole of the culture and that served the protection of individual freedom' (Reimann 1990, 842).

According to Savigny, historical study shows that the evolution and progress of society has led to lifestyles, as well as social and economic life, becoming more complex. As a result, the law has become more abstract and technical in order to respond to increasingly complex situations. This development has also necessitated the involvement of trained jurists. In other words, Savigny explained that even though the law originated from the people and was an expression of their cultural characteristics, it had to be managed by jurists after lifestyles and social and economic life became more complex. Savigny (1831, 28) stated that:

> With the progress of civilization, national tendencies become more and more distinct, and what otherwise would have remained common, becomes appropriated to particular classes; the jurists now become more and more a distinct class of the kind; law perfects its language, takes a scientific direction, and, as formerly it existed in the consciousness of the community, it now devolves upon the jurists, who thus, in this department, represent the community. Law is henceforth more artificial and complex, since it has a twofold life; first, as part of the aggregate existence of the community, which it does not cease to be; and, secondly, as a distinct branch of knowledge in the hands of the jurists.

This evolution of law over time has not been an artificial design based on rational thinking; rather, it has been an organic development. Even though Savigny argued that law first emerged and developed according to the unique spirit of the people, he also recognized that its later evolution was largely attributed to jurisprudence. Despite the emergence of increasingly complex social and economic relationships in advanced societies, as well as the increasingly prominent role of jurists in the development of law, Savigny did not think that the law should abandon its historical development or the spirit of the people as it progresses. In other words, he believed that even with the emergence of more complexities in society, the jurists tasked with improving the law could not completely separate it from the national spirit. In fact, Savigny claimed that since the history and experiences of the nation played a main role in the formation of the law, it cannot be 'changed arbitrarily' by jurists (Kantorowicz 1937, 332).

In his arguments against codification, Savigny claimed that 'no amount of state authority could produce a real, suitable, or stable code if the political element were not mature' (Kutner 1972, 287). He emphasized that since the German territories were not yet unified in the early 19th century, efforts to achieve codification based on 'a sound system of law,' which aims for 'the unity of the nation, and the concentration of its scientific efforts,' would only 'produce the desired unity for one half of Germany, and separate the rest by a line of demarcation, more strongly marked than before' (Savigny 1831,

182). He also pointed out that codification efforts in the early 19th century were premature, because the German territories of that time were occupied by many small states, whose respective laws were at different stages of development and lacked uniformity. More specifically, the laws of each state were determined by the spirit of their own people. Savigny (1831, 179) argued that 'a code is a much greater work, and that a higher degree of organic unity [of people] must be required of it.' He concluded that if the law had been codified in these small German states, it would have subsequently delayed the organic evolution and growth of the law in Germany after unification had taken place. Basically, Savigny rejected Thibaut's defense of the ahistorical theory of law, as well as his defense of reason as the main element of legal science in codifying the law in German territories.

Additionally, Savigny was opposed to 'plans for codification on the ground that the "state of the public mind" of the German people was "deficient" in "the law-making faculty" because it lacked the legal consciousness upon which to base the new legislative formulation' (Kutner 1972, 287). He explained that the formation of a good code required 'a highly developed study of law so that the code could be an adequate interpretation of the living law,' and he believed that German jurists lacked this kind of 'technical expertise' (ibid.). That is to say, according to Savigny (1831, 66), German territories lacked that which was 'necessary to the formation of a good code.' He also pointed out that Thibaut disregarded all the technical inadequacies of his time in his efforts to bring about codification.

There were also other disagreements between Savigny and Thibaut related to their codification debate. For instance, the HSJ defended 'communitarian anthropology,' because they held the view that 'the individual drives its identity entirely from its place in society and history' (Beiser 2011, 215, 243). According to Savigny, an individual is 'nothing more than a part of a larger whole,' which can include being 'a member of a family, of a people or of a state' (Small 1923B, 730). To be more precise, he explained that 'the well-being of every organic being, (consequently of states,) depends on the maintenance of an equipoise between the whole and its parts-on each having its due' (Savigny 1831, 58). He also noted that 'a lively affection for the whole can only proceed from the thorough participation in all particular relations; and he only who takes good care of his own family, will be a truly good citizen' (ibid.). Contrary to the historical school, the philosophical school supported 'atomistic anthropology,' as it regarded the 'individual as independent and self-sufficient' entity (Beiser 2011, 215, 243).

Another major point of contention between the historical school and the philosophical school was the latter's defense of natural law, which is based on universality principles. Basically, natural law theory relied on reason as the basis of law without taking account of the social and historical backgrounds of people and nations, or their particular spirits. Contrary to the views of the philosophical school, Savigny (1831, 23) did not believe that 'an ideal legislation for all times and all circumstances' could ever be established. In fact, he claimed that assuming that law was universal was wrong and illusionary. Furthermore, in his critique of the universality principle, Savigny (1831, 135) stated that people saw their 'thoughts in a false light of universality and originality. There is only the historical sense to protect us against this.'

According to Savigny, law was not fixed forever; rather, it changes with the progress and evolution of society. He explained that 'legislation itself, and jurisprudence' are 'accidental and fluctuating nature; and it is very possible that the law of tomorrow may not at all resemble the law of today' (Savigny 1831, 23). In other words, laws are not of universal validity, nor can they be applied anywhere or at any time. Savigny (1831, 135) was worried about the ambitious views of the PSJ when it came to the universality of law, particularly out of concern that human beings could lose their 'individual connection with the great entirety of the world and its history' if a law was accepted and applied universally.

Savigny concluded that implementing the legal code of another country in Germany would be a grave error. He emphasized the point that much like languages, law evolves organically across history based on the particular spirit of people and creates bonds based on common sets of beliefs, values, and convictions. Neither language nor law can be applied to other people and countries, as both develop with the evolution of a nation and disappear with its subsequent destruction. In fact, the diversity of laws between communities based on their particular historical developments is to be expected. According to Savigny, imposing the rules of one country in another country is not only imprudent, it is also unsuitable to the spirit of its people. Ultimately, he was successful in convincing 'German legal scholars to abandon their precipitate embrace of the Code Napoleon, and to explore the medieval and Roman roots of their own law' (Rodes 2004, 166). He maintained that the codification of the laws of German states via Napoleonic Code was not necessary as long as the law was in dynamic progress. Furthermore, he argued that it was up to each state to determine when the time was right for the codification of its laws.

The Historical School of Jurisprudence and the German Historical School of Economics

Savigny's work in legal science provided 'a pattern for the parallel science of economics' (Neff 1950, 356). More precisely, the integration of the features of the HSJ into political economy aimed to achieve the same result 'as the method of Savigny and Eichhorn has attained in jurisprudence' (Ashley 1894, 102). In the 19th century, there was a belief among scholars that once the historical approach was 'properly cultivated' in economics, 'it will never be quite abandoned' (Ashley 1894, 104). In Germany, 'the historical method' was originally 'passed' on 'from the lawyers' to the economists in the works of Roscher, who studied jurisprudence and philology at the universities of Göttingen and Berlin between 1835 and 1839 (Ashley 1908, 7). He sought 'to build a historical economics along the lines' of the HSJ (Schumacker 1934, 373). In other words, the impact of the HSJ was very visible in 'the case of Roscher, who took arguments from the jurists and attached importance to what he considered to be a close parallelism between the situations in the legal and the economic fields' (Schumpeter 2006, fn8, 399). He basically inherited his views about the transformation of political economy into a historical science from Savigny. In fact, Roscher's *Outline for Lectures of Political Economy* was accepted as an extension of the concepts of the HSJ to the discipline of economics, as he applied the historical method of the HSJ into political economy.

In addition to Savigny, Roscher also relied on the works of Justus Möser (1720–1794), whom he considered to be the founding father of the HSJ, as well as the greatest German national economist of the 18th century. Furthermore, Roscher's views about the historical approach were also influenced, to some extent, by the works of Eichhorn, Gößchen, and Leopold Ranke (Wolowsky 1878, 30). He even dedicated his first book, *Leben, Werk und Zeitalter des Thukydides* (1842), to Ranke. Ultimately, Roscher's importance to the development of the Historical School of Economics was not only attributed to his efforts in applying the 'laws of economics' to trade, 'agriculture,' and various other industries, but also on account of the fact that he derived the methods and purposes of this school of thought from those of the HSJ (Senn 2005, 76). Roscher and his followers basically took on 'the name Historical School, in order to ally themselves with the great reformers' in HSJ (Ely 1883, 233).

Theorists of the GHSE adopted the historical method of the HSJ, which maintains that 'every historical event was to be analyzed as to its particular features, especially its national aspects' (Pribram 1983, 213). Similar to their counterparts that adhered to the HSJ, they were of the opinion that various aspects of the social and economic development of a nation were outcomes of the spirit of its people. That means economics is not an abstract science that is shaped purely by the reason and rational thinking of individuals. On the contrary, it is an historical science that is shaped by the common spirit of people. Therefore, by adopting the historical approach of the HSJ, the GHSE was moving away from an abstract individualistic approach and toward one that is collectivist. In fact, much like the HSJ, adherents of the GHSE were of the view that changes in the economic circumstances of a nation and its institutions were not outcomes of the arbitrary will of a person or a group of people. Instead, people, their community, and their particular historical development all played roles in shaping such changes.

Theorists of the GHSE used the historical method to discover evolutionary economic patterns and laws of development. With respect to the nature and advancement of laws in legal science, theorists of the GHSE and the HSJ were in agreement that economic laws were not universal; rather, they were particular laws that changed based on the specific characteristics of a society and its institutions, as well as the spirit of its people. In other words, since these laws were derived from the particular characteristics of a society, they were not universally applicable everywhere, at any time, and under all circumstances; instead, they were accepted as relative and evolutionary laws. That means it was entirely possible for a law to be successfully adapted to one period in the historical development of a particular place and then turn out to be completely unfit for another period or location. In order to determine the appropriate laws and patterns of development for economic life, the GHSE supported using the comparative historical approach to identify differences and similarities in the development of various forms of societal organization, including tribes, empires, and nations. This is because they believed that historical studies made it possible for people to learn from their experiences and avoid making similar mistakes when designing present-day policies and reforms.

The codification debate between Thibaut and Savigny led to accusations that the historical school was being 'hostile to the liberal spirit of modern times' (Wolowsky 1878, 33). However, the support that Roscher, Knies, and Hildebrand provided for the HSJ was 'sufficient to remove this prejudice' (ibid.). The fact that the works of members of the HSJ were 'inspired by an enlightened love for progress, do not allow of such a misconstruction' (ibid.). This is mainly because 'the historical point of view does not consist in the worship of the past, any more than in the depreciation of the present … the historical method harmonizes wonderfully well with the wants of genuine progress' (ibid.). Accordingly, adherents of the GHSE supported 'the free and creative power of man, acting within the limit permitted to it by the degrees of intelligence reached, of the development of morals, and of individual liberty' (ibid.).

The GHSE believed that the discipline of economics would be completely lost without the historical method. Notably, Roscher was convinced that the historical method was the best and most conclusive of methods, because it was concerned with time, space, and societal organization. In fact, it was his commitment to integrating the historical method of the HSJ into political economy that resulted in applied economics becoming an important aspect of the GHSE. Roscher's efforts to implement the methods of the HSJ in economics culminated in him earning the title of 'the true founder of the discipline of applied economics' (Schumacker 1934, 373). Ultimately, theorists of the GHSE applied the historical method to political economy in a way that would 'unfurl the noble banner borne by the most venerated masters of the science' (Wolowsky 1878, 29).

Conclusion

Cameralism lost its dominant status in the early 19th century after having played a significant role in the initial development of political economy, public administration, public finance, statistics, bureaucratic organization, the welfare state, and political practices and thinking in both Germany and Austria.

Nevertheless, the legacy of cameralism was not completely eliminated, as universities continued to teach cameralist science. Generally speaking, contributors to the GHSE did not try to erase the entire cameralist tradition from the discipline of political economy. In fact, many of them previously studied cameralist science at university and were inspired by its goals, principles, and approaches. For example, similar to cameralists, disciples of the GHSE were against destructive competitiveness, wasteful consumption, the overexploitation of natural resources, the destruction of the natural environment, and the laissez-faire approach. Instead, they advocated for a collectivist and ethical approach, whereby the state was the supreme authority and was fully committed to achieving the common good. Other important features of the GHSE that were deeply influenced by cameralism included the use of statistics, the development of public finance and public administration, and support for the progress of social and economic institutions, all of which were important for the development of the national economy. Furthermore, while cameralists and adherents of the GHSE supported a strong state and ruler, neither of them endorsed any form of dictatorship. Both schools of thought maintained that the ruler was not free to act as he wanted, as his actions were to be limited by his own moral and ethical commitments and the legal framework. Additionally, they were opposed to individualistic, immoral, egoistic, and unethical actions on the part of the ruled.

Theorists of the GHSE not only kept the fundamental ideas of cameralism alive, they also integrated the historical approach of the HSJ into political economy. At the same time, they distanced themselves from the dogmatic rational deliberation, natural laws, and abstract economic theories of classical orthodoxy. Instead, they focused on the historical approach so as to understand the development of social and economic institutions of society and reveal the laws of historical changes. They believed that it was impossible to properly understand these institutions without a comprehension of the historical process from which they developed.

By integrating the approaches, methods, and ideas of the HSJ and the cameralist tradition into political economy, German political economists of the 19th century were able to develop a program of economic research that was not only opposed to the ideas of the dominant English school of economics, but also managed to achieve international recognition. As a result, German universities became the centers of higher education in the discipline of political economy. Moreover, professors of the GHSE were renowned for providing a high-quality education in political economy, as well as successfully discrediting many of the principles and methods of orthodox classical economics. International journals that were published in many different languages also frequently referenced the views and ideas of the theorists of the GHSE, because they were considered reliable and respectable authorities and sources within the discipline of economics. That means serious scholars around the world had to be familiar with the principles, approaches, ideas, and methods advocated by scholars of the GHSE. In the second half of the

19th century, the impeccable reputation acquired by German universities and their professors resulted in dramatic increases in enrolments on the part of international students seeking to advance their education in political economy to the point that Germany surpassed both Britain and France in terms of the number of applications received from foreign students. Accordingly, it was accepted that 'the lead in economics' was 'passed from England and France to Germany' in the mid-19th century, and the influence of theorists of the GHSE increased significantly, both domestically and internationally (Dorfman 1955, 22). Up until the outbreak of WWI, the international success of the GHSE continued with little risk that a rival economic program of research could emerge at a similar scale of advancement and sophistication.

Notes

1 The University of Halle was founded in 1694 by Frederick III (1657–1713), who served as the first 'King in Prussia' between 1701 and 1713.

2 Political economy is an historical science that mainly studies production and exchange and their relationships with laws, traditions, and income and wealth distribution. More specifically, it examines patterns or laws of evolution of production and exchange in each individual stage of historical development in order to establish general laws. In political economy, society is not divided into economic and political arenas that are independent of each other and ethical values play an important role in economic and political decisions.

3 To increase the growth of population, cameralists focused on safeguarding justice, security, safety, economic prosperity, and property rights of all of its inhabitants, including immigrants.

Bibliography

Ashley, William J. 1894. 'Roscher's Programme of 1843.' *The Quarterly Journal of Economics*. Vol. 9, No. 1: 99–105. URL: https://www.jstor.org/stable/1883638

Ashley, William J. 1908 [1888]. *An Introduction to English Economic History and Theory*. https://socialsciences.mcmaster.ca/~econ/ugcm/3ll3/ashley/Hist1.pdf

Balabkins, Nicholas W. 1988. *Not by Theory Alone...The Economics of Gustav von Schmoller and Its Legacy to America*. Berlin: Duncker und Humblot.

Backhaus, Jürgen G. 2009A. 'Introduction.' Ed. Jürgen G. Backhaus. *The Beginnings of Political Economy: Johann Heinrich Gottlob Justi*. Erfurt: Springer. XI–XII.

Backhaus, Jürgen G. 2009B. 'From Wolff to Justi.' Ed. Jürgen G. Backhaus. *The Beginnings of Political Economy: Johann Heinrich Gottlob Justi*. Erfurt: Springer. 1–18.

Becchi, Paolo. 2009. 'German Legal Science: The Crisis of Natural Law Theory, the Historicisms, and "Conceptual Jurisprudence".' Ed. Canale, Damiano, Paolo Grossi, and Hasso Hofmann. *A History of the Philosophy of Law in the Civil Law World, 1600–1900. A Treatise of Legal Philosophy and General Jurisprudence, Vol. 9*. New York: Springer International Publishing. 185–224.

Beiser, Frederick C. 2011. *The German Historicist Tradition*. New York: Oxford University Press.

Cannan, Edwin. 1929. *A Review of Economic Theory*. London: P. S. King and Son.

Chaloupek, Günther. 2009. 'J.H.G. Justi in Austria: His Writings in the Context of Economic and Industrial Policies of the Habsburg Empire in the 18th Century.'

Ed. Jürgen G. Backhaus. *The Beginnings of Political Economy: Johann Heinrich Gottlob Justi*. Erfurt: Springer. 147–156.

Cunningham, William. 1894. 'Why had Roscher So Little Influence in England.' *Annals of the American Academy Political and Social Science*. Vol. 5, 317–334.

Dorn, Walter L. 1931. 'The Prussian Bureaucracy in the 18th Century, I.' *Political Science Quarterly*. Vol. 46, No. 3: 402–423. URL: https://www.jstor.org/stable/2143267

Dorn, Walter L. 1932A. 'The Prussian Bureaucracy in the 18th Century, II.' *Political Science Quarterly*. Vol. 47, No. 1: 75–94. URL: https://www.jstor.org/stable/2142703

Dorn, Walter L. 1932B. 'The Prussian Bureaucracy in the 18th Century, III.' *Political Science Quarterly*. Vol. 47, No. 2: 259–273. URL: https://www.jstor.org/stable/2143090

Ely, Richard T. 1883. 'The Past and the Present of Political Economy.' *Overland Monthly*. Vol. 2, No. 9: 225–235. Full View|HathiTrust Digital Library|HathiTrust Digital Library.

Haney, Lewis Henry. 1915. *History of Economic Thought: A Critical Account of the Origin and Development of the Economic Theories of the Leading Thinkers in the Leading Nations*. New York: The Macmillan Company.

Hölzl, Richard. 2020. 'Towards Ecological Statehood? Cameralism and the Human-Nature Interface in the Eighteenth Century.' Ed. Nokkala Ere and Nicholas B. Miller. *Cameralism and the Enlightenment: Happiness, Governance and Reform in Transnational Perspective*. New York: Routledge. 148–170.

Ingram, John Kells. 1888. *A History of Political Economy*. Ed. London: A. and C. Black. A History of Political Economy|Online Library of Liberty (libertyfund.org).

Jackson, Michael. 2005. 'The Eighteenth Century Antecedents of Bureaucracy, the Cameralists.' *Management Decision*. Vol. 43, No. 10: 1293–1303. doi:10.1108/00251740510634877

Jevons, W. Stanley. 1876. 'The Future of Political Economy.' *The Fortnightly Review*. Vol. 20, No. 129: 617–631. London: Chapman and Hall. https://archive.org/details/in.ernet.dli.2015.21176/page/n5/mode/2up

Justi, Johann Heinrich Gottlob von. 1760. *Die Natur und das Wesen der Staaten als die Grundwissenschaft derStaatszunft, der Policen, und aller Regierungs-Wissenschaft*. https://digital.lb-oldenburg.de/brandes/content/structure/8844.

Justi, Johann Heinrich Gottlob von. 1951 [1766]. 'System des Finanzwesens.' Ed. Arthur Eli Monroe. *Early Economic Thought: Selections from Economic Literature Prior to Adam Smith*. London: Oxford University Press. 377–399. https://hdl.handle.net/2027/mdp.39015028152489

Kanamori, Shigenari. 2009. 'Justi and Japan.' Ed. Jürgen G. Backhaus. *The Beginnings of Political Economy: Johann Heinrich Gottlob von Justi*. Erfurt: Springer. 111–116.

Kantorowicz, Hermann. 1937. 'Savigny and the Historical School of Law.' *Law Quarterly Review*. Vol. 53: 326–343.

Kutner, Luis. 1972. 'Legal Philosophers: Savigny: German Lawgiver.' *Marquette Law Review*. Vol. 55, No. 2: 281–295. http://scholarship.law.marquette.edu/mulr/vol55/iss2/5

Liedke, Herbert R. 1958. 'The German Romanticists and Karl Ludwig von Haller's Doctrines of European Restoration.' *The Journal of English and Germanic Philology*. Vol. 57, No. 3: 371–393. URL: http://www.jstor.org/stable/27707117

Miller, Nicholas B. 2020. 'Cameralism and the Politics of Populationism: Comparative Perspectives.' Ed. Nokkala Ere and Nicholas B. Miller. *Cameralism and the*

Enlightenment: Happiness, Governance and Reform in Transnational Perspective. New York: Routledge. 127–147.

Monroe, Arthur Eli. 1951. *Early Economic Thought: Selection from Economic Literature Prior to Adam Smith*. Cambridge: Harvard University Press.

Neff, Frank Amandus. 1950. *Economic Doctrines*. New York: McGraw-Hill. https://archive.org/details/economic-doctrines-frank-neff

Parry, Geraint. 1963. 'Enlightenment Government and Its Critics in Enlightenment Germany.' *Historical Journal*. Vol. 6, No. 2: 178–192.

Peukert, Helge. 2006. 'Justi's Moral Economics and his System of Taxation (1766).' *Journal of Economic Behavior & Organization*. Vol. 59: 478–496.

Pribram, Karl. 1983. *A History of Economic Reasoning*. Baltimore: The Johns Hopkins University Press.

Raeff, Marc. 1975. 'The Well-ordered Police State and the Development of Modernity in Seventeenth and Eighteenth Century Europe.' *American Historical Review*. Vol. 80: 1221–1243.

Rath, Klaus Wilhelm. 1940. 'Staat und Staatswirtschaft im kameralistischen Denken.' *FinanzArchiv: Public Finance Analysis. New Series*. Vol. 7, No. 1: 75–99. URL: https://www.jstor.org/stable/40908296

Reimann, Mathias. 1990. 'Nineteenth Century German Legal Science.' *Boston College Law Review*. Vol. 31, No. 4: 837–897. https://lawdigitalcommons.bc.edu/bclr/vol31/iss4/2

Reinert, Erik S. 2009. 'Johann Heinrich Gottlob von Justi – The Life and Times of an Economist Adventurer.' Ed. Jürgen G. Backhaus. *The Beginnings of Political Economy: Johann Heinrich Gottlob von Justi*. Erfurt: Springer. 33–74.

Reinert, Erik S. and Hugo Reinert. 2009. 'A Bibliography of J.H.G. von Justi.' Ed. Jürgen G. Backhaus. *The Beginnings of Political Economy: Johann Heinrich Gottlob von Justi*. Erfurt: Springer. 19–32.

Rodes, Robert E. 2004. 'On the Historical School of Jurisprudence.' *The American Journal of Jurisprudence*. Vol. 49: 165–184. https://scholarship.law.nd.edu/law_faculty_scholarship/858

Roscher, William. 1878 [1843]. *Outline for Lectures of Political Economy*. New York: Henry Holt & CO.Savigny, Friedrich Carl von. 1831. *Of the Vocation of our Age for Legislation and Jurisprudence*. Oxford: Bodleian Library.

Schmoller, Gustav. 1902 [1893]. *Économie Nationale, Économie Politique et Méthode*. Paris: V. Giard & E. Brière, Libraires-Éditeurs.

Schumacker, Hermann. 1934. 'The Historical School.' Ed. Seligman, E.R.A. *Encyclopaedia of the Social Sciences: Vol. 5*. New York: Macmillan. 371–376.

Senn, Peter R. 2005. 'The German Historical Schools in the History of Economic Thought.' *Journal of Economic Studies*. Vol. 32, No. 3: 185–255. www.emeraldinsight.com/0144-3585.htm

Small, Albion W. 1923A. 'Some Contribution to the History of Sociology. Section VIII. Approaches to Objective Economic and Political Science in Germany: Cameralism.' *American Journal of Sociology*. Vol. 29, No. 2: 158–165. http://www.jstor.org/stable/2764288.

Small, Albion W. 1923B. 'Some Contributions to the History of Sociology. Section II. The Thibaut-Savigny Controversy: Continuity as a Phase of Human Experience.' *American Journal of Sociology*. Vol. 28, No. 6: 711–734. URL: http://www.jstor.org/stable/2764578

Small, Albion W. 2001 [1909]. *The Cameralists: The Pioneers of German Social Polity*. Kitchener: Batoche Books.

Smith, Adam. 1979. *An Inquiry into the Nature and Causes of the Wealth of Nations*. Oxford: Oxford University Press.

Schmidt am Busch, Hans-Christoph. 2009. 'Cameralism as Political Metaphysics: Human Nature, the State, and Natural Law in the Thought of Johann Heinrich Gottlob von Justi.' *The European Journal of the History of Economic Thought*. Vol. 16, No. 3: 409–430. DOI: 10.1080/09672560903101252

Spicer, Michael W. 1998. 'Cameralist thought and public Administration.' *Journal of Management History*. Vol. 4, No. 3: 149–159.

St. Marc, Henri. 1892. *Étude sur L'Enseignement de L'Économie Politique dans les Université D'Allemagne et D'Autriche*. Paris: Armand Colin et C.

Tribe, Keith. June 1984. 'Cameralism and the Science of Government.' *The Journal of Modern History*. Vol. 56, No. 2: 263–284. Chicago: The University of Chicago Press. Stable URL: http://www.jstor.org/stable/1879090

Tribe, Keith. 1988. *Governing Economy: The Reformation of German Economic Discourse 1750–1840*. Cambridge: Cambridge University Press.

Tribe, Keith. 2002. 'Historical Schools of Economics: German and English.' *Keele Economics Research Papers*. No. 2002. https://ssrn.com/abstract=316689 or http://dx.doi.org/10.2139/ssrn.316689

Tribe, Keith. 2018. 'Cameralism.' Ed. Gilbert Faccarello and Heinz D. Kurz. *Handbook on the History of Economic Analysis Volume II: Schools of Thought in Economics*. Cheltenham: Edward Elgar Publishing. 43–51.

Wagner, Richard E. 2012. 'The Cameralists: Fertile Sources for a New Science of Public Finance.' Ed. Jürgen Georg Georg Backhaus. *Handbook of the History of Economic Thought*. New York: Springer. 123–135.

Wakefield, Andre. 2005. 'Books, Bureaus, and the Historiography of Cameralism.' *European Journal of Law and Economics*. Vol. 19: 311–320.

Wakefield, Andre. 2009. *The Disordered Police State: German Cameralism as Science and Practice*. Chicago: University of Chicago Press.

Wolff, Christian. 1750. *The Real Happiness of a People under a Philosophical King*. London: M. Cooper.

Wolowsky, Louis. 1878. 'Preliminary Essay: On the Application of the Historical Method to the Study of Political Economy.' Ed. William Roscher. *Outline for Lectures of Political Economy*. 13th Ed. New York: Henry Holt & CO. 1–48.

Ziolkowski, Theodore. 2004. *Clio the Romantic Muse: Historicizing the Faculties in Germany*. London: Cornell University Press.

3 An Overview of Fundamental Features of the German Historical School of Economics

Introduction

In the 19th century, the UK and France were undergoing rapid transitions in their modes of production from preindustrial systems to industrialized economies. This was accompanied by rapid urbanization, which led to an increase in construction projects, and an expansion in urban employment. The exploitation of the masses by a minority of wealthy elites worsened with industrialization, as the latter were able to earn more income and accumulate more wealth than ever before. The more wealth and income they acquired, 'the more they feel it necessary to gain in addition. They look upon every opposition to their wishes as an uprising against economic order in general' (Small 1923, 722).

Unfortunately, 'the growth of modern industries in Germany' during the 19th century 'led to social evils similar to those which had occurred in Britain' and France, as 'reports from the provincial authorities' indicated that in 'the manufacturing districts of Prussia the labor of children was being exploited in a disgraceful manner' (Henderson 2006, 22). Additionally, a large population of factory workers in German-speaking territories were experiencing long working hours, low wages, 'harsh factory discipline,' and bad housing conditions in cities, with many living in slums (ibid.: 38). These conditions only worsened with the intensification of competition between factory owners, which led to workers experiencing exhaustion and incurring various health problems. There was a great deal of concern about the pace of urbanization in Prussia and other German states, which resulted in a decline of the rural population alongside large increases in the number of urban dwellers, in addition to many other changes associated with the rapid transition from a preindustrial system to an industrialized one. There was also growing dissatisfaction with the narrow views and ideas being put forth by classical economics. In particular, theorists of the GHSE, who rigorously sought out solutions for the social and economic inequality and injustices being caused by these rapid transformations, rejected the classical economists' defense of universal economic laws and their reduction of man into an abstract, self-interest-oriented, one-dimensional entity, arguing that such

DOI: 10.4324/9781003247715-3

practices were in contradiction with the realities and organic development of social and economic life. They believed that political economy needed to be reformed in light of the prevailing misery and poverty of their time, as well as the inability of classical orthodoxy to resolve persistent social and economic issues. In response, nearly all theorists associated with the GHSE sought to develop a system of political economy that would have a predisposition toward achieving common welfare. They were trying to find ways to alleviate the destructive outcomes of rapid urbanization and industrialization and improve the condition of craftsmen, peasants, and factory workers.

This chapter presents some of the well-known contributors to the GHSE and explains the main arguments they put forth against methodological individualism, the laissez-faire doctrine, the deductive method, the ahistorical and value-free nature of classical economics, and socialist ideals. It also discusses their support for ethical historical economics, the inductive approach, methodological collectivism, the national economy, and the use of statistics in political economy. Overall, this chapter highlights the fact that unlike classical economics, theorists of the GHSE aimed to develop sensible economic policies and reforms that would address the common needs of all social classes in order to achieve the common good. Gaining a proper understanding of the methods, approaches, ideas, and principles supported by the well-known contributors to the GHSE is necessary in order to demonstrate the important role that this school of thought played in the development of economic thought and education in the US from the 1870s until the beginning of WWI.

The Main Contributors to the GHSE: From the Older Historical School to the Youngest Historical School

It is generally accepted that the origins of the GHSE can be traced back to a growing dissatisfaction with the narrow views and ideas of the dominant English school of economics. This discontent with classical economics is what led Wilhelm Georg Friedrich Roscher (1817–1894) to publish *Outline for Lectures of Political Economy* in 1843. It outlined the main principles and methods of the historical school and became the most influential textbook of political economy[1] in Germany throughout the second half of the 19th century. In fact, this book was 'used for a long period of time very widely in the German schools' (Mitchell 1949, 185).

From 1848 to 1888, Roscher was a professor of Practical State Sciences and Cameralistics at Leipzig University, where he taught economic theory, economic policy, public finance, statistics, and cameralism. He dedicated his life to finding a historical basis for economics, which would emphasize the need for the inclusion of the historical spirit in economic research and investigation. In doing so, he became recognized as the first economist to use the term 'historical method' in political economy (Block 1879, 706). Additionally, he was accepted as 'the first macroeconomist,' even though the term macroeconomics did not exist in the 19th century (Streissler 2001, 324–325). In:

> the first quarter-century of the life history of the historical school it was Roscher's conception of the scope and method of economics that found the widest acceptance and that best expressed the animus of that body of students who professed to cultivate economics by the historical method.
> (Veblen 1901, 74)

It was also claimed that the influence and work of Roscher were primary contributing factors to 'a veritable revolution' that had 'taken place in economic studies' in Germany (Cunningham 1894, 317). In fact, Roscher was considered to be 'the most influential of German economists, a man of very wide learning and with very considerable influence upon practical affairs and with a very large following among students' (Mitchell 1949, 185). For example, *The New York Times* wrote that Roscher possessed 'such a copious knowledge of the history of all nations, ancient and modern, as no other man of his specialty has brought to light (New York Times, 1894, p. 4)' (Senn 1995, 66). That same article stated that he lived to 'be known all over Europe as the father of that school, and to see his methods adopted in universities of every civilized land ... Scores of Americans have heard his lectures, and many American professors have been among pupils' (ibid.). Joseph A. Schumpeter (1883–1950) (2006, 483) highly praised the merits of Roscher's achievements, stating that his work:

> never fell below a highly respectable level: honest scholarship and sound common sense is written all over them, and the sympathetic understanding that his gentle and highly cultivated mind extended to all types of scientific effort helped to make them perhaps more useful to many generations of students than would have been more original productions ... On the whole, however, there is hardly another economist of that period who enjoyed so nearly universal respect inside and outside of Germany.

The value of Roscher's contributions to the development of political economy is beyond doubt, particularly in light of the fact that his ideas, views, and methods spread beyond the borders of Germany, having been adopted in the universities of many other countries (Small 2001, 6). In addition to Roscher, Bruno Hildebrand (1812–1878) and Karl Knies (1821–1898) are also known as founding fathers of the GHSE. They ended up becoming 'three of the most influential professors in Germany in the middle of the nineteenth century' (Mitchell 1949, 186). All three not only rejected 'the claim of universal validity and applicability of classical economics, but insisted that it was grossly inadequate to deal with industrialization and its social consequences, not to speak of its irrelevance, for Germany' (Balabkins 1988, 25). Roscher, Hildebrand, and Knies provided arguments against key elements and principles of classical economics, including the abstract-deductive approach, individualism, laissez-faire, and universalism. Additionally, they played crucial roles in familiarizing 'the public' with the historical approach in political economy (Seligman 1917, 161).

Roscher, Hildebrand, and Knies were considered to be among the main contributors to the Older Historical School (OHS), which emerged in the beginning of the 1840s, along with Carl Dietzel (1829–1884), Erwin Nasse (1829–1890), Lorenz von Stein (1815–1890), and Georg Hanssen (1809–1894). Members of the OHS were highly critical of 'the faulty abstract-deductive methods which they found predominant, and, while they formulated a method of their own' (Haney 1915, 410). Their ideas, concepts, methods, and teachings quickly spread through universities across Germany. Moreover, many national and international political economists were drawn to Germany so that they could study under the founding fathers of the GHSE, who 'proposed new and almost radical departures in economic thought' (Balabkins 1988, 87). This was not an unexpected development, as they were regarded as 'the great innovators of the day in their profession,' who were 'doing empirical work of considerable merit, even from the contemporary perspective' (ibid.). In particular, Hildebrand, who founded *Jahrbücher für Nationalökonomie und Statistik* (*Journal of National Economics and Statistics*) in 1863, was accepted as 'a thinker of a really high order; it may be doubted whether amongst German economists there has been any endowed with a more profound and searching intellect' (Ingram 1888, 124). His work was focused on saving economics from 'false friends,' including 'Friedrich List, Marxist socialists, and classical economics' (Balabkins 1988, 27). Meanwhile, his book *Die Nationalökonomie der Gegenwart und Zukunft* (1848) was highly valued for providing 'a masterly criticism of the economic systems which preceded, or belonged to, his time, including those of Smith, Müller, List, and the socialists' (Ingram 1888, 124). Hildebrand formulated some particularly vigorous criticisms of classical economics, which included accusations that classical economists generated destructive outcomes for society by promoting egoism, individualism, and materialism (Block 1879, 708).

Knies was recognized for his analyses and critiques of prominent classical economists, mainly Adam Smith and David Ricardo (Ingram 1888, 124). He was also well known for his opposition to socialism, as he was confident that the GHSE would eventually defeat all socialist theories. Knies was specialized in the fields of statistics, money, and credit, and taught political economy to many German and international students at Heidelberg University. In fact, he played a major role in making Heidelberg into 'a center of study and research in which the most diverse types were welcomed and made to work together' (Schumpeter 2006, 777). During his time at Heidelberg University, many prominent figures studied under Knies, including Eugen von Böhm-Bawerk (1851–1914), Friedrich von Wieser (1851–1926), John Bates Clark (1847–1938), Edwin Seligman (1861–1939), and Richard T. Ely (1854–1943). Moreover, his work on subjective utility played an important role in the eventual emergence of the Marginalist Revolution that is often associated with the works of Léon Walras (1834–1910), Carl Menger (1840–1921), and William Stanley Jevons (1835–1882) (Papadopoulos and Bateman 2011). Even though the concept of marginal utility was accepted as a decisive innovation of neoclassical economics, Knies was using it decades before the emergence of the Marginalist Revolution (Streissler 2001, 322).

The historical method developed by Hildebrand, Knies, and Roscher 'exhibited its essential features more fully in the hands of the younger generation of scientific economists in Germany' (Ingram 1888, 126). Accordingly, the Younger Historical School (YHS) emerged in the 1870s under the leadership of Gustav von Schmoller (1838–1917), who was sometimes referred to as 'the leader of the extreme left of the Historical School' (Seager 1893, 237). While the OHS focused on problems pertaining to the historical method and economic development, the YHS concentrated on the social and economic problems of their time, the study of economic institutions, the application of the historical method to practical research, and the integration of ethics into social and economic policies. However, through his work on population and the division of labor, Schmoller stood out as 'the master historian and statistician' (Seager 1893, 250). This is not particularly surprising given his educational background, which included attending Tübingen University, where he studied '*Staatswissenschaften*, a combination of public finance, statistics, economics, administrative science, history and sociology' (Balabkins 1988, 13, Richter 1996, 568). He also studied chemistry, physics, and mechanical engineering during his time at Tübingen. Subsequently, he began to work in the Wurttemberg Statistical-Topographical Office as a part of his training for the civil service (Richter 1996, 568). Consequently, he recognized the importance of statistics in political economy. In 1864, Schmoller began to work as a professor of *Staatswissenschaften* at the University of Halle (1864–1872) before subsequently joining the faculties at Strasbourg University (1872–1882) and Berlin University (1882–1913). In Germany, many of his students went on to attain prominent positions, including government ministers, public officials, directors of banks, and editors of journals.

In 1881, Schmoller became the editor of *Jahrbuch für Gesetzgebung, Verwaltung und Volkswirthschaft im Deutschen Reich*, renamed *Schmollers Jahrbuch* in 1913, which was 'the leading German journal for politics and economics' (Tribe 2002, 9). Then, in 1883, he became a member of the *Prussian Staatsrat* (Council of State), where he devoted much of his work to Prussian administrative and economic history, and had 'an unprecedented influence over economic and social policy making through a system of professional and advisory organisations he helped establish' (Backhaus 2007, 13). He was 'the most conspicuous economist of the chief university in the capital of Germany, and much of the time the closest adviser of the government' (Mitchell 1949, 195). In fact, 'nobody occupied so important a situation in German society as Schmoller did' (ibid.). He was not only accepted as a social reformer and 'a great scholar very widely read and a person of strong understanding, but also a person who was in close and vigorous touch with what were in his day the guiding forces in German life' (ibid.). It could even be said that Schmoller's 'life and work closely reflected the history of the Empire' (Grimmer-Solem 2010A, 10).

In addition to being an historian, a political economist, and a statistician, Schmoller was also a great philosopher who played a main role in developing ethical economics (Seager 1893, 250). During his lifetime, Schmoller was globally renowned as one of the most respected and important economists in the history of economic thought (ibid.: 237). It was also claimed that 'the spirit and purpose of the German historical economists' was expressed in '*Grundriss der Allgemeinen Volkswirtschaftslehre* (part 1, 1900; part 2, 1904)' (Ashley 1908, 9). This two-volume book was widely considered to be 'one of the great books on economics at the end of the 19th century which sums up in a most effective fashion an enormous amount of detailed work and has a very considerable substantive value' (Mitchell 1949, 200). In it, Schmoller focused intensively on developing 'economic science through historical, descriptive, and factual material in order to relate it fully to the other social sciences,' which he also discussed in some of his other publications (Neff 1950, 360). Over the course of his career, Schmoller also wrote about a variety of other issues such as social justice, the history of Prussian economics, the historical development of enterprises, the nature of property, the reasons behind economic development, the evolution of social and economic institutions, the relationship between economics and ethics, the economics of families, the social and economic divisions of labor, social classes, the distribution of wealth, the formation of social classes, international trade, competition, labor laws, wages, and the national economy.

It has also been argued that Schmoller was the original creator of the modern welfare state. He played a major role in the establishment of some of 'the most advanced welfare legislation' in the world during the rule of Otto von Bismarck (1815–1898), who was Germany's first chancellor between 1871 and 1890 (Backhaus 1988, 5, Balabkins 1988, 50). He was also credited with being 'the father' of 'Institutionalism' in the US (Schumpeter 2018, 275). This is because 'Schmoller made a lasting impression on many of' the American students who flocked to 'German universities by the thousands' (Balabkins 1988, 50). After they returned home, these former students of Schmoller played a major role in developing economic thought and reforming the ways in which political economy was taught and studied at American universities.

Lujo Brentano (1844–1931) was also among the main contributors to the YHS. He studied law and economics at the University of Göttingen before entering the Prussian Office of Statistics in Berlin. Ultimately, he ended up working at universities in 'Berlin, Breslau, Strasbourg, Vienna,' and Munich, before succeeding Roscher at Leipzig University, when the latter resigned his post in 1888 (Grimmer-Solem 2010B, 10). Similar to other theorists of the GHSE, Brentano also warned 'German businessmen, journalists, and academics that laissez-faire was not a cure-all for the social ills of rapid industrialization and that welfare legislation might be in order soon' (Balabkins 1988, 30). That said, his work generally focused on the roles of trade unions and various social programs in the achievement of common welfare.

Adolf Gotthilf Wagner (1835–1917), who studied jurisprudence and political science at the universities of Göttingen and Heidelberg, was also known as a leading member of the YHS. He was 'the editor and, to a large extent, the writer, of a *Handbook on Political Economy*,' and reputed to be one of the original founders of public finance (Seager 1893, 238). According to Wagner, the achievement of the common good had to be the starting point in political economy. That said, he did not believe that the common good could be adequately satisfied via the free market system, which led him to oppose economic liberalism and support positive state action. Wagner advocated for protective trade measures, public ownership, and the state provision of social and economic programs and services. Even though he defended public ownership, he also supported private property ownership, so long as it served 'the best interests of society' (Seager 1893, 244).

Johannes E. Conrad (1839–1915) was another important member of the YHS, who first taught at the University of Jena, before later joining the University of Halle, where he succeeded Schmoller. Despite receiving an offer of employment from the University of Göttingen, he elected to stay on at the University of Halle, where he remained until his death. He was one of the co-organizers of *Verein für Sozialpolitik* and director of *Jahrbücher für Nationalökonomie und Statistik*, a scientific journal published in Germany since 1863. Another prominent member of the YHS was Adolf Held (1844–1880), whose research focused on taxation. In fact, his work on an 'advanced program of social security' played a major role 'in Bismarck's legislation of sickness, accident, invalidity, and old age insurance' (Dorfman 1955, 21). This is not particularly surprising, given that members of the YHS featured prominently in the formation of Bismarck's social and economic policies.

The YHS also included Karl Friedrich Hermann Rosier (1834–1894), Conrad Gustav Cohn (1840–1919), Karl Theodor von Inama-Sternegg (1843–1908), Albert Schäffle (1831–1903), Hans von Scheel (1839–1901), and Gustav Schönberg (1839–1908) (Ingram 1888, 127). Subsequently, the generation that followed the YHS was labeled the Youngest Historical School, which included Werner Sombart (1863–1941), Arthur Spiethoff (1873–1957), Max Weber (1864–1920), Georg Hanssen (1809–1894), Wilhelm Lexis (1837–1914), Karl Bücher (1847–1930), and Georg Friedrich Knapp (1842–1926). There were some notable differences between the ideas held by the older, younger, and youngest generations of the GHSE, with some being more conservative in their policies and reforms, whereas others were more liberal. However, their diverging views and policies are not discussed in this book, as it primarily focuses on identifying and explaining their converging views and ideas on the methods, approaches, principles, and goals of political economy.

Fundamental Methods, Approaches, Values, and Policies Supported by the GHSE

In the 19th century, members of the GHSE were dissatisfied with the narrow views, approaches, methods, policies, and ideas being put forth by the dominant English school of economics. In order to find solutions for the social and economic inequalities and injustices being caused by rapid urbanization and industrialization, theorists of the GHSE sought to develop a program of economic research that was based on the historical inductive approach, national economy, ethical values, the collectivist approach, and empirical and statistical methods. The following sections discuss these features of the GHSE, which significantly shaped the development of the discipline of economics and led to one of the most important methodological debates that occurred in the history of economic thought during the last decades of the 19th century. Unfortunately, a majority of economists have been ignorant of this methodological debate and its importance to the history of economic thought and the development of the discipline of economics.

Inductive versus Deductive Approach

Since WWII, methodological debates and disagreements between supporters of the inductive and deductive approaches have fallen completely out of fashion within the discipline of economics. It is rare to find anything on this subject in economic textbooks, while major economic journals have shown little interest in publishing work on methodological issues. That is unfortunate, because a proper understanding of the methodological debate pertaining to the inductive (empirical) and deductive (abstract) approaches is crucial if one is to become a well-rounded economist. In fact, it was argued that 'only those who fail to realize the situation at that time-so hard to understand at the present-who can regard as futile and meaningless the controversy regarding induction and deduction, statistical and historical method' (Ely 1910, 65). Although the methodological debate on the inductive and deductive approaches has been severely neglected by neoliberal economists, it has generated many discussions and publications throughout the history of economics among scholars from different schools of economic thought.

The methodological debate on the inductive and deductive approaches was considered to be very important by many prominent economists, including Adam Smith (1723–1790), David Ricardo (1772–1823), Jeremy Bentham (1748–1832), Thomas Robert Malthus (1766–1834), Auguste Comte (1798–1857), 'Karl Marx, Carl Menger, Alfred Marshall, Gustav von Schmoller, Werner Sombart, Max Weber,' and William Stanley Jevons (1835–1882) (Hodgson 2001, 22). Smith made use of history and statistics in his writings while also expressing an interest in historical spirit and historical investigation. Nevertheless, he mainly used the deductive method in *Wealth of Nations*. Ultimately, he employed the deductive method in this book in order to point out universal facts about human nature and nature in general. The deductive method was also used by Ricardo, who was widely considered to be the successor to Smith. In the history of economic thought, one of the most important debates on methodology emerged between theorists from the Austrian School of Economics (ASE) and the GHSE, which lasted for decades and reached its peak in the 1880s. This debate was labeled the 'methodological battle (*Methodenstreit*) between Schmoller's defence of the empirical and inductive method and Menger's defence of the abstract, theoretical, and deductive method' (Filip 2018, 108).

Much like the natural sciences, the deductive method develops theories based on abstract and ahistorical assumptions and premises. In political economy, the deductive approach takes:

> its ultimate facts, its premises, from other sciences, from common and familiar experience, or from the declarations of consciousness, proceeds from these and from definitions to evolve an economic system without any further recourse to the external world, save perhaps as furnishing tests of the validity of the reasoning.
>
> (Ely 1884, 8)

In other words, it starts from 'a new idea, put up tentatively, and not yet justified in any way'; then 'an anticipation, a hypothesis, a theoretical system' emerges from this idea, after which 'conclusions are drawn by means of logical deduction' (Popper 2002, 9). Subsequently, 'these conclusions are then compared with one another and with other relevant statements, so as to find what logical relations (such as equivalence, derivability, compatibility, or incompatibility) exist between them' (ibid.). That means the deductive method starts with a general statement (hypotheses) and then tests all possibilities in order to reach a precise conclusion or a singular (or particular) statement. It then treats the singular statement as though it were a universal (or general) statement. Essentially, the deductive approach develops 'the solution of specific problems' from the original singular statement (Mayo-Smith 1886, 105).

Scientists develop theories and make predictions based on this singular statement, which is accepted as universal. They assume that if the theory is valid (or true), then it is also valid for any other particular observation. In other words, supporters of the deductive method believe that if the universal statement is correct for a particular group, then it must also be correct for every other group and every single person that comprises each of those groups. For example, classical economists assume that all economic agents are motivated by self-interest maximization 'that there is freedom of competition, that capital and labour are transferable' (Ashley 1908, 8). Based on these assumptions, which they accept as universally valid, 'they deduce certain hypothetical conclusions -conclusions, that is to say, only true so far as the assumptions are true; and then they hope, by introducing this and that limitation, to arrive at an explanation of particular problems' (ibid.).

As for the inductive method, 'instead of beginning with certain hypothetical principles of human nature it professes to start' from the particular facts of history and statistics (Newcomb 1884, 301). More precisely, the inductive method passes from particular (or singular) statements, 'such as accounts of the results of observations or experiments, to universal statements, such as hypotheses or theories' (Popper 2002, 4). It starts from the particular statement, where multiple features and characteristics of a particular phenomenon or situation are identified through the collection of historical facts and large-scale statistical data. Then, scientists study these facts and data in order to discover patterns and regularities, which are used to determine whether or not the particular statement is valid. Once the validity of a particular statement is confirmed via the study of large-scale historical facts or experience, the scientist can then make a generalization or universal statement. However, conclusions reached according to the inductive method do not 'acquire absolute and inevitable validity' (Louzek 2011, 457). This is because it remains a possibility that 'a fact that contradicts the postulated general law will appear in the future. In that case, the theory in question is refuted and should be replaced with a new, more credible theory' (ibid.). Contrary to the inductive approach, the abstract-deductive method does not require the verification of conclusions via experience. This is on account of the fact that the deductive method is 'based on certain assumptions, which are set beforehand and that often need not correspond to experience' (ibid.: 456).

Classical economists claimed that political economy was a deductive science, and as such, there was no place for inductive methods. However, theorists of the GHSE, particularly Roscher, Hildebrand, and Knies, claimed that classical economic theories isolated society and individuals from a multitude of their real features and characteristics because they were based on the abstract-deductive method. They maintained that economic investigation cannot be confined to the abstract-deductive method, because individuals and societies cannot be completely separated from reality and empirical facts, nor can they be reduced to one or two specific characteristics. Furthermore, given that human beings, societies, and their institutions do not have artificially determined fixed existences, they are not static, meaning that they evolve across history, in different places, and at distinct paces and directions. Since predictions made by deductive methods are based on the acceptance of certain assumptions and conditions, any changes in real-world conditions would invalidate their results. That would suggest that any economic theory that is constructed via the elimination of multiple features of society or individuals is illusory and represents 'only one portion of a complex organism, all whose parts and their actions are in a constant relation of correspondence and reciprocal modification' (Ingram 1888, 122).

Roscher, Hildebrand, and Knies were opposed to the deductive approach for making generalizations and claiming that universal laws of development existed. In particular, Roscher (1878V1, 110) maintained that there could not be universal laws, suggesting that 'there can no more be an economic ideal adapted to the various wants of every people, than a garment which should fit every individual.' He pointed out that, in reality, there are many 'different ideals as there are different types of people' (ibid.). Roscher, Hildebrand, and Knies argued that the universalization of a statement based on a singular statement should not allow supporters of the deductive method to claim that a theory is sufficient enough to explain all other particular circumstances or phenomena. Furthermore, they explained that current facts and institutions of society would not prove helpful in gaining an understanding of contemporary problems, nor would they contribute to finding solutions for them, because the current achievements and failures of the economic system are also outcomes of historical development. According to Knies, the economic system must:

> be regarded as passing through a series of phases correlative with the successive stages of civilization, and can at no point of this movement be considered to have attained an entirely definitive form; that no more the present than any previous economic organization of society is to be regarded as absolutely good and right, but only as a phase in a continuous historical evolution.
>
> (Ingram 1888, 125)

For him, each economic system belonged to its own historical time and represented a stage in the development of civilization. Similarly, Hildebrand claimed that economic theories were not absolute; rather, they were relative, belonging to their particular time, place, and spirit. That is to say, there are no universal economic laws or theories, as various forms of social organizations have evolved very differently across history and places. Accordingly, their truths and principles are not universally valid across places and times either. That means each economic system was simply a part, passage, or phase in the long and continual evolution of civilization. In other words, a dominant or leading economic doctrine should not be accepted as 'complete and final, but only as representing a certain stage in the unfolding or progressive manifestation of the truth' (ibid.).

Since political economy did not possess the scientific features of the natural sciences, Roscher, Hildebrand, and Knies supported historical induction instead of the abstract-deductive method, which led to applied economics becoming an important aspect of the GHSE. According to them, political economists should 'first of all master historical technique' (Schumpeter 2006, 775). That means they should 'dive into the ocean of economic history in order to investigate particular patterns or processes in all their live details, local and temporal' (ibid.). In fact, Roscher argued that investigating and observing the current actions and decisions of individuals were not sufficient for gaining a proper understanding of societies in terms of their beliefs, customs, practices, laws, institutions, and economic and social successes and failures. This is because current economic phenomena and circumstances were outcomes of historical developments, meaning that political economy could not be limited to the investigation of current economic developments and relationships (Roscher 1843). It was also necessary to study the earlier stages of civilization and the historical developments and achievements that shaped modern societies. By doing so, political economists could reveal general conclusions that would help find remedies to current social and economic problems.

In *Leben, Werk und Zeitalter des Thukydides* (1842), Roscher recognized that empirical and genuine scientific knowledge could only be obtained through the inductive method, which led him to focus on the application of the methods of the natural sciences to the social sciences. More specifically, he applied the historical inductive method in order to obtain scientific knowledge about social and economic facts and processes. Roscher was fully aware that 'the social sciences deal with complex phenomena,' matters, and events, as well as complex relationships between people, which meant that 'unlike in the natural sciences, it was very uncommon' to repeat or to reproduce exactly the same experimental conditions or have repeated observations (Filip 2018, 110). Regularities can be maintained in the natural sciences, because experiments are conducted in controlled laboratory environments where variables can be isolated, restricted, and manipulated. As such, an experiment can always be recreated, because it relies on processes and procedures that can be repeated, which means identical results can be obtained. Meanwhile, two identical sets of conditions are unlikely to occur in the case of social phenomena. That is to say, since the experimental method could not be applied to the social sciences, the inductive method was needed to discover regularities and similarities by gathering large-scale data and facts (Milford 1995, 38–39). This method was called 'experimental,' even though experiments could not be conducted in the same manner as in the natural sciences (Ely 1883, 233, 263).

In order to justify the application of the inductive method to the social sciences, Roscher explained that 'the theoretical social sciences are the theory of history,' and much like the natural sciences, history is a 'positive science' (Filip 2018, 110). He further added that similar to any positive science, the goal of history is 'the discovery of strictly universal knowledge that is proved true, and his naturalistic account of the methodological principles of history explains that inductive methods make this possible' (Milford 1995, 38). Roscher believed that in political economy, the historical inductive method could 'be used to absorb empirical regularities into the theory' (Filip 2018, 109).

According to Roscher, political economists needed to gather large-scale data about a society by studying its moral laws, institutions, and political, cultural (including customs, habits, and traditions), linguistic, and legal developments, which represent 'the empirical basis on which the theoretical building is erected' (Milford 1995, 33). After an abundance of facts have been gathered, a political economist had to 'arrange and classify the facts' in a way that would assist him in his observations (Ely 1883, 234). He would then compare 'his conclusions with external facts, not simply for the sake of testing the accuracy of his reasoning, but also in order to ascertain whether the generalization itself was made on sufficient grounds' (Ely 1884, 9). He continuously tests 'all generalizations' against 'new facts gathered from new experience' (Ely 1883, 234). More specifically, the political economist cautiously compares hypotheses with facts, so as to discover economic regularities, trends, general principles, patterns, or laws of development (or 'the Laws of Becoming') (Balabkins 1988, Pribram 1983, 213, Tribe 2003, 173).

For the GHSE, it did not matter if a political economist did not reach 'general principles,' because, in the end, new information will have been gained, which 'in itself will be of value' (Mayo-Smith 1886, 115). 'This is a great advantage' over the abstract-deductive approach, which, when 'it was wrong, was altogether wrong and misleading' (ibid.). That means, contrary to the deductive approach, the inductive approach still provides valuable information and another perspective while also broadening people's 'views of the relations of society' when the political economist fails to reach general principles (ibid.). Furthermore, the inductive method prevents 'the science from degenerating into a mere' collection of 'stereotyped formulae, and the practice of the science into the mechanical application of these formulae to many communities and under certain circumstances' (ibid.: 116).

According to the historical inductive approach, ancient Greek city-states, feudalism, mercantilism, capitalism, industrialization, and emerging nations all progressed based on different economic theories. This is because of the fact that an economic theory might be suitable for one period, but not others. Consequently, comprehending what previous empires, nations, and civilizations valued and sought to achieve, and what courses of action they took in the aftermath of their successes or failures, could be helpful when it comes to understanding the problems of a society. The goal of the historical inductive approach was to study the experiences of past societies, so that any lessons learned could be applied to discovering patterns of development. In other words, the empirical analysis of large-scale facts and data would make it possible to understand the reasons behind the establishment of different institutions of society, as well as their progress and development (St. Marc 1892, 11).

Members of the OHS, along with many of their followers, were opposed to 'the excessive reliance on the abstract-deductive method of reasoning and dogmatic application of conclusions to policy' (Cardoso and Psalidopoulos 2016, XVIII). However, some of their successors did not share the same view, and 'proclaimed a belief in the abstract and unhistorical nature of existing economic thought, while going some way to develop analyses of trades, commerce and administration that demonstrated the existence of determinate stages of economic development' (Cook and Tribe 2016, 301). For example, Schmoller criticized the deductive method because it was based on inadequate principles that could lead to the wrong conclusions. He was opposed to 'deductions from premises based on the theoretical activity of a fictitious economic man,' as he believed that 'man was the actual man as revealed by observation, history, and the analyses of scientists' (Neff 1950, 361). He also argued that 'in broad-based economics, speculative deduction' was not 'very helpful' (Balabkins 1988, 63). Nevertheless, he did not necessarily reject its use outright. In fact, Schmoller (1902C, 305) stated that induction and deduction were both required for science, 'just as both the right and left foot were needed for walking.' Consequently, he rejected the notion of substituting the inductive method for the deductive method and vice versa. He relied on 'induction from historical and statistical observation with deduction from the known properties of human nature' (Neff 1950, 500). Accordingly, Schmoller (1902C, 306) maintained that economists who claimed that their discipline was a purely deductive science, similar to physics and geometry, only thought about the simplest man's inclinations and motives, in addition to the most advanced aspects of economics, like theories of exchange or money value, which could be adequately explained by the deductive approach. However, he argued that complex social and economic phenomena and institutions of the state cannot be simplified through the hypothetical-deductive method. Schmoller was of the view that addressing most complicated phenomena, like social questions, required induction, as it leads toward wider and more profound investigation. This is due, in part, to the fact that complicated objects and phenomena are influenced by very diverse factors.

Erwin Nasse (1887, 505) also did not completely reject the deductive approach, as he pointed out that a 'great majority of German economists would not limit political economy to the conclusions which can be reached deductively, nor to the description of the economic conditions of the past or present, nor to comparative economic history.' Meanwhile, Wagner underlined that it was false to use the deductive approach exclusively, as he considered both approaches to be 'the common property of all science' (Wagner 1891, 329). He accepted 'the need of induction side by side with deduction' (Wagner 1891, 320). According to him, the inductive and deductive approaches 'together form political economy as a science' (ibid.: 327). However, Wagner (1891, 320) warned 'against hasty generalization, against exclusive reasoning' based on the abstract-deductive approach.

Even though the GHSE aimed to discover historical laws and patterns of development, its theorists were against the formulation of universal abstract laws of development and their universal acceptance by all nations across history. They believed that it was not possible to have universal measures of progress, because contextual and historical differences between the socioeconomic systems of distinct civilizations and countries prohibited the uniform development of history. Each society is different across history and geographical locations, and the particularity of each society engenders new situations and problems. That said, solutions for new problems require new assumptions that take the specific characteristics of each society into consideration. Without the historical inductive approach of the GHSE, economics would have remained abstract and blind to the defects of the models of classical economics, which were unfit for the social realities of 19th-century Germany.

Methodological Collectivism versus Methodological Individualism

Classical economists, who supported methodological individualism, regarded individuals as independent and atomic decisions-makers. They believed that individuals can achieve the best possible outcomes for themselves by pursuing their own interests. Moreover, even though they favored the goals and interests of individuals over collective ones, they argued that individuals also contributed to attaining the common interests of society when they achieved their own personal interests. According to classical economists, the universal pursuit of individual self-interests was the prevailing determining factor of economic success. Therefore, societies achieve the best possible outcome by safeguarding the conditions that allow for the maximization of individual interests. They further claimed that 'nearly all human acts' are self-interest oriented (Newcomb 1884, 298). Consequently, classical economists rejected any interference in society on the part of an external authority aimed at coercing individuals into achieving a predetermined end.

Adherents of the GHSE argued that the main weakness of classical economics was its defense of the idea of an abstract, self-interest-oriented, individualistic man, which is completely disconnected from the realities of social and economic life. They were particularly critical of classical economists for ignoring all other factors that shaped human actions. Meanwhile, the GHSE completely rejected the assumption that self-interest maximization was a universal property of human action. Its members maintained that this abstraction was an oversimplification of human nature that largely invalidated the theoretical foundations of classical orthodoxy. According to Roscher (1878V1, 104), when man is focused solely on advancing his self-interests, he loses his moral character and 'degenerates into egotism,' 'acquisitiveness,' and 'covetousness.' He strongly criticized 19th-century classical economists for their support of methodological individualism, labeling them 'unworthy successors of Adam Smith' (Dorfman 1966, 88). Roscher further claimed that these individuals treated political economy 'as if man were "merely an exchanging animal," or as if human society were led by a blind, selfish pecuniary interest, removed from all the varying conditions of time and place, of national and social organization' (ibid.). This reductive view of 'the average man' as a self-interest maximizer was a very attractive and useful assumption, because it provided classical economists 'with a few easily managed formulas, which enabled' them to falsely 'solve all social problems at a moment's notice, and at any time to point out the only true and correct policy for all governments, whether in the present or the past, whether in Europe or Asia, Africa or America' (Ely 1883, 226).

Theorists of the GHSE rejected the view that the best results for society as a whole are 'to be gained under a regime in which each individual' pursues his own self-interest (Small 1923, 712). To the contrary, they regarded individual self-interest maximization as the source of some of the most egregious forms of social and economic inequality, injustice, poverty, and misery, all of which were destructive to the welfare of the community (Schmoller 1904, 57). In fact, Schmoller (1902B, 3) was of the view that the individual was not the center of social and economic life, nor should he be. Accordingly, he claimed that classical economists had a 'naive overweening confidence' in 'the omnipotence of the individual and of the individual life' (Schmoller 1894, 733). For them, 'out of the blind struggle of selfish individuals peaceful society should grow out' (ibid.: 722). Meanwhile, Schmoller (1894, 723) stressed that there was no peace or harmony in a society founded on the pursuit of individual self-interests because, when 'selfish impulses combat each other, natural masses tend to destroy each other.' Moreover, he argued that:

> the idea that economic life has ever been a process mainly dependent on individual action, -an idea based upon the impression that it is concerned merely with methods of satisfying individual needs -is mistaken with regard to all stages of economic civilization, and in some respects it is more mistaken the further we go back in history.
>
> (Schmoller 1902B, 3–4)

As such, Schmoller (1990, 139) was opposed to the universal application of self-interest maximization for 'all times, climates, races and peoples.' He argued that even though the reductive views of classical economists accepted the individual as a self-interest maximizing entity, in reality, human beings have 'higher intellectual, aesthetic and moral' goals by nature (Schmoller 1894, 700). Individuals bestow on 'life those ideal aims, from them grow those conceptions which accompany and influence all human life, all actions, all institutions, as ideal visions of what ought to be' (ibid.). This is the way to facilitate the development and progress of society and its institutions.

In his own opposition to methodological individualism, Knies, who was known as 'the most determined critic of the classical school's' pursuit of self-interest maximization as a universal principle, explained that economic activities and the economic institutions of society are determined by the particular spirit of the people, which is neither universal nor static (Neff 1950, 359). Similarly, Hildebrand pointed out that humans are social and historical beings, and there are many other factors aside from self-interest maximization that affect the decisions they make. Accordingly, he believed that methodological individualism was completely disconnected from the realities of actual life. That is to say, it was unrealistic to rely on self-interest maximization to explain the actions of all individuals over the duration of their lives.

Instead of methodological individualism, adherents of the GHSE supported methodological collectivism, which values the totality or unity of all the people that comprise a society. This is because they did not see society as a collection of separate individuals; rather, they regarded people as members of the community. Based on methodological collectivism, the common goal is achieved via the unity of the goals and ends of many individuals. In other words, people's actions are guided by the mutual interests of their community as opposed to the pursuit of self-interest maximization. This is true regardless of the size of the particular societal organization in question, whether it be a family, clan, village, city, region, nation, or empire. To underline the importance of the community in an individual's life, actions, and decisions, Wagner argued that 'the conditions of economic life of the community' determined the limits of the economic actions and goals of individuals (Adams 1886, 80). Furthermore, Schmoller (1894, 708) pointed out that a person's 'every word, every idea, every conception' were not the outcomes of 'an individual, but of a social process.' Even the greatest genius 'thinks and feels as a member of the community; ninety per cent of what he possesses is a trust conveyed to him by forefathers, teachers, fellow-creatures, to be cherished and bequeathed to posterity' (ibid.). According to Schmoller (1894, 708), only 'the smallest part of our thoughts originates in ourselves, and that we draw, as it were, from a public storehouse, and participate in a universal generation of thoughts to which each individual makes only a comparatively scanty contribution.'

Adherents of the GHSE believed that anybody seeking to understand the evolution of economic life needed to consider the complex relationships that individuals had with other people, their social and economic institutions, their unique historical development, their moral and ethical values, and their culture and customs. According to them, man was 'the actual human being such as history and surrounding circumstances have made him, with all his wants, passions, and infirmities' (Leslie 1875). This is because each person is a part of the community they reside in, where there is shared history, social commitments, duties, culture, traditions, beliefs, values, and customs, all of which are components of the particular spirit of the people that plays an important role in their choices with respect to their social and economic activities. Schmoller (1902B, 78) believed that the desire to unite individual interests for the purpose of achieving collective interests was why:

> the strife of towns and territories had been softened and moderated with time, until, on the foundation of still greater social bodies, the states, it had passed into a moral influence, and an obligation to educate and assist the weaker members within the larger community.

That means societal organization was an outcome of a certain solidarity of interests, whereby an economic activity should contribute to the achievement of the common good. Even though theorists of the GHSE defended methodological collectivism, the achievement of the common good did not rule out the achievement of individual goals. This is because collective goals were attained by following the universal will, which provided individuals with the means by which to achieve their own personal goals and objectives.

The Laissez-Faire Approach versus National Economy

After the Napoleonic wars, Germany continued to confront serious economic difficulties. In particular, the delay of industrialization in Germany relative to its trading partners led to imported cheap goods dominating

German markets, primarily those originating in the UK. It was during this period, when 'German-speaking people were seeking' a road to 'economic development that would be free from the British dominance,' that the GHSE emerged (Hodgson 2001, 58). In order to address their growing social and economic problems, Germans had to choose between protective economic policies and a *laissez-faire/laissez-passer* approach, the repeated maxim of classical economics, which advocated for the government to abstain from 'all interference in industrial life' in favor of leaving 'things alone' and letting 'them take care of themselves' (Ely 1883, 226). In fact, Germans closely examined the social and economic effects of laissez-faire policies in industrialized England and France and determined that it was in the best interest of Germany to avoid following in their footsteps. More specifically, they concluded that the combination of rapid industrialization and the laissez-faire approach were responsible for exacerbating poverty, misery, and social and economic inequality. They were of the view that these kinds of destructive outcomes were inevitable, because classical orthodoxy did not care about the achievement of the common good or the development of 'a system of national' economy; rather, it dealt exclusively with the maximization of 'the wealth of individuals' (Cunningham 1894, 318). In reality, they did not think that free exchange and a *laissez-faire* system could exist anywhere. In fact, they believed that the notion of a *laissez-faire* system achieving progress and the common good in the absence of any state intervention was a utopian fantasy.

Adherents of the GHSE argued that 'the accumulation of wealth in the hands of capitalists was by itself inadequate to fulfill the requirements of national well-being' (Balabkins 1988, 111). However, they were simultaneously opposed to the radical and immediate transformation of the 'economic constitution of society in the interest of the proletariat' via revolutionary movements (Ingram 1888, 128). For example, Schmoller cautioned about:

> the threat from social revolution engendered by the division between employer and worker, propertied and propertyless classes, and suggested that popular economic beliefs concerning commercial freedom and economic individualism could well create even greater disorder, rather than the rosy future they imagined.
>
> (Tribe 2002, 10)

He opposed socialism because it presupposes:

> a disappearance of all divisions of labor and occupation, of all differences of race, talents, capabilities, of abolition of city and country, a wiping out of all the more highly endowed as well as the disappearance of all raw and minor forces, with, so far as possible, a future breeding system which will produce wholly like human beings of a mediocre type.
>
> (Schmoller 1915, 519)

He believed that this kind of system would negatively impact societies by hindering development and progress, leading to a loss of balance and engendering disasters. Roscher (1878V1) held similar ideas, as he argued against the nationalization of all factors of production and the abolition of private property ownership. He stated that 'such a system does not suffice to insure the real productiveness of a nation's economy' (Roscher 1878V1, 267). That said, he was not opposed to all forms of public ownership, explaining that it could serve a great number of people instead of one exclusive user in certain cases.

In order to help Germany catch up to the leading industrialized countries in the 19th century while simultaneously ensuring a less damaging transition from an agrarian-based economy to an industrialized one, theorists of the GHSE envisaged an 'intermediate standpoint,' as they were 'opposed alike to social revolution and to rigid laisser faire' (Ingram 1888, 129). That is to say, they wanted to have 'new social arrangements, the need of social reform in opposition to social revolution on the one hand and to rigid laissez-faire on the other' (Dorfman 1955, 21). As such, the GHSE regarded state regulations in the economy as a necessity if they wanted to avoid relying on the *laissez-faire* approach. More specifically, they sought to develop the national economy (*Nationalökonomie*) in order to achieve the general interests of the population. They believed that many of the destructive outcomes associated with private business practices ought to be curbed by a strong government, which should also be tasked with providing social and economic programs and services.

Even though the national economy was a fundamental feature of the GHSE, it is important to recall that up until the early 19th century, Germans had 'no sense of Germany as a country, nor of Germans as compatriots. They were Westphalians and Hanoverians and Prussians and Saxons and Bavarians and Austrian' (Small 1923, 53). However, despite the existence of this plurality of states, the people in these territories were educated 'in nationalistic theory and practice for centuries' (Small 1923, 306). In fact, Germans had been systematically focusing on determining the proper role of the state and establishing limits for state actions in order to achieve economic development in the German territories and common happiness for their inhabitants since the early days of cameralism. In other words, the seeds of becoming a 'conscious of collective Germany' based on the national spirit were already being planted by the cameralists (Small 1923, 53). That means the work of 19th-century political economists aimed at achieving a national economy, in the 'sense of connections with the German past and of interdependence with all the Germans in the present,' was already largely accomplished (ibid.). Subsequently, the political and economic situation that emerged led to the rise of economic nationalism in Germany in the 19th century, with theorists of the GHSE largely contributing to the construction of its national economy.

Theorists of the GHSE believed that establishing the conditions that would facilitate the development of the national economy was the main concern of political economy. Thus, they dedicated their lives to 'the development of the industrial life of nations' (Cunningham 1894, 318). That said, they also acknowledged that the national economy did not only concentrate on the actions of the state, it also took account of the actions of its citizens, because they work together in order to form the nation and the national community. Nonetheless, the GHSE maintained that only the state was capable of improving the general welfare of its population by reducing social and economic tensions and uniting people.

Schmoller clearly indicated his preference for national economics, which could guide the state in its social policy over a utopian laissez-faire system. Similarly, Hildebrand wanted to turn economics into 'the science of national development' (Neff 1950, 358). He, along with many other adherents of the GHSE, valued national solidarity and the historical continuity of the nation. They believed that a strong sense of national continuity and community were essential to the development of the national economy. These sentiments were exemplified by Roscher (1878V1, 84) when he stated:

> The public economy of a nation grows with the nation. With the nation, it blooms and ripens. Its season of blossoming and of maturity is the period of its greatest strength, and, at the same time, of the most perfect development of all its more important organs.

Roscher (1878V1) accepted individuals as parts of one great whole, and believed that the organization of this whole of people via the state would achieve the common good. For him, the state was an organic social entity with a duty to achieve the unity of all its members along with their common good, neither of which could be adequately attained under a laissez-faire system. To ensure this unity, the state had to be strong enough to maintain a system that would protect the security of its citizens. That is not to say that the state role was limited to the maintenance of order. In particular, Schmoller explained that while the role of the state would 'vary from narrow to broad, according to the circumstances of civilization,' it must always be 'the most tremendous institution for the education of the human race' (Small 1923, 716). He further argued that the state must be 'the leading intelligence, the responsible centre of public sentiment, the acme of existing moral and intellectual powers, and therefore can attain great results' (Schmoller 1894, 735).

Schmoller (1894, 735) had complete confidence in the notion that 'the great statesman and reformer, the far-seeing party chief and legislator' could achieve 'extraordinary things, not directly, not immediately, but through a wise and just transformation of the economic institutions they can greatly influence the administration of incomes and property.' Furthermore, he argued that the state should have 'a strong direct influence on the distribution of incomes and wealth as the greatest employer of labor, the greatest property holder, or the administrator of the greatest undertakings' (ibid.: 734). It should also exercise 'the greatest indirect influence on law and custom, on all social institutions' (ibid.). That means state power could be deployed to exercise its authority over virtually all areas of national life in order to achieve the development of the national economy. However, these types of positive state actions were only legitimate if they played a role in the achievement of the common good in instances when it could not have otherwise been effectively achieved via individual efforts.

Even though Schmoller defended state regulations and interventions aimed at controlling international trade and limiting unfair business practices, he was not completely opposed to free trade. He recognized that the long, violent, and destructive conflicts that transpired in Europe from 1600 to 1800 led to the economic arena of the time being dominated by protective trade measures (Schmoller 1902B). That is to say, towns, cities, and nations implemented protective trade measures meant to exclude foreign wares. He also pointed out that, from 1750 to 1800, England attained 'the summit of its commercial supremacy' not by practicing laissez-faire economics, but 'by means of its tariffs and naval wars, frequently with extraordinary violence, and always with the most tenacious national selfishness' (ibid.). Meanwhile, Roscher (1878V2, 438) supported a 'wisely conducted protective system' to combat the evils of the international competitive market. However, he acknowledged that free trade was advantageous to 'a people's nationality the moment they have attained to the maturity of manhood' (ibid.). In fact, he described free trade as a feature of 'highly civilized nations,' for which 'the desire for a protective system must be looked upon as a symptom of disease' (ibid.: 447).

Generally speaking, adherents of the GHSE did not reject free trade, though they did not believe that it would generate immediate economic growth without the support of some state-imposed protective trade measures. According to them, if international competition threatened the prosperity of domestic production, then protective trade measures were justified in order to strengthen the ability of these industries to compete with foreign companies. That means the ultimate goal of protective trade measures was to improve and secure a prosperous future for domestic production. Adherents of the GHSE defended a variety of state measures intended to protect domestic production, including the nationalization of strategic industries, and the protection of infant industries, particularly those facing strong foreign competition. Accordingly, they endorsed Bismarck's implementation of import tariffs on a wide variety of industrial and agricultural goods aimed at protecting the domestic market from international competition.

To achieve the development of the national economy, theorists of the GHSE called on political economists to master different branches of the natural sciences in order to facilitate the better use of natural and human resources. In particular, they supported better management and technical innovation in the manufacturing and agriculture sectors for the purpose of conserving natural resources. According to them, classical economics did not value the better management and protection of natural resources aimed at serving the needs of the inhabitants of the country; rather, it motivated the enrichment of a few individuals through the reckless exploitation of natural resources at the expense of the masses.

In addition to the better management and protection of natural resources, the GHSE also supported the development of human resources so that everyone could participate 'in all the higher goods of civilization' (Small 1923, 716). To do so, its adherents advocated for state policies designed to protect the interests of farmers, agricultural workers, traditional craftsmen, and small businesses. Schmoller endorsed such policies, because they promoted the advancement of such workers in modern industrial societies and provided them with opportunities to achieve their own development of individuality. Additionally, other theorists of the GHSE maintained that the state had an ethical duty to intervene in order to achieve the development of individuality among the ruled. Consequently, they supported a state role in improving the moral, spiritual, institutional, and economic development of individuals (St. Marc 1892, 11). To be more specific, the GHSE supported positive state actions that would assist in the development of individuality via education, the promotion of 'intellectual and æsthetic culture,' the enforcement of 'provisions for public health and regulations,' and the safeguarding of 'the labourer against the worst consequences of personal injury' (Ingram 1888, 128).

Many theorists of the GHSE, including Schäffle, Wagner Schmoller, Knapp, and Brentano, supported the state implementation of social reforms and policies designed to: 'protect the weaker members of society, especially women, children, the aged, and the destitute, at least in the absence of family maintenance and guardianship'; elevate the lower classes; and overcome the economic inequality, poverty, and misery that was widespread in Germany at that time (Dorfman 1955, 21, Ingram 1888, 128). Before Bismarck came to power, German 'wages were low, taxes high, work scarce, and the entire economic existence of the lower classes uncertain and full of anxiety' (Ely 1882, 507). Workers felt insecure, because they had very few protections when it came to their employment, which left them vulnerable in the event that their ability to work was affected by factors like poor health, injury, or old age. If citizens found themselves facing poverty, illness, or helplessness, they were essentially on their own, as society did not 'accept any responsibility towards' them beyond 'the usual provisions for the poor' (Yefimov 2009, 14). Theorists of the GHSE were enthusiastic about Bismarck's nation building social and economic reforms in Germany, as well as his rejection of laissez-faire policy. In particular, they supported Bismarck's view that 'the economic links between the German states should be strengthened and should be used to cement political unity' (Henderson 2006, 45). They also agreed that the state had a duty to protect workers against injustices and exploitation in the workplace and 'guarantee the safety of their earnings' (Ingram 1888, 128).

Roscher (1878V2) supported state regulations to protect worker rights in order to achieve social and economic justice. For example, he called for 'the strict justice of the state, which should protect members of the unions from all tyranny by their leaders, and from violations of the legal rights of non-members' (ibid.: 93). He also supported a guaranteed 'equitable minimum of wages' by the state (ibid.: 94). Meanwhile, Schmoller recognized the importance of worker associations and trade unions in terms of protecting and representing the rights and interests of the labor classes. He believed that trade unions were necessary in order to humanize working conditions through such means as improving health and safety regulations in factories. He also advocated for improving the living conditions of the lower classes via the implementation of publicly financed social programs and services (St. Marc 1892, 35). Similar to Schmoller, Brentano was of the view that people without wealth, jobs, and capital needed state assistance. Accordingly, he supported an insurance system for workers that safeguarded them against illness, injury, work accident, disability, old age, unemployment, death, and more.

In response, Bismarck passed 'the first welfare laws' in 1883 and 'welfare capitalism was launched' (Balabkins 1988, 113). In fact, he introduced programs and services for 'compulsory State insurance against accidents, sickness and old age' before any other advanced country (Henderson 2006, 45). As a result, 'the Prussian state offered cutting-edge social services' in all corners of its territories, which had 'an appreciable impact on the welfare of workers' (Clark 1995, 485–486). These services provided:

> German workers a feeling of security. If a workman had an accident or fell ill his family was no longer plunged into poverty. The health of the workers improved. They enjoyed a higher standard of living, better housing conditions, improved sanitation and more thorough medical attention.
>
> (Henderson 2006, 57)

Bismarck continued his efforts to further improve the working conditions of laborers, which included limiting excessive working hours, prohibiting child workers, and improving wage rates. Theorists of the YHS of economics actually played a particularly important role in guiding Bismarck's understanding of 'the nature of the social consequences of the industrial revolution' (ibid.: 45). In fact, 'his favorite adviser in economic matters' was 'Professor Adolf Wagner, the most socialistically inclined of the professional socialists (*Kathedersocialisten*)' (Ely 1882, 510). Incidentally, Wagner admired Bismarck for a long time before becoming his economic advisor (ibid.). The social and economic reforms continued 'into the early 1890s, when the new administration under William II and Chancellor Caprivi enacted labour laws that brought progress in the areas of industrial safety, working conditions, youth protection and arbitration' (Clark 1995, 485). Managing all of these social and economic programs and services required a large number of public workers, which resulted in the Prussian ministry of public works becoming 'the largest employer in the world' in 1913 (ibid.).

Adherents of the GHSE generally agreed that the state should have an active positive role in society, whereby it would design and implement economic policies in order to achieve the conditions of common welfare. At the same time, they maintained that any positive state actions should not threaten the conditions of freedom. If freedom were to be suppressed, then the foundation of all national moral, cultural, and spiritual progress would be inhibited, as would any future evolution of the national culture (Brentano 1881, 103). That is to say, theorists of the GHSE believed that positive state action should not be used to constrain and coerce people, because they accepted the state as an ethical institution, which they considered to be an indispensable condition of human progress. They believed that achieving the development of the national economy required the triumph of ethics in society with the assistance of the state.

Ethical Economics

The treatment of ethical values was one of the main points of contention between the GHSE and many of the other prominent economic schools of thought, including classicals, neoclassicals, neoliberals, ordo-liberals, and the ASE. None of those schools of thought required any moral or ethical relationships in the economic arena, because they considered economics to be a value-free science. In other words, they pushed moral and ethical values away from political economy. To the contrary, the GHSE, particularly members of the YHS, was often referred to as 'the ethical school,' because its adherents intentionally adopted 'an ethical ideal, and endeavor to point out the manner in which it may be attained, and even encourage people to strive for it' (Ely 1886, 46). Accordingly, they were strongly opposed to the idea that human beings were atomistic, self-interest oriented, and purely materialistic by nature. They believed that the prevalence of this type of human behavior was 'responsible for many social evils' during the periods of rapid industrialization and urbanization in France and Britain, including extreme social and economic inequalities, 'pauperism, poverty and inhuman working conditions' (Cardoso and Psalidopoulos 2016, XVII).

Wagner criticized classical economists for defending 'economic self interest as a natural force in the economic world just as gravity is in the physical world' (Small 1923, 709). He believed that treating the pursuit of self-interests as a universal characteristic of human behavior led classical economists to eliminate ethical judgments from economics, along with a number of other factors that shaped people's decisions and actions. Meanwhile, Hildebrand criticized the unethical and materialistic tendencies of classical economists and argued that political economy had to concern itself with moral and ethical judgments. As for Knies (1883, 436), he was of the view that since an individual's entire life often revolves around their economic activities, particularly finding solutions to various economic issues and problems, it was necessary to recognize that political economy belonged with the moral sciences. More precisely, he strongly believed that 'political economy cannot be conclusive until it consciously and deliberately organizes itself as a moral science' (Small

1923, 707). Similarly, Schmoller maintained that economics was a 'historico-ethical' discipline (Schumpeter 2006, 780). He explained that the framework for the social and economic institutions of modern society was originally established and developed in the family before evolving to suit the needs of small towns, villages, territories, and states, all of which are forms of ethical societal organizations. These institutions 'regulate and direct social and economic life' (Peukert 2001, 76). The smaller the moral community, like the case of a 'primitive culture,' then 'the simpler and clearer their purpose, the more evident become the qualities, according to which moral judgment compares and classifies men' (Schmoller 1894, 720). However, the emergence of increasingly complex modern societies over time resulted in moral qualities often being overlooked, particularly under the guidance of classical economics. As such, Schmoller thought that in a complex modern world, unrestricted competition, individualism, acquisitiveness, laissez-faire doctrine, and egoism of classical economics would lead to a 'crisis for the whole morality of the advancing people' (Small 1923, 722). Broadly speaking, Schmoller believed that the more that economics emphasized the individual pursuit of self-interests, the more the entire economic system and its institutions would assume the character of individual goals and concerns, as opposed to collective goals and concerns guided by ethical values. He stressed that moral and ethical values were essential for all types of communities, particularly in a complex modern world.

Schmoller (1894, 705–706) explained that life in the community is one of the things that distinguishes human beings from animals, as it requires the development of a common spirit of the people, which is shaped by a variety of characteristics, including language, history, memories, literature, education, cultural practices, customs, common sentiments, and moral and ethical values (Schmoller 1902B, 47). That said, moral and ethical values were among the most important factors in the development of the spirit of the people. Schmoller (1902C, 285) went on to explain that the spirit of people then shapes various social and economic institutions, as well as the types of enterprises, the division of the labor force, the formation of different economic classes, and the organization of the market, industries, and trade. In turn, these institutions played important roles in raising ethical and moral awareness, which is essential for everyday practical reasoning and guiding people's decisions and actions in their families, communities, and businesses (St. Marc 1892, 30). Meanwhile, the state is supposed to demonstrate a higher moral-ethical worldview in its own decisions and actions in order to achieve the common good, as it, along with its institutions, plays a key role in regulating the behaviors of individuals and facilitating social and economic progress (ibid.: 29).

Schmoller (1902A, 46) believed that the most advanced civilizations valued ethical and moral practices by individuals and on the part of their social and economic institutions. He was also of the opinion that transforming social and economic institutions into ethical and moral ones would play a major role in addressing class struggles, as well as social and economic injustices (Schmoller 1915, 505). Furthermore, Schmoller claimed that real economic development was dependent upon the advancement of the social and economic institutions of society, which is correlated with the progress and evolution of ethics (St. Marc 1892, 96). In other words, the progress of the national economy was directly related to the progress of ethical practices. Schmoller concluded that the destructive outcomes of economic actions would not be tolerated in highly advanced civilizations; rather, they would be prevented by limiting economic activities to some extent via moral and ethical values and the legal framework.

Contrary to classical economics, adherents of the GHSE believed that the pursuit of individual self-interests only accounted for a fraction of the motivation behind human actions. To be more precise, they acknowledged that an overriding desire to maximize personal self-interests could be an identifying feature of a particular society during a certain period; however, this same society might be strongly criticized and deemed immoral and unethical by other societies and/or periods. This is due to the fact that every phase in human history could have its own 'conventional standards of valuation for human qualities and deeds, virtues and vices; it conventionally values this kind of action more highly than that, and so demands accordingly in one case greater rewards or greater honors, in another severer punishments' (Schmoller 1894, 708). Schmoller believed that these 'conventional standards of valuation' were basically 'the starting-point of every judgment of justice' (ibid.). Meanwhile, he suggested that a lack of moral and ethical commitments was the origin of all evil in society (St. Marc 1892, 30). Similar to Schmoller, other members of the GHSE did not separate ethics and moral values from political economy. In particular, theorist of the YHS insisted on 'the necessity of accentuating the moral element in economic study' (Ingram 1888, 127). That means the GHSE gave political economy a normative character. They were highly supportive of the notion that the state should play a more decisive role in fostering the development of the economy based on an ethical orientation.

Ethics and Social and Economic Inequalities

Moral and ethical values were necessary in order to judge the actions of people and determine whether they are vices or virtues. Schmoller (1894, 700, 737) accepted justice as 'the virtue of virtues,' explaining that 'the conception of justice grows out of necessary processes in our soul and necessarily influences economic life.' Roscher (1878V2, 210) also discussed the role of virtues and vices in social and economic life. He explained that vices, particularly intemperance, were 'detrimental to a nation's economy' and resources, as they 'directly or indirectly increases the demand for commodities' (ibid.: 210–211). In general, Roscher supported the virtuous 'practice of frugality in every day life' to achieve justice (ibid.: 211).

Schmoller (1894, 700) believed that, much like other virtues, the concept of justice is not 'imparted to men by some revelation'; rather, 'it is the necessary product of our moral intuition and our logical thinking, and in so far it is an eternal truth, manifesting itself ever new yet ever similar metamorphoses.' He highly valued justice, 'in the form of moral and religious sense of duty,' in shaping the daily activities of 'practical life' (ibid.: 724). He believed that through 'higher justice and better institutions humanity is educated up to higher forms of life' (ibid.: 733). Moreover, Schmoller (1894, 736) was of the view that justice is 'connected with the highest and best that we think, imagine and believe.' He further explained that people 'eternally seek it, eternally battle for it, and though ever progressing, never reach it, so the idea of justice has no resting, determined existence on earth' (ibid.). That means the concept of justice is 'always an ideal conception, to which reality may approach, but which it will never attain' (ibid.: 700). Schmoller believed that when life had more economic justice, economic culture would possess a more ethical character. He explained that economic inequalities emerged from historical causes, as every state in every period of historical development always experienced 'class contrasts, class struggles, and class domination' based on ethnicity, religion, race, occupation, income, and wealth (Schmoller 1915, 504). Schmoller (1894, 730) pointed out that:

> For thousands of years the selfish impulses of those who in the social struggle of competition are the stronger have demanded unconditional freedom of contract, and this demand is always opposed by public conscience and the demand of the weaker, which establishes the conception of *justum pretium*, which requires a governmental regulation of prices, statutes on usury, considerations for the *laesio enormis*, public control of abuses in trade and traffic, a restriction of exploitation.

Adherents of the GHSE were worried about the wealthy elite classes expanding their power and influence over society. In particular, they were preoccupied with the possibility of monopolies and cartels extending their abusive and exploitive authority, which would further enable them to push misery, poverty, and dehumanizing conditions onto the working classes. More specifically, the GHSE observed 'the growing power of corporations,' studied 'the tendency of wealth to accumulate in a few hands,' and witnessed 'the development of evil tendencies in certain classes of the population' (Ely 1883, 234). In doing so, they sought to determine whether or not it was 'desirable for a central authority to limit the power of corporations, or to take upon itself the discharge of new functions' (ibid.).

Schmoller was worried about the rich elite classes seeking to control the government. He specifically warned that 'the higher economic classes have always understood more or less how to develop customs and laws in their favor, how thereby to increase their incomes and their property, how to give themselves an advantage in commercial intercourse' (Schmoller 1915, 507).

For example, the privileged classes could buy the press, install agents into political processes and elections, and corrupt politicians into making decisions that serve their own interests. Meanwhile, Schmoller (1915, 507) pointed out that 'the lower classes have always been most unfavorably situated for that sort of influence.' This imbalance of power meant that wealthy elites could successfully influence and change the rules and laws in ways that would further their interests at the expense of the poor masses. Schmoller argued that this would lead to the emergence of extreme social and economic inequality, which would not only be unethical, but also eventually result in the destruction of freedom and undo all of the progress made by the social and economic institutions of the state. To demonstrate the correlation between ethical practices and social and economic progress, Schmoller pointed out that when inequality expands, the practice of moral and ethical values declines and the enjoyment of cultural and artistic activities and products deteriorates. Conversely, when inequality is reduced, there is an increase in the number of people who are interested in art, enjoy advances in sciences, practice ethics, and exhibit refined manners.

Roscher (1878V2, 176) was also worried about expanding social and economic inequalities, as he argued that the economic prosperity of a people could only be achieved 'when no citizen is so rich that he can buy the others, and no one so poor that he might be compelled to sell himself.' He further added that 'when inequality increases because the lower classes absolutely decline, there is no use in talking any longer about the prosperity of the nation' (ibid.). Wagner recognized that poverty, misery, suffering, welfare, wealth, and prosperity will always coexist in this world (St. Marc 1892, 58). He also acknowledged that 'there will always be differences in property which cannot be traced back to actual merit or personal fault' (Small 1923, 710). He believed that it was the task of political economists 'to diminish the evils that grow out of this fact and to keep the existing inequalities from increasing' as much as possible (ibid.). Accordingly, Wagner emphasized the importance of integrating ethical and moral judgments into the economic decisions and actions of people and enterprises. He also argued that state policies and reforms needed to be guided by ethical judgments if a more egalitarian and just society was to be achieved. That said, he maintained that the proper role of the state was 'neither passivity nor indiscriminate intervention, but constant watchfulness and throwing of its weight from case to case against injustice' (ibid.: 709).

Schmoller (1894, 706) was cognizant that the judgment of equality or inequality is always 'a very complicated one.' Although there will always be demands and efforts to end various forms of injustice and social and economic inequalities, he acknowledged that it was impossible to eliminate them altogether. Accordingly, his main focus was not to achieve equality, but rather 'to reconcile individual and common interests, freedom and justice, property and work, the aristocratic position of the powerful and the rich with the democratic position of the masses' (Schomoller 2018, 229). He made it explicitly clear that he rejected the classical orthodoxy and socialism as solutions to the growing social and economic inequalities that prevailed in Germany at that time. More specifically, he argued that there could be no peace, harmonious relationships, or common happiness within the laissez-faire system of classical orthodoxy or via the equal distribution of wealth and income and the abolishment of private property advocated by socialism. Schmoller was also fully aware that a temporary increase in wages would not solve social and economic inequalities or bring about justice. In fact, he believed that:

> a just assessment of taxes, a just distribution of the burdens for the improvement of highways, of the duty of military service, a just gradation of wages are much easier to attain than a just distribution of the total incomes and wealth.
>
> (Schmoller 1894, 734)

Accordingly, he focused on improving the living and working conditions of labor, specifically stating that (Schmoller 1915, 525):

> we have either to crush the laborers down to the level of slaves, which is impossible, or we must recognize their equal rights as citizens, we must improve their mental and technical training, we must permit them to organize, we must concede to them the influence which they need in order to protect their interests.

Schmoller (1902A, 34–36) believed that the gap between the upper and lower classes could be significantly reduced by advancing civilization in a way that is guided by ethical values. That said, he argued that limiting 'the acquisitive forces; to the greed of the strong and the rich, and to the growing economic differences of income and their causes' was crucial if social and economic justice is to be achieved (Schmoller 1915, 523). The achievement of justice also required the state and its institutions to be committed to the provision of public services and programs that facilitated the ethical, social, and cultural development of the masses. He argued that 'the state-controlled school system and the entire legal and constitutional order are the chief leverages for social progress' and the attainment of social and economic justice (ibid.). If progress and harmonious development were hindered by social and economic inequalities at some point, he called for the imposition of state regulations on the activities of the business classes, as well as the improvement of the social and economic institutions of society, in order to avoid revolutionary tendencies and achieve a more humane and just society. Schmoller (1894, 733) was convinced that 'the great epochs of economic progress are primarily connected with the reform of social institutions' rather than revolution. Essentially, the goals of such reforms are to establish a good relationship between the social classes, make sure that the principles of justice are respected, and improve the moral and ethical practices of the masses (Schmoller 1902A, 105).

According to theorists of the GHSE, moral and ethical values were a fundamental part of political economy. They believed that moral and ethical values ought to guide people in their relationships with others and their environments. In fact, all members of society, including its rulers, needed to integrate ethics into their decisions and actions in order to achieve common ends. That would suggest that moral and ethical values should govern 'the external and internal life' of the inhabitants of a nation (Schmoller 1894, 719). They should also provide guidance when it comes to shaping the laws, institutions, and policies of the state. Ultimately, the adherents of the GHSE believed that practicing moral and ethical values in economic activities would result in better outcomes for the entire society. According to Schmoller (1894, 735), this type of ethical economics was the only way for the state to prevent 'its best intention destroyed by a thousandfold formal injustice' caused by the pursuit of individual self-interests in a laissez-faire system.

The Role of the GHSE in the Development of Mathematical Economics and Statistical Research

Efforts to transform the discipline of economics into a branch of the natural sciences intensified after WWII. Consequently, economics has been accepted as a discipline of the natural sciences since the 1950s. Generally speaking, mainstream economists believe that the origins of mathematical economics and the application of statistics to their discipline can be traced back to the works of English mathematical economist William Stanley Jevons (1835–1882), French mathematical economist Léon Walras (1834–1910), and American mathematical economist Irving Fisher (1867–1947). In reality, one could argue that the development of mathematical economics and the application of statistics to economics were significantly influenced by the historical inductivism of the GHSE. However, even before the GHSE, cameralists were already applying statistics and the approaches of the natural sciences to political economy (Small 2001, 444). More specifically, it is often accepted that Johann Heinrich Gottlob Justi (1717–1771), who was the first scholar of the administrative census in Germany, played an initial role in the use of statistics in economics.

The contributions made by Germans to the development of mathematical economics was recognized by Jevons (1876, 626), who was accepted as the father of mathematical economics. He stated that a number of economists from Germany made 'attempts towards a mathematical theory' in economics (ibid.). However, he also pointed out that 'their works have been almost unnoticed' and 'forgotten' (ibid.). In fact, some of the theorists of the GHSE have been recognized as 'forerunners of the modern econometrics studies' (Senn 2005, 194). For instance, Roscher was accepted as the 'econometrician' of the GHSE 'in the sense that he presented – frequently very well chosen, quantitative – evidence on every point he made' (Streissler 2001, 316). Meanwhile, Knies relied on mathematical economics in his discussions about use value and exchange value. Additionally, Schmoller (1902C) recognized that the methods of the natural sciences and mathematics were a necessary auxiliary means for solving economic questions and discovering the laws of the phenomenon at issue. He also considered the application of statistics to political economy, as well as other social sciences, to be one of the most important developments of last few centuries (ibid.: 277). In particular, Schmoller (1902C, 277) believed that statistical charts, diagrams, and tables were crucial when it came to comparing different variables, measuring their influences, and providing a solid foundation when making economic decisions.

Among GHSE contributors, Roscher (1878V1, 102) emphasized that:

> it would be much more in harmony with the intellectual tendencies of the time, to adopt a mathematical mode of treatment in Political Economy, involving, as such a mode of treatment does, not the matter of the science, but only a formal principle.

Roscher (1878V1, 103) pointed out that, like mathematics, political economy:

> swarms with abstractions. Just as there are, strictly speaking, no mathematical lines or points in nature, and no mathematical lever, there is nowhere such a thing as production or rent, entirely pure and simple. The mathematical laws of motion operate in a hypothetical vacuum, and, where applied, are subjected to important modifications, in consequence of atmospheric resistance. Something similar is true of most of the laws of our science; as, for instance, those in accordance with which the price of commodities is fixed by the buyer and seller. It also, always supposes the parties to the contract to be guided only by a sense of their own best interest, and not to be influenced by secondary considerations. It is not, therefore, to be wondered at, that many authors have endeavored to clothe the laws of Political Economy in algebraic formulæ.

Even though Roscher (1878V1, 104) recognized some of the advantages of mathematical economics, he maintained that its use as a 'mode of expression diminishes as the facts to which it is applied become more complicated.' In particular, he noted that 'the portraying of national' economy with mathematical economics would 'soon become so complicated, as to make all further progress in the operation next to impossible' (ibid.). He further pointed out that there are always 'many and important facts in national life,' which cannot be subjected to numerical calculation (ibid.: 94). Thus, while Roscher supported the use of mathematics in political economy, he advised for it to be limited. In fact, many theorists of the GHSE only supported the limited use of mathematics in political economy, because they were of the opinion that people's decisions and actions were too complex to be realistically represented by mathematical models. In other words, they believed that the usefulness of mathematical economics was limited, because it requires regularities or correlations, which are very rare in real social and economic life. For instance, even though Schmoller (2018, 216) supported the limited use of mathematics, he was critical of advanced mathematical economics, because it failed to understand or appreciate man's true nature and 'his place in the world and in history,' which are important if one is to 'comprehend the state and society, to recognize the overall effect of spiritual forces, to understand the course of customs, law, and institutions.' He also argued that the exclusive use of advanced mathematical models 'usually disable the scholar to judge matters political and economic' (Herbst 1965, 137). As such, he advised that mathematical models be used with caution. According to Schmoller, mathematical modeling can be useful if there are no structural changes in social and economic institutions. However, mathematical economics essentially becomes useless when there are no regularities or structural and spontaneous changes occur, because economists will have to deal with unknown causes, meaning that 'economic phenomena cannot be predicted as physical phenomena can' (Newcomb 1884, 299).

In addition to mathematics, adherents of the GHSE supported the use of statistics to some extent in order to provide insights, gain an understanding of social and economic problems, and address policy issues. They believed that properly comprehending economic developments and progress necessitated the collection and analysis of large amounts of statistical data. Consequently, they accepted statistics as a useful tool when it came to understanding and explaining changes in variables of social and economic life in different societal organizations across history. To be more precise, they combined historical knowledge and statistics into a critical and analytical tool to help them find solutions for a wide range of social and economic issues and problems of their time.

Many adherents of the GHSE were involved with statistical research associations and institutions, which played a significant role in the development of empirical investigation into social and economic problems. At that time, Germany boasted a number of statistic research institutions (also known as statistical bureaus) that were important when it came to training the theorists of the GHSE. For example, the statistical bureau of Prussia (*Preußischen Königlichen Statistischen Büros*, 1805–1934) opened in Berlin in 1805. Then, in 1862, the statistical office of Berlin (*Statistisches Bureau der Stadt Berlin*) was established.[2] In 1864, Bruno Hildebrand founded the Thuringian Statistical Office in Jena. Subsequently, in 1872, the statistical bureau of the German Empire (*Kaiserliches Statistisches Amt*) was created. Next, the State Sciences Society (*Staatswissenschaftliche Gesellschaft*) was established by Schmoller and his colleagues in 1883. These statistical bureaus were closely connected with each other and often exchanged views and ideas. They also organized seminars to train students in statistics. Furthermore, their members travelled internationally to acquire additional training and advance their knowledge.

Adherents of the GHSE generally received their training in statistics in the seminars of Gustav Rumelin (1815–1889) and Ernst Engel (1821–1896). Specifically, Hildebrand, Knies, Schmoller, Held, Knapp, and Brentano were among the members of the GHSE who attended Engel's seminars in Berlin. Engel, who acquired much fame for creating the Engel Curve (Engel's Law), was one of the most important German statisticians. He was widely regarded as the intellectual father of statistical empiricism, and served as director of the statistical bureau of Prussia from 1860 to 1882.[3] Many of the political economists who were trained in Engel's seminars went on to teach statistics at various German universities. For example, Knapp, who was a member of the Youngest Historical School, taught statistics at the universities of Leipzig and Strasbourg. He is known for contributing to the development of mathematical economics by using mathematical equations and statistics to estimate social and economic indicators. Additionally, Schmoller gave lectures in statistics in Strasbourg, while Held taught the subject in Bonn.

One of the main reasons why theorists of the GHSE played such an important role in the development of statistics and empirical economic research was because they viewed them as pathways to obtaining scientifically rigorous solutions in economics. More precisely, they believed that statistics were necessary for establishing the foundations of theories in political economy. Accordingly, they focused on acquiring quantitative and qualitative knowledge that would allow them to depict various aspects of social and economic life through statistics. More specifically, they used statistical methods to implement a number of social reforms and policies to address a variety of issues, including severe income inequality, poverty, child mortality, prostitution, worker protection, homelessness, universal education, counteracting the negative outcomes of rapid urbanization, affordable housing, and improving living standards.

Even though adherents of the GHSE played an important role in the early development of mathematical economics and the use of statistics in their discipline, their contributions have been largely forgotten. Eventually, modern economists lost touch with the original reasons why political economists supported these practices in the first place, which was to combine historical knowledge and statistics into a critical and analytical tool that would help them find solutions to a wide range of social and economic issues and problems of their time. By making mathematics into the essence of economics instead of employing it as a useful tool as was originally intended by the GHSE, neoliberal economists have come to believe that anything expressed in mathematical terms or equations must not only be correct, but also universal. The extensive representation of the economic world through the methods, presentations, and language of mathematics has resulted in current economists generally possessing a poor and limited understanding of society, social phenomena, and economics in general.

Conclusion

Most of the books and articles published by theorists of the GHSE demonstrated that many of them were great savants. Their readers would marvel at their extensive knowledge in a variety of areas, including literature, the natural sciences, geography, history, politics, culture, and traditions. These great savants and scholars saw political economy as the science of the laws of development for both the economy and economic life, which could be used to effectively achieve common welfare. Their goals included finding better ways to describe people's 'economic nature and economic wants, to investigate the laws and the character of the institutions which are adapted to the satisfaction of these wants, and the greater or less amount of success by which they have been attended' (Roscher 1878V1, 111). They believed that since the economic and societal organization of each historical stage is different than those of others, there cannot be an absolutely valid system that should be universally adhered to by all forms of societal organization across history. Accordingly, they called for the complete abandonment of universal economic laws, individualistic assumptions, the laissez-faire doctrine, and highly abstract ahistorical deductive methods, all of which were promoted by classical economics. Adherents of the GHSE also rejected the classical view that political economy was a value-free discipline. In fact, they believed that economic progress and ethics complemented one another.

Theorists of GHSE addressed the common needs of all social classes by trying to achieve general welfare and national solidarity via the historical inductive method, methodological collectivism, and ethical economics. In fact, they ended up changing the method of investigation in political economy by collecting empirical data and dedicating themselves to historical and statistical studies. Additionally, they deemed state reforms, regulations, and policies as indispensable tools for the development of the national economy, which was crucial for the achievement of common welfare. In fact, all state reforms, regulations, and policies were supposed to be evaluated based on historical studies, statistical analyses, and ethical judgments to ensure that they would contribute to the achievement of common welfare. Furthermore, since the development of the national economy was dependent on a country's natural resources and human capital, theorists of the GHSE not only valued material investments aimed at improving productivity and the effective management of natural resources, they also advocated for the improvement of human capital via the provision of public education and training. They also supported positive state interventions designed to 'enforce provisions for public health,' regulate 'production and transport,' 'protect weaker members of society,' 'guarantee the safety of earnings,' promote 'intellectual and aesthetic culture,' improve working conditions, and so on (Ingram 1888, 128). Ultimately, their efforts played a major role in establishing the original foundations of the modern welfare state, particularly those of some members of the YHS.

For most of the 19th century, the GHSE was the great stimulating force of political economy that broadened the scope of economics and attracted the attention and interest of international students and academics. However, since the dominance and influence of the GHSE started to decline in the early 20th century, little or no attention has been paid to the important contributions that this school of thought has made to the development of the discipline of economics. At the same time, it is not overly surprising that the discipline of economics has neglected the role of the GHSE in its development in this way, since most economists of the 20th and 21st centuries have failed to value the importance of learning from the history of economic thought and the history of economics.

Notes

1 Roscher (1878V1, 87) defined political economy as 'the science which has to do with the laws of the development of the economy of a nation, or with its economic national life.'
2 https://www.statistik-berlin-brandenburg.de/publikationen/aufsaetze/2012/HZ_201201-01.pdf.
3 https://www.statistik-berlin-brandenburg.de/publikationen/aufsaetze/2012/HZ_201201-01.pdf.

Bibliography

Adams, Henry Carter. 1886. 'Economics and Jurisprudence.' Ed. Richard T. Ely. *Science Economic Discussion*. New York: The Science Company. 80–91.
Ashley, William J. 1908 [1888]. *An Introduction to English Economic History and Theory*. https://socialsciences.mcmaster.ca/~econ/ugcm/3ll3/ashley/Hist1.pdf
Backhaus, Jürgen. 1988. 'Preface.' Ed. Nicholas W. Balabkins. *Not by Theory Alone... The Economics of Gustav von Schmoller and Its Legacy to America*. Berlin: Duncker und Humblot. 5–8.
Backhaus, Jürgen G. 2007 [1989]. 'Gustav von Schmoller and Social Economics.' *International Journal of Social Economics*. Vol. 16: 6–16.
Balabkins, Nicholas. 1988. *Not by Theory Alone...The Economics of Gustav von Schmoller and Its Legacy to America*. Berlin: Duncker und Humblot.
Block, Maurice. 1879. 'Les deux écoles économiques.' *Académie des Sciences Morales et Politiques*. 705–733. https://hdl.handle.net/2027/uiuo.ark:/13960/t5cc77h71
Brentano, Lujo. 1881. *Der Arbeiterversicherungszwang: Seine Voraussetzungen und seine Folgen*. Berlin: Carl Habel.
Cardoso, José Luís and Michalis Psalidopoulos. 2016. *The German Historical School and European Economic Thought*. New York: Routledge.
Clark, Christopher. 1995. *Iron Kingdom: The Rise and Downfall of Prussia, 1600–1947*. London: Penguin Books.
Cook, Simon and Keith Tribe. 2016. 'Historical Economics.' Ed. Gilbert Faccarello and Heinz D. Kurz. *Handbook on the History of Economic Analysis Volume II: Schools of Thought in Economics*. Elgaronline: 295–312. DOI: https://doi.org/10.4337/9781785367366.0002
Cunningham, William. 1894. 'Why had Roscher So Little Influence in England.' *Annals of the American Academy: Political and Social Science*. Vol. 5: 317–334.
Dorfman, Joseph. 1955. 'The Role of the German Historical School in American Economic Thought.' *The American Economic Review*. Vol. 45, No. 2: 17–28.
Dorfman, Joseph. 1966. *The Economic Mind in American Civilisation. Volume III. 1865–1918*. New York: The Viking Press.
Ely, Richard T. 1882. 'Bismarck's Plan for Insuring German Laborers.' *International Review*. Vol. 12: 504–520.

Ely, Richard T. 1883. 'The Past and Present of Political Economy.' *The Overland Monthly Series*. Vol. 2, No. 9: 225–235. The Overland monthly. ser.2:v.2 (1883). - Full View | HathiTrust Digital Library | HathiTrust Digital Library.

Ely, Richard T. 1884. *The Past and the Present of Political Economy*. Baltimore: N. Murray, Publication Agent.

Ely, Richard T. 1886. 'Ethics and Economics.' Ed. Richard T. Ely. *Science Economic Discussion*. New York: The Science Company. 44–56.

Ely, Richard T. 1910. 'The American Economic Association 1885–1909.' *American Economic Association Quarterly*. Vol. 11, No. 1: 47–111. Papers and Discussions of the Twenty-Second Annual Meeting: Being the Twenty-fifth Anniversary of the Founding of the Association. URL: https://www.jstor.org/stable/3000023

Filip, Birsen. 2018. 'The German Historical School of Economics and the Foundations and Development of the Austrian School of Economics.' Ed. Robert Leeson. *Hayek: A Collaborative Biography: Part XIII: 'Fascism' and Liberalism in the (Austrian) Classical Tradition*. Cham: Palgrave Macmillan, 79–128.

Grimmer-Solem, Erik. 2010A [2003]. 'Introduction.' Ed. Erik Grimmer-Solem. *The Rise of Historical Economics and Social Reform in Germany 1864–1894*. Oxford Scholarship Online. DOI: 10.1093/acprof:oso/9780199260416.001.0001

Grimmer-Solem, Erik. 2010B [2003]. 'What was the Historical School? A Critical Reassessment.' Ed. Erik Grimmer-Solem. *The Rise of Historical Economics and Social Reform in Germany 1864–1894*. Oxford Scholarship Online. DOI:10.1093/acprof:oso/9780199260416.003.0002

Haney, Lewis Henry. 1915. *History of Economic Thought: A Critical Account of the Origin and Development of the Economic Theories of the Leading Thinkers in the Leading Nations*. New York: The Macmillan Company.

Henderson, William Otto. 2006 [1961]. *Industrial Revolution on the Continent: Germany, France, Russia 1800–1914*. Oxon: Routledge.

Hodgson, Geoffrey M. 2001. *How Economics Forgot History: The Problem of Historical Specificity in Social Science*. New York: Routledge.

Ingram, John Kells. 1888. *A History of Political Economy*. London: A. and C. Black. A History of Political Economy | Online Library of Liberty (libertyfund.org)

Jevons, W. Stanley. 1876. 'The Future of Political Economy.' *The Fortnightly Review*, Vol. 20, No. 129: 617–631. London: Chapman and Hali. https://archive.org/details/in.ernet.dli.2015.21176/page/n5/mode/2up

Knies, Karl. 1883. *Politische Oekonomie vom geschichitlichen Standpuncte*. Osnabrück: Otto Zeller.

Leslie, T. E. Cliffe. 1875. 'The History of German Political Economy.' *Fortnightly Review*. https://socialsciences.mcmaster.ca/econ/ugcm/3ll3/leslie/leslie04.html

Louzek, Marek. 2011. 'The Battle of Methods in Economics: The Classical *Methodenstreit*: Menger vs. Schmoller.' *American Journal of Economics and Sociology*. Vol. 70, No. 2: 439–463.

Mayo-Smith, Richmond. 1886. 'Methods of Investigation in Political Economy.' Ed. Richard T. Ely. *Science Economic Discussion*. New York: The Science Company. 104–122.

Milford, Karl. 1995. 'Roscher's Epistemological and Methodological Position Its Importance for the *Methodenstreit*.' *Journal of Economic Studies*. Vol. 22, No. 3/4/5: 26–52.

Mitchell, Wesley Clair. 1949. *Lecture Notes on Types of Economic Theory: Vol. II*. New York: Kelley.

Nasse, Erwin. 1887. 'The Economic Movement in Germany.' *The Quarterly Journal of Economics*. Vol. 1, No. 4: 498–506. URL: https://www.jstor.org/stable/1879345

Nau, Heino Heinrich. 2000. 'Gustav Schmoller's Historico–Ethical Political Economy: Ethics, Politics and Economics in the Younger German Historical School, 1860–1917.' *The European Journal of the History of Economic Thought*. Vol. 7, No. 4: 507–531. ISSN 0967–2567 print/ISSN 1469–5936 online © 2000 Taylor & Francis Ltd.

Neff, Frank Amandus. 1950. *Economic Doctrines*. New York: McGraw-Hill. https://archive.org/details/economic-doctrines-frank-neff

Newcomb, Simon. 1884. 'Two School of Political Economy.' *The Princeton Review*. Vol. 60: 291–301. The Princeton review. ser.4 v.14 (1884). Full View|HathiTrust Digital Library|HathiTrust Digital Library.

Papadopoulos, Kosmas and Bradley W. Bateman. 2011. 'Karl Knies and the Prehistory of Neoclassical Economics: Understanding the Importance of "Die Nationaloekonomische Lehre vom Werth" (1855).' *Journal of the History of Economic Thought*. Vol. 33, No. 1: 19–35. doi:10.1017/S105383721000061

Peukert, Helge. 2001. 'The Schmoller Renaissance.' *History of Political Economy*. Vol. 33, No. 1: 71–116. Durham: Duke University Press.

Popper, Karl. 2002 [1945]. *The Open Society and Its Enemies*. London: Routledge.

Pribram, Karl. 1983. *A History of Economic Reasoning*. Baltimore: The Johns Hopkins University Press.

Richter, Rudolf. 1996. 'Bridging Old and New Institutional Economics: Gustav Schmoller, the Leader of the Younger German Historical School, Seen With Neoinstitutionalists' Eyes.' *Journal of Institutional and Theoretical Economics*. Vol. 152, No. 4: 567–592. URL: http://www.jstor.org/stable/40751932

Roscher, William. 1842. *Leben, Werk und Zeitalter des Thukydides*. Göttingen: Vandenhoeck und Ruprecht.

Roscher, William. 1843. *Outline for Lectures of Political Economy*. New York: Henry Holt & CO.

Roscher, William. 1878V1 [1843]. *Principles of Political Economy V1*. 13th Ed. Translation by John J. Lalor. New York: Henry Holt & CO.

Roscher, William. 1878V2 [1843]. *Principles of Political Economy V2*. 13th Ed. Translation by John J. Lalor. New York: Henry Holt & CO.

Schmoller, Gustav. 1865. 'Die Arbeiterfrage.' *Preußische Jahrbücher*. Vol. XV: 32–63.

Schmoller, Gustav. 1894 [1881]. 'The Idea of Justice in Political Economy.' *Annals of the American Academy: Political and Social Science*. Vol. 4: 697–737.

Schmoller, Gustav. 1902A. *Lettre Ouvert à M. Heinrich von Treitschke, 1874–1875*. Paris: V. Giard & E. Brière, Libraires-Éditeurs.

Schmoller, Gustav. 1902B [1884]. *The Mercantile System and Its Historical Significance: Illustrated Chiefly from Prussian History*. London: MacMillan and Co.

Schmoller, Gustav. 1902C [1893]. *Économie nationale, Économie politique et méthode*. Paris: V. Giard & E. Brière, Libraires-Éditeurs.

Schmoller, Gustav. 1904. *Grundriss Der Allgemeinen Volkswirtschaftslehre, Vol II*. Leibzig: Duncker & Humblot.

Schmoller, Gustav. 1915. 'Schmoller on Class Conflicts in General.' *American Journal of Sociology*. Vol. 20, No. 4: 504–531. Chicago: University of Chicago Press. Stable URL: https://www.jstor.org/stable

Schmoller, Gustav. 1990 [1913]. *Charakterbilder*. Munich: Duncker & Hurnblot.

Schmoller, Gustav. 2018 [1897]. 'Changing Theories and Fixed Truths in the Field of State and Social Sciences and Contemporary German Political Economy.' *Journal of Contextual Economics*. Vol. 138: 213–232. Berlin: Duncker & Humblot.

Schumpeter, Joseph A. 2006 [1954]. *History of Economic Analysis*. The Taylor & Francis e-Library. ISBN 0-203-98391-2 Master e-book ISBN.

Seager, Henry Rogers. 1893. 'Economics at Berlin and Vienna.' *Journal of Political Economy*. Vol. 1, No. 2: 236–262. URL: https://www.jstor.org/stable/1817770

Seligman, Edwin R. A. 1917. *The Economic Interpretation of History*. New York: Columbia University Press.

Senn, Peter R. 1995. 'Why had Roscher So much Influence in the USA Compared with the UK.' *Journal of Economic Studies*. Vol. 22, No. 3/4/5: 53–105.

Senn, Peter R. 2005. 'The German Historical Schools in the History of Economic Thought.' *Journal of Economic Studies*. Vol. 32, No. 3: 185–255. www.emeraldinsight.com/0144-3585.htm

Small, Albion W. 1923. *Some Contributions to the History of Sociology*. Chicago: University of Chicago Press.

Small, Albion W. 2001 [1909]. *The Cameralists: The Pioneers of German Social Polity*. Kitchener: Batoche Books.

St. Marc, Henri. 1892. *Étude sur L'Enseignement de L'Économie Politique dans les Université D'Allemagne et D'Autriche*. Paris: Armand Colin et C.

Streissler, Erich W. 2001. 'Rau, Hermann and Roscher: Contributions of German Economics around the Middle of the Nineteenth Century.' *European Journal of History of Economic Thought*. Vol. 8, No. 3: 311–331.

Tribe, Keith. 2002. 'Historical Schools of Economics: German and English.' *Keele Economics Research Papers*. No. 02. ISSN 1352-8955.

Tribe, Keith. 2003. 'The German Historical School: The Historical and Ethical Approach to Economics.' *History of Political Economy*. Vol. 35, No. 1: 173–194.

Veblen, Thornstein. 1901. 'Gustav Schmoller's Economics.' *The Quarterly Journal of Economics*. Vol. 16, No. 1: 69–93.

Wagner, Adolf. 1891. 'Marshall's Principles of Economics.' *The Quarterly Journal of Economics*. Vol. 5, No. 3: 319–338. URL: https://www.jstor.org/stable/1879612

Yefimov, Vladimir. 2009. 'Comparative Historical Institutional Analysis of German, English and American Economics.' *Munich Personal RePEc Archive*. http://mpra.ub.uni-muenchen.de/48173/

4 German-Trained American Political Economists and the Influence of the German Historical School of Economics

Introduction

In the second half of the 19th century, 'the progress of Germany became the wonder of the world,' as it assumed a leadership position 'in industry and trade, in literature and education, in military growth and civil administration' (Kinley 1918, 5). German professors achieved a 'degree of perfection... that astonishes the world,' while their universities acquired impeccable international reputations for providing very attractive learning environments and high-quality teaching (Dorfman 1955, 22). Accordingly, this became accepted as the beginning of 'a golden period' of 'ambition without hatred' in Germany, when large numbers of foreign students came to the country to study in all disciplines and encountered a friendly and welcoming environment (Simkhovitch 1938, 53).

From the 1870s up until the beginning of WWI, German universities held supremacy over their counterparts in Britain and France when it came to the quality of teaching and the enrollment of international students. Basically, 'no country in Europe' could rival Germany in many academic disciplines (Rowe 1890, 78). In the case of political economy, German universities achieved remarkable development due to the work and efforts of the theorists of the German Historical School of Economics (GHSE), who became global leaders in the discipline. In addition to international students, many Germans were also trained under the GHSE, including government officials, members of social and economic institutions, and anybody else who wanted to obtain a higher education in political economy.

The GHSE was at 'its apex' in the latter part of the 19th century, when 'it stood unrivaled in the number and high quality of scholars who were devoting themselves to research and teachings in the various branches of economics' (Ferguson 1950, 154). During that time, international students seeking 'advanced teaching in economics' went to Germany, 'since in England there was very little systematic teaching of economics, and no graduate qualification as in Germany; while the French university system was then (and still is) firmly linked to a closed educational and cultural system' (Tribe 2002, 2). In other words, 'men from most parts of the civilized world, who wished to equip

DOI: 10.4324/9781003247715-4

themselves for professional work in economics, flocked in large numbers to Germany for postgraduate study' (Ferguson 1950, 154). More specifically, these ambitious foreign scholars and students of political economy came to Germany to obtain an advanced education under the theorists of the GHSE and to 'work as free scholars in an expanding world' (Simkhovitch 1938, 53). The international success of the GHSE continued without the possibility of a rival economic program of research emerging at the same scale of advancement and sophistication until the outbreak of WWI.

Political economy departments at German universities not only attracted large numbers of international students who wanted to obtain an advanced education in the discipline, they also became the models for many countries around the world. After those international students completed their studies and training, they returned to their home countries and brought their newly acquired knowledge, experiences, and ideas with them. That means the influence of the GHSE was manifested through the modification of opinions, which led to changes in the way political economy was taught and learned in many different countries (Ingram 1915, 131). More specifically, German-trained young men from a number of nations were able to help 'bring forward economic science, from its old position' (Dunbar 1891, 397). In this way, 'the methods and principles' of the GHSE gained ground in many countries, including the US, Italy, France, England, and Japan (Ely 1883, 234). In case of the US, 'no one of the moral science' made 'a more rapid or solid gain than political economy, either in the extent and importance of its scientific investigations, or in the dignity of method and spirit which characterizes its work, or in its educational value' (Dunbar 1891, 397).

This chapter focuses on German-trained American political economists, who played significant roles in the development of economic thought from the late 19th century up until the outbreak of WWI. It begins by briefly providing information about some of the distinguished American economists who studied political economy at German universities under the theorists of the GHSE. It also explains why these returning economists were not satisfied with the classical orthodoxy that was dominant among American political economists at that time. It then presents some of striking similarities in the methods, approaches, policies, reforms, goals, values, and ideas defended by these returning American economists and those advocated by the GHSE.

Why Did the GHSE Attract American Students and Scholars?

In the 19th century, American society was becoming more industrialized and urbanized. There was also a growing interest in economic problems, as young American men were worried about the destructive outcomes associated with the industrialization process, which motivated them to try to find ways 'to avoid the ills that disfigured England's factory and machine age and threatened the Anglo-American tradition of liberty' (Dorfman 1955, 17). In fact, the destructive outcomes of industrialization observed in England led them to lose faith in the ability of classical economics to provide the appropriate policies and reforms needed to successfully offset similar results in the US. That also means critics of classical economics were already present in the US prior to the arrival of significant numbers of Americans who went to Germany to advance their education and training under the theorists of the GHSE.

There were a number of factors that made Germany the exclusive destination of choice for American students and academics seeking to further their education and training abroad. While the German reputation for providing great hospitality played a role in this phenomenon, the most important reason was the prominent status of German undergraduate and graduate programs when it came to providing an advanced level of education due, in large part, to the unparalleled international reputation of the theorists of the GHSE (Devine 1894, 87). At that time, it was accepted that Germany was the only country in which 'systematic academic training in political economy had begun' (Mason and Lamont 1982, 391). However, even before the GHSE achieved international prominence, Americans were paying close attention to the social and economic changes that were transpiring across the Atlantic by following European newspapers, journals, books, and periodicals. By doing so, they became informed about the great triumphs and successes of the GHSE when it was still rising in stature, which inspired many young American men to learn more about this school of thought.

Like many of their international peers, Americans were interested in getting a higher education in Germany instead of France or England due to the perception that 'no other country' was 'so interesting to the political economist as Germany' (Ely 1882, 519). At that time, the work of theorists of the GHSE represented the rise of 'a new creative power' in political economy (Ely 1883, 233). It was even claimed that the discipline of political economy obtained its 'truly scientific basis' from this new movement, which was initiated through the works of Wilhelm Georg Friedrich Roscher (1817–1894), Bruno Hildebrand (1812–1878), and Karl Knies (1821–1898) (Seligman 1886A, 18). There was also a great deal of appreciation for 'the amount of actual knowledge, historical and theoretical, imparted' by Gustav von Schmoller (1838–1917), Lujo Brentano (1844–1931), Adolf Held (1844–1880), Adolf Gotthilf Wagner (1835–1917), Johannes Conrad (1839–1915), and many other theorists of the GHSE (Seligman 1886A, 19).

The contributions of the GHSE to the 'positive knowledge of the economic institutions and customs of the different parts of the world' was striking (Ely 1883, 234). Its theorists essentially introduced 'a new spirit and purpose' into political economy, and many American men were delighted with this fundamental alteration to the spirit of the discipline (ibid.). The GHSE was clearly experiencing unprecedented success, as evidenced by the fact that 'an ever increasing number of college graduates were going to Germany for advanced work' (Dorfman 1955, 22). Living and studying in Germany demonstrated 'the importance of linking book knowledge and practical experience' for young American students and academics (Ely 1938, 187). In fact, unlike the classical economics of England, which had its influence 'communicated by the importation and the republication of books,' the influence of the GHSE was largely transmitted through personal networks and interactions (Devine 1894, 87). In 1876, the successes enjoyed by the GHSE led Harvard economics professor Charles Franklin Dunbar (1830–1900) to suggest that 'the lead in economics' was 'passed from England and France to Germany' (Dorfman 1955, 22).

Since American students and academics were interested in acquiring advanced knowledge in the area of political economy, including the methods and techniques developed by the theorists of the GHSE, they were being 'constantly drawn to Germany,' where they could enroll in classes on historical and statistical investigation (Ely 1882, 519). They relied heavily on the work of Roscher in order to acquire 'information about early phases of German economic thought' (Small 2001, 5–6). His work was particularly influential in the development of American economics between 1865 and 1914 (Senn 1995, 60). During this period, three of his books were translated into English and widely used as textbooks at universities: *Outline of Lectures on Political Science According to the Historical Method; Principles of Political Economy*; and *The Spanish Colonial System*. In fact, Roscher was 'admired' by many 'on account of his reverence for his predecessors' (Seligman 1889, 545). His astonishing 'historic learning enabled him to explain much that had been dark' (Seligman 1889, 545).

In addition to Roscher, Schmoller, 'the master historian and statistician,' was highly revered by many German-trained American political economists, though his influence 'was at its peak' between 1870 and 1910 (Seager 1893, 249). It was mainly those American students with an interest in ethical economics and 'historical and statistical researches' that chose to attend Schmoller's classes (ibid.: 241). These students had a particularly high opinion of his teachings, views, knowledge, and writing (Seager 1893). However, it has been claimed that his 'importance and influence' in the development of the GHSE could not be 'appreciated by one who has never heard him lecture' (ibid.: 251). In fact, Schmoller's lectures received exceptionally high praise for giving 'the student not merely a valuable set of historical notes, but also a grasp of the deeply underlying principles and tendencies,' which was deemed 'truly admirable' (ibid.: 250). His lectures were 'attractive, not so much for the truths they contain…as because of the manner in which these truths are expressed' (ibid.: 249). His students pointed out that even if someone was opposed to some of Schmoller's ideas, anybody would be 'impressed by the consummate manner' in which he presented them (ibid.: 251). Many German-trained American political economists did not hide their admiration for Schmoller's achievements in political economy, as it was widely believed that 'whatever be the final judgment of later generations of economists on the schools and doctrines of our day, there can be no doubt that here has been a great task set for himself by a man of great gifts, and worthily accomplished' (Taussig 1905, 501).

American students who were interested in socialism, money and banking, public finance, and practical political economy often chose to study in Wagner's classes (Seager 1893, 241). To be more precise, his courses on money and banking mainly focused on 'the history, nature and function of moneys, the history and statistics of the production of the precious metals,' etc. (ibid.: 245). Meanwhile, his courses on practical political economy concentrated on 'agriculture, manufacturing industry, trade and transportation, laying down general rules to guide the action of the state in its relation to these industries' (ibid.: 244). During his lectures, Wagner would provide 'a wealth of striking illustrations and interesting facts borrowed from the economic histories of all countries' (ibid.: 243). Consequently, much like many of his contemporaries at the GHSE, Wagner's classes were 'crowded with students from all over the world. Russians, Poles, Bulgarians, Italians, English, Japanese and Americans flocked to hear him' (Simkhovitch 1938, 51). Meanwhile, Conrad's classes mainly focused on the economics and statistics of the modern agriculture sector. His lectures and seminars also attracted and 'stimulated a large number of distinguished students, many of whom were Americans' (Ely 1938, 40). Students from the US also had high praise for Knies, because his classes on statistics and money at University of Heidelberg gave 'the historical method a scientific standing' (Clark 1886, 35). Americans also studied under many other prominent contributors of the GHSE. In fact, between 1870 and 1890, of the 76 American economists at 28 leading colleges and universities across the US, '53 studied in Germany' and attended the classes and lectures of these prominent political economists that adhered to the GHSE (Parrish 1967, 5).

Notable American Economists Who Studied under the Theorists of the GHSE

In the 19th century, classical economics disseminated its ideas and spread its influence throughout the US almost exclusively by having the publications of its theorists read and studied in the classrooms of American universities. Meanwhile, the influence of the GHSE was mainly attributed to the personal interactions that occurred between the Americans that lived and studied in Germany and the adherents of the GHSE that they came into contact with, including their professors and fellow students. At that time, it was indispensable for Americans to reside and study in Germany for a few years if they wanted to have a successful academic career in political economy, as well as a number of other disciplines (Devine 1894, 87). After completing their studies in Germany and returning to the US, these Americans 'naturally expected their foreign residence to give them an advantage in the competition for a position at home' (Herbst 1965, 4). One of the most prominent German-trained American political economists who played a key role in the development of the discipline of economics in the US was Richard T. Ely (1854–1943).

After graduating from Columbia College in 1876, Ely went to Germany in order to further his education in 1877 and remained there for three years. He began by learning the German language in Kiel before moving on to the University of Halle, where he studied philosophy, psychology, history, and political economy. During his time in Halle, Ely met Simon Nelson Patten (1852–1922), who had come to Germany to join his friends Edmund Janes James (1855–1925) and Joseph French Johnson (1853–1925), who were already studying there. It was through Patten that Ely met professor Conrad, who was teaching at the University of Halle (Ely 1938, 39, St. Marc 1892, 63). After Halle, Ely moved on to Heidelberg, where he completed his PhD in political economy in 1880 under the guidance of Knies.

Ely (1938, 37, 40) confessed that he was motivated to go abroad to Germany in order 'to find the absolute truth.' For him, studying there felt like entering 'into a new heritage of freedom, and a certain joyous expansion was one of the most pronounced feelings' that he had ever experienced (ibid.). He believed that 'in the atmosphere of the German universities there was room for growth and encouragement of the development of individuality, which was something new' to him and the other American students (Ely 1910, 69).

After returning to the US, Ely worked at the Political Economy department of Johns Hopkins University from 1881 to 1892, where he taught the History of Political Economy. Then, in 1892, Ely was appointed professor at the University of Wisconsin, where he also served as director of the School of Economics, Political Science, and History until 1925. During his time at Wisconsin, he was able to introduce his students to the spirit of teaching and studying that he experienced as a student in German universities. While Ely wrote many articles and books on a number of different topics, including socialism, labor movements, social reforms, and monopolies, his most well-known publications were: *French and German Socialism in Modern Times*, 1883; *Monopolies and Trusts*, 1883; *Labour Movement in America*, 1883; *Taxation in American States and Cities*, 1888; and *Socialism and Social Reform*, 1894 (Ingram 1915, 173). Ely's publications 'purposefully enabled him to reach millions of people who could not attend his classes in the university' (Taylor 1944, 134). Ultimately, Ely managed to significantly shape American economic thought, the economics profession, and the way it is taught, as well as economic policies, not only through his books, but also on account of the fact that he taught many generations of economists at Johns Hopkins University and the University of Wisconsin.

There is no doubt that Ely played a major role in transferring the economic thinking of the GHSE from Germany to the US. He also had a significant impact on 'the formation of a sound public opinion regarding the economic problems which have confronted' Americans during the last quarter of the 19th century (Ingram 1915, 174). Among his most notable contributions to the development of economics in the US was being one of the founding fathers of the American Economic Association (AEA) in 1885 and serving as its president in 1900–1901. Ely also featured prominently in efforts to improve the conditions of the American labor classes. Furthermore, many of his former students went on to become important 'journalists, leaders in many branches of social reform, experts in taxation, the control of monopolies, credit institutions, appraisals, home ownership, rural land tenure, agricultural economics, and many other fields' (Taylor 1944, 134). They included future president Woodrow Wilson, the 'prominent sociologist Edward A. Ross,' reformers Frederic C. Howe and Albert Shaw ([Theodore] Roosevelt's advisors), 'the historian Frederick Jackson Turner, John Finley, who became editor of the New York Times, David Kinley, who became president of the University of Illinois, and Dr. Henry Taylor, who became chief of the Bureau of Agricultural Economics' (Fine 1957, 240). Ely also influenced key progressive figures, including Robert La Follette and Theodore Roosevelt, though the former never studied in his classes (ibid.). In addition to 'the Progressive movement,' the New Deal also attested 'to Ely's significance as a precursor of twentieth-century reform' (ibid.).

John Bates Clark (1874–1938), who was accepted by 'many authorities as the most distinguished American economist,' graduated from Amherst College in 1872. Then, from 1872 to 1875, he studied under Wilhelm Roscher in Leipzig and under Johannes Conrad and Karl Knies at University of Heidelberg (Neff 1950, 390, 503). Consequently, he was highly influenced by the views and methods of the GHSE. Clark returned home in 1875, and then worked at Carleton (1877–1881), Smith (1882–1893), Amherst (1892–1895), and Johns Hopkins from 1892 until 1895. He then joined Columbia University in 1895, where he played a major role in the development of the economics department until his retirement in 1923 (ibid.: 390). He also served as president of the AEA in 1894–1895. Similar to the adherents of the GHSE, Clark accepted that economics had an ethical element to it. Later in his career, he became known for his contribution to marginal utility theory. More specifically, Clark was credited with conceiving 'his own version of marginal utility to the inspiration of his German teacher, Karl Knies' (Dorfman 1955, 28). He also ended up being particularly influential on the economic views of Edmund Janes James.

James received his doctorate in political economy from the University of Halle in 1877 under the supervision of Conrad. Then, in 1883, he was appointed professor of public finance and administration in the Wharton School of Finance and Economy at the University of Pennsylvania. The following year, he was elected as a member of the National Council of Education. Subsequently, from 1891 to 1895, he served as 'President of the American Society for the Extension of University Teaching, an association organized to promote the introduction and development of University Extension methods of instruction throughout' the US (Annals of the American Academy of Political and Social Science 1896, 79). During his presidency, in the US, 'the number of lecture courses rose from 42 in 1890–91 to 126 in 1894–95; while the number in attendance increased from 7400 to 20,000' (ibid.).

In 1896, James left the University of Pennsylvania for the University of Chicago. Then, in 1902, he became president of Northwestern University, where he strongly promoted scholarly achievements. In particular, he sought to:

> raise the University to international attention by hosting world-class scholars and researchers. During his administration, the newly developed graduate program to promote academic and experimental research became the first program in the nation to receive its own appropriation from a state legislature.[1]

In 1904, he left Northwestern and 'became president of the University of Illinois,' where he established the University of Illinois Press (Kinley 1949, 48). James was regarded as 'the greatest American university president of his day' (ibid.). In fact, President Abbott Lawrence Lowell (1856–1943) of Harvard University described him as 'the man under whose inspiring touch the University of Illinois has risen to the front rank among American universities' (ibid.).

Among his other notable achievements, James was a member of the American Philosophical Society. He was also one of the founding members of the AEA in 1885 and, in addition to contributing to its publications, served as its first vice president in 1885 before becoming its president during 1910–1911 (Annals of the American Academy of Political and Social Science 1896, 79). Furthermore, James was one of the founding members of the American Academy of Political and Social Science, as well as its inaugural president from 1889 to 1901. He was also editor of the *Annals of the American Academy of Political and Social Science* and a known contributor to the *Cyclopaedia of Political Science, Political Economy and United States History* (Annals of the American Academy of Political and Social Science 1896, 79). Over the course of his career, James published many articles in English and German on a variety of issues such as the public education system, immigration and emigration, factory laws, machinery, finance, labor rights, labor unions, insurance, the history of political economy, the federal regulation of railways, the forestry industry, and transportation system in the US. Moreover, some of his publications aimed at improving the American system of higher education discussed topics like the requirements and features of PhD programs in Germany, and the teaching of political economy in German universities.

Another important German-trained figure in the discipline of economics was Simon Nelson Patten, who obtained his PhD in political economy at the University of Halle in 1877 under Conrad. In fact, he later dedicated his book *The Premises of Political Economy: Being a Re-examination of Certain Fundamental Principles of Economic Science* (1885) to 'his teacher and friend, Dr. Johannes Conrad…to whose kind encouragement and inspiring example his many students owe so much.' During his time studying in Germany, Patten (1916, 4) observed that adherents of the GHSE were 'the most ardent of the new groups of moderns' in the university lectures and seminars that he attended. He also considered himself to be 'more ardent' than most other students 'for the new culture' he was experiencing in Germany (ibid.). After returning home, Patten was appointed professor at the Wharton School of Economics in the University of Pennsylvania, where he worked from 1888 up until his retirement in 1917. During that period, Patten ended up enjoying close relationships with Ely and James after they had initially become acquainted while studying together under the theorists of the GHSE at the University of Halle. In 1884, Patten and James were inspired to organize an association similar to *Verein für Sozialpolitik*, but ultimately failed (Ely 1938, 132–135). Later, with the same inspiration, Patten, James, and Ely founded the AEA in 1885. Subsequently, Patten was its president in 1908–1909.

Frank William Taussig (1859–1940) graduated from Harvard in 1879, before going on to study Roman law and political economy for one semester at the University of Berlin. He then went back to Harvard University, where he studied law from 1883 to 1886. Taussig began teaching political economy at Harvard in 1886 and remained there until 1935, when his chair was succeeded by Joseph Schumpeter (1883–1950). His teaching was very influential 'on the course of American economic thought and action. Practically every Harvard student of economics studied under him' (Dorfman 1966V3, 270). Taussig's views, approaches, and teaching were highly influenced by Wagner and Schmoller. In fact, his most renowned graduate course was dedicated to 'a critic of classical and neo-classical writers' (ibid.). Taussig admitted to writing 'a most encouraging letter' to Ely after reading a scathing review of his book *The Labor Movement in America* (1886) in *The Nation*, which was written by astronomer, mathematician, and teacher of political economy Simon Newcomb (1835–1909), who defended abstract mathematical economics, the laissez-faire approach, and the invisible hand theory. Newcomb went so far as to accuse Ely of being a socialist and describe the book as 'the ravings of an anarchist or the dream of a socialist' (Dorfman 1966V3, 163, Ely 1936, 146). In response, Taussig immediately sent 'his application' for membership in the AEA (Ely 1936, 146).

Taussig established the foundations of modern trade theory in the US, largely on account of his original work 'on the history of tariff legislation' (Adams 1884, 89). He was also the editor of the *Quarterly Journal of Economics* from 1889 to 1890 (ibid.). Furthermore, he played a major role in influencing American public policy, as he became an unofficial adviser on economic and commercial policy to President Woodrow Wilson and was appointed 'the first chairman of the United States Tariff Commission' from 1917 to 1919 (Carlson 1968, 104). In fact, Taussig accompanied President Wilson to the Versailles Peace Conference at the end of WWI, serving as his economic advisor in drafting some of the economic requirements that were included in the Treaty of Versailles in 1919. Taussig also served as president of AEA during 1904–1905 (Ely 1936, 146).

Richmond Mayo-Smith (1854–1901) was an American statistician and sociologist, who studied in Berlin during 1875–1877 and then in Heidelberg in 1878. In 1877, he was offered the Chair in Economics and Statistics in the Faculty of Political Science at Columbia college, which was about to be established, on the condition that he completed his graduate studies in Germany (Dorfman 1955, 18). This could be interpreted as a 'formal acceptance' of the great reputation that the GHSE had within the American academic community (ibid.). Shortly thereafter, Mayo-Smith completed his studies in Germany and assumed his position as professor of Political Economy and Social Science at Columbia College in 1878.

Over the course of his academic career, Mayo-Smith played a major role in the development of how statistics was taught in the US, as well as its application to the social sciences. In fact, he taught the first course on statistics at an American university in 1880, and continued to do so until 1901. In 1889, Mayo-Smith became the vice president of the AEA, a position that he held until his death. The following year, he became:

> a member of the National Academy of Sciences, which prior to this had usually selected only scholars in the pure and natural sciences. He was also an active member of the International Statistical Institute and was elected an honorary fellow of the Royal Statistical Society.[2]

Herbert Baxter Adams (1850–1901) obtained his PhD in political science at Heidelberg University in 1876. He actually met Clark while studying at Heidelberg. Once Adams returned to the US, he was offered a post at Johns Hopkins University. Based on his experiences as a student, he came to regard the German graduate education program as a model that should be emulated at American universities. In fact, he was credited with being one of the first American scholars to introduce the types of seminars that were prevalent in Germany at American universities. Adams also played an instrumental role in 'organizing the American Historical Association' and was 'probably never happier than when bringing an institution into existence' (Ely 1910, 56).

Edwin Robert Anderson Seligman (1861–1939) graduated from Columbia College in 1879 and went on to study at universities in Berlin, Paris, and Heidelberg until 1882. He actually studied under Knies during his time at the University of Heidelberg. Subsequently, he went back to Columbia to obtain his PhD. He then became a professor of political economy at Columbia University, where he worked from 1891 until 1931. In fact, both Seligman and Clark played major roles in the development of the economics department at Columbia University. Seligman's views were highly influenced by the theorists of the GHSE, as well as H.B. Adams and Ely. During his career, Seligman was accepted as a founding father of American Institutionalism. He also played an important role in establishing the AEA and served as its president during 1902–1903. Seligman was also a significant player in the creation of the American Association of University Professors. Additionally, he was the editor of the *Political Science Quarterly Journal*. He also worked for the Bureau of Labor Statistics and in 1916 became a fellow of the American Statistical Association (ASA).

Henry Carter Adams (1851–1921) obtained his PhD at Johns Hopkins University in 1878. He then completed a postdoc in Berlin and Heidelberg from 1878 to 1879, which involved studying with Wagner, Held, and Engel. While in Germany, Adams was able to publish his thesis, which was entitled 'Zur Geschichte der Besteuerung in den Vereinigten Staaten von Amerika in der Periode von 1789–1816 in the *Zeitschrift für die gesammte Staatswissenschaft*.'[3] In fact, he received high praise for this publication from Wagner, who happened to be the editor of that particular journal. At that time, publishing in a German journal was a very important step in the career of an academic, as doing so brought international respect and recognition for their work. Once he returned home, Adams worked at Cornell University from 1880 to 1887. During that period, he also occasionally lectured on political science at the University of Michigan. Then, from 1887 up until his death, he worked as a professor of political economy and finance at the University of Michigan. He also served as president of the AEA in 1896–1897, and became chief statistician for the new Interstate Commerce Commission, where his work focused on railroad accounting and regulation, as well as the protection of labor rights.

Henry Walcott Farnam (1853–1933) graduated from Yale University in 1874. He returned to Yale in 1876 to study Roman law and economics. Subsequently, he went abroad to further his education at universities in Berlin, Strassburg, and Göttingen. During his time at Berlin University, his doctoral thesis was evaluated by Schmoller in 1878. Shortly thereafter, in 1880, Farnam began his career as a professor of political economy at Yale University, where he remained until 1918. His classes mainly focused on public finance, labor organization, and protective labor laws. Much like theorists of the GHSE, Farnam (1913) supported historical ethical economics. Aside from the GHSE, he was also influenced by Clark's political economy. Over the course of his career, Farnam established *The Yale Review* in 1892 and was president of the AEA in 1911–1912.

In 1890, economic historian Edwin Francis Gay (1867–1946) graduated from the University of Michigan, where he studied history and philosophy. He then went off to Germany and studied under the theorists of the GHSE in Berlin and Leipzig for 12 years. In 1902, he obtained his PhD from the University of Berlin, having written his dissertation under the supervision of Schmoller. Gay adopted Schmoller's view that a political economist does not only focus on 'the relationships between man and material goods,' but also on the relationships among men (Balabkins 1988, 100). Ultimately, Gay's dissertation received the 'highest honors from the University of Berlin,' and Schmoller wanted to have it published (ibid.: 101). However, this did not happen, because Gay did not complete all of the necessary steps to prepare 'the dissertation for publication' (Mason and Lamont 1982, 406). In 1902, Gay returned to the US, where he taught at Harvard until 1917 and then again from 1924 to 1936. During his first stint, Gay was a principal advisor to Harvard President Charles William Eliot (1834–1926) in his efforts to launch the Harvard Graduate School of Business Administration, which occurred in 1908.[4] He was also appointed the first Dean of the Harvard Business School (Carlson 1968, 106).

Gay also had a number of other notable accomplishments, foremost among them being that he was credited with establishing the Master of Business Administration (MBA) as an academic degree at Harvard in 1908. He was also a member of the Council of Foreign Relations and directed the US government's Central Bureau of Planning and Statistics, which was established in 1918. Additionally, Gay was among the cofounders of the National Bureau of Economic Research in 1919 and served as its first president. He was also president of the AEA in 1929–1930, and then became the first president of the Economic History Association in 1940. Gay was clearly a very influential political economist and 'he radiated his German scholarship all over the country. He was particularly successful in stressing the significance of the "contiguous fields" surrounding the core of economics' (Balabkins 1988, 101). During his career, Gay supported ethical and historical economics and argued against the abstract individualistic approach of classical economics, all of which were consistent with the views of his former professors in Germany.

Charles Franklin Dunbar (1830–1900) graduated from Harvard College in 1851. In 1869, he went to study in Germany and England for two years, before being given the first chair in political economy at Harvard College in 1871 (Taussig 1901). He was uniquely qualified for 'his new duties,' as, at that time, there was 'a rare chance to find a man better equipped' than him due to the lack of 'systematic training in economics' at American institutions (Taussig 1904, X). In 1876, Dunbar was elected Dean of Harvard College and remained in that post until 1882. Then, in 1886, Harvard University established the *Quarterly Journal of Economics* and Dunbar was appointed as 'its editor, and remaining in charge from 1886 to 1896' (Taussig 1901, 573). Subsequently, 'in 1890,' after 'the enlarged and remodelled Faculty of Arts and Sciences was organized' at Harvard University, he became its first Dean and remained in that post until 1895 (Taussig 1904, XI). Dunbar also served as president of the AEA in 1893–1894. During the 'later period' of his career, it was often the case that 'he turned' to the theorists of the GHSE (ibid.: X).

Arthur Twining Hadley (1856–1930) was a student of political science at Yale under William Graham Sumner (1840–1910) before going on to the University of Berlin, where he studied history and political science under Wagner from 1877 to 1879. When he returned to the US in 1879, Hadley joined the faculty of Yale University, where he became a professor of political science (1886–1891), a professor of political economy (1891–1899), and first Dean of the Graduate School (1892–1895).[5] He was 'inaugurated as first lay President of Yale University in 1899,' and retained that position until 1921.[6] Over the course of his career, Hadley also became president of the AEA in 1898–1899, as well as a member to the American Philosophical Society. Furthermore, he also became editor of the Department of Foreign Railroads for *The Railroad Gazette* in 1887 and remained as such until 1899. He actually published a number of articles on railways and welfare states, with the most well known among them being 'Railway Transportation: Its History and its Laws' and 'Economics: An Account of the Relation between Private Property and Public Welfare.' Like his German professors, Hadley highly praised historical studies and ethical economics. However, he did not trust the power of the state, as was the case with his former professor Sumner.

Henry Rogers Seager (1870–1930) graduated from the University of Michigan in 1890. He then studied under H.B. Adams and Ely at Johns Hopkins University before going overseas to further his education in Halle, Berlin, and Vienna for a year. During his brief time in Europe, he was particularly impressed with Wagner's lessons about public finance and socialism and Schmoller's historical and statistical classes. Subsequently, he returned to the US and completed his PhD under Patten at the University of Pennsylvania in 1894. That same year, he started to teach political economy at the Wharton School of the University of Pennsylvania. In 1902, Seager left Pennsylvania after accepting a post in the political economy department at Columbia University, where he taught Labor Problems and 'Corporation and Trust Problems' (Dorfman 1966V4, 166). He was also president of the AEA in 1922–1923, in addition to becoming president of the American Association for Labor Legislation. Seager (1893, 236) was heavily influenced by the GHSE, as evidenced by his opinion that, since the publication of Roscher's *Grundriss* in 1843, 'Germany has been the scene of an almost uninterrupted struggle for supremacy between conflicting opinions concerning the most fundamental questions in political economy.'

Jeremiah Whipple Jenks (1856–1929) graduated from the University of Michigan in 1878 and then obtained his PhD from the University of Halle under Conrad in 1885. Jenks held professorships at both Cornell University and New York University. Like the GHSE, he supported historical ethical economics. Outside of the academic setting, he was appointed as an expert on Asia for the US Treasury during the presidency of Theodore Roosevelt. He also prepared many reports on currency, worker compensation, child labor, and immigration policies for the government. Jenks was also president of the AEA in 1906–1907.

Elisha Benjamin Andrews (1847–1917) studied under professors of the GHSE in Berlin and Munich between 1882 and 1883 (Barber 1993, 88). In fact, 'he immersed himself thoroughly in the doctrines' of the GHSE, and this was evident in his teaching and in the textbook he wrote entitled *Institute of Economics* (1889) (ibid.). In his lectures at Brown and Cornell, he focused on the views and methods of Roscher, Knies, Schaeffe, and Wagner (ibid.). He believed that the GHSE displayed great merit in refuting the laissez-faire doctrine and 'the old notions of human nature and social institutions as fixed creations' (ibid.). Andrews was also 'among the charter members' of the AEA (ibid.: 90). During his career, he strongly supported state regulations against monopoly power and the improvement of working conditions for the labor class.

Ernest Ludlow Bogart (1870–1958) obtained his PhD at the University of Halle and then went on to 'the University of Illinois from Princeton in the fall of 1909 as Associate Professor of Economics' at the recommendation of Kinley.[7] He also became president of the AEA in 1930-1931. His book, *The Economic History of the United States* (1907), was:

> adopted by Dr. Kinley prior to his joining the faculty at the university: it was the second text in American Economic History ever to be written, and would bring Dr. Bogart the immediate distinction of being one of the top Economic Historians in the country.[8]

Edward David Jones (1870–1944), who was accepted as the first professor of marketing in the US, was a student of Ely at the University of Wisconsin before going off to Germany to study under Engel, Knies, and Conrad in 1894–1895 (Bartels 1951). When he returned to the US, he gave lectures on political economy and statistics at the University of Wisconsin from 1895 to 1901. Afterwards, he accepted a post at the University of Michigan in 1901 at the invitation of Henry Carter Adams (Dickinson 1951, 535). While there, Jones started to teach the first-ever marketing classes in the US, which were mainly influenced by the views of theorists of the GHSE.

Thomas Nixon Carver (1865–1961) attended Johns Hopkins for two years and took economics courses under David Kinley and 'a course in Roman history under Dr. Herbert B. Adams' (Carver 1949, 95). During his first year at Johns Hopkins, he followed 'Ely in his espousal of the historical method' and did 'a lot of reading' on the subject (ibid.: 97). However, he did not complete his PhD at Johns Hopkins; instead, he did so at Cornell in 1894. Subsequently, Carver went to study in Berlin (ibid.: 137). While there, he was particularly impressed with seminars on taxation by Wagner and economic history by Schmoller, noting that their classes were very crowded (ibid.: 138). Carver started to work at Harvard in 1900 and remained there for 32 years. During this time, he served 'two periods as chairman of the Department of Economics (1901–1903 and another period of three years in the twenties)' (ibid.: 212). He also 'acted as editor of the Quarterly Journal of Economics from 1901–1904 and again from 1918–1922' and served 'as chairman of the Division of History, Government, and Economics for two terms, 1903–1906 and 1929–1932' (ibid.). Additionally, Carver was president of the AEA in 1916–1917 and worked as its secretary-treasurer for five years. Over the course of his career, Carver was recognized for making contributions to the development of marginal utility theory. In fact, he admitted being influenced by Clark's principle of marginal utility theory of value (ibid.: 97). He also contributed to agricultural and rural economics, monetary policy, the distribution of wealth, religion, taxation, social justice, the role of the state, etc. Furthermore, he supported statistical economics while pointing out that he used 'facts and figures only to bolster his argument' (Carlson 1968, 109).

There were also a number of American political economists who studied under the theorists of the GHSE, but then followed a different direction after they returned home to the US. An example was Frank Albert Fetter (1863–1949), a leading economist in the first decade of the 20th century who obtained his PhD from the University of Halle in 1894. After he returned to the US, he worked at the universities of Cornell, Stanford, and Princeton. During his time at Princeton, he was chairman of the Interdisciplinary Department that included courses on history, politics, and economics. He was also president of the AEA in 1912–1913. Despite having studied in Germany, Fetter's views were more closely aligned with those held by economists of the Austrian School.

Vladimir G. Simkhovitch (1874–1959) studied at Halle, where he attended the lectures of Wagner. During that time, 'the students of economics had a club of their own, and in this "Staatswissenschaftlicher Verein"' was organized by Simkhovitch (1938, 52). Subsequently, he moved to the US in 1898 after obtaining his PhD. Then, in 1904, he started to teach economic history at Columbia University. Simkhovitch was highly influenced by Wagner's socialist ideas and became known as a socialist economist.

Bernard Moses (1846–1931) obtained his BA from the University of Michigan in 1870, and then studied in Berlin, Leipzig, and Heidelberg. He completed his PhD at Heidelberg in 1873, thereby becoming 'the first American economist to obtain a Ph.D. in Germany' (Cookingham 1993, 274). Then, from 1876 to 1890, he taught two courses in political economy at the University of California, Berkeley. In 1880, he founded the *Berkeley Quarterly: A Journal of Social Science*, which only survived for two years (ibid.: 275). Moses was a supporter of historical ethical economics. However, he believed that the historical approach was 'necessary but not sufficient in understanding problems of political economy' (ibid.: 274). Contrary to many other political economists trained under the theorists of the GHSE, Moses was not involved in the foundation or activities of the AEA.

There were also a number of American political economists that studied under the theorists of the GHSE, whose contributions to the development of the discipline of economics are not particularly well known. For example, John Christopher Schwab (1865–1916) went to Germany to study under the theorists of the GHSE at the universities of Berlin (1887–1888) and Göttingen, obtaining his PhD from the latter in 1889. After returning to the US, he became a professor of political economy at Yale, where he began editing *The Yale Review* in 1892.[9] In 1901, he published *The Finances of the Confederate States of America (1861–1865)*, which was accepted as 'a valuable addition in the field of economic history.'[10] Meanwhile, Abram Piatt Andrew (1873–1936) obtained his master's degree and doctorate from Harvard before setting off to Europe to study at universities in Halle, Berlin, and Paris. After returning to the US, he played an important role in reforming the American banking system. Subsequently, he went back to Europe and studied at the central banks of Germany, Britain, and France. Additionally, Roland Post Falkner

(1866–1940) graduated from the Wharton School of Finance and Economy at the University of Pennsylvania before studying political economy in Berlin, Leipzig, and Halle. When he returned home, he taught accounting and statistics at the University of Pennsylvania, and eventually played a major role in the development of statistics in the US. John Henry Gray (1859–1946) was another American economist who obtained his PhD in Germany, doing so under Conrad at the University of Halle. Afterwards, he worked was a professor of economics at Northwestern University, Carleton College, and the University of Minnesota. He also became president of the AEA in 1914–1915. Then there was Carl Copping Plehn (1867–1945), who completed his undergrad at Brown and then obtained his PhD from the University of Göttingen in 1891. He embraced the historical inductive approach and ethical economics (Cookingham 1993, 274). Subsequently, he worked as a professor of public finance at the University of California from 1893 to 1937, during which time he taught a variety of subjects, including European history, the history of economics, finance, and taxation. It should be noted that the University of California established its Economics Department in 1902. Plehn was also president of the AEA in 1923–1924. It has been claimed that 'for more than thirty years he exerted a significant influence on tax practice in California.'[11] Plehn also played a major role in 'shaping the system of contributory retiring allowance which protects members of the faculty at the present time.'[12] As it turned out, 'he was one of the last of that generation of scholars in economics to include study at German universities as a significant part of their education.'[13] Furthermore, Winthrop More Daniels (1867–1944) graduated from Princeton in 1888, and then studied at Leipzig University from 1899 to 1890. When he returned to the US, he worked as an instructor of Economics and Social Science at Wesleyan University from 1891 to 1892 before becoming a professor of Political Economy at Princeton, where he remained until 1911. Finally, Carleton Hubbell Parker (1878–1918) was a German-trained political economist at Berkeley, who previously obtained his PhD at Heidelberg in 1912. While in Germany, he developed an interest in the relationship between labor and employers. Consequently, he was 'involved as a mediator' in many labor disputes in the US (Cookingham 1993, 279). Unfortunately, he died very young and his work has been largely forgotten.

A number of American economists who were trained at universities in the US were also familiar with the legacy of the GHSE, because they were exposed to its principles and ideas through professors that studied in Germany. In particular, many of Ely's students at Johns Hopkins and the University of Wisconsin played a major role in the successful development and improvement of the discipline of economics based on the ideas, goals, methods, and approaches of the GHSE. Some of the notable individuals who were influenced by Ely at Johns Hopkins University included Albert Shaw, Edward Webster Bemis, Edward Alsworth Ross, Amos G. Warner, C. H. Haskins, William A. Scott, David Kinley, T. K. Worthington, Charles H. Levermore, and Charles F. A. Carrier, just to name a few. The extent to which Ely instilled some of the fundamental ideas of the GHSE into his former students eventually became evident in their teaching styles and publications (Adelstein 1993, 313, Ely 1938, 159). Another noteworthy student of Ely at Johns Hopkins University was Albion Small (1854–1926), who completed his PhD in 1889. He previously studied political economy and history in the universities of Leipzig and Berlin from 1879 to 1881 (Balabkins 1988, 102). While Small did not make a mark in the field of economics after completing his studies, he did play a fundamental role in the development of sociology in the US. In 1892, he was invited to 'set up a new department of social science at the University of Chicago' (ibid.). In fact, it was 'the first department of its kind in the US' (ibid.). Later, he founded the *American Journal of Sociology*, which he edited and frequently contributed to over the period spanning 1895–1926.

Henry Brayton Gardner (1863–1939) was a former student of Ely at Johns Hopkins, where he obtained his PhD in 1890. He was highly influenced by the views of 'Walker, Ely, Taussig, Jevons and Marshall' (Barber 1993, 91). After graduating, Gardner taught at Brown University from 1890 to 1928, and served as president of the AEA in 1919–1920. Additionally, David Kinley (1861–1944), who was known as one of the key contributors to American institutionalist economics, served as president of the AEA in 1913–1914. In fact, Kinley was significantly influenced by Ely's lectures and views at both Johns Hopkins University and the University of Wisconsin. Initially, he was a graduate student of Ely at Johns Hopkins University. Ely made 'it possible for Kinley to study for two years at this institution, and he carried Kinley with him for another year of study when he transferred to Wisconsin,' where he obtained his PhD in 1893 (Haig 1949, 8). While at Wisconsin, Kinley became 'both a fellow in economics and an extension lecturer' (ibid.). Looking back, Kinley (1949, 24) stated that Ely not only invited him to accompany him to the university of Wisconsin, he also did everything possible to make his 'way easy and successful.' He further stated that 'no teacher could have done more' for him than Ely (ibid.). Subsequently, he went to Germany in 1900–1901 and visited 'Berlin Munich, Halle, Leipzig, and Göttingen' (Kinley 1949, 44). Although Kinley (1949, 42) had 'the pleasure of hearing Dr. Adolph Wagner lecture' in Berlin, it is important to point out that he did not study or obtain a degree at any German university, as the objective of his visit was to collect information about the 'educational aims and methods' of German political economy departments.

When Ely was accused of teaching socialism and promoting socialist ideals in a letter prepared by 'the State Superintendent of Education in Wisconsin,' which was published in the New York edition of the *Nation* in 1894, Kinley defended him (ibid.: 30). He pointed out that the attack on Ely was weak and based on 'prejudices rather than on accurate information' (ibid.: 30). In fact, he was certain that this attack was 'untrue' from the outset, because he heard 'most of Ely's lectures' at Johns Hopkins and the University of Wisconsin (ibid.). Kinley viewed his defense as 'discharging a debt of gratitude and affection, and defending' their profession; at 'Ely's request,' he employed the 'Hon. Burr Jones, one of Madison's ablest lawyers' (ibid.: 31). In the end, 'the trial broke down, and not only was Dr. Ely fully exonerated but the regents adopted a resolution in favor of freedom of discussion in teaching' (ibid.).

John Rogers Commons (1862–1945) was one of Ely's most important former students from Johns Hopkins University who completely embraced the approaches, ideas, and methods of the GHSE. Commons would go on to be known as an American institutional economist and serve as president of the AEA in 1917–1918. He admitted to choosing 'Johns Hopkins University largely because of his admiration' for Ely (Lafayette 1962, 17). In fact, Commons (1963, 40) confessed that he initially decided to study at Johns Hopkins University after reading 'an editorial attack on Professor Ely, in *The Nation*, for his so-called socialism,' which was written by Newcomb. He believed that 'Newcomb's charges against Ely's labor sympathies' were baseless (Lafayette 1962, 18). In 1904, Commons joined Ely at the University of Wisconsin. He considered working with Ely at the University of Wisconsin to be his 'new birth' and acknowledged that many of his own ideas and writings were inspired by Ely's 'new economics' (Commons 1963, 44, 97). Ely's intellectual influence contributed to Commons having a high appreciation for the work of the theorists of the GHSE. Actually, 'he naturally explored their works before formulating any theory of his own' (Lafayette 1962, 177). Even though Commons (1963) did not study in Germany, he was fluent in German, which enabled him to extensively read the works of German economists.

Among all of Ely's former students, Commons may have played the most significant role in conveying the methods and ideas of the GHSE to his own students (Yefimov 2009, 38). Much like the theorists of the GHSE, he provided many arguments against classical liberalism in his writings and teaching while also underlining the importance of historical ethical economics. During his time at Wisconsin, Commons ended up supervising or co-supervising the 'completion forty-six PhD' degrees (ibid.: 40). Some of his former students went on to become professors in the economics department of the University of Wisconsin. Among them, Sumner H. Slichter and Selig Perlman played major roles in the development of Wisconsin Institutionalism along with Commons (ibid.: 39).

Davis Rich Dewey (1858–1942), brother of philosopher John Dewey (1859–1952), studied at Johns Hopkins University under Ely and Henry Baxter Adams and obtained his PhD in 1886 (Adelstein 1993, 311). He was highly influenced by the GHSE, and remained so right up until his death (ibid.: 312). In 1887, he was appointed as an instructor of history and political science at Massachusetts Institute of Technology (MIT). Then, Dewey was named head of the department of economics and statistics at MIT in 1907, and worked in that capacity until 1933. Dewey was also secretary of the ASA from 1886 to 1906 and the editor of the *American Economic Review* from its founding in 1911 until 1940. In fact, he was present at the preparation of 'the original statement of principles of the AEA,' along with Ely and its other founding fathers, and remained strongly attached to the organization for the rest of his life (ibid.). He also served as president of the AEA in 1909–1910.

Allyn Abbott Young (1876–1929) completed his PhD at the University of Wisconsin under Ely in 1902. During that time, he was also influenced by William A. Scott and Charles H. Haskins, who were previously students of Ely at Johns Hopkins University. After completing his studies, Young worked as a professor at the economics departments of the universities of Wisconsin, Harvard, Cornell, and Washington. Additionally, he was head of the economics department at Stanford University between 1906 and 1910 (Carlson 1968, 106). It should be noted that 'Young was the most highly respected economics professor at Harvard. Under him a considerable number of the outstanding students wished to write their doctors' theses. His reputation as a scholar and as a teacher was well deserved' (ibid.). Some of Young's former students who later rose to prominence included Bertil Ohlin, Frank H. Knight, Nicholas Kaldor, and Lauchlin Currie. Later in his life, Young became president of the ASA in 1917 and the AEA in 1925–1926. Furthermore, in 1919, he went to the Versailles Peace Conference with President Wilson as 'chief of the Division of Economics and Statistics of the American Commission to Negotiate Peace' (Dorfman 1966V4, 222).

In 1893, Charles Jesse Bullock (1869–1941) went to the University of Wisconsin to obtain his PhD under Ely. After graduating, he taught at Cornell, before joining Harvard in 1903. During his time at the latter, Bullock became 'chairman of the Harvard University Committee of Economic Research' (Carlson 1968, 108). He mainly published about public finance and was recognized as an authority on the subject.

Henry Ludwell Moore (1869–1958) obtained his PhD from Johns Hopkins University in 1896. During his graduate studies, he was significantly influenced by Clark, having taken his classes on the economic theory of distribution (Stigler 1968). He also attended classes taught by Henry Baxter Adams covering German history, Prussian history, and railway problems. Later, he went on to study under Carl Menger in Vienna. After completing his studies, he worked as a professor of political economy at Johns Hopkins University and Columbia University. Moore was considered an early pioneer of econometrics, as he influenced Henry Schultz (1893–1938) who was credited with introducing the subject to the University of Chicago.

Francis Amasa Walker (1840–1897) was drawn to German-trained American academics on account of disagreements he had with adherents of classical orthodoxy. Although he did not study under the theorists of the GHSE, Walker held many of the views espoused by their American disciples, as he defended ethical economics, methodological collectivism, and the historical approach, while also valuing social justice and advocating for the rights of the working class, which included calling for limits on working hours, improvements in working conditions, and higher earnings. Over the course of his career, Walker was a professor of political economy at Yale University, a statistician, and a journalist, while also attaining 'the rank of brigadier general during the Civil War' (Barber 1993, 143). In fact, he served as Chief of the Bureau of Statistics from 1869 to 1870. Subsequently, Walker, who was 'the first statistician' from the US, was invited 'in 1872 to join the faculty of the Sheffield Scientific School of Yale College with the title of "Professor of Political Economy"' (Barber 1993, 143, Dorfman 1966V3, 102). He was also credited with teaching one of America's first courses in statistics at the Yale Graduate School (Adelstein 1993, 301). While working at Yale, Walker wrote a letter to Ely in which he claimed that he was 'treated at times even contemptuously by the Old Guard and felt keenly the injustices that had been done him' (Ely 1936, 147). He specifically identified Sumner as being hostile to him during that time. Eventually, the hostility he encountered at Yale College motivated him to leave the school.

In 1877, Walker taught a series of lectures on monetary policies at Johns Hopkins University, which led him to develop close relationships with American disciples of the GHSE (Adelstein 1993, 304). Then, in 1881, he played a major role in the establishment of a political economy department at MIT (ibid.: 305). That same year, Walker became president of MIT, a post that he retained until his death. In 1882, he became president of the ASA, before being elected as the first president of the AEA in 1885. Members of the AEA accepted Walker as 'a leader,' who was 'far more than any other man, prepared the way for the development of future thought in economics in the United States' (Ely 1910, 88). This is likely why he ended up serving as its president for the first seven years of its existence. Also of note, in 1891, he was elected 'Vice-President of the National Academy of Sciences; in 1893, he was President-adjunct of the International Statistical Institute at its session in Chicago' (Dunbar 1897, 436). It was widely believed that 'General Walker's contributions to economic theory' would have 'lasting value' (ibid.: 445). There is no doubt that he was able to change the scene of the discipline of economics by breaking 'the crust of the old economics' (Dunbar 1897, 444, Ely 1936, 147).

During the early development of the discipline of economics in the US, leading theorists such as Henry Carter Adams, Clark, James, Patten, Ely, Seligman, Seager, Mayo-Smith, and Walker represented the most striking characteristics of American economics. Although American economists were no longer particularly interested in studying in Germany in the early decades of 20th century, they continued to be influenced by the American scholars that were trained in Germany in prior decades. For instance, institutionalist Thorstein Bunde Veblen (1857–1929) was influenced by Ely, Henry Baxter Adams, Clark, and Dewey (Adelstein 1993, 311). Similar to adherents of the GHSE, Veblen was opposed to the simplistic view of economic men advocated by classical economics, believing instead that the individual was formed historically through social interactions with others, habits, culture, and institutional restrictions on behavior. Wesley Clair Mitchell (1874–1948), another institutionalist who was one of the founders of the National Bureau of Economic Research in 1920 and president of the AEA in 1924–1925, was also exposed to the views, ideas, goals, and methods of the GHSE, largely through the influences of Veblen and Dewey. In addition to Veblen and Mitchell, other well-known institutional economists included Schumpeter, Wassily Leontief, Gottfried Haberler, Sumner H. Slichter, Alvin H. Hansen, John M. Clark, Rexford G. Tugwell, Gardiner C. Means, and Clarence E. Ayres. All of them were influenced at some level, directly or indirectly, by works, ideas, and methods of the GHSE. While it is extremely difficult to uncover all the details about the extent to which the GHSE affected economists who never studied in the classes of its theorists, it is evident that the GHSE had a major influence on the intellectual formation of many American economists.

American Economists on the Methods, Values, and Policies of the GHSE

Many young American economists attributed the economic problems of the 19th century to the arbitrary and unrealistic assumptions of classical orthodoxy that dominated national policies and the curriculums of colleges and universities (Walker 1891). To modernize political economy, they abandoned classical orthodoxy in favor of the GHSE, which was a 'vigorous political economy' that was 'grappling with the problems' of their time (Ely 1883A, 233). These American economists that followed 'the German, statistical, or historical school' became known as disciples of the New School (Newcomb 1884, 300). However, not all German-trained American political economists became adherents of the New School.

Adherents of the New School also called themselves 'the Historical school, taking the name used' by their 'German teachers' (Ely 1936, 145). Moreover, members of the New School were also labeled 'the young rebels' (ibid.: 147). Ely was considered to be the leader of the New School, while some of its main disciples were Seligman, Mayo-Smith, Henry Carter Adams, James, Clark, and Patten (Coats 1985, 1703, Ely 1936, 145). According to the New School, the older generation of economists, known as the Old School, prevented real progress, because they adhered to the outdated principles and assumptions of classical orthodoxy.

Hadley, Sumner, and Newcomb were the main adherents of the Old School, which was influenced by classical economics in an extreme form (Ely 1936, 143). In particular, they strongly advocated for the free trade and laissez-faire approach that were promoted by classical economics. Naturally, they were disturbed by the thoughts and ideas being put forth by the New School, especially its defense of positive state action as a necessary condition of social and economic progress. In response, they accused adherents of the New School of being 'unscientific pamphleteers and strident propagandists for social reform, rather than scholars' (Barber 1993, IX). In fact, they even went so far as to regard the New School as 'a menace to the welfare of the country' (Ely 1936, 143). However, while the discipline of political economy was flourishing, thanks to the influence of the GHSE, 'the few older adherents of the orthodox school' continued to 'pursue their way peacefully, seemingly unconscious of the attacks made upon them, but gradually losing touch with the mass of educated men' (Seligman 1889, 544). Seligman (1889, 544) suggested that young economists who supported the Old School were in 'reality suffering a delusion' (ibid.). Meanwhile, Ely (1936, 145) argued that they 'entirely misunderstood' the new economists who supported 'historical, statistical, and inductive research.'

Members of the New School supported ideas, policies, and methods that were similar to those advocated by the GHSE. In doing so, they wanted to find solutions to 'the rapidly changing American situation' based on everything that they had learned in Germany (Coats 1985, 1703). Meanwhile, they were very critical of the principles and methods of classical economics and sought 'to overthrow the entrenched "Clerical Ricardian" orthodoxy' of the Old School, 'which had hitherto dominated college textbooks' (ibid.). Seligman (1886A, 19) argued that the GHSE had freed itself 'from the yoke of a method which had now become sterile, the new school, devoid of all prepossessions, devoted itself to the task of grappling with the problems which the age had brought with it.' He also accused the Old School of being blind to the relationship between economic theory and changing social and material conditions (Seligman 1886B). As for other prominent members of the New School, James (1886, 24) criticized devotees of the classical orthodoxy for strictly adhering to their fundamental principles 'as if they were law and gospel,' while Mayo-Smith (1886, 105) claimed that classical economists clung to outdated 'old ideas' and 'old formulae.' Furthermore, Patten (2003, 60) believed that the mistake of classical economists could be found in 'their low ideal.' That is to say, they think that 'we have almost reached the limit of our progress, and hence our economy should conform to a static ideal' (ibid.). To the contrary, Patten argued that economic progress is dynamic.

Adherents of the New School rejected 'not merely a few incidental conclusions of the English school, but its method and assumptions, or major premises—that is to say, its very foundation' (Ely 1883, 234). They argued that 'the system of Political Economy' that was 'imported from England' and taught at American colleges did not have 'universal assent to which its scientific character and the eminence and influence of its expounders would seem to entitle it' (Newcomb 1884, 291). Consequently, many adherents of the New School believed that German methods, values, policies, and ideas were 'greatly to be admired' and advocated for them to be 'appropriated' (Adams 1879, 294). Even though some American economists recognized that 'the principles upon which' German economics and finance were based might be 'inappropriate to the political and industrial conditions' of the US, many of them still embraced its fundamental principles, methods, and ideas (ibid.). The following section discusses historical studies, the inductive method, positive state action, ethics, and methodological collectivism, all of which were features of the GHSE and became necessary characteristics of the New School.

Historical Studies

Under the leadership of the New School, political economy ceased to be a branch of the natural sciences (Herbst 1965, 135). This is because its adherents believed that political economy should be concerned with men and their relationships with each other. For example, much like theorists of the GHSE, Mayo-Smith (1886, 119) was of the view that it was not possible to 'cultivate political economy without at the same time cultivating the other branches of social science, especially political science and jurisprudence.' That means political economists should study 'the facts of economic life as they actually exist, blended with the political, legal, and social life' (Mayo-Smith 1886, 120). Similarly, Seligman was of the opinion that jurisprudence, history, politics, ethics, and economics were all closely related. According to him, 'legal development is inexplicable apart from economic forces' and 'economic phenomena take place within a legal framework' (Seligman 1910, 32). Additionally, Gay confessed that writing his dissertation under the supervision of Schmoller taught him that 'economics could be brought into close interrelation with psychology, ethics, history, and political science to produce a real science of society' (Balabkins 1988, 100). Furthermore, Seager, Patten, James, and Ely also had high praise for the theorists of the GHSE, because of the emphasis they placed on the study of related sciences, including history, jurisprudence, ethics, politics, law, and philosophy. Clearly, members of the New School were of the belief that political economy should not be 'theoretical, deductive, or mathematical, but must of necessity be descriptive and historical' science that is entangled with other branches of social sciences (Herbst 1965, 135). Its adherents also thought that historical studies could play a major role in understanding the diverse social and economic theories and policies of other nations across history (Patten 1891, 102). This is because historical studies demonstrated that 'the production and distribution of wealth are influenced by many forces which are not economic in the usual acceptance of the term,' such as philosophy, politics, ethical values, law, customs, and cultural practices (Farnam 1913, 123). This view was opposed to the idea 'that there is but one system of political economy, the doctrines of which hold true for every civilization' (Patten 2003, 7). Like the GHSE, adherents of the New School explained that each society is different across history and that the particularity of each society engenders new situations and problems, which require distinct solutions. That is to say, since the economic and societal organization of each historical stage was different, there could not possibly be an absolutely valid system that should be universally adhered to by all nations across history. Thus, in order to properly understand a problem and find an appropriate solution, it is necessary to observe, compare, and analyze past events and facts.

In his defense of historical studies, Seligman (1910, 25) argued that political economy deals with 'man' who is 'a product of history; economic institutions, like all other social facts, have their roots in the past.' He highly valued historical studies, because he believed that lessons learned from the past could guide people in both the present and the future. He further claimed that historical studies could help people identify the conditions that could facilitate progress or lead to retrogression (Seligman 1910). Meanwhile, Taussig (1888) was of the view that historical studies could help provide an understanding of the errors that people and nations committed in their social and economic lives, and determine how those errors could be avoided in the future. He explained that when one analyzes a prolonged historical stretch of customs, values, cultural practices, law, and restrictions among people in a certain period, including primitive man, the ancient world, the Middle Ages, the Renaissance, and the emergence of the mercantile system, it becomes obvious that there was never a 'universal applicability of economic laws' (Taussig 1905, 501). All of these historical periods were fundamentally different in terms of their goals, problems, and priorities. Seligman (1886B) pointed out that these fundamental differences meant economic theories are not absolute, but relative. Since economic theories are developed based on the historical study of the particular social, political, and economic conditions of different societal organizations, they are not universally applicable anywhere or at any time.

Patten explained that historical studies could demonstrate that each nation experiences a different economic situation based on its particular environment, geographical position, and historical development. Each nation also undergoes its own particular period of transition, where its customs, laws, habits, and beliefs are modified or disappear. Furthermore, Patten (1885, 74) believed that historical studies could teach us how people's desires and characters change with time and space. He noted that people's 'tastes and inclinations change with alterations' in their 'ideas or surroundings, and what is natural in one group of circumstances is most unnatural in another' (ibid.: 76). Even if the change were to occur within the lifetime of an individual, something that was previously liked or enjoyed by that person could easily become something that is disliked or unnatural. The study of historical changes in institutions, moral spirit, and the desires and tastes of people could help political economists discover laws of economics and formulate better economic policies and reforms that might be beneficial for one nation, though they might not be suitable for others.

Contrary to the GHSE, which accepted economic policies and laws as relative and ephemeral, classical economics regarded them as 'absolute' and universal, in that they could 'conform to the conditions of every nation in all stages of its progress' (Patten 2003, 12). However, the rise of the New School displaced this conception of political economy, as its adherents no 'longer seek after a universal economy which will be good under all industrial conditions, but for one that is fitted to the people of a particular nation in a particular stage of its development' (ibid.). For them, a policy that was 'good for one nation at a particular time is no longer regarded as sufficient evidence that it will be good for other nations, or for other times' (ibid.). Patten (2003, 12) stressed that 'the causes of national prosperity must be studied under the peculiar conditions of each nation, and the separate problems which its economy brings forward must be solved by a study of its own economic conditions.' Farnam (1913, 77) also highlighted the importance of historical studies, as he recognized that 'each great period of the world's history' had an 'economic ideal,' which became 'part of the mores of the time and country.' Furthermore, Seligman (1886A, 2) pointed out that 'each period of economic life must be treated by itself, both in regard to the truth or falsity of the doctrine itself, and in regard to the applicability of the particular theory in question.' Similarly, Dunbar (1904, 40) believed that 'the economic theories of any generation must be regarded primarily as the outgrowth of the peculiar conditions of time, place, and nationality' and that 'no particular set of tenets can arrogate to itself the claim of immutable truth.' He emphasized the importance of historical studies in political economy when he stated that 'the development of the industrial life of nations and of their economic institutions, and the causes which, in all that relates to material life, make one nation a different historical product from another' (ibid.: 44).

Mayo-Smith (1886, 114) was convinced that the goal of political economy should be to systematize the knowledge of the past, which was obtained through historical and comparative study, 'as rapidly as possible, so as to reach general principles of economic life.' According to him, 'the chief merit of the new school' was its historical study of the 'degree of civilization, custom, law, etc.' of different nations, which 'the older economists neglected' (ibid.: 113). Mayo-Smith (1888, 244) explained that historical study reveals 'the formation and modification of social institutions,' as well as the motivations behind people's choices of action in different civilizations. It also 'discloses relations of cause and effect' and provides 'indications of the direction of human development' (ibid.).

The Inductive Approach versus the Deductive Approach

In the US, members of the Old School accepted the deductive approach as the starting point of political economy in order to make it into a branch of the natural sciences. Based on the deductive approach, truths are deduced 'from certain premises by a logical process' (Dunbar 1904, 34). However, these truths are 'limited by their own complete logical statement to cases where the conditions originally premised are present, and not controlled by any others' (ibid.). In other words, truths are attained only under specified conditions. Therefore, the truths derived from the deductive approach are far from universal, because they require a specific set of conditions to exist. Accordingly, these truths should not be treated as though they are universally applicable to any time or in any place, because they were created based on the particular development of the society being studied (Adams 1886, 4).

Supporters of the deductive method defended a singular approach to political economy. Even though the outright rejection of the inductive approach inhibited scientific inquiry and constrained 'the progress of political economy,' they continued to use the deductive approach exclusively (Dunbar 1886, 18). The most successful opposition to the deductive approach occurred in Germany, as the GHSE adhered to the inductive method. Meanwhile, in the US, the inductive method gained support due to the fact that 'political economy, as pursued by the deductive method,' had 'seriously disappointed the hopes which formerly centred around it' (ibid.: 9). This disappointment was not only attributed to 'the extravagance of the hopes, but also by reason of its own sterility in results' (ibid.). In fact, 'the inadequate basis' upon which classical economics rested in the US, with its support of the abstract deductive method, was partly 'responsible for the growth of the German Historical School' and its backing of the inductive approach (Clark 1886, 35, 203).

Ely (1883, 233) highlighted that the abstract deductive approach and the 'à priori doctrines or assumptions' of classical economics were 'cast aside' by the disciples of the GHSE. Contrary to the supporters of the deductive approach, the GHSE did not 'expect to discover general economic laws by the historical method'; moreover, they denied that 'such laws existed' (Farnam 1913, 28). Similarly, adherents of the New School argued that since the abstract deductive method was based on only a few hypotheses with respect to human nature, any economic laws derived from it were too narrow to be considered universal. Accordingly, they were opposed to the premise of formulating universal abstract laws of development that all nations across history and time should adhere to. They also questioned the classical economics assumption that 'all economic phenomena' were subject to 'a few formal laws' (Newcomb 1884, 293). Ultimately, members of the New School argued that classical economists failed to take account of how 'these laws' were 'modified or even reversed in practice' (ibid.). In response, they abandoned 'the dry bones of orthodox English political economy for the live methods of the German school' (Ely 1883, 235). Moreover, they believed that the inductive approach would not lead political economists toward extremes like classical orthodoxy and socialism did.

Much like theorists of the GHSE, members of the New School maintained that the inductive method allowed for the study of 'the present in the light of the past' (Ely 1882, 519). That is to say, they adopted 'experience as a guide, and judged of what was to come by what had been' (Ely 1883, 233). Based on the inductive approach, they observed 'external phenomena' and gathered statistical and historical data in order to study social, economic, and financial questions (ibid.). They collected facts and data about the phenomena of society:

> not merely as means of increasing the sum of human knowledge, but as means of grasping a certain series of laws and principles by which, if properly applied, the phenomena of society may be modified and guided, and the future condition of society improved.
>
> (Patten 1891, 103)

They were of the opinion that the inductive method was the best way to understand the reasons behind men's actions in a society with continuously changing social and economic conditions.

Similar to the theorists of the GHSE, Mayo-Smith considered the inductive method to be 'comparative,' in that it compares 'economic institutions performing the same function among different nations of the same degree of civilization, in order to discover which is the best' (Mayo-Smith 1886, 107). It is also 'statistical,' as it collects data to form the basis of its knowledge about 'man and nature' and 'it uses this knowledge for the purpose of guiding and helping its investigations' (ibid.). Mayo-Smith (1886, 107) also explained that the inductive approach 'carefully observes the limits of time and place, and abstains from asserting its principles to be either universal or perpetual.' Accordingly, many of the adherents of the New School believed that the triumph of the inductive method would be fruitful for political economy, as it could allow political economists to 'escape the sterility' of the abstract deductive method (ibid.: 114).

Adherents of the New School did not really state 'explicitly how far they would go in flinging away deduced principles' (Taussig 1888, 232). However, many of them were not completely opposed to the use of the deductive approach. Some of 'the leading writers of the new school' accepted the use of the deductive method 'in some way and to some extent,' while also acknowledging that it was not separable from the inductive approach (Dunbar 1904, 41–42). For example, even though Patten was concerned that 'various leaders in the formation' of the AEA supported the deductive approach, whereas historical studies and the inductive approach were 'very little cultivated' among them, he did not support the complete elimination of the deductive approach from political economy (Ely 1910, 66). More precisely, he believed that while they had 'the right idea' in their decision to focus on 'concrete facts' instead of abstract doctrines, both the deductive and inductive methods were indispensable to political economy (Patten 1891, 101). In fact, Patten (1891, 100) stated that 'science has the greatest educational value that uses both deductive and inductive reasoning and properly combines them.' Similarly, Ely supported the use of both methods as long as they could solve problems that economists were concerned about. For him, the deductive approach could be useful as long as the premises were carefully developed. Taussig (1888, 232) shared parallel views, as he claimed that no 'real and serious disagreement exists between the deductive economists and the advocates of exclusively historical and practical treatment.' Additionally, Farnam (1913, 12) did not support the complete exclusion of the deductive approach from political economy, as was advocated by some of the theorists of the GHSE.

According to Seligman (1910, 27, 28), it would be a mistake to assert any predominance between inductive and deductive methods, as 'neither can be successfully divorced from the other.' He argued that supporters of the deductive approach often made their generalizations quickly, and 'through their failure to make allowance for the numberless counteracting tendencies, often gave an appearance of unreality to their conclusions' (ibid.: 28). He also pointed out that supporters of the inductive approach sometimes 'exaggerated the difficulty of reaching general laws at all, and have left us to wander aimlessly in the forest of facts, putting off to an ever-distant day their analysis and utilization' (Seligman 1889, 1910, 28). In fact, Seligman (1910, 28) claimed that it was those political economists who used both the inductive and deductive approaches that accomplished 'a real advance.' He maintained that 'the more tolerant and wiser economists' in 'all countries recognize that both the historical and the comparative method on the one hand, and the deductive method on the other' were 'not mutually exclusive, but complementary; and that the use of each method in turn is of the utmost value in the elucidation of different problems' (Seligman 1912, 158). For example, he pointed out that when it came to problems related to 'land tenure, e.g., the historical and comparative method is indispensable; in discussing such a problem as the incidence of taxation the historical and comparative method is useless' (ibid.). Thus, he advised students of political economy to familiarize themselves with both methods and hoped that 'the political economy of future generations will be a combination of Schmoller and Ricardo' (Balabkins 1988, 68).

In discussing the deductive and inductive approaches, Hadley (1896, 23) explained that 'the old antithesis between deductive and historical schools' was 'giving place to a distinction between static and dynamic problems' (ibid.). In the case of a static problem, it is assumed that 'the character and institutions of a people remain fixed while the relations between the individual members change' (ibid.). Meanwhile, in a dynamic problem, political economists take 'account of the progressive changes in national character which result from the altered conditions of individuals' (ibid.). Hadley (1896, 23) believed that the world finally recognized 'the true position and importance of economic history' in his time. As such, he argued that it was pointless to separate economists 'into deductive and historical schools' (ibid.). In fact, he pointed out that all of the good economists of his time were employing 'both methods by turns,' guiding their choice according to 'the character of the problem' being investigated (ibid.).

Even though some adherents of the New School were convinced that the dogmatic defense of the deductive approach by classical economists obscured the progress of the discipline of economics, not all its members had a negative view of using both approaches. In other words, much like Schmoller and Wagner, many of the adherents of the New School defended the use of both approaches and argued that it was absurd to exclusively use one while completely discounting the other. They believed that had the supporters of classical orthodoxy understood this absurdity, a reconciliation between inductive and deductive methods would have been a simple matter. However, despite the efforts of the New School, neoliberal economists have worked tirelessly to make economics into a branch of the natural sciences for most of the 20th century. That is to say, they essentially imported the methods of the natural sciences into economics and focused on studying economics from the deductive side while disregarding the importance of the inductive approach for economic research.

The New School on the Laissez-Faire Approach

Before the GHSE, Americans were mainly influenced by 'the older political philosophy of laissez-faire and non-interference' (Taussig 1911, 434). In particular, *Wealth of Nations*, which had more 'influence in forming the character of the Nineteenth Century than any other one book published,' garnered significant support for the laissez-faire doctrine in the US (Adams 1884, 20). This book served as the intellectual foundation for 'the establishment of a system of industrial freedom' (ibid.). Defenders of laissez-faire were of the opinion that 'any interference on the part of the state with economic activity would be injurious to economic life' (Adams 1879, 290). They not only opposed state interference, but also associated it with misgoverning and socialism. They also believed that the laissez-faire policy was 'the true policy' of government (ibid.). In fact, prior to the influence of the GHSE in the US, government officials often referenced the laissez-faire approach in their 'speeches, pamphlets and letters' (Adams 1884, 21).

Adherents of the New School believed that the doctrine of laissez-faire was 'a part of the old economic system,' which assumed that there was 'a body of economic doctrines good for every people in every age' (Patten 2003, 12). According to Ely (1883, 226, 1938, 139), '*Laissez faire, laissez passer*-let things alone, let them take care of themselves,' which 'was the oft-repeated maxim of *à priori* economists,' implied that 'laws of economic life were "natural laws" like those of physics and chemistry.' However, adherents of the New School believed that classical economists went too far when they claimed that the laissez-faire approach was a natural law. Taussig (1886, 35) argued that it was a 'great mistake to treat' the laissez-faire approach like a natural law, and it was an even 'greater mistake to treat it as a law of political economy.' In his own opposition to the laissez-faire approach, Clark (1886, 219) explained that nothing could 'be wilder or fiercer than an unrestricted struggle of millions of men for gain, and nothing more irrational than to present such a struggle as a scientific ideal.' He also argued that 'false economic teachings' based on classical economics 'blinded the people' in the US to the destructive outcomes of the laissez-faire system (Clark 1879, 163). He even went so far as to state that the 'most savage form of competition' was tolerated by law under the laissez-faire system of the US (ibid.: 165). For Clark, this type of competition resulted in many extreme forms of evils. Meanwhile, Patten (1888, 690) labeled the laissez-faire approach a primitive notion. He argued that supporters of laissez-faire viewed the state as a necessary evil in national life and sought to limit its actions, including the provision of public services and programs intended to facilitate social and economic development.

Taussig (1911, 321) attributed the unprecedented growth in the power of the American business classes, as well as 'the backwardness' of labor legislation and its administration in the US, to the dominance of the laissez-faire approach. More specifically, he explained that swift changes in the 'social and industrial conditions of the last generation or two, the influx of immigrants and the growth of manufactures' led to rapid expansions in labor problems and the power of business classes, which could not be adequately addressed via the laissez-faire approach (ibid.). Adams (1887) was also worried about the unprecedented growth in the power of the business classes under the laissez-faire system. In particular, he was concerned that the rise of corporate power menaced 'the stability of society, by controlling in their favor legislation' (Adams 1887, 532). According to Adams (1887, 502), the laissez-faire approach turned the government into a 'weak and inefficient' entity that became obedient to the orders of private interests. He argued that:

> a weak government placed in the midst of a society controlled by the commercial spirit will quickly become a corrupt government; this in its turn reacts upon commercial society by encouraging private corporations to adopt bold measures for gaining control of government machinery.
> (ibid.)

Adams predicted that, in another century, the kind of power that corporations were exercising under the laissez-faire system would be regarded as a violation of freedom and a threat to the raison d'être of the government. He believed that the goal of political economy should not be to intentionally make the government 'weaker, or more corrupt and more inefficient, by continuing to preach the illogical doctrine of laissez-faire' (ibid.: 475–476). In fact, he supported positive state action to mitigate the growing power of corporations. Ely agreed with him and made it clear that the power of private enterprises should never undermine state action. As for Seligman, he supported state intervention when 'the powers of state themselves are threatened...by corporate monopolies' (Dorfman 1955, 27).

According to James (1887, 54), whenever governments adopted a system of 'laissez- faire of letting everything take care of itself,' it ended 'disastrously in a thousand ways' (ibid.). Ely (1883, 226) also expressed concerns about the destructive social and economic consequences of the government abstaining from 'all interference in industrial life,' including various forms of inequality, injustice, unemployment, and misery. In fact, he went so far as to state that 'no doctrine... ever made a more complete fiasco than the maxim, Laissez faire, laissez passer, when the attempt was seriously made to apply it in the state' (ibid.: 230). He argued that the laissez-faire policy was unsound in morals and kept people in ignorance, pointing out that it resulted in the 'moral and physical degradation of large classes' at English factories, particularly the bankruptcy of the 'morality of women' and outcomes that were 'destructive of the health of children' (ibid.: 231). According to him, this immoral and exploitive degradation of the social and economic conditions of the people would 'shame any country calling itself civilized and Christian' (ibid.).

Ely (1883, 235) agreed with the GHSE view that classical economists used the *laissez-faire* approach 'as an excuse for doing nothing while people starve, nor allow the all-sufficiency of competition as a plea for grinding the poor.' He believed that the GHSE aimed to somehow 'return to the grand principle of common sense and Christian precept. Love, generosity, nobility of character, self- sacrifice, and all that is best and truest in our nature have their place in economic life' (ibid.). Accordingly, he maintained that the theorists of the GHSE were 'humanitarians and wanted to help bring about a better world in which to live,' which allowed them to see the evils of the laissez-faire approach (Ely 1936, 145). He further added that they were no longer allowing 'the science to be used as a tool' to implement social and economic policies in 'the hands of the greedy and the avaricious for keeping down and oppressing the laboring classes' (Ely 1883, 235).

Walker (1889B, 29) argued that the laissez-faire doctrine was 'imported into American thought, wrought a great deal of mischief.' However, he conceded that there could be some rare exceptions where the laissez-faire approach could be applied, provided that doing so clearly profited the public interest. In his opposition to the laissez-faire doctrine and his support of state regulation and intervention, Patten (1888, 690) warned that 'activity on the part of the state' should not be 'detrimental to the harmonious development of each individual' and their freedom. Meanwhile, James (1886, 43) argued that support for the laissez-faire approach prevented the state from 'undertaking certain great reforms.' He was of the view that it was 'perfectly possible' to allow the state to interfere 'in such a way as to promote and create industry' (ibid.). According to him, state interference would be permitted in instances where not doing so would 'stop' progress and allow 'retrogression set in' (ibid.).

Adherents of the New School believed that the laissez-faire approach advocated by the Old School should be replaced with 'carefully studied' state interference and regulations. In other words, rather than promoting the laissez-faire approach, which does not improve the common welfare, more emphasis needed to be placed on state regulations and interventions aimed at advancing the general well-being of the people. Taussig (1911, 435) pointed out that 'the success of regulation depends on the quality of the individuals' who regulate them. Accordingly, he believed that the people with regulating authority needed to have 'stable tenure of office and adequate salaries. They should be chosen not by popular election, but by executive appointment' (ibid.). Having said that, he noted that these requisites were often neglected in the US.

For adherents of the New School, being critical of the classical orthodoxy 'in an environment of laissez-faire, where businessmen controlled the boards of trustees of private universities, was not easy' (Balabkins 1988, 104). Nevertheless, they continued to oppose the laissez-faire doctrine and defend state regulations in order to achieve the common welfare. In the final decades of the 19th century, it was believed that the rise of the New School meant that the laissez-faire doctrine had lost 'its position, and will probably never be reinstated' (Mayo-Smith 1886, 105). Moreover, the defeat of the laissez-faire approach was accepted as the definitive 'triumph of the new over the old' school (ibid.). This was confirmed by Clark (1914, 5) in 1914, as he stated that 'extreme laissez-faire policy once dominant in literature and thought, now finds few persons bold enough to advocate it or foolish enough to believe in it.'

Positive State Action

During the last few decades of the 19th century, members of the New School were concerned about the growing power and wealth of corporations that often engaged in reckless and destructive business practices, as well as the rise of a large proletariat in the cities that endured deplorable working conditions and miserable lifestyles. In their quest to find solutions to the growing social and economic inequalities and misery of their time, they turned to the work of leaders of the GHSE in the area of the national economy. Similar to theorists of the GHSE, adherents of the New School were opposed to the classical economist view that the state was 'a purely negative factor in economic and social life' (James 1886, 25). To the contrary, both schools of thought supported positive state actions in many areas of life that were intended to secure common welfare (Patten 1916, 21). They were also in agreement that positive state actions should be designed to improve and develop various sectors of the national economy, including health care, education, social services, agriculture, forestry, transportation, commerce, manufacturing, and finance. Ultimately, both the GHSE and the New School supported state regulations that sought to achieve prosperity and progress (ibid.). Of note, James (1886, 25) argued that state interference was an 'absolutely essential condition of human progress.' That said, he emphasized that state regulations needed to be beneficial and positive for society as opposed to being repressive and negative. This is because positive state actions threatened the unjust and unfair practices of the business classes, which contributed to the achievement of common welfare.

According to Patten (2003, 41), obstacles that hindered economic progress needed to be removed in order to achieve development in society. As such, he supported an active state role in addressing such obstacles as rapidly as possible. Otherwise, if left unchecked, these obstacles would inhibit society from progressing, resulting in 'a gradual diminution in the average return for labor and a more unequal distribution of wealth' (ibid.). Patten (2003, 60) also clarified that 'whatever obstacles to economic progress the nation must overcome to reach a higher civilization can, with the aid of an education, be overcome with less protection, and the period of protection will also be shortened.'

Clark primarily focused on the role of the state in terms of eliminating the evils of competition so as to improve labor rights. He explained that whenever employers have a bargaining advantage, they will exploit workers by paying them low wages that are below the value of labor's marginal product.

He even suggested that much of the bargaining power held by employers 'resembles the robbing of defenseless persons' (Clark 1879, 164). As such, he called on the state to enact labor laws that reduced working hours, prohibited child labor, and provided 'indemnities for injuries' (Clark 1914, 19, 22). He also supported 'sanitary regulations' and the strengthening of 'pure-food laws' to improve the living conditions of the working class (ibid.: 19). Ely held similar views, as he stated that 'the inadequate action of competition in regulating and controlling great corporations gives another excuse for governmental interference' (Ely 1883, 232). Additionally, Walker highlighted that, under imperfect competition, the ability of the labor classes to react to 'the impulses of self-interest was seriously reduced' (Dorfman 1966V3, 105). However, while he supported perfect competition, he also believed that the state had to maintain the conditions of a competitive market. In other words, the government was supposed to have a corrective role in the marketplace. Walker (1890) also supported the formation of labor unions to offset the destructive outcomes of imperfect competition by establishing more of a balance in economic power. He also highlighted the importance of trade unions and 'strikes' in facilitating perfect competition and promoting the 'common interest' (Walker 1889A, 268). He argued that 'if the laboring class are active, alert and aggressive in the pursuit of their interests, the employing class will be continually sifted' (ibid.: 267). However, if 'the laborers are ignorant, stupid, inert, great numbers of incompetent men will get into the control of industry, and sustain themselves there, at the expense of the community, and of the laboring class in particular' (ibid.). In this case, not only will the working classes become poorer, but so will their 'master' (ibid.: 268).

Kinley (1949, 141) believed that state regulations aimed at ensuring fairness and justice became increasingly necessary as a society and its institutions progressed. In particular, he supported state legislation 'against monopolies, unfair advertising, predatory acts of groups, and other evils' (ibid.). He also argued that the achievement of fairness and justice would be in 'the best economic, social, and moral interest of all classes,' including employers (Kinley 1893, 12). According to Kinley (1893, 17), defending protective labour laws, standing for social and economic justice, and protecting the land and natural resources of a nation from 'industrial evils' are all intended to achieve common welfare. Meanwhile, Adams (1887) claimed that destructive outcomes emerge when competition is mostly confined to a handful of large corporations instead of many small-sized enterprises under a system of laissez faire. Additionally, Seligman maintained that the state had 'a duty to interfere where free competition ends disastrously' (Dorfman 1955, 27). He believed that the complexities of modern life meant that the state regulation of 'many business enterprises on behalf of producers, of consumers, of investors or of the general public' was a necessity (Seligman 1910, 169). Ultimately, the goal of state regulation was to ensure the conditions of 'liberty through the attainment of equality and responsibility' (ibid.). Seligman (1910, 169) maintained that state regulations aimed at securing the conditions of general freedom were justified in cases of: business laws that 'give the operatives a fair chance'; railway regulations that seek to 'secure equal treatment of shippers; supervision of banks, insurance companies and other corporations is designed to enforce financial responsibility.'

Seligman supported the state ownership of natural monopolies, including electricity, water, gas, and postal services. However, James (1887, 54) was concerned about 'artificial monopolies,' as he believed that they would 'continually grow worse unless it be made to grow better' by the state. He was particularly worried about monopoly power in strategic areas, such as railroads, telegraphs, express companies, telephone companies, oil companies, coal companies, gas, water, etc. Accordingly, he supported state interference, as well as state administration, in these important areas of the economy. Adams (1879, 293) also called for an active state role in the administration of 'railroads, telegraphs, post, and express; in the management of public domains and forest.' He explained that 'those enterprises that are undertaken by the State and carried on as private enterprises, with the single exception that they are carried on not for profit to the State, but in the interest of the people' (ibid.).

Ely also promoted the use of laws to limit the power of private corporations. He advocated for the abolishment of 'private monopoly and substitution therefore of public ownership and management of all those enterprises which are by nature monopolies like railways, gas and electricity, telegraph, telephone' (Ely 1938, 252). He pointed out that publicly owned and operated railways functioned very well in Germany. However, it should be noted that Ely's defense of the 'nationalisation of the railroads' and the public ownership of monopolies were influenced by his former teacher Wagner (Herbst 1965, 190). To the contrary, Hadley (1886) did not support state ownership for the purpose of mitigating the destructive outcomes associated with monopolies, despite describing how frightening monopoly power can be for the masses. In fact, he believed that state-owned monopolies often became abusive and destructive themselves. As a result, he argued that since large producers had a responsibility to the public, they should be subject to public regulations (Hadley 1888, 591). Clark (1914, 10) also argued that a 'monopoly of any sort is hostile to improvement, and in this chiefly lies the menace which it holds for mankind.' He was opposed to both private and public monopolies in any industry, stating that:

> if a public monopoly were to exist in every part of the industrial field, the per capita income would grow less, and that it would be only a question of time, and a short time at that, when the laborers would be worse off than they are now.
>
> (ibid.)

To protect the public, Clark supported the regulation and reformation of monopolies so as to offset their growing and damaging power. He also relied heavily on the moral improvement of people in order to mitigate the destructive practices of monopolies. Meanwhile, James (1887, 79) believed that if it was necessary to have monopoly power 'in order to secure the interests of the public, this monopoly should be within the control and management of the public.' He also argued that it was an imperative duty of the state to assume the management of strategic industries to achieve progress and common welfare.

James was opposed to a small state, because he believed that it would inevitably degenerate into misery, and halt the social and economic progress of society (James 1886, 31). In fact, he claimed that all economic progress was the outcome of an active role on the part of the state (ibid.: 26). According to James (1886, 33), a bigger state becomes necessary when the institutions and interactions in a society become 'more complicated.' More precisely, as a society advances and progresses, the 'government will be so improved that the state can safely undertake to a larger and larger extent the exercise of this collective action' (ibid.). At the same time, James (1887, 82) made it clear that the 'proper functions of government' are not 'absolute, but relative, and they change with an advancing civilization.'

Ely (1938, 136) was of the opinion that positive state action was an indispensable condition of human progress. In fact, he believed that state action was necessary in 'every time of distress' (Ely 1883, 231). He even went so far as to claim that all reforms and progress 'in the social and economic institutions of Great Britain' were 'accomplished only by the direct, active interference of government in economic affairs' (ibid.). According to Ely (1883, 231), even though such forms of state interference violate 'all the principles of *laissez faire* economists,' they 'are nevertheless applauded by the wisest and best men of all lands.'

Like the Germans, Ely supported the state provision of education, as he did not regard the state as a violator of academic freedom; rather, he considered it to be a promoter and guardian of academic freedom. He believed that if the state had 'the duty of seeing' the new generation educated, then this role should be supported in order to 'enable it to accomplish its duty effectually' (Ely 1880, 259). However, while Ely (1895, 70) was not worried about state involvement in the education system, he was very concerned about powerful classes hindering academic freedom and independence in the study of economies and other disciplines. In fact, he cautioned that 'large and powerful classes interested in the present condition of things' would always be opposed to any changes intended to achieve the common good (ibid.).

Similar to the theorists of the GHSE, Ely highly valued the provision of various social security services and programs by the state, such as insurance against accidents, sickness and old age, labor laws to ensure workplace safety and better working conditions, and youth protection. When addressing the implementation of social security programs by Otto von Bismarck (1815–1898), Ely (1882, 520) commented that 'we may be sure that the same social problems which now vex Germany will one day confront us' in the US. It is not surprising that Ely valued Bismarck's social and economic policies so highly, as did a number of other German-trained American scholars, because some of their GHSE professors had roles in their design and establishment, including Knies and Schmoller (both served in their parliaments), and Wagner and Conrad (both were economic advisors of Bismarck). For American scholars of the New School, 'the example of Bismarck's Germany, with its fervent nationalistic spirit, was the one to follow' (Herbst 1965, 191).

Farnam (1888, 288) also supported publicly funded social services and programs, as he believed that 'the state should, as far as possible, endeavor to strike at the root of pauperism rather than to merely prune its branches.' That said, he suggested that 'the state should be exceedingly cautious in applying methods of relief,' and 'it should not hesitate to go beyond the simple giving of relief' (ibid.). In this way, 'the amount of relief needed in the future' will decrease (ibid.). Hadley (1896) also supported publicly funded social services and programs, because he thought they played a significant role in the achievement of public happiness. Like the theorists of the GHSE, he held the view that 'the true basis for an estimate of a nation's wealth is be found in the enjoyments of its members' (Hadley 1896, 4).

Seligman (1910, 170) focused on the role of the state in the imposition of protective trade measures and the improvement of 'real productive efficiency.' He explained that 'if the relative inequality of two countries in the production of a certain commodity is great, free trade may hinder in the weaker country the growth of an industry which might become relatively profitable or even highly necessary' (ibid.). Accordingly, he supported protective state measures that would help build up 'the industry to the point where there will be a domestic competition' (ibid.). Meanwhile, Taussig (1883) concentrated on trade restrictions designed to protect infant industries. To be more precise, he argued that it was necessary and legitimate to shield an infant industry if 'the causes which prevent the rise of the industry' are not natural and permanent obstacles to its flourishing (Taussig 1883, 8). In other words, if artificial obstacles 'temporarily prevent the rise of the industry,' then its protection by the state was justified (ibid.: 10). Patten (2003, 41) also supported the protection and development of infant industries. He explained that since people's wants and goals are not static, and they do not 'wish merely for the same few articles that their ancestors had,' the development of new industries was a necessity (ibid.). Patten (2003, 42) stressed that these new industries need state 'protection and encouragement' when they are in their infancy.

Patten argued that 'free trade doctrines are not really based upon the best economic knowledge of today' (Patten 2003, 13). As an example, he explained that trade restrictions were often accepted as measures that prevented each nation from enjoying the benefits of commerce. However, he maintained that this view was far from the truth, stressing that advocates of protective trade measures were not intent to 'destroy foreign trade' (ibid.). In fact, they sought to 'develop foreign trade as much as their opponents' did (ibid.). Patten also argued that since all nations are fundamentally distinct from one another, their trade policies should also be very diverse. That means the success of free trade in a given nation does not 'prove that it would be beneficial' for all nations (ibid.: 8).

Ely also supported positive state actions for environmental reasons. He did not believe that people always pursued their self-interests. However, when they did, he argued that it was false to assume that they would always contribute to the best interests of society as a whole. Consequently, he supported state intervention in instances where individual and general interests did not harmonize. For example, he argued that the state interference was necessary for 'preserving our forests' because 'the ordinary laws of supply and demand' were not adequately doing so (Ely 1883, 232). Other adherents of the New School also advocated for forest conservation projects on the part of the state. Among them, Adams emphasized that 'corporations could not undertake such a task because the fruits of the investment were too remote' (Dorfman 1955, 26). Meanwhile, Hadley (1896, 45) attributed an important role to the state in developing the domestic economy in a manner that would help avoid food scarcity and starvation. According to him, this would require the state to play a crucial part in improving the 'utilization of the products of the land' (ibid.). Hadley (1896, 45) argued that this could be achieved by enabling the agriculture sector to cultivate 'the land' in a way that will 'furnish larger crops.' He also supported state action in making 'improvements in clothing and shelter' (ibid.).

Adams (1887, 494) believed that it was a mistake to accept 'the state as a necessary evil,' like classical economists did, or to regard 'the state as an organism complete within itself,' as was the case with the adherents of the GHSE. Instead, he argued that:

> both state action and the industrial activity of individuals are functions of the complete social organism. The state is not made out of the chips and blocks left over after framing industrial society, nor does industrial society serve its full purpose in furnishing a means of existence for the poor unfortunates who are thrust out of the civil or the military service. (ibid.)

Adams stressed that the state needed to be an ethical agent in order to have an active role in regulating economic activities and providing social services and programs. He pointed out that it was possible to have a positive state action aimed at achieving the common welfare in Germany, because 'the best talent of the people' were 'drawn into the public service' (ibid.: 535). In fact, Germans considered working for the nation in pursuit of the common welfare to be a highly prestigious and respectable occupation. Ely (1938) held similar views to those of Adams, explaining that students in Germany would try to get the highest grades and win distinctions in their final exams in the hopes of acquiring a job in the civil service. This was 'a question of high social esteem that they felt would be obtained in the civil service rather than in private employment' (Ely 1938, 259). Essentially, the goal in Germany was to attain the best civil service possible while cultivating the right spirit among civil servants. However, the US failed to achieve a comparable civil service because American society developed in 'the opposite direction,' with individual success and interests being highly praised, while the common good was not considered to be particularly important (Adams 1887, 535). Consequently, the 'civil service' in the US ended up being 'so poor that an official has no social position, while a business man who accumulates money is generally regarded with deference' (ibid.). Furthermore, the salary paid by the state was 'nothing when compared with what men of ordinary talent' could earn, 'either as profit if engaged in business on their own account, or as salary if working for a private employer' (ibid.: 536). To prevent the corruption of public workers, Adams advised for a well-educated and 'well-paid civil service,' which would play a major role in restoring 'the harmony between state and private service' (Dorfman 1955, 26).

Adherents of the New School accepted the state as 'an educational and ethical agency whose positive aid' was 'an indispensable condition of human progress' (Ely 1938, 136). At the same time, they recognized that common welfare has been among the most abused concepts by decision-makers and despots across history. The government had to serve its people as opposed to behaving as though it was their master. In other words, even though they supported positive state actions intended to achieve common welfare, they were conscious that governments have a proclivity for despotic tendencies. As such, they supported a legal framework to limit state actions. They also advocated for well-trained and ethical public servants, as well as a selfless and virtuous ruler. Broadly speaking, all adherents of the New School wanted to have positive state action in order to achieve the common good of society, though there were some disagreements among them as to what the exact limits of that state action should be. Ultimately, the efforts of the New School contributed to significantly expanding the positive role of the state in the first decades of the 20th century, which was among the biggest achievements of this school of thought. In fact, their work essentially prepared the groundwork for the welfare state that emerged in the US during the 1930s.

Ethical Values

The dominance of classical orthodoxy resulted in a decline of moral sentiment in the discipline of economics, the practices of the 'business community,' and society in general (Adams 1887, 502). More specifically, the laissez-faire approach, the unrestrained activity of private enterprises, methodological individualism, and unlimited 'free competition,' all of which were advocated by classical economists, disregarded the role of moral and ethical values in economics (Adams 1879, 291). Similarly, adherents of the Old School, who were disciples of classical orthodoxy in the US, did not give any consideration to the idea of man as an ethical being, nor did they care about improving society based on motivations that were guided by ethical values

(Patten 1891, 103). In fact, one of the main differences between the Old School and the New School was that the latter sought 'the establishment of a new relation between ethics and economics' (Ely 1886, 70). Like theorists of the GHSE, members of the New School focused on studying mankind from an ethical standpoint, while also highly valuing the application of moral and ethical values in economics.

Ely argued that the stripping of ethics from political economy on the part of classical economists resulted in some of the worst characteristics of man, such as the unrestrained pursuit of self-interests, being accepted as fundamental and universal principles of human behavior. To the contrary, he maintained that 'the ethical ideal' was 'the most perfect development of all human faculties in each individual, which can be attained' (Ely 1886, 50). Meanwhile, Dunbar (1904, 35) suggested that the progress of political economy in the US was delayed by the widespread adherence to classical economics, as its supporters ignored all higher purposes and duties, while devoting all of their work and effort to 'the pursuit of wealth alone' (ibid.). Kinley (1949, 140) also contended that the complete absence of ethics among the considerations for an individual's choice of action resulted in destructive outcomes for the common interest across history. He explained that 'the plea that the best results will be produced' by laissez-faire falls to 'the ground, and the actual circumstances of life constitute a necessity for interference, in order to produce an ethical social life' (Kinley 1893, 9). According to him, advanced civilizations are correlated with the feeling of being part of a community, as well as the practice of ethical and moral values for the purpose of achieving common welfare for all (ibid.: 13). As for Patten (1888), he explained that classical economists only achieved a temporary benefit for a few people by excluding moral judgments from economics, while the masses were forced to endure many detrimental outcomes. To be more precise, he claimed that if individual temptations were not restricted and simply allowed to be fully realized, then people would enjoy 'intense present pleasures' that could result in many evils (Patten 1896, 103). According to Patten, moral and ethical ideals would create motives by which temptation would be resisted. He further argued that these ethical and moral 'ideals which raise men's thoughts above temptation would become the great social forces' (ibid.: 107). Patten (1896, 125) was also of the opinion that moral and ethical practices were the best way to achieve 'the highest form of life.'

Seligman (1889, 544) believed that there were no conflicts between economic and ethics, because political economy was not an 'exact or a purely abstract science'; rather, it was an ethical science. In other words, political economy cannot be separated from ethics (Seligman 1910, 6). In fact, he believed that economic actions and economic institutions should be shaped by ethics so as to achieve common welfare (ibid.: 31). Seligman (1917, 126) also maintained that people across history were moved by 'ethical considerations' and that 'all progress' resulted from 'the attempt to realize the unattainable, the ideal, the morally perfect.' Thus, he concluded that the acceptance of economics as an ethical discipline was 'the basis of social progress' (Seligman 1910,

698). Meanwhile, Patten (1896, 125) stressed that social and economic progress required 'checking the influence of the degrading tendencies in our present economic and social environment, and in educating the public up to higher moral and political standards' (Patten 1890, 27). According to him, moral and ethical values had a significant role in economics, even going so far as to argue that they are 'the real source from which so many economic motives spring' (Patten 1888, 689). Gay was also highly supportive of ethical economics. He claimed that economic decisions and actions are part of social life, and as such, must be guided by ethical judgments. As for Ely, he also supported the ethical evolution of society and emphasized the importance of ethical economics in the achievement of the collective good. For him, 'the sphere of economic activity of any society is determined by the laws and mores of the society, and the moral standards of its individual members' (Kinley 1949, 140). Kinley (1949, 140) not only supported ethical economics, but also regarded it as a necessary component of progress and the achievement of the common interest. Consequently, he argued that if ethical outcomes are to be achieved, then an 'extension of the role of government in the economic life' of Americans was necessary due to 'the growing complexity' of the economic system (ibid.: 141). Furthermore, Clark (1886, 41) argued that the 'growing complexity of the economic process' meant there was 'an increasing need of moral force.' More precisely, the complexity of social and economic life in advanced civilizations necessitated 'a growing subordination of brain and members to the dictates of moral law' (ibid.: 42).

Clark (1914, 26) believed that perfect competition was the best guarantee of the general welfare of the people. However, he underlined that unrestrained competition was not only unethical and destructive, but it also produced disastrous consequences for society. In fact, he argued that 'competition without moral restraints is a monster' (Clark 1886, 151). According to Clark (1879, 162), before the influence of the GHSE took hold in the US, 'moral influence' was less instrumental, 'less powerful and less pervasive in America.' Meanwhile, in Europe, 'moral forces' played an important role in 'limiting competition more and more' after the GHSE came to prominence (Clark 1879, 160). In particular, Clark (1879, 160) noted that 'a farther development of moral force suppressed open robbery' by the business classes in Germany and England. As such, he advocated for a greater emphasis on moral and ethical values to limit the destructive outcomes of free trade and competitive markets in the US. In fact, he believed that 'the greatest social wealth' depended on the moral and ethical commitments of society (Clark 1886, 86). He also maintained that higher moral and ethical principles should be 'recognized' and consciously adopted by all if the evils of capitalism were to be remedied (Clark 1879, 165). Moreover, Clark (1886, 173) contended that:

> justice in the division of products, equality in exchanges, must become the aim of social effort. The gain will be both material and moral; the change which makes workmen richer will make all classes better; and what is of more importance, it will open the way for continued progress.

Meanwhile, Patten believed that the desire for economic welfare becomes strong when ethics play an important role in society. In turn, the achievement of economic welfare would create demand for economic justice and equality.

Adherents of the New School believed that the combination of the laissez-faire approach, the unrestricted pursuit of self-interests, and the elimination of ethics from economics, as advocated by classical economics, resulted in the prevalence of insatiable wants for acquisitiveness, power, and wealth, and led to the emergence of a corrupt and incompetent state that could not be trusted to achieve the common good. Contrary to classical economists, they supported ethical economics, which revolutionized political economy based on the works of the GHSE. The ethical economics taught by Schmoller, Conrad, Wagner, and Knies led to adherents of New School respecting the importance of ethics in political economy (Ely 1910, 77). In fact, with the dominance of the GHSE in the discipline of political economy, no economist of repute 'would attempt to ignore the ethical aspects' of economics in the last few decades of the 19th century (Hadley 1896, 23). Even when it came to defenders of individualism and socialism, 'instead of asserting the complete independence of economics and ethics,' they would 'insist on the close connection between the two sciences' (ibid.). It could even be said that there was nearly a general consensus among political economists that 'nothing could be economically beneficial which was ethically bad, because such economic benefit could be only transitory' (ibid.). They also accepted that 'nothing could be ethically good which was economically disastrous, because in this case also destruction must ensue with equal certainty' (ibid.).

Methodological Individualism

Like the classical economists of England, disciples of the Old School only took the interests of individuals into consideration while largely neglecting those of the community. In England, 'the philosophy of individualism permeates all thought, the presumption is in favor of private enterprise; in Germany, where the state is the center of all interests, the presumption lies in the opposite direction' (Adams 1887, 493). This contrast between the classical economics of England and the GHSE was very important for adherents of the New School. Like members of the GHSE, they argued that in political economy, there is no 'natural law of self-interest in the same sense' of 'the natural law of gravitation. The one is dependent on man, the other is independent of man' (Seligman 1910, 25). Accordingly, the New School questioned the classical economics assumption that human beings are entirely self-interest oriented. In doing so, they argued that classical economists oversimplified economic relationships in order to make it easier to construct political and economic laws. Specifically, Ely (1883, 226) claimed that an inadequate and reductive view of 'the average man' was very attractive for classical economists, because it provided them 'with a few easily managed formulas, which enabled' them 'to solve all social problems at a moment's notice, and at any time to point out the only true and correct policy for all governments, whether in the present or the past, whether in Europe or Asia, Africa or America.'

Adherents of both the GHSE and New School believed that real-life individuals were very different from the abstract, self-interest maximizing economic agents assumed by classical economics. They believed that classical economists had inadequate conceptions of man, because the reasons and motivations behind the 'activities of men cannot be determined by assuming that man is a being of a certain kind' (Clark 1886, 33). To the contrary, neither the GHSE nor the New School considered man to be purely 'an exchanging animal' with 'a single unvarying interest, removed from all the real conditions of time and place a personification of an abstraction' (Leslie 1875). For instance, Clark (1886, 34) was in agreement with the GHSE, as he stressed the necessity of building political economy on 'a permanent foundation of anthropological fact.' According to him, historical and anthropological studies would reveal that 'the assumed man' of classical economics does not 'resemble the real one in several important respects, and that there is not only a possibility, but a moral certainty' that 'the assumed man is too mechanical and too selfish to correspond' with the man of the real world (ibid.: 34–35). Clark pointed out that real people are not independent of their surroundings or community where they have social relationships with other individuals. In actuality, people are guided by many different motives in different areas of life aside from the strict pursuit of self-interests, as defended by classical economics. To the contrary, their wants, desires, values, goals, decisions, and actions are shaped by unselfish forces of society, which have generated many benefits for people across history, including filling 'the land with schools, churches, art museums, hospitals...for social improvement' (ibid.: 45).

Seligman (1910, 4) acknowledged that it is an undisputable fact that people are motivated by the satisfaction of their individual 'wants with the smallest possible effort' in their economic lives. However, he criticized classical economists for reducing man into an entity that is driven solely by the pursuit of individual self-interest maximization while excluding all other possible incentives (Seligman 1886A). According to Seligman (1910, 5), an examination of the actual motives in people's economic lives reveals 'widely varying effects at different times and places, as well as in different individuals or classes at the same time or place.' In particular, he pointed out that history has countless cases where 'nations, like individuals, have acted unselfishly and have followed the generous promptings of the higher life' (Seligman 1917, 126). Similarly, Ely (1883, 229) also argued that the pursuit of individual self-interests was not always 'the force which moves great masses.' He strongly disagreed with classical economists that 'the only motive for human action' is 'the motive of self-interest' (Ely 1887, 10). To be more precise, he maintained that self-interest is 'the motive of the economic activity of men-but by no means of all men; it promotes the common welfare-but by no means in all cases' (Ely 1884, 37). With that in mind, Ely (1883, 229) stated that:

> any scientific method must strive to take into account *all* of men's motives and *all* the conditions of time and place in framing economic laws concerning men's actions. The nearer it comes to this "all," the more precise it is, the nearer it attains to its ideal. To neglect other motives, and consider self-interest alone, is absurd.

Contrary to the narrow-minded commitment that classical economists displayed for methodological individualism, Ely pointed out that people do not always act based on their personal self-interests. He suggested that other forces that could move people included moral and ethical commitments, national honor, principles, patriotism, politics, language, literature, compassion, traditions, and customs. Ely (1883, 228) specifically stated that:

> all men may be more or less selfish, but he who is thoroughly so, even in business transactions, is so rare as to be despised by the vast majority of mankind. During the late "hard times," hundreds of manufacturers continued business chiefly for the sake of their employees. Even great corporations, with their proverbial lack of feeling, are far from utterly disregarding the welfare of those in their employ.

This was in direct contradiction with the views expressed by classical economists, who believed that individuals are 'most truly benefiting others in pursuing their own egotistic designs' (ibid.: 227). Adams (1887, 482) countered that it was false to accept the notion that 'when a man advances his own interests or what he believes to be his own interests, he thereby necessarily advances the interests of society.' Furthermore, Ely (1887, 10) was frustrated that classical economics did not make any effort to 'ascertain how men actually do act; it only undertook to philosophize respecting the results, provided they acted in a certain assumed manner.' In fact, he suggested that classical orthodoxy became worse than 'an apostate in religion' (Ely 1883, 226).

Ely (1884, 37) argued that 'the economic system, based on the exclusive consideration of self-interest, is full of self-contradictions.' He further claimed that the universal acceptance of such a system by classical economists almost 'deified a monstrosity known as the economic man, that it looked upon laissez-faire as a law of beneficent providence, and held that free trade must be received as an ethical dogma' (Ely 1910, 64). Meanwhile, Ely (1883, 234) highly praised the fact that theorists of the GHSE accepted 'man as man, and not wealth' and focused on the achievement of his true welfare as a member of the community.

Ely (1884, 37) described methodological individualism as a 'strange psychology' that 'destroys the unity of the mind!' According to him, the fact that people reside in communities means that there are many other factors that affect their decisions and actions aside from self-interest maximization. He explained that theorists of the GHSE supported methodological collectivism, because they recognized 'the divine element in the associations' of people in 'towns, cities, states,' and nations (Ely 1883, 234). They were 'animated by a fixed purpose to elevate mankind, and in particular the great masses, as far as this can be done by human contrivances of an economic nature' (ibid.). Additionally, Kinley (1893, 7) argued that 'the idea that all are equally able to care for their own interests' is 'an utterly baseless belief.' He claimed that this was 'an unattainable and an undesirable ideal' (ibid.). In fact, he believed that only classical orthodoxy and its supporters could believe in such an idea. According to Kinley (ibid.: 9), the pursuit of self-interest maximization is not beneficial when people are:

> really oppressed, either unintentionally by stronger competitors, or deliberately by the selfishness of those who think their own "success" more important than the health and happiness and good character, and perhaps the lives, of some whom chance or dire necessity has put in their power.

Meanwhile, Hadley (1896, 15) argued that methodological individualism was destructive to the unity of the community, as it promoted unlimited increases in the possessions and wealth of individuals. In his own opposition to methodological individualism, Patten (1895, 120) argued that 'self-interest is active in the child from the very beginning' and that this kind of behavior needed to be discouraged and restrained at 'every stage through life.' He pointed out that, contrary to the classical economists who worshipped self-interest maximization, Germans accepted 'the sacrifice of self-interest to the higher social life' as 'the first duty of a man, and that no personal motive should weigh in the scale against it' (Patten 1916, 19). Patten (1916, 20) further stated that 'the spirit of calculation and self-aggrandizement' were 'absent when the higher interests of Germany' were 'endangered, or when the cultural life of the people' was 'threatened.'

The New School on Socialism

Since adherents of the New School and the GHSE supported a more just society, they were worried about the destructive outcomes of the laissez-faire approach and methodological individualism, including misery, injustice, and inequality. According to them, the laissez-faire approach and methodological individualism were used to further the interests of the already rich elite classes at the expense of the poor and hard-working people. For example, under classical economics, factory owners appealed to 'the principles of political economy' to avert strikes that could improve working conditions and raise wages (Mayo-Smith 1886, 118). Members of the New School and the GHSE believed that it was 'a mistake to formulate scientific principles so absolutely that they can be used in this way' (ibid.).

Adherents of the New School advocated for the working and living conditions of the masses to be improved through ethical state reforms, as opposed to some kind of socialist revolution. However, they recognized that it would be difficult for the state to implement protective labor laws in the US on account of the fact that the laissez-faire approach was strongly supported by Old Economists and deeply ingrained in the social and economic practices of Americans. Therefore, even though adherents of the New School were anxious to follow the example of Germany, they had a hard time trying to introduce similar welfare legislation in the US, because Americans were not ready for it. In other words, the 'German welfare legislation of the 1880s was acceptable in Germany,' but not in the US (Balabkins 1988, 102). Nevertheless, Farnam (1913) supported the introduction of similar welfare legislation in the US. He pointed out that under the laissez-faire system, neither patent laws, which motivate invention and innovation, nor corporation laws, which 'encourage production on a large scale and give the investing capitalist the benefit of a limited liability,' were advantageous for the whole population (Farnam 1913, 171). He was particularly concerned that the laissez-faire system allowed for some to profit handsomely while not being held accountable for any injury or death from the accidents, negligence, and disease caused by their economic activities (ibid.). In order to achieve economic progress, Farnam (1913, 88) defended collective bargaining and protective labor laws prohibiting 'child labor, limiting the hours of employment, limiting the age of employment, etc.' More broadly, Farnam (1913, 89) supported a legal framework that protected the rights of the working classes and established 'a standard' that changed 'the conditions of competition, and made it impossible for the employer' to violate labor laws.

Commons also supported state reforms that ensured fair competition and improved the working and housing conditions of the labor class (Dorfman 1966V3, 280). For example, he defended reduced working hours, unemployment insurance, compensation for work-related injuries, and a minimum wage (ibid.: 292). In fact, Commons defended 'so many important proposals for social legislation that he has been called "the intellectual origin of the movement toward the welfare state"' in the US (Lafayette 1962, 3). One could argue that the role he played in establishing social security programs and services aimed at achieving common welfare in the US was similar to that of Schmoller in Germany (Yefimov 2009, 39).

Hadley (1896, 60) also advocated for the foundation of a 'system of compulsory insurance' to support and protect American employees and their families, which would be similar to the one that already existed in Germany. Additionally, Adams highly supported the formation of labor unions so that workers could protect their rights by strengthening their bargaining power relative to employers. He also supported legislation to 'remove serious abuses in the factory' (Dorfman 1955, 26). Adams believed that such measures would guarantee the conditions of personal freedom and secure 'to men an enjoyment of the fruits of their labor' (ibid.). Meanwhile, Clark (1914, 19) concentrated on supporting labor rights by reducing work hours, providing 'protection for the workers and indemnities for injuries.' He stressed that such laws and regulations needed to be 'strengthened and more fully enforced' (ibid.). Seager also supported labor unions and the protection of labor rights, including the reduction of working hours, and an improvement in wages and other working conditions, particularly in sweatshops. He also supported the child labor 'amendment in 1925' (Dorfman 1966V4, 166).

Ely also defended the labor movement, because he believed that it would improve working conditions. More broadly, he claimed that 'the amelioration of the condition' of the working classes was dependent upon 'the labor organization, the school, the state, and the church' (Farman 1886, 684). That said, he regarded the existence of labor movements and trade unions as 'the strongest force outside of the Christian church, making for the practical recognition of human brotherhood' (ibid.). In his own defense of labor rights, Patten (1888, 698) argued that 'a reduction in the hours of labor elevates the moral nature,' and 'the elevated moral nature increases the estimate of future welfare.'

Generally speaking, adherents of the New School defended social justice, as did the theorists of the GHSE. To achieve it, they supported the public provision of health care and education, unemployment insurance, the establishment of labor unions, and the legislation of insurance to protect against sickness, accidents, invalidity, and old age. However, their advocacy for social justice did not mean that adherents of the New School were supporters of socialism. Like theorists of the GHSE, they supported state regulations while opposing socialist revolutions, which would entail the elimination of the private property ownership, a more active state role, and the elimination of economic freedom. Essentially, members of the New School were concerned about the destructive outcomes of socialism on the development and progress of societies, just like they were in the case of classical economics. They were fully aware that the public ownership and management of everything in an economic system was 'ruinous,' while allowing everything to be owned by 'private enterprise' was 'equally ruinous' (James 1887, 55).

Efforts on the part of the New School aimed at improving the working conditions of the labor classes, as well as their support for state reforms that provided social services and programs, were 'dubbed socialistic or anarchistic' and 'communistic, or bolshevistic' by adherents of the Old School (Balabkins 1988, 102, Dorfman 1966V4, 166). As such, members of the New School often experienced a lack of academic freedom and other difficulties due to their support for state regulations and interventions. They were also targets of hostility on account of their advocacy for labor rights and protections, including calls to abolish child labor and expressions of support for labor unions, strikes, and labor movements. Furthermore, their support for the public ownership and management of natural monopolies was very unpopular among adherents of the Old School and certain special interest groups. There were 'a number of high-profile cases in which academic appointments were placed in jeopardy and—more often than not—were lost' due to the lack of academic freedom (Barber 2001, 228). For example, in 1881, Walker was pressured to resign from his position as chair of political economy at Yale due to the hostile attitude of Sumner. In fact, while he was working at Yale, Walker wrote a letter to Ely in which he admitted that he was 'treated at times even contemptuously by the Old Guard and felt keenly the injustices that had been done him' (Ely 1936, 147). He also confessed that:

> before its foundation he felt himself alone. After the AEA was founded, he stood among friends. Instead of finding himself more isolated in the face of hostile criticism, he had a forum for the sympathetic discussion of views, where the things that he said helped a hundred others and where he, in turn, was helped by what others said and did. What was true in the case of Walker was true in the case of many others.
>
> (Ely 1910, 98)

Henry Carter Adams also endured difficulty on account of his opposition to the laissez-faire approach and his defense of labor rights at the University of Cornell, where he worked from 1880 until 1887. Ultimately, he was fired from Cornell for having socialist views. In 1888, German-trained Elisha Benjamin Andrews (1847–1917) left Brown University and joined the University of Nebraska because of 'academic freedom difficulties' (Cookingham 1993, 284). Furthermore, Ely moved from Johns Hopkins to the University of Wisconsin in 1892 because of a hostile environment and false accusations that he was a socialist. Then, in 1894, Ely was accused of teaching socialism and promoting strikes and boycotts at the University of Wisconsin, which actually led to him being subjected to a trial. Additionally, Edward Alsworth Ross (1866–1951), a former student of Ely at Johns Hopkins, was dismissed from the University of Stanford due to his support for state intervention and reforms aimed at improving the rights and living conditions of the working class (Cookingham 1993, 283). Another former student of Ely, Commons, was dismissed from the University of Chicago. 'Edward W. Bemis (at the University of Chicago)' was also let go on account of his support for social and economic justice (Barber 2001, 228).

Ely (1899, 167) valued the fact that socialism helped 'men to picture to themselves an ideal society' and 'familiarized them with the idea of social change.' He also pointed out that, contrary to the 'individual side of economic life' defended by classical economics, socialists highlighted the importance of 'the social side of economic life' (ibid.). While Ely (1886, 70) undoubtedly recognized that socialists made significant contributions to economic knowledge, he clarified that among those who were 'known as the new school of political economists,' there was not 'a single one who could be called an adherent of socialism.' In fact, he believed that 'pure socialism' was not being advocated by any 'teacher of political economy in any American college or university' (Ely 1886, 70). However, Ely was also critical of American economists who were 'neither on the side of the rich nor on that of the poor, neither a partisan of the class of employers nor a partisan of the class of employees' (ibid.: VII). He even went so far as to describe them as little more than mere office workers without any opinions and exhibiting no concern about the consequences of their work on society. With that in mind, Ely (1886, X) underlined that in order 'to understand any organism better than others,' one must have 'opinions about it which differ from those ordinarily current' views.

Even though Clark (1886, 199–200) admitted that 'the socialistic ideal has a beauty that captivates the intellect which fairly grasps it,' he was nonetheless concerned that socialism would eliminate personal freedom, which led him to oppose a socialist revolution. In reality, he deemed socialism to be impractical and undesirable. Taussig (1911, 435) was also opposed to socialist revolutions, electing instead to support social and economic reforms. He agreed with the theorists of the GHSE, who maintained that the best alternative to the public ownership of the socialist system was state regulation and reform. Furthermore, Patten (1885, 70) opposed socialist revolutions in favor of the state provision of public services and programs designed to improve the skills and knowledge of people. He believed that the training and education of people in such ways would lead to the emergence of 'new qualities in men' (ibid.). In turn, these new qualities would result in 'a great increase of the opportunities to labor, and an enlarged return for labor in the field of employment' (ibid.).

Seligman (1910, 656) criticized socialism for forgetting about the individual while exaggerating the role of the state. In fact, he went so far as to claim that if socialism was ever realized in practice, it would be 'the death knell of economic advance and true social betterment' (ibid.: 658). He was particularly opposed to the socialist ideas of eliminating private property and competitive industry, as he was of the opinion that these were important factors in the progress and development of societies. According to Seligman (1917, 108), 'private property and private initiative' were 'the very secrets of the whole modern movement.' Nevertheless, he still wanted to have a society that was characterized by social and economic justice and equality. That said, like theorists of the GHSE, he made it clear that justice did not require the equal redistribution of incomes or wealth. Instead, Seligman (1910, 164) relied on the development of a 'sense of social solidarity' and responsibility in order to eliminate social and economic inequalities. Contrary to classical economists, he argued that freedom without responsibility was destructive, and as such, advocated for 'real economic liberty' which is accompanied by equality and responsibility (ibid.: 165). He also pointed out that 'liberty without equality and responsibility may mean advance for the few and retrogression for the many' (ibid.).

Adams (1879, 291) was also highly critical of 'extreme socialists' who claimed that labor was 'the source of all wealth, and therefore, that all wealth belongs to the laborer' that controlled all economic activity in society. That said, he did not oppose all socialist ideas. Like Wagner, Adams (1879, 285) recognized that socialism had an important place in 'the historical development of Political Economy, just as the Mercantile System, the System of the Physiocrats, or the English System of Private Economy.' He argued that socialism was not just 'an ideal, a dream, like Plato's ideal state, or Sir Thomas More's Utopia,' it had 'actual economic and political results' (Adams 1879, 285). These results were evident in the German Empire's politics and economy during the reign of Bismarck (ibid.). However, while Adams accepted that Bismarck's Germany was 'an example of efficiency and enlightened reform' and was impressed by some of its achievements, he was opposed to the way that Germans worshipped the state (Dorfman 1955, 25). He maintained that the US should avoid 'the centralizing tendency of German Economy' because it was 'opposed to the ideas upon which the government is founded' (Adams 1879, 294). At the same time, he warned that 'another century of unrestrained activity of private enterprise will itself contradict the theory of freedom, and destroy' the government (ibid.). In the end, he highly valued the coexistence of public and private ownership, both of which he considered to be necessary 'to the development of a highly organized society' (Dorfman 1966V3, 168).

Adherents of the New School were often labeled socialists when they called for the working conditions of the labor classes to be improved or supported state reforms that provided social services and programs aimed at achieving the common good. In reality, they wanted to achieve social and economic progress by carefully observing the effects of a given course of action rather than trying to instigate a socialist revolution. In fact, they were opposed to socialist revolutions and believed that the best way to prevent socialism was to improve the working and living conditions of the masses. In the end, their efforts resulted in a number of advancements in social justice in the US, including the 'movement for the conservation of natural resources, the demand for protective labor laws,' and the regulation of railroads and other public services (Seager 1904, 36).

Conclusion

The American economy was already experiencing the effects of industrialization in the last few decades of the 19th century, including the rapid accumulation of power and wealth by corporations that often engaged in destructive business practices, as well as the emergence of a large proletariat in the cities that endured deplorable working conditions and miserable lifestyles. Young American men were acutely aware of the fact that they lacked the adequate economic knowledge and proper approaches, methods, and values required to resolve the pressing problems of their time. Moreover, they did not have academic institutions that could provide them with appropriate training in political economy. In response, they looked to further their education abroad, with many electing to obtain advanced training in Germany. These individuals were attracted by the progress and developments that were being achieved by theorists of the GHSE in areas like statistics, national economy, ethical economics, and public finance. By that time, the GHSE had already acquired an international reputation for leading the great historical movement that transpired in Germany during the last half of the 19th century.

Studying political economy under the theorists of the GHSE opened up an entirely new world for Americans, as the boundaries of economics were expanded to unprecedented levels through the historical approach. They came to cherish the methods, ideas, values, reforms, approaches, and policies of the GHSE while blaming classical orthodoxy for many of the ills that plagued their time. In fact, they used historical ethical economics to formulate strong arguments against the laissez-faire system, the abstract deductive approach, and methodological individualism. When they returned home after completing their studies, these Americans, who came to be known as the New School, wanted to adapt what they learned during their time in Germany to the US. Much like theorists of the GHSE, adherents of the New School believed that historical ethical economics would not allow self-oriented greedy people to use political economy for their own gain and to oppress the masses. Furthermore, they were also of the view that historical ethical economics would not support the laissez-faire approach, where a state does nothing while many people live in misery and abject poverty.

The fact that the GHSE was a proponent of developing the national economy was appealing to many of the Americans that were studying in Germany, because they highly valued the national interests of their own country. The influence of the GHSE led members of the New School to believe that the government needed to play an important role in controlling monopolies and ensuring that competition was fair and ethical. The New School also supported an active state role in the provision of social services and programs. Furthermore, they advocated for labor protections, including the reduction of working hours, higher wages, the provision of unemployment insurance, compensation for work-related injuries, and the freedom to join trade unions in order to improve their working conditions. Without the efforts of the adherents of the New School, the US would not have become the type of welfare state that was witnessed in the 20th century.

There is no doubt that adherents of the New School managed to facilitate remarkable development in political economy, both as an academic discipline and a profession, and exert significant influence over state policies in the US. In fact, it could be argued that these German-trained American political economists revolutionized political economy in the US, in part by ingraining the principles, methods, and ideas of the GHSE in their own students. However, despite the immense influence that the New School exerted on American society from the end of the 19th century until the outbreak of WWI, only a few aspects of methods, ideas, and goals of the GHSE were ultimately retained in the long run.

Notes

1 University of Illinois System. 'James 1904–1920.' https://www.uillinois.edu/president/history/about_the_presidents/james.

2 https://www.encyclopedia.com/people/social-sciences-and-law/economics-biographies/richmond-mayo-smith.

3 Johns Hopkins University. 1879. *Annual Report of the Johns Hopkins University*. Baltimore: John Murphy & Co.
4 *The Harvard Graduates Magazine*. December 1902. Vol. 11: 247–248.
5 Archives at Yale. 'Arthur Twining Hadley, President of Yale University, Records.' https://archives.yale.edu/repositories/12/resources/2590.
6 Ibid.
7 Illinois University Department of Economics. 'Bogart, Ernest L.' https://economics.illinois.edu/spotlight/historical-faculty/bogart-ernest-l.
8 Ibid.
9 Archives at Yale. John Christopher Schwab family papers: Collection: John Christopher Schwab family papers | Archives at Yale.
10 Ibid.
11 Online Archive of California. 'Carl Copping Plehn, Economics: Berkeley.' http://texts.cdlib.org/view?docId=hb696nb2rz&doc.view=frames&chunk.id=-div00047&toc.depth=1&toc.id=.
12 Ibid.
13 Ibid.

Bibliography

Adams, Henry Carter. 1879. 'Socialism: The Position of Socialism in the Historical Development of Political Economy.' *The Penn Monthly*. Vol. X: 285–294. #299-Penn monthly. v.10 1879. Full View|HathiTrust Digital Library.

Adams, Henry Carter. 1884. *Taxation in the United States, 1789–1816*. Baltimore: N. Murray, Publication Agent.

Adams, Henry Carter. 1886. *Outline of Lectures upon Political Economy*. Ann Arbor: Press of Register Publishing House.

Adams, Henry Carter. 1887. 'Relation of the State to Industrial Action.' *American Economic Association*. Vol. 1, No. 6: 471–549. Baltimore: The Press of Guggenheimer, Weil & Co.

Adelstein, Richard P. 1993. 'Mind and Hand: Economics and Engineering at the Massachusetts Institute of Technology.' Ed. William J. Barber. *Breaking the Academic Mould: Economists and Higher Learning in the Nineteenth Century*. New Brunswick: Transaction Publishers. 290–317.

The Annals of the American Academy of Political and Social Science. 1896. Vol. 7: 78–86. URL: https://babel.hathitrust.org/cgi/pt?id=njp.32101057051276&view=1up&seq=5

Balabkins, Nicholas W. 1988. *Not by Theory Alone: The Economics of Gustav von Schmoller and Its Legacy to America*. Berlin: Duncker und Humblot.

Barber, William J. 1993. *Economists and Higher Learning in the Nineteenth Century*. New Brunswick: Transaction Publishers.

Barber, William J. 2001. 'Economists and Professional Organisations in Pre-World War I America.' Ed. Massimo M. Augello and Marco E. L. Guidi. *The Spread of Political Economy and the Professionalization of Economists: Economic Societies in Europe, America and Japan in the Nineteenth Century*. London: Routledge. 216–232.

Bartels, Robert. 1951. 'Influences on the Development of Marketing Thought, 1900–1923.' *Journal of Marketing*. Vol. 16, No. 1: 1–17.

Carlson, Valdemar. 1968. 'The Education of an Economist before the Great Depression: Harvard's Economics Department in the 1920's.' *The American Journal of Economics and Sociology*. Vol. 27, No. 1: 101–112.

Carver, Thomas Nixon. 1949. *Recollections of an Unplanned Life: Autobiography of T.N. Carver.* Los Angeles: The Ward Ritchie Press.

Clark, John Bates. 1879. 'Business Ethics, Past and Present.' *New Englander.* Vol. CXLIX: 157–168.

Clark, John Bates. 1886. *The Philosophy of Wealth: Economic Principles Newly Formulated.* Boston: Gin & Company.

Clark, John Bates. 1914. *Social Justice without Socialism.* New York: Houghton Mifflin Company.

Coats, Alfred William. 1985. 'The American Economic Association and the Economics Profession.' *Journal of Economic Literature.* Vol. 23, No. 4: 1697–1727. URL: http://www.jstor.com/stable/2725706

Cookingham, Marry E. 1993. 'Political Economy in the Far West: The University of California and Stanford University.' Ed. William J. Barber. *Breaking the Academic Mould: Economists and Higher Learning in the Nineteenth Century.* New Brunswick: Transaction Publishers. 266–289.

Commons, John Rogers. 1963 [1934]. *Myself. The Autobiography of John R. Commons.* Madison: The University of Wisconsin Press.

Devine, Edward T. 1894. 'Economic Science in America.' *University Extension Bulletin: A Record of Current University Extension Work.* Vol. 1–2, No. 5: 86–88. Philadelphia: The American Society for the Extension of University Teaching. https://babel.hathitrust.org/cgi/pt?id=mdp.39015086683797&view=1up&seq=65

Dickinson, Z. Clark. 1951. 'The Department of Economics.' Ed. Wilfred B. Shaw. *The University of Michigan: An Encyclopedic Survey.* Ann Arbor: University of Michigan Press. 532–544.

Dorfman, Joseph. 1955. 'The Role of the German Historical School in American Economic Thought.' *The American Economic Review.* Vol. 45, No. 2: 17–28.

Dorfman, Joseph. 1966V3. *The Economic Mind in American Civilisation. Volume III.* 1865–1918. New York: The Viking Press.

Dorfman, Joseph. 1966V4. *The Economic Mind in American Civilisation. Volume IV.* 1918–1933. New York: The Viking Press.

Dunbar, Charles F. 1886. 'The Reaction in Political Economy.' *Quarterly Journal of Economics.* October: 1–27.

Dunbar, Charles F. 1891. 'The Academic Study of Political Economy.' *Quarterly Journal of Economics.* July: 397–416.

Dunbar, Charles F. 1897. 'The Career of Francis Amasa Walker.' *Quarterly Journal of Economics.* July: 436–448.

Dunbar, Charles F. 1904. *Economic Essays.* New York: Macmillan & CO., LTD.

Ely, Richard T. 1880. 'American Colleges and German Universities.' *Harper's New Monthly Magazine.* Vol. LXI, No. 362 (July, 1880): 253–260.

Ely, Richard T. 1882. 'Bismarck's Plan for Insuring German Laborers.' *International Review.* Vol. 12: 504–520.

Ely Richard T. 1883. 'The Past and the Present of Political Economy.' *Overland Monthly.* Vol. 2. No. 9: 225–235. The Overland Monthly. ser.2:v.2 (1883). Full View|HathiTrust Digital Library|HathiTrust Digital Library.

Ely, Richard T. 1884. *The Past and the Present of Political Economy.* Baltimore: N. Murray, Publication Agent.

Ely, Richard T. 1886. 'The Economic Discussion of Science.' Ed. Richard T. Ely. *Science Economic Discussion.* New York: The Science Company. 68–79.

Ely, Richard T. 1887. 'Report of the Organization of the American Economic.' *American Economic Association*. Vol. 1, No. 1: 5–46.

Ely, Richard T. 1895. 'On Methods of Teaching Political Economy.' Ed. G. Stanley Hall. *Methods of Teaching History*. Boston: D. C. Heath & Company. 61–72.

Ely, Richard T. 1895. *The Strength and Weakness of Socialism*. Cleveland: Chautauqua Press.

Ely, Richard T. 1910. 'The American Economic Association 1885–1909.' *American Economic Association Quarterly, 3rd Series*. Vol. 11, No. 1: 47–111. New York City: American Economic Association. URL: https://www.jstor.org/stable/3000023

Ely, Richard T. 1936. 'The Founding and Early History of the American Economic Association.' *The American Economic Review*. Vol. 26, No. 1: 141–150. URL: https://www.jstor.org/stable/1807774

Ely, Richard T. 1938. *Ground under our Feet*. New York: Macmillan.

Farnam, Henry W. 1886. 'Review of R.T. Ely's *The Labor Movement in America*.' *Political Science Quarterly*. Vol. 1: 683–687.

Farnam, Henry W. 1888. 'The State and the Poor.' *Political Science Quarterly*. Vol. 3, No. 2: 282–310. URL: https://www.jstor.org/stable/2139034

Farnam, Henry W. 1913. *The Economic Utilisation of History*. New Haven: Yale University Press.

Ferguson, John M. 1950 [1938]. *Landmarks of Economic Thought*. New York: Longman's Green and Company.

Fine, Sidney. 1957. *Laissez faire and the General-welfare State; A Study of Conflict in American Thought, 1865–1901*. Ann Arbor: University of Michigan Press.

Hadley, Arthur Twining. 1886. 'Private Monopolies and Public Rights.' *The Quarterly Journal of Economics*. Vol. 1, No. 1: 28–44. URL: https://www.jstor.org/stable/1883107

Hadley, Arthur Twining. 1888. 'Some Difficulties of Public Business Management.' *Political Science Quarterly*. Vol. 3, No. 4: 572–591. URL: https://www.jstor.org/stable/2139113

Hadley, Arthur Twining. 1896. *Economics: An Account of the Relations between Private Property and Public Welfare*. New York: G. P. Putnam's Son.

Haig, Robert Murray. 1949. 'Introduction.' Ed. David Kinley. *The Autobiography of David Kinley*. Urbana: University of Illinois Press. 7–11.

Herbst, Jurgen. 1965. *The German Historical School in American Scholarship: A Study in the Transfer of Culture*. New York: Ithaca.

Ingram, John Kells. 1915 [1888]. *A History of Political Economy*. London: A. and C. Black. A History of Political Economy | Online Library of Liberty (libertyfund.org)

James, Edmund Janes. 1886. 'The State as an Economic Factor.' Ed. Richard T. Ely. *Science Economic Discussion*. New York: The Science Company. 24–43.

James, Edmund Janes. 1887. 'The Relation of the Modern Municipality to the Gas Supply.' *American Economic Association*. Vol. 1, No. 2–3: 53–122.

Kinley, David. 1893. *The Ethical Basis of Labor Legislation*. Boston: Christian Social Union. https://babel.hathitrust.org/cgi/pt?id=uiug.30112062843617&view=1up&seq=7&skin=2021

Kinley, David. 1918. *The Aims and Claims of Germany*. Illinois: College of Agriculture.

Kinley, David. 1949. *The Autobiography of David Kinley*. Urbana: University of Illinois Press.

Lafayette, G. Harter Jr. 1962. *John R. Commons: His Assault on Laissez-faire*. Oregon: Oregon State University Press.

Leslie, T. E. Cliffe. 1875. 'The History of German Political Economy.' *Fortnightly Review* (July, 1875).

Mason, Edward S. and Thomas S. Lamont. 1982. 'The Harvard Department of Economics from the Beginning to World War II.' *The Quarterly Journal of Economics.* Vol. 97, No. 3: 383–433.

Mayo-Smith, Richmond. 1886. 'Methods of Investigation in Political Economy.' Ed. Richard T. Ely. *Science Economic Discussion.* New York: The Science Company. 104–122.

Mayo-Smith, Richmond. 1888. 'Statistics and Economics: Outline of Statistical, Science with Especial Reference to the Use of Statistics in Political Economy and Social Science.' *Publications of the American Economic Association.* Vol. 3, No. 4/5: 7–127. URL: https://www.jstor.org/stable/2560511

Neff, Frank Amandus. 1950. *Economic Doctrines.* New York: McGraw-Hill. https://archive.org/details/economic-doctrines-frank-neff

Newcomb, Simon. 1884. 'Two School of Political Economy.' *The Princeton Review.* Ser.4, Vol. 14: 291–301. The Princeton review. ser.4 v.14 (1884). - Full View | HathiTrust Digital Library | HathiTrust Digital Library

Parrish, John B. 1967. 'Rise of Economics as an Academic Discipline: The Formative Years to 1900.' *Southern Economic Journal.* Vol. 34, No. 1: 1–16. URL: https://www.jstor.org/stable/1055330

Patten, Simon Nelson. 1885. *The Premises of Political Economy: Being a Re-examination of Certain Fundamental Principles of Economic Science.* Philadelphia: J. B. Lippincott Company.

Patten, Simon Nelson. 1888. 'The Present Condition of Economic Science, and the Demand for a Radical Change in its Methods and Aims.' *Political Science Quarterly.* Vol. 3, No. 4: 687–690. URL: https://www.jstor.org/stable/2139118

Patten, Simon Nelson. 1890. 'The Decay of State and Local Governments.' *The Annals of the American Academy of Political and Social Science.* Vol. 1: 26–42. URL: https://www.jstor.org/stable/1009057

Patten, Simon Nelson. 1891. 'The Educational Value of Political Economy.' *Publications of the American Economic Association.* Vol. V, No. 6: 100–115.

Patten, Simon Nelson. 1895. 'The Teaching of Economics in the Secondary Schools.' *American Economic Association.* Vol. 10, No. 3: 119–138. URL: https://www.jstor.org/stable/2485652

Patten, Simon Nelson. 1896. 'The Theory of Social Forces.' *The Annals of the American Academy of Political and Social Science.* Vol. 7: 1–151. URL: https://www.jstor.org/stable/1009418

Patten, Simon Nelson. 1916. *Culture and War.* New York: B. W. Huebsch.

Patten, Simon Nelson. 2003 [1890]. *The Economic Basis of Protection.* Kitchener: Batoche Books.

Rowe, Leo S. 1890. 'Instruction in Public Law and Political Economy in German Universities.' *The Annals of the American Academy of Political and Social Science.* Vol. 1: 78–102.

Seager, Henry Rogers. 1893. 'Economics at Berlin and Vienna.' *Journal of Political Economy.* Vol. 1, No. 2: 236–262. URL: https://www.jstor.org/stable/1817770

Seager, Henry Rogers. 1904. *Principles of Economics.* New York: Henry Holt and Company.

Seligman, Edwin R. A. 1886A. 'Continuity of Economic Thought.' Ed. Richard T. Ely. *Science Economic Discussion.* New York: The Science Company. 1–23.

Seligman, Edwin R. A. 1886B. 'Change in the Tenets of Political Economy with Time.' *Science-Supplement.* Vol. 12, April: 375–382.

Seligman, Edwin R. A. 1889. 'Reviewed Work(s): Zur Litteraturgeschichte der Staats-und Sozialwissenschaften. by Gustav Schmoller.' *Political Science Quarterly.* Vol. 4, No. 3: 543–545. URL: https://www.jstor.org/stable/2139153

Seligman, Edwin R. A. 1910. *Principles of Economics: With Special Reference to American Conditions.* New York: Longmans, Green, and Co.

Seligman, Edwin R. A. 1912. 'The Seminar: Its Advantages and Limitations.' *Journal of Political Economy.* Vol. 20, No. 2: 153–162. URL: https://www.jstor.org/stable/1820512

Seligman, Edwin R. A. 1917. *The Economic Interpretation of History.* New York: The Columbia University Press.

Senn, Peter R. 1995. 'Why had Roscher so much influence in the USA compared with the UK.' *Journal of Economic Studies.* Vol. 22, No. 3/4/5: 53–105.

Simkhovitch, Marry Kingsbury. 1938. *Neighborhood: My Story of Greenwich House.* New York: Norton.

Small, Albion W. 2001 [1909]. *The Cameralists: The Pioneers of German Social Polity.* Kitchener: Batoche Books.

St. Marc, Henri. 1892. *Étude sur L'Enseignement de L'Économie Politique dans les Université D'Allemagne et D'Autriche.* Paris: Armand Colin et C.

Stigler, George. 1968. 'Works by Moore: Supplementary Bibliography.' *The International Encyclopedia of Social Sciences.* https://www.encyclopedia.com/social-sciences/applied-and-social-sciences-magazines/moore-henry-l

Taussig, Frank William. 1883. *Protection to Young Industries as Applied in the United States. A Study in Economic History.* New York: Press of G. P. Putnam's Sons.

Taussig, Frank William. 1886. 'The State as an Economic Factor.' Ed. Richard T. Ely. *Science Economic Discussion.* New York: The Science Company. 34–38.

Taussig, Frank William. 1888. 'A Suggested Rearrangement of Economic Study.' *The Quarterly Journal of Economics.* Vol. 2, No. 2: 228–232. URL: https://www.jstor.org/stable/1879492

Taussig, Frank William. 1901. 'Proceedings of the American Academy of Arts and Sciences.' *American Academy of Arts & Sciences.* Vol. 36, No. 29: 569–557. URL: https://www.jstor.org/stable/20021619

Taussig, Frank William. 1904. 'Introduction.' Ed. Charles F. Dunbar. *Economic Essays.* New York: Macmillan & CO., LTD. VII–XVII.

Taussig, Frank William. 1905. 'Schmoller on Protection and Free Trade.' *The Quarterly Journal of Economics.* Vol. 19, No. 3: 501–511. URL: https://www.jstor.org/stable/1882664

Taussig, Frank William. 1911. *Principles of Economics Vol.2.* New York: Macmillan Company.

Taylor, Henry C. 1944. 'Obituary: Richard Theodore Ely: April 13, 1854--October 4, 1943.' *The Economic Journal.* Vol. 54, No. 213: 132–138.

Tribe, Keith. 2002. 'Historical Schools of Economics: German and English.' *Keele Economics Research Papers.* No. 2002/02. SSRN: https://ssrn.com/abstract=316689 or http://dx.doi.org/10.2139/ssrn.316689

Walker, Francis A. 1890. 'Mr. Bellamy and the New Nationalist Party.' *Atlantic Monthly.* Vol. 65, No. 388: 248–262.

Walker, Francis A. 1889A. *First Lessons in Political Economy.* New York: Henry Holt and Company.

Walker, Francis A. 1889B. 'Recent Progress of Political Economy in the United States.' *Publications of the American Economic Association*. Vol. 4, No. 4: 17–40. URL: https://www.jstor.org/stable/2485572

Walker, Francis A. 1891. 'The Tide of Economic Thought.' *American Economic Association*. Vol. 6, No. 1–2: 15–38. URL: https://www.jstor.org/stable/2560447

Yefimov, Vladimir. 2009. 'Comparative Historical Institutional Analysis of German, English and American Economics.' *Munich Personal RePEc Archive*. http://mpra.ub.uni-muenchen.de/48173/

5 The Early Establishment of Political Economy Departments at American Colleges and Universities

Introduction

In Germany, political economy was 'most assiduously and most fruitfully cultivated during the last fifty years' of the 19th century (Seager 1893, 239). However, the origins of its development can actually be traced back to the 18th century, when many universities in Germany started to offer the systematic study of political economy. In fact, the first two known chairs of political economy in the world were established in Halle and Frankfurt in 1727 (Streissler 2001, 313). Looking ahead to the middle of the 19th century, German universities succeeded in 'maintaining the first place' in the world when it came to teaching, learning, and conducting advanced research in political economy due to the work and effort of adherents of the German Historical School of Economics (GHSE) (Dunbar 1891, 399). As a result, political economy students and scholars from around the globe went to Germany to study and obtain a higher education under the theorists of the GHSE. The international reputation garnered by the GHSE also led to journals from many countries that were published in a number of different languages, frequently referencing them as reliable sources (St. Marc 1892, 2).

Compared to Germany, the development of political economy as an academic discipline was delayed in the US. German-trained American political economists were not satisfied with the quality of education and teaching being offered in the area of political economy at American universities. They were convinced that the American way of teaching political economy did not promote the development of critical thinking and creativity, which, in turn, inhibited the production of original work within the discipline. In response, they introduced the ideas, methods, and goals of their 'instructors and associates' from the GHSE, 'not in a formulated exact system, but in the form in which they had been impressed' upon them (Devine 1894, 87). They essentially integrated many of the features they witnessed and experienced in the political economy departments of German universities into the curriculums of their own universities in the US. This chapter begins by explaining how German-trained American political economists facilitated the establishment of successful economics departments at a variety of colleges and universities

DOI: 10.4324/9781003247715-5

across the US during the 1880s and 1890s. In doing so, it identifies a number of American political economists who played important roles in the development of these newly established economics departments, and outlines some of their key contributions. It also describes how the number of courses offered at these newly established economics departments increased rapidly, as did the number of teachers working at them and the number of enrolled students. Furthermore, this chapter highlights a number of key features of these newly established economics departments at American institutions of higher learning, including some of the specific classes being offered, the importance of the German language, the adoption of the seminary method, the teaching of statistics, the creation of PhD programs, and the provision of adequate university library resources.

Newly Established Political Economy Departments at American Universities

From the 16th century to the last few decades of the 19th century, American universities were not oriented toward scientific research or advancing new knowledge, creativity, and critical thinking. In fact, 'economics as an independent discipline was a rather wilted flower' for about the first 100 years of its existence (Balabkins 1988, 88). During that time, studying in 'economics was generally regarded as dull and fruitless' and American universities did not even have undergraduate or graduate schools in political economy (Haney 1915, 515). In the rare instances where political economy was taught 'in the colleges' of the US prior to the onset of German influence, it 'was almost invariably considered an adjunct to philosophy or moral philosophy' or theology departments (Mason and Lamont 1982, 384). This is not surprising, given that Christianity actually had a significant influence on the development of political economy in the US since the 17th century, because American universities emulated the systems employed at British universities before German influence took hold. This is due to the fact that they were established at a time when the American territories were still colonies of Great Britain. During this period, when classical economics and Christianity were influential in the discipline of economics, members of the 'clerical school of academic economists worked closely with a group of wealthy and prominent men of affairs' to defend the laissez-faire approach as a universal law of economic evolution and advocate for the implementation of 'laissez-faire as an American system of economics' (Furner 1975, 37). Their ultimate goal was to facilitate 'the joint creation of academics who domesticated English classical economics as a scientific substitute for moral philosophy and American businessmen who needed just such a rationale for the developing industrial economy' (ibid.: 36).

Prior to being influenced by the GHSE, American universities and colleges would typically offer a 'brief course in Political Economy' conducted by 'the Professor of Moral and Intellectual Philosophy [Cocker], who would prefer to confine himself to his own special work' (Dickinson 1951, 532). To be more precise, most teachers of political economy were ministers or preachers, because the clerical school exercised influence over academia at that time. That was made possible by the fact that the requirements to obtain a degree or gain employment as a professor were much less stringent at American universities relative to their German counterparts. In fact, 'almost any one could teach political economy, no special training being necessary,' as a graduate degree was not even a criterion for obtaining a professorship at American universities and colleges (Haney 1915, 515). Richard T. Ely (1883, 226) went so far as to state that the quality of education in political economy was so poor that teaching classical economics required only a few hours of study 'to make of the village schoolmaster both a statesman and a political economist.' He further noted that 'neither high attainments nor previous study and investigation were required even in a professor of the science' (ibid.). That is to say, being 'familiar with the subject' was by 'no means indispensable' for instructors (Haney 1915, 515). It was sufficient to read 'one good book' in order to become an economist or economic teacher (Ely 1938, 125). As such, an education in political economy required little more than 'a well-arranged text-book, together with some effort on the part of the teacher and attention on the part of the pupil' (Haney 1915, 515). Teachers would basically read the passages from the textbook and students learned 'by heart a few truisms' (Ely 1889, 61). Consequently, the economics education being offered at American colleges failed to help students 'understand the practical questions of the day,' such as 'labor strikes, trusts,' financial matters, and issues related to banking and money (Patten 1895, 132). In effect, studying political economy was often deemed to be impractical and useless. Furthermore, 'all the teaching of political economy' amounted to about an hour a week in 'any department of the rich and powerful college' in the US (Ely 1889, 61). These factors are likely among the main reasons why the political economy taught at American colleges and universities was often described as 'barren' or called 'the "dismal" science and sometimes "dry bones"' (Ely 1910, 67).

Most American students usually went to 'college merely because their parents sent them'; at the same time, their parents did not believe that studying political economy provided good prospects for earning a decent living (Farnam 1887, 69). The fact that there was little possibility for a fruitful career as an economist in the US represented a real hindrance to those individuals who wanted to dedicate themselves to the field. Consequently, any American student who wanted to take courses 'in history, politics, political economy, mathematics, physics, philosophy, or in any one of many other studies lying outside of the three professions, law, medicine, and theology,' had to go to Europe (Ely 1880, 256). Ely (1880, 257) warned that until Americans adopted 'a satisfactory system' of education, 'thousands of parents will continue to educate their children in Europe.' This was particularly true in the case of American economists, as training in Germany was crucial if they wanted to secure academic work and promotions.

Before the influence of the GHSE took hold at American academic institutions, well-known political economists like Charles Franklin Dunbar (1830–1900), John Bates Clark (1874–1938), Arthur Twining Hadley (1856–1930), and many others never had 'more than one undergraduate course in political economy, never earned more than a four year degree, all traveled abroad' (Parrish 1967, 4, fn.11). In fact, in 1870, all American colleges and universities across the entire nation only offered a combined 18 economic courses (ibid.). The following decade, only the most prestigious American institutions employed one or two instructors 'teaching political economy' (ibid.: 3, fn.23). Moreover, 'economics did not become a separate department at several major universities until the 1890s or even later' (Ely 1910, 67). Meanwhile, in 1890, the University of Berlin, on its own, boasted 'twenty-one lecturers, who give an aggregate of 102 hours' of instruction each week, in addition to the work done in the seminars (Rowe 1890, 80). In light of these disparities, it becomes clear that American students were not able to obtain an education in political economy domestically that was on par with what was being offered by German universities at that time. Furthermore, the dismal state of political economy in the US, both as a profession and an academic discipline, meant that Americans contributed 'virtually nothing to the development of economic theory' until the 20th century (Balabkins 1988, 88). It also suggests that decisions on important economic matters in the US were being made by politicians who knew nothing about the subject.

Many young Americans were unhappy with the unfruitfulness of studying and teaching at their domestic universities. In response, they went to Germany in order to advance their knowledge and education under the guidance of the theorists of the GHSE (St. Marc 1892, 1–2). They eventually returned to the US 'as the missionaries of the new cult' that would guide a new generation of American economics students (Walker 1899, 310). For example, Richard Theodore Ely (1854–1943) (1910, 80) confessed that while he had 'little notion' of what he was 'to get in Germany' when he set off, he had 'very definite notions' when he returned. He explained that he came back in 'open revolt against the traditional concepts' of economics 'and found the narrow self-satisfied attitude of the American very trying' (ibid.). He was particularly frustrated that 'many good people' at American universities were blindly attached to the classical orthodoxy (ibid.: 259).

Edmund Janes James (1855–1925), who received his doctorate in political economy from the University of Halle in 1877 under Conrad, was also frustrated that American colleges and universities did not have the kind of education system that prevailed in the political economy departments across Germany, which provided excellent training and encouraged critical thinking and original research; instead, they elected to impose a uniform curriculum on students along with a homogeneous and monotone teaching method (James 1882, 262). Ely (1880, 260) agreed, but clarified that the presidents and professors of the best American institutions should not be blamed 'for not doing more,' because it was the institutions themselves that lacked 'favorable circumstances for a high development.' He claimed that if American academics had 'the same advantages as the German professors, they would not do less in advancing science'; unfortunately, they were 'less independent than the German professors' (ibid.). Ely (1938, 132) believed that American professors were 'denied the right to exist scientifically,' because followers of the Old School exercised 'a very large influence,' particularly 'in university circles.' This sad state of affairs in higher education delayed the progress and 'development of economics in the United States' (Ely 1936, 142).

The opinions expressed by James and Ely with respect to the situation of the discipline of economics at American institutions were actually very common among German-trained American economists. After experiencing how economics was taught and studied at German universities, 'the group of young rebels who returned from Germany about 1880' were disappointed with the 'barrenness' and 'the sterility of the old economics which was being taught in the American colleges' (Ely 1936, 143, 1938, 132). However, they were also hopeful that the situation could be remedied and committed to fighting against those who stood 'in the way of intellectual expansion and of social growth' (Ely 1938, 132). Essentially, these young Americans, who were filled with the ideas and methods of the GHSE, wanted to 'inject new life into American economics' (ibid.). Their ultimate goal was to transform their colleges and universities in ways that would help them attain the prestigious status enjoyed by the universities in Germany. More precisely, they wanted to rectify the backwardness that afflicted the discipline of economics in the US by freeing it from the narrowness of classical economics to the fullest extent possible, while also improving how political economy was taught and studied.

In their efforts to reform the discipline of economics in the US, German-trained American political economists essentially relied on their German experiences to transform their domestic universities and 'colleges into German universities' (Ely 1880, 254). Accordingly, 'the German methods of teaching, including the lecture system, were generally adopted' (Laughlin 1912, 169). American institutions effectively underwent 'a complete transformation,' which helped raise the quality of education being offered in the US (Dunbar 1891, 400). German-trained American political economists played instrumental roles in shaping the political economy departments at many American universities and colleges, including Columbia, Wisconsin, Pennsylvania, Johns Hopkins, Michigan, Cornell, Massachusetts Institute of Technology (MIT), Harvard, and Yale. Thus, 'a new impetus was given to the development' of political economy at American universities, as almost all of the teaching staff, with few exceptions, spent some time at German universities in pursuit of a higher education (Ingram 1915, 172).

Charles Franklin Dunbar (1830–1900), who 'turned to German writers' during the latter part of his career, started to teach political economy at Harvard College in 1871 after spending two years in Europe (Taussig 1904, X). When he initially arrived at Harvard, he had to teach his classes 'under the head of Philosophy,' as there was no dedicated department of political economy at that time (Eliot 1900, 478). Later that same year, Dunbar was appointed the first chair of political economy at Harvard University (Scott 1889, 188). Then, during 1872–1873, his political economy courses, which focused on connecting political economy with history, were being offered in the political science department (ibid.). In 1876, he was made Dean of the Faculty of Harvard College, remaining as such until 1882. In 1875, Harvard awarded its first PhD in political economy to Stuart Wood (1853–1914), despite the fact that it still did not have an independent political economy department. However, 'after awarding its first Ph.D. in political economy in 1875, Harvard did not award another for 20 years' (Parrish 1967, 7).

In 1882, Dunbar went back to Europe, and his absence resulted in James Laurence Laughlin (1850–1933) being appointed as an assistant professor the following year. Previously, Laughlin had been a student of Dunbar at Harvard before going on to complete his PhD dissertation under the supervision of Henry Carter Adams (1851–1921) at Johns Hopkins University in 1876. Frank William Taussig (1859–1940) also began teaching at Harvard University in 1883 after having studied political economy at the University of Berlin, where he was highly influenced by Wagner and Schmoller. He continued to teach at Harvard until 1935. After Dunbar returned from Europe, his plans for 'the development of his department in the University became apparent to the academic world' (Eliot 1900, 479). In 1890, he became the first Dean of the Faculty of Arts and Sciences at Harvard University, a post that he retained until 1895 (Taussig 1904, XI). In 1892, the Department of Economics was officially established at Harvard University, followed by the creation of a graduate program in political economy in 1894. Dunbar continuously sought to increase 'the number of teachers and courses' being offered in political economy (Eliot 1900, 479). Over the course of his 28 years at Harvard, Dunbar was 'a complete collegiate instrument for training young Americans in Political Economy, the first such instrument ever constructed' (ibid.: 480). During that time, the progress and development of political economy at the Harvard was a direct outcome of 'Dunbar's sagacity, sobriety, and fairness' (ibid.).

Sir William James Ashley (1860–1927) was a well-known English political economist who joined Harvard University in 1892 and taught there until 1901. During that time, he ended up holding the first known Chair in Economic History in the world (Harvard University 1897–1898). Prior to joining Harvard, Ashley was a supporter of historical economics in Britain along with John Kells Ingram (1823–1907), Thomas Edward Cliffe Leslie (1825–1882), and William Cunningham (1849–1919). Ashley not only translated some of Schmoller's works into English, but the two of them also shared many similar views. In particular, Ashley supported ethical economics and believed that political economy should include both deductive and inductive methods. According to Ashley (1893, 8), Harvard was among the first American universities to 'see the wisdom of having both attitudes-the theoretical and the historical-represented in a great institution of learning.' Furthermore, he claimed that teachers at Harvard showed 'a confidence in free inquiry, and an understanding of the true nature of a university,' thereby resembling the theorists of the GHSE (ibid.). In 1902, the courses on economic history that Ashley taught at Harvard University were taken over by Edwin Francis Gay (1867–1946), who obtained his PhD from the University of Berlin under the supervision of Schmoller that same year after having studied with the theorists of the GHSE in Berlin and Leipzig for 12 years. His 'first courses at Harvard were Medieval Economic History, Economic History of Europe (from 1500), and Nineteenth Century German Economic Thought' (Mason and Lamont 1982, 406). He ended up teaching at Harvard from 1902 to 1917 and once again from 1924 to 1936. During his first stint at the institution, Gay served as a principal advisor to Harvard President Charles William Eliot (1834–1926) when he launched the Harvard Graduate School of Business Administration in 1908.[1] He was also appointed the first Dean of the Harvard Business School in 1908.

The teaching of political economy at Harvard gradually improved since the 1870s. In the early 1890s, Taussig (1892–1893, 116) pointed out that 'Ten years ago, the Department of Political Economy had one professor and one instructor, neither giving all of his time to the subject. At present, the Department of Economics has three professors and two instructors.' He further noted that the number of political economy courses being offered at Harvard increased from 'two to a dozen, with a corresponding development in the variety of topics treated,' while the number of students also rose significantly (Taussig 1892–1893, 116–117). Taussig (ibid.) mainly attributed this progress to 'the change in name, from Political Economy to Economics,' which also involved in 'an enlargement of the range of subjects' being offered at the department.

In the beginning of the 20th century, the economics department of Harvard University continued to appoint new professors, which corresponded with the enrollment of more students and additional courses being offered (Ripley 1903, 246). At that time, it was generally accepted that Harvard had 'the strongest department of economics in the country' (Carver 1949, 142). In 1902, Thomas Nixon Carver (1865–1961) began to work at Harvard, having previously studied at Johns Hopkins University under David Kinley (1861–1944), Herbert Baxter Adams (1850–1901), and Ely, before completing his PhD at Cornell in 1894. Carver ended up working at Harvard for 32 years, during which time he served 'two periods as chairman of the Department of Economics (1901–1903 and another period of three years in the twenties)' (ibid.: 212).

Charles Jesse Bullock (1869–1941), who obtained his PhD in economics from the University of Wisconsin in 1895 under the supervision of Ely, joined the economics department of Harvard University in 1901. He eventually became one of the leading economists at Harvard. In 1902, William Zebina Ripley (1867–1941) was hired to teach a course in Statistics, which attracted a great deal of interest. Prior to that, he obtained his PhD at Columbia

University in 1893. In 1910, Allyn Abbott Young (1876–1929) joined the department as a visiting professor, having previously completing his PhD at the University of Wisconsin under Ely. Young became 'the most highly respected economics professor at Harvard. Under him a considerable number of the outstanding students wished to write their doctors' theses' (Carlson 1968, 106).

Johns Hopkins was one of the oldest universities in the US. It was also among the earliest to be modeled after 'German research universities' in order to 'provide a domestic alternative to the Migration of Americans to Germany for graduate study' (Barber 1993, 11). In 1876, it became the first university in the country to establish a graduate program in political economy, largely due to the work and efforts of Ely (Carver 1949, 111). Henry Carter Adams was 'the first registrant' in the program, as well as the first economist to obtain a PhD from Johns Hopkins in 1878; the second political economy PhD would not be awarded for another ten years (Parrish 1967, 7). In fact, it was Francis Amasa Walker (1840–1897) who conducted Adams's doctoral examination (ibid.: 6–7). Walker played a major role in the development of the economics department at the school. In particular, he taught a series of lectures on monetary policy, which led him to develop close relationships with American disciples of the GHSE (Adelstein 1993, 304). It was recognized that his 'teaching of economics on a university basis at Johns Hopkins ... helped to create a group of younger scholars who soon filled the chairs of economics throughout the country' (Seligman 1911, 388).

In 1881, German-trained Ely and Herbert Baxter Adams, who obtained his PhD in political science from Heidelberg University in 1876, started to teach at Johns Hopkins University, where they worked 'well together,' as they shared many common interests and views (Barber 1993, 213). They wanted American universities to have seminaries and libraries, as well as a spirit of teaching and conducting research, comparable to those that they witnessed and experienced during their time in Germany. While at Johns Hopkins, Ely and Herbert Baxter Adams were able to utilize the influence of the GHSE and the growing role of the New School to attract many students to the university. In 1891, Ely requested that political economics be separated from history to become its own stand-alone department at Johns Hopkins. However, his proposal was rejected on the basis that 'the time has not yet come to constitute a department of political economy distinct from the department of historical and political science' (ibid.: 222). Subsequently, Johns Hopkins officially established a separate political economy department in 1901.

In 1892, Ely left Johns Hopkins after teaching political economy there for a little over a decade in order to join the University of Wisconsin. One of the main reasons for his departure was the hostile attitude of Simon Newcomb (1835–1909), who was opposed to Ely's defense of historical ethical economics and heavily criticized his defense of labor rights and movements. The same year that Ely left, John Bates Clark, who studied under Roscher, Conrad, and Knies between 1872 and 1875, began to teach political economy at Johns Hopkins, but then left for a position at Columbia University in 1895. Henry Ludwell Moore (1869–1958) joined the faculty of Johns Hopkins in 1896 and taught classes covering German history, Prussian history, and railway problems. Previously, he obtained his PhD at Johns Hopkins, where he was significantly influenced by Clark and Herbert Baxter Adams. Moore also studied with Carl Menger for one year in Vienna before completing his PhD.

In the 19th century, Johns Hopkins played a major role in the development of 'American economics far greater than that of any other institution in the land' (Barber 1993, 224). During his time there as a professor, Ely ended up influencing many important economists and other prominent figures who studied under him, including 'Woodrow Wilson, Newton D. Baker, John H. Finley, Charles Levermore, E. A. Ross, John R. Commons, W. A. Scott, Albert Shaw, Albion W. Small, David Kinley' (Taylor 1943, 2). In fact, it was claimed that 'no man in the United States has done so much' as Ely 'to bring economic thought down out of the clouds and into contact with actual human concerns' (Ely 1938, 230–231). Unfortunately, the success that the economics department at Johns Hopkins University experienced under German-trained economists, particularly Ely and Herbert Baxter Adams, was largely forgotten in the 20th century.

When Ely (1938, 180) arrived at the University of Wisconsin in 1892, he set out to 'establish a school' of economics. He wanted to provide his students with a broader approach to life and economics than what classical economics could offer, as he was of the view that 'better economic knowledge' would eventually 'bear its fruits in better citizenship' (ibid.: 187). Under Ely's leadership, the school of economics at the University of Wisconsin was 'preparing to challenge' the supremacy of the Faculty of Political Science at Columbia, which was established in 1880, and the School of Political Science at the University of Michigan, which was established in 1881 (Henderson 1993, 326). During his time at Wisconsin, which spanned the period of 1892–1925, Ely encouraged his students to study under the theorists of the GHSE. However, he was also able to introduce the spirit of his past German professors to his students and colleagues in the department of political economy. He did this by exclusively advocating the ideas, methods, and approaches of the GHSE in his classes, speeches, and publications. In particular, he promoted the 'look and see method' of the GHSE, which played a key role in the development of the political economy department of the University of Wisconsin. Additionally, Ely managed to influence many people to some extent through his defense of ethical historical economics and the social aspects of Christianity, which he often discussed in his classes and books (Taylor 1943).

When Ely left Johns Hopkins for the University of Wisconsin in 1892, he brought some of his most promising students with him to work on the establishment of an economics department, including David Kinley (1861–1944), William Amasa Scott (1862–1944), and Charles J. Bullock (1869–1941). Shortly before that, in 1890, Charles Homer Haskins (1870–1937) was appointed as an instructor at the University of Wisconsin after completing his studies at

Johns Hopkins. He later became a full professor and remained at Wisconsin until 1902. In 1904, Ely invited John Rogers Commons (1862–1945), another former student of his from Johns Hopkins University, to work at Wisconsin. Commons (1963, 44, 97) acknowledged that many of his own ideas and writings were inspired by Ely's 'new economics,' and he confessed that working with Ely at the University of Wisconsin was his 'new birth.' During his time at Wisconsin, Commons supervised or co-supervised the 'completion forty-six PhD' (Yefimov 2009, 40). Additionally, Selig Perlman (1888–1959), who obtained his PhD at Wisconsin in 1915, played a key role in the development of Wisconsin institutionalism along with Commons (ibid.: 39).

Some of Ely's former students from the University of Wisconsin went on to become professors at its political economy department. For example, Allyn Abbott Young, who obtained his PhD under Ely at Wisconsin, ended up joining the department after graduating. Two other former students of Ely from the University of Wisconsin that obtained prominent positions at its political economy department were Max Otto Lorenz (1876–1959) and Edward David Jones (1870–1944). Lorenz was known for developing the Lorenz curve. Meanwhile, Jones went to Germany to study under Engel, Knies, and Conrad before returning to the University of Wisconsin, where he gave lectures on political economy and statistics from 1895 to 1901. Furthermore, in the 1890s, University of Wisconsin graduate Helen Page Bates (1860–1933) started to teach at the economics department, followed by Henry C. Taylor (1873–1969), another Wisconsin alumnus, in 1901. Many of these economists were influenced by the ideas, methods, goals, and approaches of the GHSE to some degree, which is not surprising given that Ely sought to make the economics department of the University of Wisconsin into a replica of the ones that existed at German universities. Ultimately, the appointment of so many professors who were influenced by the GHSE led to the political economy department at the University of Wisconsin becoming highly prestigious in the US. In fact, 'the University of Wisconsin became a pioneer in the training of persons for public administration' (Lafayette 1962, 253).

Another political economy program that rapidly gained prominence in the US due to the influence of the New School was at Stanford University, which was founded in 1885 and began teaching economics in 1891. In 1892, Amos G. Warner (1861–1900), who completed his PhD at Johns Hopkins under the supervision of Ely, became head of the new Department of Economics and Social Science at Stanford. Edwin A. Ross (1866–1951), another Johns Hopkins alumnus who obtained his PhD under Ely, also joined the department in 1893 and taught political economy. Subsequently, in 1906, Young, another former student of Ely, became head of the Department of Economics and Social Science at Stanford University and remained in that position until 1910. A number of German-trained American political economists also joined the economics department at the school during that period. For example, Edward Dana Durand (1871–1960) joined in 1898 after completing his PhD at Cornell University and then studying under Wagner at Berlin University.

Stanford also hired Frank Albert Fetter (1863–1949), who obtained his PhD from the University of Halle in Germany in 1894.

German influence was also present in the early days of the economics department at Yale University. In fact, in the first decade of the 20th century, out of:

> 116 economists and sociologists at Yale, 59 had studied at some point in Germany, with 20 earning Ph.Ds; of 80 listing their most important muse, 30 indicated the historical school, and 23 the scientific and historical method combined. They noted their influences as Wagner, Schmoller, Conrad, Roscher, and Knies.
>
> (Herbst 1965, 130–131)

In 1872, Walker, who was highly influenced by the GHSE, was invited 'to join the faculty of the Sheffield Scientific School [connected with Yale College] with the title of "Professor of Political Economy"' (Barber 1993, 143). That same year, William Graham Sumner (1840–1910) also started to work at Yale College, which became a university in 1887. In fact, Walker and Sumner took the first chairs of political economy at the school when they arrived in 1872. Sumner was an adherent of the Old School and focused on teaching classical economics. Meanwhile, Walker, who was a leading American economist and statistician, introduced one of the first courses in statistics in the country at the Yale Graduate School (Adelstein 1993, 301).

Despite the fact that Sumner exhibited a hostile attitude toward the New School, a number of its adherents joined the economics faculty at Yale while he was there. For example, Henry Walcott Farnam (1853–1933) began his career as a professor of political economy at Yale in 1880 after having obtained his PhD under the evaluation of Schmoller. He remained there until 1918 and was credited with establishing *The Yale Review* in 1892. Arthur Twining Hadley (1856–1930), who previously studied under Wagner at the University of Berlin, also joined Yale where he became a professor of political science (1886–1891), a professor of political economy (1891–1899), and the first Dean of the Graduate School (1892–1895). He was also 'inaugurated as first lay President of Yale University in 1899,' and held on to that position until 1921.[2] Furthermore, John Christopher Schwab (1865–1916) became a professor of political economy at Yale, where he began editing *The Yale Review* in 1892[3] after obtaining his PhD at the University of Göttingen in 1889. Yale also hired Irving Fisher (1867–1947) as a professor of mathematics and political economy. He remained there for the entirety of his career, during which time he made notable contributions to the development of methodologies of quantitative empirical research, which were highly influenced by the works of the GHSE. Previously, Fisher attended Yale as a student from 1888 to 1891, where he studied under leading political economists Hadley and Farnam. However, he also studied under Sumner. After obtaining his PhD in 1891, Fisher went to study in Berlin during 1893–1894, due in part to a desire to improve his German so that he could read books written by theorists from the GHSE and the Austrian School of Economics.

In 1881, Walker felt pressured to resign from his position as chair of political economy at Yale due to the hostile attitude of Sumner. After his resignation, he became president of MIT, and remained as such until his death in 1897. During that time, he played a major role in the establishment of a political economy department at the school. In 1885, Walker met Davis Rich Dewey (1858–1942) at the founding of the American Economic Association (AEA) and invited him to come work at MIT. Dewey, who previously studied under Ely and Herbert Baxter Adams at Johns Hopkins University, accepted the offer and became a professor of economics and statistics at MIT shortly thereafter. Subsequently, he served as head of the department of economics and statistics at MIT from 1907 to 1933. Walker and Dewey played instrumental roles in the development of the economics department at MIT, as well as efforts to attract the best students to it.

Charles Herbert Levermore (1856–1927), another former student of Ely from Johns Hopkins where he obtained his PhD in 1885, also played an important role in the development of economics at MIT. Like Walker and Dewey, he was committed to the historical approach and ethical economics. In 1900, astronomer Henry Smith Pritchett (1857–1939) became president of MIT shortly after the death of Walker in 1897. He immediately began implementing major changes at the university that reflected the high value he placed on branches of the natural sciences for facilitating the progress and development of society. Pritchett wanted the teaching of social sciences to be connected to the branches of the natural sciences. However, these new changes negatively affected all of the progress that was achieved by Dewey and Walker, who accepted political economy as an ethical and historical science. In the end, Dewey managed to retain the most important ideas and approaches of the New School, thereby saving economics at MIT from Pritchett's efforts to make it into a branch of the natural sciences (Adelstein 1993, 317).

The political economy department of the University of Chicago was founded in 1892. In its early years, very few of its academics were influenced by the GHSE compared to the newly established economics departments at other American institutions. In 1892, Laughlin, who was an adherent of the Old School, was appointed as the inaugural head of the department of Political Economy at the University of Chicago. He brought Thorstein Bunde Veblen (1857–1929) and Robert Franklin Hoxie (1868–1916), two of his former students, with him. The three of them were early contributors to the development of the department. Edward Webster Bemis (1860–1930), an adherent of the New School and a former student of Ely at Johns Hopkins, also became a professor of economics at Chicago in 1892. However, he was concerned about being 'placed in a position of subordination to Laughlin,' given that they belonged to two contrasting schools of economic thought (Barber 1993, 249). His instinct was correct, as their relationship was strained from the outset and only deteriorated over time (Barber 1993, 251). In the 1890s, Laughlin admitted to distancing himself from the 'dangerous doctrines associated with the organizers' of the AEA; however, he eventually ended up joining the organization in 1904 (ibid.: 248). Bemis left the department in 1895. That same year, he stated that 'the University of Chicago was the captive of big business interests and that they, in turn were responsible for Bemis's undoing' (ibid.). In 1893, Edmund Janes James, who was an adherent of the New School, left the University of Pennsylvania in order to work at the University of Chicago.

In 1925, the Department of Political Economy at the University of Chicago officially became the Department of Economics. Eventually, the Chicago School of Economics became the leading school of economic thought and the most prominent advocate of a free market economy. Its economists and their ideological commitment to free market capitalism have influenced not only the academic world but also public opinion and the public policies of American presidents and the leaders of many other countries around the world.

In 1881, the School of Political Science was set up within the Department of Literature, Science, and the Arts at the University of Michigan. In addition to political economy, it also offered classes in subjects like history and international law. Henry Carter Adams, who obtained his PhD at Johns Hopkins University and studied in Berlin and Heidelberg, became the first president of the School of Political Science the same year that it was established. As it turned out, the creation of a School of Political Science was premature, as it came to an end in 1889. However, this was not the end of political economy at the University of Michigan, as courses in the subject continued to be taught. In fact, Henry Carter Adams continued to teach political economy and finance at the school until 1921 (Dickinson 1951). It is widely accepted that 'Adams was a pioneer among American economists in the development of syllabi and texts in various political economy courses' (ibid.: 541).

In 1892, Fred M. Taylor (1855–1932), who studied under Ely and Herbert Baxter Adams at Johns Hopkins, began teaching political economy at the University of Michigan with the support of Henry Carter Adams. Subsequently, in 1901, Edward David Jones, who trained under Ely at the University of Wisconsin before heading off to Germany to study under Engel, Knies, and Conrad, accepted a post at the Department of Political Economy and Sociology of the University of Michigan at the invitation of Henry Carter Adams. In 1909–1910, Political Economy and Sociology were separated into their own independent departments at the university.

German influence had a strong presence in the early days of Cornell University. Charles Kendall Adams (1835–1902), who studied history in Germany, served as president of Cornell University from 1885 until 1892. During that period, he looked to the German education system as a model and supported historical and ethical studies (Ely 1938, 202). In fact, the political economy department employed many adherents of the New School.

For example, Henry Carter Adams taught political economy at Cornell from 1880 until 1887, when he was fired for having socialist views. Additionally, Fetter was hired at Cornell after obtaining his PhD from the University of Halle in Germany in 1894. Jeremiah Whipple Jenks (1856–1929) also held a professorship at Cornell University after graduating from the University of Michigan in 1878 and then obtaining his PhD from the University of Halle under Conrad in 1885. Another adherent of the New School, who was also a former student of Ely, that ended up working as a professor in the economics department of Cornell was Young. Furthermore, Laughlin taught political economy at Cornell from 1890 to 1892, while Ross, who also previously studied under Ely, joined the faculty in 1892. In 1895, Cornell hired Bullock, another past student of Ely. Adams, Fetter, Jenks, and Bullock all promoted historical ethical economics in their teachings and publications.

The Wharton School of Finance and Economy, which was established at the University of Pennsylvania in 1881, was also significantly influenced by the GHSE. That same year, Albert Sidney Bolles (1846–1939), who was inspired by the German education system and historical economics, joined the department to teach business classes. However, it was ultimately James, who arrived two years later in 1883, that played a major role in the development of the political economy department, based on the ideas and principles of the GHSE.

His ultimate goal was to bring an advanced political economy education program to the Wharton School of Finance and Economy that was on par with those headed by the GHSE. Accordingly, he introduced the first research seminary at the University of Pennsylvania in 1885, which was based on those of the GHSE. Under his influence, 'its corps of instructors was largely increased, the subjects of instruction multiplied, and its curriculum extended from two years to four, changes which were followed by a large increase in the number of students' (Annals of the American Academy of Political and Social Science 1896, 79). His hard work also meant that 'statistics, journalism, sociology, transportation, municipal government, jurisprudence, and politics was added to the work in history, economics, and finance' (ibid.). Furthermore, James encouraged his students to improve their knowledge and skills by going abroad to study at German universities. Thanks to the efforts of James, 'the Wharton School of Finance and Economy became not only a successful department for higher commercial education, but also one of the leading centres for the study of economics and politics in the United States' (ibid.).

James brought Simon Nelson Patten (1852–1922) to the University of Pennsylvania in 1888. Patten, who obtained his PhD in political economy under Conrad at the University of Halle in 1877, remained at the University of Pennsylvania until his retirement in 1917. During that time, he played a major role in the development and improvement of political economy at the school. Ely (1936, 159) stated that while Patten was 'something of a rough diamond in his early days, he did such remarkable work both as teacher and writer' at the University of Pennsylvania. In fact, Patten was 'the originator of the idea of schools of experimental economics and he founded and lived with the Wharton School' (Tugwell 1923, 186). Ultimately, he significantly contributed to enhancing the reputation of the Wharton School in the US. Roland Post Falkner (1866–1940), who was a German-trained political economist, also joined the faculty of the University of Pennsylvania in 1888 to teach accounting and statistics after having previously graduated from the Wharton School of Finance and Economy and then going abroad to study political economy in Berlin, Leipzig, and Halle. Falkner was able to utilize the advanced training he received from Conrad at Halle to significantly influence the development of statistics at the University of Pennsylvania and in the US in general. In fact, he was credited with being 'the first man to hold a leading American university post devoted exclusively to statistics, at the Wharton School of the University of Pennsylvania' (Dorfman 1955, 23). Henry Rogers Seager (1870–1930) also taught political economy at the Wharton School of the University of Pennsylvania from 1894 to 1902 after studying at Johns Hopkins University, going abroad to Halle, Berlin, and Vienna, and finally completing his PhD at the University of Pennsylvania under Patten in 1894. In 1902, he left Pennsylvania in order to work at Columbia University.

John William Burgess (1844–1931) played an instrumental role in shaping the economics department at Columbia University. In 1871, he went to Europe to study 'history and public law at Göttingen, Leipzig, and Berlin' under theorists of the GHSE (Columbia Law Times 1893, 123). After completing his education, he worked at Columbia from 1876 to 1912, during which time he founded the *Political Science Quarterly* in 1886. He also played a significant role in establishing the Faculty of Political Science in 1880, which was intended to train students for the public service. The creation of this faculty was primarily 'responsible for Columbia's transition from a college to a university' in 1896.[4] Burgess was highly influenced by the style and method of education he witnessed during his time at German universities. As such, he basically implemented those 'same methods of instruction' at Columbia University (Columbia Law Times 1893, 124). In the end, the changes that Burgess instituted at the School of Political Science at Columbia University set 'an example which has since been followed by a considerable number of American colleges' (ibid.).

Richmond Mayo-Smith (1854–1901) studied in Berlin from 1875 to 1877 and then in Heidelberg in 1878. In 1877, he was offered the Chair of the Economics and Statistics in the Faculty of Political Science at Columbia College, which was about to be established, on the condition that he completed his graduate studies in Germany. After he joined Columbia, he ended up having a significant influence on the way statistics was taught and applied to the social sciences in the US. In fact, he was credited with teaching the first course on statistics at an American university in 1880, which he continued to do until his death in 1901 (Herbst 1965, 140).

After graduating from Columbia College in 1879, Edwin Robert Anderson Seligman (1861–1939) went on to study at universities in Berlin, Paris, and Heidelberg until 1882. Subsequently, he went back to Columbia to obtain his PhD. After graduating in 1885, he remained at Columbia University, where he taught political economy from 1891 to 1931. Seligman's views were highly influenced by the theorists of the GHSE, as well as Ely and Herbert Baxter Adams. In fact, Seligman's dedication to improving the way political economy was taught along with his work as editor of the *Political Science Quarterly* were key factors in the establishment of the Department of Economics at Columbia University. In 1895, Clark joined Seligman at Columbia, and the two of them played important roles in the development of its economics department.

In 1902, Henry Ludwell Moore was hired as a professor of political economy at Columbia University, where he taught the elementary principles of statistics. Previously, in 1898, Vladimir G. Simkhovitch (1874–1959) became a professor of economic history at the school after studying at Halle where he attended the lectures of Wagner. He was particularly influenced by Wagner's socialist ideas and actually became known as a socialist economist (Simkhovitch 1938). Edward Thomas Devine (1867–1948) also joined the faculty at Columbia University after completing his PhD in economics under Patten at the University of Pennsylvania in 1889 and then studying for one year in Germany. The combined efforts of Moore, Seager, Devine, and Seligman helped the economics department at Columbia University achieve a leading role in the US until the end of WWI. Their teachings and publications focused on historical ethical economics and multidisciplinary studies, thereby reflecting the influence of the GHSE.

David Kinley (1861–1944), who was significantly influenced by Ely's lectures and views at both Johns Hopkins and Wisconsin, arrived at the University of Illinois in 1893 to start working at its newly established department of economics. In 1893–1894, it offered seminars and courses on 'the principles of economics, public finance, state and local taxation in the United States, money, sociology,' and 'social pathology' (Kinley 1949, 29). The following academic year, courses on 'practical economic problems, financial history of the United States, railroad problems, statistics, and social problems' were added (ibid.). Additionally, Ernest Ludlow Bogart (1870–1958), who obtained his PhD at Halle, joined the University of Illinois 'in the fall of 1909 as Associate Professor of Economics' at the recommendation of Kinley.[5] Bogart's text 'Economic History of the United States,' published in 1907, was adopted by:

> Kinley prior to his joining the faculty at the university: it was the second text in American Economic History ever to be written, and would bring Dr. Bogart the immediate distinction of being one of the top Economic Historians in the country.[6]

During his career, Kinley consistently made efforts to improve the department of economics of the University of Illinois based on the German model.

Before German influence took hold, there was not 'much teaching' of political economy going on at American universities and colleges (Patten 1895, 131). However, returning German-trained American political economists significantly improved the quality of the education and teaching of political economy being offered at American institutions by implementing changes based on the German model. They became leaders in their field, and as such, contributed to the progress of their discipline by establishing the new foundation of economics in the US. In doing so, they founded successful economics departments at a variety of colleges and universities across the US during the 1880s and 1890s. Their efforts also resulted in a multiplication in the number chairs available at political economy departments in colleges and universities throughout the country. In 1880, only three scholars 'in the 28 leading schools "devoted most of their time to political economy" by 1890 there were 20 chairs in the subject, and 51 by 1900' (Coats 1985, 1700). In fact, each university had 'either an independent chair of Political Economy or a combined chair of economics and history, or some other subject' by 1890 (Devine 1894, 88). Then, in early 20th century, 'institutions like Columbia, Harvard, Yale, Chicago, and Wisconsin' had 'from six to ten professors of economics and social science, together with a corps of lecturers, instructors, and tutors' (Seligman 1911, 388). Additionally, all of the reforms and changes that were implemented resulted 'in the six or eight leading American institutions the number of hours of instruction given per week to economics has increased on the average six or seven fold since 1876' (Dunbar 1904, 54). The expansion and improvement of political economy departments at American universities, which contributed to better teaching and an increase in high-quality academic research, would not have been possible without the influence of the GHSE.

Teaching in the Newly Established Political Economy Departments of American Universities

The GHSE not only inspired the establishment of institutions of higher education in the US, it also influenced the content and methodology of teaching and practicing political economy across the country. Before German influence took hold, Americans believed that the responsibility of teachers at universities was 'putting into the minds of their students a certain number of text-books' (*Illinois School Journal* January 1882, 13). They were not 'expected to make new discoveries' or contribute to the progress of knowledge (ibid.: 14). Essentially, students could 'never acquire more than a text-book knowledge,' because they were not given a 'chance to develop' their capacities, knowledge, and skills to the fullest extent possible (ibid.: 13). This was the case at every American college and university, and German-trained Americans were very unhappy with this state of affairs. To remedy this situation, they wanted make the newly established political economy departments into replicas of the ones they experienced in Germany. This involved adopting many of the features that characterized an education in political economy under the leadership of the GHSE, including similar courses, language requirements, seminary methods, and adequate library resources, all of which would contribute to the advancement of knowledge and academic research.

Courses and Language Requirements at Newly Established Economics Departments

German-trained American political economists were particularly impressed with the freedom and 'all possible assistance' that was 'given to those who aim to do original work' in Germany, despite the fact that the universities were state institutions (James 1882, 262). They highly valued the freedom that prevailed at the political economy departments of German universities, where students had 'the greatest choice in the selection' of their studies (Farnam 1887, 67). Members of the New School found this type of freedom, which was an integral part of higher education in Germany, to not only be 'novel but very refreshing and delightful' (Ely 1910, 77). They believed that this level of academic freedom helped German universities gain international prominence and success, because it encouraged creativity and motivated the publication of original work. To the contrary, the lack of academic freedom available at US institutions of higher learning prevented American political economists from achieving progress until around the 1870s. Ultimately, followers of the New School thought that academic freedom would help students develop an interest in scholarly duties of their 'own free will, uncoerced by regulations or supervision' (Herbst 1965, 21).

In supporting academic freedom, disciples of the New School believed that it was important to offer students a variety of courses to choose from, so that they could select the ones that would best serve their needs depending on their plans for the future. Like theorists of the GHSE, Walker (1889) advocated for a multidisciplinary education to be offered in the political economy departments of American universities. Mayo-Smith (1899, 2) agreed, as he maintained that 'almost all social phenomena have an economic interest.' Additionally, James was of the view that providing a greater diversity in the courses being offered would allow for a higher degree of specialization, which would entice more students to obtain a university degree in political economy. In turn, he believed that having more highly specialized university graduates would stimulate advances and progress in American society as a whole. Meanwhile, Patten (1895, 120) described history and sociology as 'cousins' of economics, while geography and physics were its 'half-brothers.' He supported the notion of having students train in these different disciplines as early as high school in order to facilitate the 'conscious study of the development of economic ideas' (ibid.). Therefore, the students enrolled in the newly established economics departments of many American universities were required to understand the relationships that political economy had with other disciplines, including political science, jurisprudence, history, philosophy, anthropology, religion, and ethics (Ely 1889). Additionally, disciples of the New School wanted to teach specialized political economy courses similar to those offered at German universities, which included a 'series of lectures on the following subjects: History of Political Economy, Theoretical Political Economy, Practical Political Economy (the discussion of the economic problems of modern society), Science of Finance, Statistics, Police Supervision,' Economic Institutions, and Administration (James 1882, 261). Adherents of the New School, 'whether their writings tend to be deductive or inductive,' also taught their students to use the 'look and see' method that was favored by the GHSE (Ely 1936, 149). They also unanimously supported the idea of relativity, which was an important feature of the GHSE when it came to explaining different economic policies over time.

Before German influence became widespread, little economic history was taught in the US. However, adherents of the New School expected their students to demonstrate a profound knowledge of the history of political economy. As such, they adopted some of the courses that were being offered in Germany on the history of economics and economic thought at their own institutions. This provided American students at newly established political economy departments with the opportunity to study subjects like Ancient and mediaeval commerce, crusades and the renaissance, and colonial policy, among others. For instance, Seligman focused on teaching the history of economics and finance at Columbia University. In those courses, he taught the works and ideas of a wide range of theorists and thinkers, including Plato, Aristotle, Xenophon, Cato, Seneca, Cicero, Aquinas, Petty, Locke, Quesnay, Gournay, Turgot, Mirabeau, Smith, Tucker, Hume, Cantillon, Stewart, Malthus, Ricardo, Jones, Mill, Say, Sismondi, Cournot, Bastiat, Herrmann, List, Roscher, Knies, Hildebrandt, Rogers, Jevons, Leslie, Toynbee, Marshall, Wagner, Schmoller, Held, Brentano, Cohn, Schäffle, Menger, Böhm-Bawerk, Wieser, Walras, George, Walker, Clark, Patten, and Adams (Columbia University 1905–1907, 27). Some of the notable books that his students were expected to familiarize themselves with included Wagner's *Politische Oekonomie* (1876), Roscher's *Nationaloekonomik des Ackerbaues* (1867) and *Nationaloekonomik des Handels* (1881), and Ernst Engel's *Das Zeitalter des Dampfes in technisch-statistischer Beleuchtung* (1881).

Even though many of the original contributors to the development of political economy at the University of Chicago were not really adherents of the New School, courses on history of economics were still being offered in the early years of the department. Some of these courses included the Origin and Development of the Historical School and the History of Political Economy in Germany, the History of the Development of Economic Thought, the History of Socialistic Theories, and Recent German Systematic Writers such as Wagner, Cohn, Schmoller, Schäffle, and Menger (University of Chicago Press 1892). Of note, the course on the Origin and Development of the Historical School and History of Political Economy in Germany focused on studying the character of political economy and its relationships with ethics, political science, and sociology. It involved having students study the methodologies of Mill, Menger, Wagner, and Schmoller, among others, with 'special attention being devoted to Knies, *Die Politische Oekonomie vom Geschichtlichen Standpunkte*' (ibid.: 10). Meanwhile, the course on German Economic Thinking concentrated on 'the earlier writers, Rau, von Thünen, and Hermann' (ibid.). Students taking this course had to work closely with Wagner's *Volkswirthschaftslehre*, Schmoller's *Ueber einige Grundfragen des Rechts und der Volkswirthschaft*, Schäffle's *Bau und Leben des socialen Körpers*, and Menger's *Grundsätze der Volkswirthschaftslehre.* Furthermore, the course on Recent German Systematic Writers aimed to help students 'appreciate the spirit, quality, and tendency of German economic thinking' and broaden their 'view of fundamental economic ideas' (ibid.: 12).

Between 1892 and 1901, Ashley taught classes on the History of Economics at Harvard University, which always had a large number of students enrolled in them. These courses covered a wide range of topics, including:

> the economic theories of Plato and Aristotle; the economic ideas underlying Roman law; the mediaeval church and the canonist doctrine; mercantilism in its diverse forms; "political arithmetic;" the origin of the belief in natural rights and its influence on economic thought; the physiocratic doctrine; the work and influence of Adam Smith; the doctrine of population as presented by Malthus; Say and the French school; and the beginnings of academic instruction in economics.
>
> (Harvard University 1897–98, 33)

Ashley also gave lectures on the Middle Ages to Mediaeval Economic History of Europe, conducted seminaries on Roscher, and taught selected works of Wagner and Schmoller (ibid.: 31, 34). Additionally, Laughlin (1885, 9–11) taught classes at Harvard University that required students to study some of the prominent books written by political economists since the 18th century, including Mill, Roscher, Smith, and Ricardo.

In its early years, the University of Stanford offered many courses covering different periods of the history of economics. To be more precise, some of those courses included 'A History of Tariff Legislation in the United States,' 'A History of Agriculture and Prices,' 'History of Economic Theories,' 'A History of Industry, including Trades Unions, Guilds, Factory Systems, Strikes, Arbitration, Labor Organizations, etc.' (Leland Stanford Junior University 1894, 59).

Up until the early decades of the 20th century, the newly established economics departments at Johns Hopkins, Wisconsin, Harvard, Columbia, and other prominent universities offered courses on socialism, communism, the socialist movement in Europe, the history of modern socialism, and the labor movement in Europe. For example, the Communism and Socialism courses offered at Harvard University during 1892–1893 focused on French and German socialism, as well as Ely's views on socialism. At Columbia

University, Clark taught a course that criticized scientific socialism, which was comparable to Wagner's class on the critique of socialism being offered in Berlin (Columbia University Bulletin 1897, 68). Clark also taught 'Communistic and Socialistic Theories,' where students studied 'the works of St. Simon, Fourier, Proudhon, Owen, and Lassalle' as well as 'Marx's treatise on capital' (Columbia University 1905–1907, 35). In this course, students also had to be familiar with ancient labor movements, mediaeval and early modern labor movements, economic causes of the French Revolution, the life and teachings of Saint-Simon, France's social and economic situation under Louis XVIII and Charles X, etc.

Newly established political economy departments in the US also offered classes on the social and economic problems of the time. For instance, Devine taught a course called Poverty and Dependence in the Social Economy at Columbia University, which focused on improving the social and economic conditions of the masses. Basically, this class emphasized the importance of 'Charity organization; social settlements; housing reform; the elimination of disease; the restriction of child labor; and the prevention of overcrowding, and especially the congestion of population in the tenement-house districts of the great cities' (Columbia University 1905–1907, 32).

The criteria for obtaining a PhD at the newly established economics departments in the US were comparable to those required by German universities. Up until the first few decades of the 20th century, the general examination for a PhD at American universities typically required students to demonstrate a robust understanding of the works of Ancient Greek philosophers and the theories, policies, and methods of the GHSE. They also had to master the following subjects: Economic Theory, Economic History, Public Finance, International Trade and Tariff Policy, History of Political Theory, Money, Banking, Crises, the Economics of Corporations, the Economic History of the 19th century, and the History of Modern Socialism.

Proficiency in foreign languages also became a criterion for obtaining a PhD in political economy at American universities. This is because German-trained Americans were very impressed by the fact that political economy students in Germany were required to have some knowledge of Latin and 'modern languages as a prerequisite to the degree of Ph.D.' (James 1888, 614). At the universities of Berlin, Bonn, Göttingen, and Königsberg, it was prescribed that 'if the thesis relates to topics connected with classical and Oriental philology and antiquities or ancient history and philosophy it must be written in Latin' (ibid.: 615). For all other topics, the faculty could 'accept a thesis in German,' but the candidate may still 'be required at the public examination to show that he can read and translate a passage assigned him from some Roman classic' (ibid.). When foreign students underwent examinations in German universities, in addition to proving their ability to study in German, it was also possible for them to be made to demonstrate a capability to translate from Greek or Latin as a condition for obtaining their degrees (ibid.: 614). In fact, improving their proficiency in the German language was one of the main reasons why many foreign students and academics of political economy went to Germany during the dominance of the GHSE. They wanted to be able to comprehend many of the important books, articles, and papers that were being published in German. Since German was the language of the international scientific community, prominent academics of the time often published their research in German in order to gain international recognition. German was also usually the main language used at international conferences and congresses along with French and English to some extent (Ruggles 1863).

Laughlin (1912, 172) was critical of the fact that only a few of the students that obtained undergrad degrees from the political economy departments of American universities possessed the ability to read in French and German. Meanwhile, Ely (1889, 69) argued that in order to have 'the advanced investigation, a knowledge of foreign languages, especially of German, is indispensable' at American institutions of higher learning. Given the importance of the German language in the international scientific community, German-trained American political economists believed that American universities should be staffed with professors and teachers that were fluent or proficient in German, as well as French. They also wanted American economics students to possess a working knowledge of German, because they were expected to read and comprehend the original works of German political economists. Since many of the books written by theorists of the GHSE were not translated into English, Ely (1889) advised economic students to learn German so that they could read and comprehend important texts like Roscher's *System der Volkswirthschaft*, Wagner's *Lehrbuch der politischen Oekonomie*, Knies's *Die politische Oekonomie vom geschichtlichen Standbuhkte* and *Geld und Credit*, Schmoller's *Ueber einige Grundfragen des Rechts und der Volkswirthschaft*, and Schönberg's *Handbuch der politischen Oekonomie*. Eventually, efforts on the part of the disciples of the New School led to German becoming the 'second language' that was 'required by all major American institutions granting the Ph.D. in economics,' at least until the outbreak of WWII (Senn 1989, 263). During that period, it was common practice for students to be asked to translate, interpret, or explain quotations attributed to German economists of the 19th century that were written entirely in German.

Following the decay of the GHSE, learning German was no longer necessary in the discipline of economics in the US. This turned out to be a significant problem when it came to spreading the work and ideas of the GHSE, because the books and articles written by its theorists were rarely translated into English with a few exceptions, because German was the language of the academic world for most of the 19th century. In fact, in the early decades of the 20th century, 'only three articles, a booklet on mercantilism,' and 'a condensed' version of Schmoller's Grundriss were 'translated into English' (Peukert 2001, 71). With the decline of the GHSE, the German language all but disappeared from the curricula of American universities and colleges as a requirement for obtaining a PhD. Since 1920, the 'only new language that American economists' had to learn aside from English was mathematics (Balabkins 1988, 111). This 'deplorable linguistic deficiency among American economists today deprives them of the ability to learn from other economists' who published in different languages (ibid.: 107).

The Rise of Statistics in Political Economy

It is often accepted that Johann Heinrich Gottlob Justi (1717–1771), who was the most important contributor to cameralism and 'the first theoretician of the administrative census' in Germany, played a pioneering role in the application of statistics to economics (Chaloupek 2009, 151). However, the word statistics was first coined by 'Gottfried Achenwal, professor of law and politics at Göttingen, in his work entitled "*Staatsverfassung der heutigen vornehmsten Europaischen Reiche und Völker,*" of which the first edition bears date 12th April, 1749' (Guy 1865, 478). He specifically used the term to identify those disciplines that focused on 'the extent, limits, subdivisions, and natural relations of States, their advantages, their history, and their origin' (Guy 1865, 479). In the 19th century, the main contributions to advances in statistics in Germany occurred at statistical bureaus. In 1805, the Statistical Bureau of Prussia (Prussian Statistical Bureau) (*Preußischen Königlichen Statistischen Büros*, 1805–1934) was opened in Berlin. Then, in 1862, the statistical office of Berlin was established (*Statistisches Bureau der Stadt Berlin*).[7] Two years later, in 1864, Bruno Hildebrand founded the Thuringian Statistical Office in Jena. Subsequently, the statistical bureau of the German Empire (*Kaiserliches Statistisches Amt*) was created in 1872. Additionally, the State Sciences Society (*Staatswissenschaftliche Gesellschaft*) was founded by Schmoller, who 'collected archival materials and wrote statistical and economic monographs for almost twenty-five years of his academic career, from 1864 to 1887' (Balabkins 1988, 54). In 1888, a government-funded statistical organization called *The Archiv fur soziale Gesetzgebung und Statistik* was established by Ernst Engel (1821–1896), 'one of the most famous economists of Europe,' who acquired much notoriety for creating the Engel Curve (Engel's Law) (Dorfman 1955, 18). These various statistical bureaus were closely connected with each other and often exchanged views and ideas. They also organized seminars to provide students with training in statistics, while their members travelled internationally in order to acquire further training and advance their knowledge.

German statistical bureaus ended up publishing a large 'amount of original work' (Adams 1884, 80). These publications were of 'international significance, by reasons of the lessons which they teach' (ibid.). Anyone interested in a comparative analysis of:

> the subject of national or municipal finance; the relations of church and school; sanitation; insurance; trade and commerce; industries; population; land and climate; cities; development of the science of statistics; statistical congresses; markets; fairs; genealogies of royal families; tables of mortality; education; administration, etc.
>
> was 'richly rewarded by consulting the published works' of statistical bureaus.
>
> (ibid.)

Engel was widely regarded as 'the greatest of living statisticians' and the intellectual father of statistical empiricism at the GHSE (Ely 1883, 233). From 1860 to 1882, he served as director of the Statistical Bureau of Prussia, which was recognized as the central authority on statistics in the Prussian territories (Meitzen 1889, 57). Under his direction, the Statistical Bureau of Prussia organized seminars focusing on original research. In his own seminary, Engel was clearly committed to the statistical training of 'university graduates who qualified for admission to the higher branches of the civil service' (Dorfman 1955, 18). Basically, 'the government offices of the statistical bureau' became 'laboratories of political science' (Adams 1884, 80). Like many adherents of the GHSE, Engel also played an important role in the development of empirical investigation into social and economic problems for the purpose of designing effective policies and reforms.

Among theorists of the GHSE, Knies was 'one of the earliest advocates of the development of statistics,' and many American political economists were highly influenced by his views and teachings (Ely 1936, 145). Meanwhile, Wagner, who applied 'the statistical method to banking problems,' argued that 'statistics were to be applied' to all social and natural phenomena so as to determine causal relationships (Haney 1915, 482, Herbst 1965, 138). According to him, large-scale data could be used to explain different aspects of economic variables or economic phenomena, which could help gain an understanding of the development of institutions of society.

German students had the advantage of studying at universities and training at statistical bureaus where they could hone the skills needed for 'this profession; in which the civil service' gave 'place and rank, and recognition and promotion' to those who excelled as statisticians (Walker 1899, 141). Meanwhile, many of the Americans studying in Germany benefited from taking statistical seminars conducted by Engel, Conrad, Knies, Schmoller, and Wagner (James 1882, 262). These American students ended up supporting the use statistics in order to maintain scientific accuracy. Moreover, they came to regard statistics as a tool for observing regularities and irregularities and discovering causal relationships, which could be helpful in designing social and economic reforms and policies (Mayo-Smith 1899). In fact, Mayo-Smith (1888, 386) stated that statistics was 'a valuable auxiliary in the work of depicting the evolution of economic institutions, or of describing the present economic condition of the world.' He also pointed out that in 'inductive science, the importance of the statistical method becomes still greater' (ibid. 387). Mayo-Smith further argued that, 'with the extension of statistical inquiry and the refinements in statistical method, statistics promise to be of constantly increasing value' (ibid.).

Ely, who was a member of the statistical bureau of Prussia and attended the statistics lectures of Engel and Wagner at Berlin University, advocated for statistics to be taught at the newly established political economy departments of American universities. This position was strongly supported by a number of members of the New School, including Dewey (1889, 364) who argued that by studying statistics, 'the student will undoubtedly gain a far more lasting knowledge of the subject matter.' In fact, he went so far as to suggest that 'the study of Statistics should be made the very backbone' of economic education (ibid.: 365). Similarly, Farnam (1913, 32) was highly supportive of the use of statistics, stating that the ideal of economists must be 'to express in numerical form.' Meanwhile, Patten (1891, 100) insisted that since political economy was an inductive and historical science, it needed to focus on statistics to the fullest extent possible instead of mathematical economics.

Even though adherents of the New School accepted statistics as a highly useful tool for political economy, the vast majority of American economists neglected its role before this school of thought attained its dominant position in the discipline of economics (Walker 1899, 290). In fact, prior to the influence of the GHSE, Americans never did 'anything as a nation, and little in their individual capacity, to promote the cultivation of statistics' (ibid.: 149). In the 1860s, the Congress of the US had not yet 'established a distinct Bureau of Statistics,' even though statistics were 'the very eyes of the statesman, enabling him to survey and scan with clear but comprehensive vision, the whole structure and economy of the body politic' (Ruggles 1863, 8). At that time, it was almost impossible to fathom that in the future, 'America may at least approach in scientific accuracy and philosophical arrangement, the more mature and perfect performances of the statisticians of Europe' (ibid.: 14).

Walker played a major role in the development and use of statistics in the US, particularly 'the extension and improvement of the statistical service' of the American government (Falkner 1897, 3). In fact, he was credited with teaching one of America's first courses in statistics at the Yale Graduate School (Adelstein 1993, 301). He also published the *Statistical Atlas* in 1870, which earned him the respect of many statisticians and scholars of his time. Furthermore, he worked for the American census, where his goal was 'not only to improve the quality of the census, but to make it a complete record of the social and economic condition of the people' (Falkner 1897, 3). Walker believed that statistics was 'a method' that historians, sociologists, and political economists could use to 'confidently and surely to reduce from thousands of pages closely packed with figures some hitherto unsuspected law of human life or conduct' (Herbst 1965, 140).

Walker (1899, 150) pointed out that unlike in Germany where working in statistical offices usually required a PhD, the US did not employ trained statisticians, and 'the work was in the hands of those who necessarily were ignorant of the elementary principles attending the collection and compilation of statistics and the administration of statistical service.' He further explained that the absence of formal training in statics meant that Americans lacked 'elementary knowledge of the subject which was necessary to save them from making great errors of judgment, and sometimes monstrous errors in their conclusions' (ibid.). He pointed out that while the American government spent 'tens of millions upon the collection, compilation, and publication of statistics,' it never invested significantly 'in training and preparing the men who should conduct the statistical service of the country' (ibid.: 149). Walker (1899, 150) stressed that it was illogical for the American government to spend 'enormous sums' for statistics, as well as 'statistical service in other departments of the government,' while at the same time doing nothing to facilitate the formation of proficient statisticians. This lack of training was responsible for Americans suffering 'an enormous loss of resources' and 'great impairment of the validity, accuracy, and comparability' of their statistics at the national, state, and municipal levels relative to European countries (ibid.: 150–151). Walker (1899, 151) also underscored that American 'colleges and universities' did not contribute to rectifying this situation by training statisticians. Mayo-Smith (1888, 413) concurred, claiming that one 'cannot have scientific statistical results unless' one employs 'scientifically trained statisticians.'

During their education and training in Germany, American students were very impressed with the statistical techniques that were developed by the Germans. In fact, the influence of the GHSE was a key factor that led American scholars to start paying serious attention to the field of statistics, which had been largely neglected in the US up to that point. In the 1880s, German-trained Americans pushed for statistics to be taught at all colleges and universities, because they believed that it was a very useful tool that would enable political economists to formulate 'correct economic policy' and reforms (Mayo-Smith 1888, 385). After returning home from Germany in 1879, 'Henry Carter Adams became the first statistician of the Interstate Commerce Commission and devised its pivotal accounting system which served as a model for the regulation of public utilities here and throughout the world' (Dorfman 1955, 23). The following year, in 1880, Columbia University offered the first course on statistics at an American university, which was conducted by Mayo-Smith, who continued to teach the subject until his death in 1901. During that time, his statistics courses were very well received by students at Columbia. Furthermore, his books in statistics, including *Science of Statistics* (1895), *Statistics and Sociology* (1895), and *Statistics and Economics* (1899), were very influential on the development and application of statistics in the social sciences at American universities.[8] Additionally, the introduction of Ripley's course on statistics at Harvard University in the 1880s attracted a great deal of interest, which was very promising 'for the future of economic studies in Harvard' (Carver 1902, 248). Then, in 1891, Falkner was appointed as an associate professor of statistics 'at the Wharton School of the University of Pennsylvania,' which meant he was 'the first man to hold a leading American university post devoted exclusively to statistics' (Dorfman 1955, 23).

In addition to the newly established political economy departments at many American universities, the American Statistical Association (ASA) also played a major role in introducing statistical studies at colleges and universities across the country (Walker 1899, 301). This organization aimed to promote 'the discussion of statistical methods, statistical results, and statistical principles among the members' (Walker 1899, 152, 154). It also prepared students for employment in the provision of statistical services by the government. Despite its crucial role, the ASA never had 'any funds. Now and then the treasurer sent bills to members for their small fees toward the expenses of a hall or of a meeting' (ibid.:152).

Eventually, Americans became devoted to statistical research and investigation to an 'exceptionally high degree,' with national and state statistical bureaus 'opening in every direction' (Walker 1899, 145). By the end of the 19th century, there was no country where 'the work of the statistician' was 'held in greater honor' and respect than in the US (ibid.: 141). In early 20th century, 'the forecasting service' became highly influential in the US and:

> its methods and techniques were copied and admired by the London and Cambridge Economic Service, the Institute of Statistics at the University of Paris, *the Institut für Konjunkturforschung* in Berlin, and in similar organizations in Rome, Vienna, Padua, and elsewhere.
>
> (Mason and Lamont 1982, 414)

Although the empirical and statistical methods of the GHSE became important parts of mainstream economics in the 20th and 21st centuries, the original contributions of this school of thought to the application of statistics within the discipline of economics have been largely forgotten.

The Establishment of PhD Programs based on the German Model

German-trained American political economists were highly involved in setting up graduate programs at some of the most prestigious universities across the US. After returning from Germany, they proceeded to engage in a debate to determine the precise criteria that should be met in order to be awarded a PhD in their discipline. It was believed that this debate would benefit significantly from examining 'the condition of things in Germany,' given that 'the degree of Doctor of Philosophy is pre-eminently a German degree' (James 1888, 611). At German universities, a PhD was the highest academic degree that could be attained. Acquiring one required an advanced education, scientific training, creativity, and the writing and defense of an original thesis. Furthermore, having a PhD was not only a 'requirement for university teaching' in Germany, it was also 'important for entry into some parts of state administration' (Tribe 2002, 4). James (1888, 611) explained that prior to German influence, a PhD in the US was regarded to a large:

> extent as an honorary degree, and given away so lavishly to men of high station and low station, and, indeed, of no station at all, that those who hold it on examination are almost ashamed of it, and finally, in order

> to defend themselves, have adopted the expedient so long in vogue in England of writing after their degrees the name of the university from which it is taken.

Many of the economics graduate programs that were established at American institutions toward the end of the 19th century adopted the German model. At that time, earning a PhD at a typical American institution required students to take courses for three years, write and defend a thesis, pass an oral exam, and master a foreign language (e.g., French, German, or Latin). In the US, the first PhD in political economy was awarded at Harvard in 1875, while 'Yale awarded the second in 1877' and 'Johns Hopkins awarded the third' in 1878 (Parrish 1967, 7). Subsequently, a total of 'five institutions awarded' 11 PhD degrees in political economy in the 1880s, while another 'twelve institutions awarded 95 degrees' in the 1890s (ibid.: 11). These early PhD degrees were experimental, in a sense. In hindsight, it appears that they may have been premature, as evidenced by the fact that:

> after awarding its first Ph.D. in political economy in 1875, Harvard did not award another for 20 years. After its first degree, Yale did not award another for seven years. The Johns Hopkins did not award a second political economy Ph.D. until after a lapse of ten years.
>
> (ibid.: 7–8)

Nevertheless, the establishment of a PhD degree played an important role in fortifying and justifying 'the new professorships in political economy' in the US (ibid.: 8).

In 1897, a comparison of political economy programs at German and American universities revealed that the requirements for acquiring a PhD were most stringent at the University of Berlin relative to all other universities in both countries (Columbia University Bulletin 1897, 67). At the same time, 'the requirements for the degree of PhD' were found to be 'higher in several American institutions than in the average German university' (ibid.). In fact, it was argued that 'the progress of American universities' was so rapid at the end of the 19th century while the entrance requirements had 'so largely increased, that the bachelor's degree' was 'actually approaching the German doctorate in essential worth' (ibid.). The possibility of obtaining a quality PhD at an American institution of higher learning actually slowed the number of students leaving the country to study political economy in Germany. However, it was really the beginning of WWI that completely dissuaded American economics students from traveling to Germany in search of a higher education.

The Introduction of the German Seminary Method at American Political Economy Departments

Before coming under German influence, education at American universities was based on 'the old-fashioned system of daily examinations, in which the students' were 'interrogated like witnesses,' and their learning experience was very 'mechanical' (Farnam 1887, 71). Unfortunately, this kind of education system was damaging to 'the interest of the student, no less than to kill originality and suggestiveness on the part of the teacher' (ibid.). Accordingly, German-trained Americans were very impressed with the seminaries (*Seminarium*) they experienced in Germany, which were a major part of the system of higher education in that country that were credited with motivating creative and original scientific research (Adams 1884, 64).

Initially, 'the seminary was a nursery of theology and a training-school for seminary priests' (ibid.). The original mediaeval seminaries were supposed to 'impart to the students a comprehensive knowledge of particular topics' and 'teach them methods of special work' (Seligman 1912, 153). As it turns out, the German seminaries of the 19th century were 'only modifications' of their mediaeval predecessors (Adams 1889, 142). In other words, the seminaries at German universities were outcomes of 'the development of the old scholastic method of advancing philosophical inquiry by the defense of original theses' (Adams 1884, 64). The first seminary in Germany was founded at 'Goettingen in 1733, by Gesner the famous Latinist,' and it served as 'the model for all later ones' (ibid.). In the 1830s, German historian Leopold von Ranke (1795–1886) and a number of other scholars played key roles in spreading the concept of historical seminary training through 'all the universities in Germany' (ibid.: 65).

Seminaries became one of the most important aspects of the scientific activity that professors and students of the GHSE engaged in (St. Marc 1892, 101). To be accepted into a German seminary, students had to be earnest about their studies, as 'idlers or dilettantes' were not admitted (*Illinois School Journal*. March 1882, 14). Since seminaries were 'gratuitous and private, the professors' had 'the right to refuse admittance to any they choose' (ibid.). Students were also 'subject to expulsion by the board of control for failure to discharge any obligations, for inadequate work, or for misuse of the library' (Adams 1884, 69).

In practice, seminaries were essentially supplements to lectures, where experienced masters would teach their 'young apprentices the deft use of the tools of the trade' (Adams 1884, 70). The real purpose of the seminar was to 'teach the student how to handle his material and by interpretation or discovery to make a contribution to the store of existing knowledge' (Seligman 1912, 157). It also encouraged the free expression of ideas, creativity, critical thinking, and the spirit of scientific independence. Basically, seminaries stimulated the appetites of students when it came to performing original work and developing their skills in academic research (ibid.). Seminaries also allowed professors to advance their specializations, while also giving them more time to devote to their own research and writing. Typically, there were two types of work that prevailed in the German seminary for political economy: 'the writing of short theses (*Kleine Arbeiten*) or the critical reading of some document or documents, more frequently of some chronicler or chroniclers' (Adams 1884, 71). Each seminar also generally allocated a half-hour 'to the review of current periodical and other scientific publications' (Seligman 1912, 157). This was done to ensure that students experienced 'increased familiarity with the recent literature' (Seligman 1892, 4). The rest of the time was dedicated to investigations conducted by participants, who had to present the results of their research and 'get the benefit of criticism and discussion' (Taussig 1912, 165).

Based on his experiences at the University of Heidelberg, Herbert Baxter Adams (1884, 68) claimed that the seminary method employed by Knies mainly consisted of 'reading and discussion of original papers by his pupils upon assigned topics.' In the seminary, 'the professor selects a list of subjects for theses from the field of his special line of investigation and assigns them to the students, the latter's particular tastes being generally consulted' (ibid.: 71). Then, 'the professor points out the sources and authorities, and the student consults with him whenever difficulties arise in the preparation of the work' (ibid.). Furthermore, Adams (1884, 79) commented on the importance of the statistical seminary in Berlin, which trained 'university graduates who have passed the examinations required for entrance to the higher branches of the civil service.' German statistical seminaries also included participants who were already 'doctors of philosophy' and 'public officials' (Seager 1893, 246). Adams (1884, 69) was also impressed by the quality of seminaries at Bonn, where 'all members are expected to be present, although no individual student makes more than one contribution during a semester.' There was undoubtedly 'a unification of their work,' which provided a benefit for the instructors and participants alike (Taussig 1912, 163). When it came to seminaries, Taussig (ibid.: 169) supported oral presentations, but was strongly opposed to 'the reading of papers,' arguing that to 'read from manuscript at the meetings' was 'deadly' and 'appalling.' Taussig (ibid.) went so far as to contend that if students are unable to present their research without reading, they should not 'be allowed to persist in preparation for the teaching profession, or even in a career of research.'

German-trained American political economists highly valued 'a social side to a German Seminar' (Seager 1893, 248). They enjoyed the fact that 'professor and students' met 'upon a footing of intimacy, the formality of the lecture room' was 'put to one side' (ibid.). In the seminar, the professor was 'not the preceptor but the coworker'; he was like 'the friend' and 'the equal' of his students (Seligman 1912, 159). On occasions where the professor did criticize his students, he guided the discussions, and it was often the case that he learned from them (ibid.). For American students, it was 'this feeling of equality, of meeting on a common fighting-ground' that constituted 'one of the most precious features of the seminar' (ibid). Seligman (1912, 159) confessed that bringing the professor 'into personal and friendly contact with the students' was 'an utter impossibility in the lecture-room' of the American university.

Unlike regular courses, where 'the university students enter the lecture-room as strangers, and depart as strangers,' seminaries gave participants 'an opportunity of gauging each other's abilities, of familiarizing each with the others' strong points, of laying the seeds of future collaboration in scientific or professional work' (ibid.: 156, 157). Herbert Baxter Adams (1884, 68) pointed out that in addition to getting scholarly training and engaging in stimulating debates, students also had a 'pleasant' and 'enjoyable' time in a friendly environment, where long-lasting friendships were made. After the seminary had concluded, the professor would sometimes invite the participants to a restaurant or their home, which allowed for the continuation of discussions in a more relaxed setting (St. Marc 1892, 102). In fact, it was these 'friendly after-gatherings that the most pleasant recollections of many of those' who studied in Germany (Seager 1893, 248).

Many prominent adherents of the New School were trained in the seminars of the GHSE, including Ely, H. C. Adams, H. B. Adams, Patten, James, Seligman, Falkner, Johnson, Seager, and Fetter. After participating in seminaries held in places like Berlin, Bonn, Heidelberg, and Leipzig, they were motivated to implement the German seminary method at American universities. Actually, they believed that university instruction was not complete without seminaries. Thus, when they were developing graduate programs for American universities, they agreed that the German seminary method needed to be adopted. Seligman (1912, 160) was of the view that the seminar was an 'adjunct to specialization,' meaning that it should be 'the work of the university, not of the college.' He believed that college students did not have 'the maturity nor the training' that were 'necessary prerequisites to independent thinking,' nor did they possess the 'linguistic and literary equipment' required for the successful utilization of 'the arts of comparison and criticism' (ibid.: 161). Accordingly, he emphasized that the seminar should be 'a strictly university method' (ibid.: 160). In fact, he wanted the seminar to be restricted to masters and PhD candidates only (Seligman 1911, 390).

In 1881, Herbert Baxter Adams was credited with being one of the first American scholars to introduce the German-type seminary in the US at Johns Hopkins University. He was followed by Taussig and Dunbar at Harvard and James at the University of Pennsylvania (Herbst 1965, 36). From there, the seminar method that was imported from Germany ended up spreading quite rapidly through American universities. Eventually, the 'advanced courses' in political economy that were being offered at American universities were 'carried' on like German seminaries (Laughlin 1912, 171). The seminaries ended up becoming revolutionary in the discipline of economics in the US, which motivated further specialization and advanced academic work. Eventually, German seminary training also spread throughout 'institutions beyond German borders' in many countries (Adams 1884, 65).

The Establishment of Adequate Libraries

German-trained Americans were captivated by the extensive library facilities that were available at the German universities and the great quantities of books and journals they possessed. First of all, they were surprised by the number of different libraries that they had access to as students in Germany, including the library of the House of Parliament, the statistical library, the university library, and the university reading room (Seager 1893, 252). They were particularly impressed by the capacity of university libraries, which boasted 'several thousand volumes' and complete collections of periodicals that could be used by the students (ibid.: 251). These libraries also had 'files of the leading German economic journals, a large assortment of government publications and an especially rich collection of works upon public finance' (ibid.: 252). Each university also had seminary libraries for its various departments. For example, political economy departments generally had 'a very complete collection of economic works' at the service of students and professors (ibid.). In fact, they contained almost 'all the important works in German, English and French bearing upon general economics' (ibid.). They also housed papers that were 'pieces for scientific purposes' (Adams 1889, 145). Moreover, the seminaries of political economy devoted 'especial attention to the collection of statistical materials, documents illustrating local, municipal, state, and national institutions; also to the collection of maps, works of historical and political geography' (ibid.: 146).

Statistical bureaus also had their own libraries. For example, the library of the Prussian Statistical Bureau was accepted as unrivaled, because it provided a 'complete guide to political science in its historical, theoretical, and practical aspects' with 'over 70,000 volumes' (Adams 1884, 81). At the time, there existed:

> far and wide no library so rich, no collection of periodicals so select, no map collection so excellent, as those in the royal bureau of statistics. All new contributions to this branch of literature, whether in Germany, France, England, Belgium, Holland, Sweden, Norway, Denmark, Russia, Italy, Spain, Portugal, North and South America were made available to the members of [its seminary].
>
> (ibid.)

The library of the Prussian Statistical Bureau also had 'a series of more than seventy special magazines of political economy, statistics, and the allied branches of industry, agriculture, commerce and trade, public; works, finance, credit, insurance, administration (municipal and national), social self help' that it made available for 'seminary-use' (ibid.).

American students pointed out that these various library resources that were available in Germany were of great service to the students of political economy. They were also impressed with how long those libraries were open. For example, most libraries in the US were only open for about an hour per day, while many of those in Germany were open for study from seven in the morning until nine in the evening (Seager 1893). It was common for students to work at the libraries for at least a few hours on most days (Adams 1889, 145). German-trained American political economists were also surprised that books could be borrowed by university students and 'retained four and, upon renewal, six weeks' (Seager 1893, 251).

Walker (1899, 289) believed that libraries were very important for 'advanced historical study.' Ely also (1889, 72) underlined the importance of libraries for both the teachers and students of political economy. That said, he recognized that relative to their German counterparts, American colleges and universities lacked adequate library facilities in terms of capacity and accessibility. This was evidenced by the fact that in 1840, Yale had '15,000 volumes, Harvard, 52,000, Columbia, 15,000,' whereas the library in Göttingen had 200,000 volumes on its own (Parrish 1967, 4). Adherents of the New School were fully conscious that the development of political economy departments at American institutions required the establishment of adequate libraries similar to the ones in Germany. Over time, the efforts of German-trained American scholars led to an expansion and enhancement of US library resources. By 1900, Harvard library had '500,000 volumes,' Columbia had '250,000,' and Cornell had 200,000 (ibid.: 9).

Conclusion

From the 16th to the early 19th centuries, many universities in the US did not have graduate schools, while the number of doctoral degrees awarded was very small, amounting to only a few students per year. However, in the last quarter of the 19th century, Americans experienced remarkable development in the academic environments of all of the disciplines that constituted the social and natural sciences, including political economy. Adherents of the New School were deeply inspired and motivated to reform the system of higher education in the US following their experiences at German universities. Accordingly, the GHSE served as a 'midwife, helping to birth the ideas which had been conceived under American conditions' (Ely 1910, 77, 1938, 145). German-trained American political economists basically imported their experiences at German universities to the US, particularly in terms of teaching and studying, in order to advance economic thinking and knowledge and to encourage the production of original research, critical thinking, and creativity. Their tireless work resulted in the establishment of political economy as an independent academic discipline at many American universities. It also led to German-inspired graduate schools and programs of political economy being set up.

In terms of specifics, members of the New School introduced German-inspired courses and language requirements at the political economy departments of American universities. They also introduced the seminary method of teaching at most newly established graduate schools. Furthermore, they played an important role in opening adequate library facilities in order to motivate advanced creative research. As a result, American institutions of higher learning essentially underwent a complete transformation when it came to the discipline of political economy. Eventually, this rapid and robust progress attracted more interest in the academic study of economics. This was evidenced by rapid expansion in the courses being offered at the newly established economics departments and graduate studies programs in the US, as well as significant increases in the numbers of teachers employed at them and students enrolled. Additionally, there was a multiplication in the number chairs at political economy departments in colleges and universities.

By the end of the 19th century, economics was being taught at all major universities in the US, many of which went on to gain international prominence in the 20th century. Many of the early graduates of these newly established American political economy departments went on to become college and university professors across the US. Ultimately, the efforts of adherents of the New School contributed to making economics into a very prestigious profession in the US, with economists occupying some of the highest academic posts, including university presidents. In fact, 'the serious and eager attention given to economic studies in America, both in Academic and political life,' at the beginning of 20th century, resulted in American economics departments attracting the attention of European students (Ely 1910, 100). Consequently, the economics departments of American universities became international models that were adopted by many universities around the world for much of the 20th century. This transition led to American universities and colleges producing large numbers of well-respected American economists.

Adherents of the New School faced an extremely difficult situation and tremendous challenges due to financial and institutional constraints, as well as their opposition to orthodox views. Nonetheless, they were able to realize extraordinary achievements in the discipline and profession of economics in the US, due in large part to the influence of the GHSE. Eventually, they became well-known respected experts in their field, to the point that the main newspapers and journals would reference their views about the economic issues and matters of their time. This chapter is a testimony to the fact that American economists are indebted to the GHSE for their many contributions to the early development of the discipline of economics, which one could never trace back in detail. Unfortunately, the achievements of both the GHSE and the New School are largely taken for granted by modern economists.

Notes

1 *The Harvard Graduates Magazine*. December 1902. Vol. 11: 247–248.
2 Archives at Yale. 'Arthur Twining Hadley, President of Yale University.' https://archives.yale.edu/repositories/12/resources/2590.
3 Archives at Yale. John Christopher Schwab family papers: Collection: John Christopher Schwab family papers|Archives at Yale.
4 Columbia250. 'John William Burgess.' http://c250.columbia.edu/c250_celebrates/remarkable_columbians/john_burgess.html.
5 Illinois University Department of Economics. 'Bogart, Ernest L.' https://economics.illinois.edu/spotlight/historical-faculty/bogart-ernest-l.
6 Ibid.
7 https://www.statistik-berlin-brandenburg.de/publikationen/aufsaetze/2012/HZ_201201-01.pdf.
8 https://www.encyclopedia.com/people/social-sciences-and-law/economics-biographies/richmond-mayo-smith.

Bibliography

Adams, Herbert Baxter. 1884. *Methods of Historical Study*. Baltimore: Johns Hopkins University studies in Historical and Political Science. Second Series. No. 1–2. The Johns Hopkins University Studies in Historical... ser.2 no.1–2 yr. 1884 mo. Jan–Feb. Full View|HathiTrust Digital Library|HathiTrust Digital Library.

Adams, Herbert Baxter. 1889. 'Special Methods of Historical Study: As Pursued at the Johns Hopkins University and Formerly at Smith College.' Ed. G. Stanley Hall. *Methods of Teaching History*. Boston: D. C. Heath & Company. 113–147.

Adelstein, Richard P. 1993. 'Mind and Hand: Economics and Engineering at the Massachusetts Institute of Technology.' Ed. William J. Barber. *Breaking the Academic Mould: Economists and Higher Learning in the Nineteenth Century*. New Brunswick: Transaction Publishers. 290–317.

Annals of the American Academy of Political and Social Science. 1896. Vol. 7: 78–86. https://babel.hathitrust.org/cgi/pt?id=njp.32101057051276&view=1up&seq=5

Ashley, William James. 1893. 'On the Study of Economic History.' Ed. N.B. Harte. 1971. *The Study of Economic History: Collected Inaugural Lectures 1893–1970*. New York: Routledge. 1–18.

Backhaus, Jürgen G. 2007 [1989]. 'Gustav von Schmoller and Social Economics.' *International Journal of Social Economics*. Vol. 16: 6–16.

Balabkins, Nicholas W. 1988. *Not by Theory Alone . . . : The Economics of Gustav von Schmoller and Its Legacy to America*. Berlin: Duncker und Humblot.

Barber, William J. 1993. *Breaking the Academic Mould: Economists and Higher Learning in the Nineteenth Century*. New Brunswick: Transaction Publishers.

Carlson, Valdemar. 1968. 'The Education of an Economist before the Great Depression: Harvard's Economics Department in the 1920's.' *The American Journal of Economics and Sociology*. Vol. 27, No. 1: 101–112.

Carver, Thomas Nixon. 1902. 'Economics.' *The Harvard Graduates' Magazine*. Vol. 11: 247–248. Full View|HathiTrust Digital Library|HathiTrust Digital Library.

Carver, Thomas Nixon. 1949. *Recollections of an Unplanned Life: Autobiography of T.N. Carver*. Los Angeles: The Ward Ritchie Press.

Chaloupek, Günther. 2009. 'J.H.G. Justi in Austria: His Writings in the Context of Economic and Industrial Policies of the Habsburg Empire in the 18th Century.' Ed. Jürgen G. Backhaus. *The Beginnings of Political Economy: Johann Heinrich Gottlob von Justi Johann Heinrich Gottlob Justi*. Erfurt: Springer. 147–156.

Coats, Alfred William. 1985. 'The American Economic Association and the Economics Profession.' *Journal of Economic Literature*. Vol. 23, No. 4: 1697–1727. URL: http://www.jstor.com/stable/2725706

Columbia Law Times. 1893. 'John William Burgess, LL. D.' Vol. VI, No. 5: 123–125. #151- Columbia law times. v.6 1892/93. Full View|HathiTrust Digital Library.

Columbia University Bulletin. 1897. 'University Notes.' Vol. XVIII: 67–69. https://babel.hathitrust.org/cgi/pt?id=uc1.b2928562&view=1up&seq=393

Columbia University. 1905–1907. *Columbia University Bulletin, 1905/1907 History, Economics and Public Law*. Courses Offered by the Faculty of Political Science and the Several Undergraduate Faculties. Announcement. New York: Columbia University. https://babel.hathitrust.org/cgi/pt?id=mdp.39015076502676&view=1up&seq=2

Devine, Edward T. 1894. 'Economic Science in America.' *The University Extension Bulletin: A Record of Current University Extension Work*. Vol. 1–2, No. 5: 86–88. *HathiTrust* Digital Library. https://babel.hathitrust.org/cgi/pt?id=mdp.39015086683797&view=1up&seq=65

Dewey, Davis R. 1889. 'The Study of Statistics.' *Publications of the American Economic Association*. Vol. 4, No. 5: 37–52. URL: https://www.jstor.org/stable/2485685

Dickinson, Z. Clark. 1951. 'The Department of Economics.' Ed. Wilfred B. Shaw. *The University of Michigan: An Encyclopedic Survey: In Four Volumes*. Ann Arbor: University of Michigan Press. 532–544.

Dorfman, Joseph. 1955. 'The Role of the German Historical School in American Economic Thought.' *The American Economic Review*. Vol. 45, No. 2: 17–28.

Dunbar, Charles F. 1891. 'The Academic Study of Political Economy.' *Quarterly Journal of Economics*. Vol. 5, No. 4: 397–416.

Dunbar, Charles F. 1904. *Economic Essays*. New York: Macmillan & Co., Ltd.

Eliot, Charles W. 1900. 'Charles Franklin Dunbar.' *The Harvard Graduates' Magazine*. Vol. VIII, No. 32: 469–484.

Ely, Richard T. 1880. 'American Colleges and German Universities.' *Harper's New Monthly Magazine*. V1: 253–260. https://babel.hathitrust.org/cgi/pt?id=msu.31293023091329&view=1up&seq=267

Ely, Richard T. 1883. 'The Past and Present of Political Economy.' *The Overland Monthly*. Vol. 2, No. 9: 225–235. The Overland Monthly. ser.2:v.2 (1883). Full View|HathiTrust Digital Library|HathiTrust Digital Library.

Ely, Richard T. 1889. 'On Methods of Teaching Political Economy.' Ed. G. Stanley Hall. *Methods of Teaching History*. Boston: D. C. Heath & Company. 61–72.

Ely, Richard T. 1910. 'The American Economic Association 1885–1909.' *American Economic Association Quarterly, 3rd Series*. Vol. 11, No. 1: 47–111. New York City: American Economic Association. URL: https://www.jstor.org/stable/3000023

Ely, Richard T. 1936. 'The Founding and Early History of the American Economic Association.' *The American Economic Review*. Vol. 26, No. 1: 141–150. URL: https://www.jstor.org/stable/1807774

Ely, Richard T. 1938. *Ground under Our Feet*. New York: McMillan

Falkner, Roland P. 1897. 'In Memoriam: Francis Amasa Walker.' *The Annals of the American Academy of Political and Social Science*. Vol. 9: 1–5. URL: https://www.jstor.org/stable/1009689

Farnam, Henry W. 1887. 'Academic Freedom in Germany.' *New Englander & Yale Review*. Vol. 46, No. 1: 67–71.

Farnam, Henry W. 1913. *The Economic Utilisation of History*. New Haven: Yale University Press.

Furner Marry O. 1975. *Advocacy & Objectivity: A Crisis in the Professionalization of American Social Science 1865–1905*. Lexington: University Press of Kentucky.

Guy, William A. 1865. 'On the Original and Acquired Meaning of the Term "Statistics," and on the Proper Functions of a Statistical Society: Also on the Question whether there be a Science of Statistics; and, if so, what are its Nature and Objects, and what Is Its Relation to Political Economy and "Social Science."' *Journal of the Statistical Society of London*. Vol. 28: 478–493. London: Harrison & Sons. https://babel.hathitrust.org/cgi/pt?id=uc1.b4148189&view=1up&seq=498

Haney, Lewis T. 1915. *History of Economic Thought*. New York: The Macmillan Company.

Harvard University. 1897–1898. 'Faculty of Arts and Sciences. Division of History and Political Science Comprising the Departments of History and Government and Economics.' Cambridge: Harvard University. Division of History, Government, and Economics: containing an announcement for [year]: Harvard University: Free Download, Borrow, and Streaming: Internet Archive.

Henderson, John P. 1993. 'Political Economy and the Service of the State: The University of Wisconsin.' Ed. William J. Barber. *Breaking the Academic Mould: Economists and Higher Learning in the Nineteenth Century*. New Brunswick: Transaction Publishers. 318–339.

Herbst, Jurgen. 1965. *The German Historical School in American Scholarship: A Study in the Transfer of Culture*. New York: Ithaca.

Illinois School Journal. 1882. 'German Student Life.' Vol. I, No. 11: 13–15. https://babel.hathitrust.org/cgi/pt?id=hvd.32044102788908&view=1up&seq=247

Ingram, John Kells. 1915 [1888]. *A History of Political Economy*. London: A. and C. Black.

James, Edmund James. 1882 (September). 'Political Economy in German Universities.' *The Nation*. 261–262.

James, Edmund James. 1888. 'The Degree of PhD. in Germany.' *The Andover Review: A Religious and Theological Monthly*. Boston: Houghton, Mifflin and Company. Vol. 9, No. 54: 611–623. https://babel.hathitrust.org/cgi/pt?id=mdp.39015070186807&view=1up&seq=4

Kinley, David. 1949. *The Autobiography of David Kinley*. Urbana: University of Illinois Press.

Lafayette, G. Harter Jr. 1962. *John R. Commons: His Assault on Laissez-faire*. Oregon: Oregon State University Press.

Laughlin, J. Laurence. 1885. *The Study of Political Economy. Hints to Students and Teachers*. New York: D. Appleton and Company.

Laughlin, J. Laurence. 1912. 'The Economic Seminar.' *Journal of Political Economy*. Vol. 20, No. 2: 169–175. URL: https://www.jstor.org/stable/1820514

Leland Stanford Junior University. 1894. *Third Annual Register, 1893–94*. Palo Alto: University Stanford.

Mason, Edward S. and Thomas S. Lamont. 1982. 'The Harvard Department of Economics from the Beginning to World War II.' *The Quarterly Journal of Economics*. Vol. 97, No. 3: 383–433. Oxford: Oxford University Press.

Mayo-Smith, Richmond. 1888. 'Wage Statistics and the Next Census of the United States.' *The Quarterly Journal of Economics*. Vol. 2, No. 4: 385–413. URL: https://www.jstor.org/stable/1879385

Mayo-Smith, Richmond. 1899. *Statistics and Economics*. New York: The McMillan Company.

Meitzen, August. 1889. 'History, Theory, and Technique of Statistics. Part First: History of Statistics.' *The Annals of the American Academy of Political and Social Science*. Vol. 1: 1–100. URL: https://www.jstor.org/stable/1008943.

Parrish, John B. 1967. 'Rise of Economics as an Academic Discipline: The Formative Years to 1900.' *Southern Economic Journal*. Vol. 34, No. 1: 1–16. URL: https://www.jstor.org/stable/1055330

Patten, Simon Nelson. 1891. 'The Educational Value of Political Economy.' *Publications of the American Economic Association*. Vol. V, No. 6: 100–115.

Patten, Simon Nelson. 1895. 'The Teaching of Economics in the Secondary Schools.' *American Economic Association*. Vol. 10, No. 3: 119–138. URL: https://www.jstor.org/stable/2485652.

Ripley, W. Z. December 1903. 'Economics.' *The Harvard Graduates' Magazine*. Vol. 12: 246. The Harvard graduates' magazine. v.12 (1903-04). - Full View | HathiTrust Digital Library | HathiTrust Digital Library

Rowe, Leo S. 1890. 'Instruction in Public Law and Political Economy in German Universities.' *The Annals of the American Academy of Political and Social Science*. Vol. 1: 78–102.

Ruggles, Samuel B. 1863. *Reports: International Statistical Congress at Berlin*. Albany: Weed Parsons & Company & Printers.

Scott, Henry E. 1889. 'The Courses of Study in History, Roman Law, and Political Economy, at Harvard University.' Ed. G. Stanley Hall. *Methods of Teaching History*. Boston: D. C. Heath & Company. 167–190.

Seager, Henry Rogers. 1893. 'Economics at Berlin and Vienna.' *Journal of Political Economy*. Vol. 1, No. 2: 236–262. URL: https://www.jstor.org/stable/1817770

Seligman, Edwin Robert Anderson. 1892. 'The Seminarium: Its Advantages and Limitations.' 30th University Convocation of the State of New York July 5–7. https://archive.org/details/seminariumitsadv00seli/page/n1/mode/2up

Seligman, Edwin Robert Anderson. 1911. 'Economics: History.' Ed. Paul Monroe (1911). *A Cyclopedia of Education*. Chicago: The MacMillan Company. 387–391.

Seligman, Edwin Robert Anderson. 1912. 'The Seminar: Its Advantages and Limitations.' *Journal of Political Economy*. Vol. 20, No. 2: 153–162. URL: https://www.jstor.org/stable/1820512

Senn, Peter R. 1989. 'What Has Happened to Gustav von Schmoller In English?' *HES Bulletin*. Vol. 11, No. 2: 252–295.

Simkhovitch, Kingsbury Marry. 1938. *Neighborhood: My Story of Greenwich House*. New York: Norton.

St. Marc, Henri. 1892. *Étude sur l'enseignement de l'économie politique dans les universités d'Allemagne et d'Autriche*. Paris: L. LaRose er Forcel.

Streissler, Erich W. 2001. 'Rau, Hermann and Roscher: Contributions of German Economics around the Middle of the Nineteenth Century.' *European Journal of the History of Economic Thought*. Vol. 8. No. 3: 311–331.

Taussig, Frank William. 1892–1893. 'Economics.' *The Harvard Graduates' Magazine*. Vol. 1: 116–117. The Harvard graduates' magazine. v.1 (1892-1893). - Full View | HathiTrust Digital Library | HathiTrust Digital Library

Taussig, Frank William. 1904. 'Introduction.' Ed. Charles F. Dunbar. *Economic Essays*. New York: Macmillan & CO., LTD.

Taussig, Frank William. 1912. 'The Conduct of a Seminary in Economics.' *Journal of Political Economy*. Vol. 20, No. 2: 163–169. URL: https://www.jstor.org/stable/1820513

Taylor, Henry C. 1943. *Richard Theodore Ely*. Chicago: Farm foundation. 1–6.

Tugwell, Rexford G. 1923. 'Notes on the Life and Work of Simon Nelson Patten.' *Journal of Political Economy*. Vol. 31, No. 2: 153–208. URL: https://www.jstor.org/stable/1822302

University of Chicago Press. 1892. 'The University of Chicago: Programme of Courses in Political Economy, 1892–1893.' The University of Chicago: Programme of Courses in Political... - Full View | HathiTrust Digital Library | HathiTrust Digital Library

Walker, Francis A. 1889. 'Recent Progress of Political Economy in the United States.' *Publications of the American Economic Association*. Vol. 4, No. 4: 17–40. URL: https://www.jstor.org/stable/2485572

Walker, Francis A. 1899. *Discussions in Economics and Statistics. Vol. II*. New York: Henry Holt and Company.

Yefimov, Vladimir. 2009. 'Comparative Historical Institutional Analysis of German, English and American Economics.' *Munich Personal RePEc Archive*. http://mpra.ub.uni-muenchen.de/48173/

6 The GHSE and the Establishment of Economic Associations and Journals in the United States

Introduction

German-trained American political economists were concerned that the way political economy was being taught and studied in the US did not motivate the development of critical thinking, creativity, and curiosity, or stimulate the production of original research and publications. To remedy this situation, they sought to emulate their German professors by establishing environments that facilitated the free exchange of ideas and fruitful academic discussions, which led many of them to become significantly involved in the founding of various economic associations and journals in the US. Other objectives of these newly established journals and associations were to unite political economists against classical orthodoxy. Basically, they were intended to be centers of new thought forces where political economists could work together to develop ideas and obtain strength through mutual support.

This chapter discusses the establishment of some of the most prominent economic associations and institutes in the US, including the American Economic Association (AEA), the American Academy of Political and Social Science (AAPSS), and the American Political Science Association (APSA). It also discusses journals and periodicals whose creations were attributed to the work and efforts of American economists who were directly influenced or inspired by the German Historical School of Economics (GHSE), including the *American Economic Association Quarterly*, the *American Economic Review*, the *Quarterly Journal of Economics* (QJE), the *Political Science Quarterly* (PSQ), and *The Yale Review*. Furthermore, this chapter explains that, in addition to establishing economic associations and journals, adherents of the New School also contributed to the development of the discipline of economics in the US by founding various institutions and research centers, as well as playing instrumental roles in the development of government legislation and policies.

The Establishment of American Economic Association

In order to properly understand the early development of the discipline of economics in the US, it is imperative to study the original establishment and

DOI: 10.4324/9781003247715-6

evolution of the AEA. Richard Theodore Ely (1854–1943) (1936, 142) argued that 'one does not have an adequate knowledge' of 'American economic thought' without understanding the early development of the AEA. In fact, he claimed that the AEA is the history of economic thought in the US (Ely 1910, 91). Prior to the establishment of the AEA, American political economists were united under the American Social Science Association (ASSA), along with other social scientists including historians, sociologists, and political scientists. The ASSA was founded in 1865 and its objectives were to assist in:

> the development of Social Science, and to guide the public mind to the best practical means of promoting the Amendment of Laws, the Advancement of Education, the Prevention and Repression of Crime, the Reformation of Criminals, and the progress of Public Morality, the adoption of Sanitary Regulations, and the diffusion of sound principles on questions of Economy, Trade, and Finance.
>
> (American Social Science Association 1866, 3)

Its members, which included academics, politicians, clerics, and businessmen, were supposed to 'to collect all facts, diffuse all knowledge, and stimulate all inquiry, which have a bearing on social welfare.'[1] Some adherents of the Old School, such as William Graham Sumner (1840–1910), were 'disenchanted with the "do-goodism" aspect of the ASSA's activities,' whereas adherents of the New School were pleased with 'the reformist dimension of the ASSA's style' (Barber 2001, 219). Eventually, the ASSA came to an end in 1912, as its membership gradually splintered off and formed their own associations. For example, political economists established the AEA in 1885, social scientists founded the AAPSS in 1889, political scientists created the APSA in 1903, and sociologists launched the American Sociological Society (ASS) in 1905.

For German-trained American economists, the goals and agenda of the ASSA were far removed from those of *Verein für Sozialpolitik* (the German Association for Social Policy), which directly inspired the establishment of the AEA. *Verein für Sozialpolitik* was a reformist organization founded by adherents of the GHSE to oppose the individualism and laissez-faire approach of the Manchester School, which was directed by Richard Cobden (1804–1865) and John Bright (1811–1889). *Verein für Sozialpolitik* was officially established in 1873, with its first congress taking place on October 6 and 7 of that same year. However, an initial meeting that led to its creation was organized in Halle, Germany, in July 1872, which involved the participation of prominent theorists of the GHSE, including Wilhelm Georg Friedrich Roscher (1817–1894), Ernst Engel (1821–1896), Bruno Hildebrand (1812–1878), Adolf Gotthilf Wagner (1835–1917), Johannes E. Conrad (1839–1915), Lujo Brentano (1844–1931), Gustav von Schmoller (1838–1917), and Friedrich Knapp (1842–1926) (Philippovich 1891, 226).

Verein für Sozialpolitik aimed to address 'broadly the social problems of industrialisation and urbanisation, involving impoverishment, class conflict, and social fragmentation' (Tribe 2002, 10). Its membership included scholars from political economy and other social sciences, trade union leaders, 'government officials, publicists, journalists,' 'manufacturers, land proprietors,' and members of political parties (ibid.). However, while this diverse group may have had significant differences of 'opinion,' they were 'united in their opposition to the Manchester school' (ibid.: 226, 231). They were also in agreement that unrestricted economic activities on the part of private businesses did not safeguard the welfare of the masses. In response, *Verein für Sozialpolitik* supported positive state actions to regulate the activities of private businesses and protect the vulnerable segments of the population. It also defended positive state actions to promote and protect the common welfare against the ideals of socialism and classical economics. Members of *Verein für Sozialpolitik* supported economic research projects and organized annual conferences. After each conference, 'commissioned studies were published in the *Verein*'s monograph series, the *Schriften des Verein für Sozialpolitik*' (Yefimov 2009, 13). In total, this association ended up financially supporting the publication of '188 monographs' prior to its dissolution in 1936 with the Nazis coming to power (Balabkins 1988, 55).

In Germany, Conrad advised the American students in his seminary to organize an association similar to *Verein für Sozialpolitik* in the US after they returned home (Ely 1910, 108). Basically, he told them that:

> the old order was passing away, and if economic students were to have any influence whatever upon the course of practical politics, it would be necessary to take a new attitude toward the whole subject of social legislation, and if the United States were to have any particular influence in the great social legislation and the great readjustment of society on its legal side which seemed to be coming, an association of this sort would have very real value.
>
> (ibid.)

Edmund Janes James (1855–1925), who was among those in attendance, was inspired by Conrad's advice and decided that he would work on creating such an association in the US as soon as possible (ibid.).

In February 1883, James visited many of the leading American institutions of higher learning to engage in conversations with some of their prominent members about the possibility of establishing an economic association of the sort suggested by Conrad (ibid.: 109). Some of the specific individuals that he engaged with included Henry Carter Adams (1851–1921) of Michigan, Arthur Lathamn Perry of Williams (1830–1905), Charles Franklin Dunbar (1830–1900), and James Laurence Laughlin (1850–1933) of Harvard, John Bates Clark (1874–1938) of Smith College, William Graham Sumner (1840–1910) and Henry Walcott Farnam (1853–1933) of Yale, Francis Amasa Walker (1840–1897) of *Massachusetts Institute of Technology* (MIT), Edwin Robert Anderson Seligman (1861–1939) of Columbia, Richard T.

Ely (1854–1943) of Johns Hopkins, and Robert Ellis Thompson (1844–1924) and Albert S. Bolles (1846–1939) of Philadelphia (ibid.). These academics agreed that such an association would be beneficial for the discipline of political economy.

The following year, in 1884, James and Simon Nelson Patten (1852–1922), both of whom received their doctorates in political economy from the University of Halle, launched an initiative to establish an organization that would be called the Society for the Study of National Economy (SSNE) which was inspired by *Verein für Sozialpolitik* (ibid.: 50). The stated objectives of the SSNE were to: 'encourage the careful investigation and free discussion of the special problems' of the national economy; facilitate 'the publication of economic monographs'; fight methodological individualism; promote methodological collectivism so as to 'secure to each individual the highest development of all his faculties'; and advocate for 'a general unity of sentiment' in order to have 'a hearty cooperation' between people (ibid.). The SSNE would also serve as an advocate for the working classes by calling for improvements to working conditions, higher wages, and limited hours. Additionally, it was supposed to play a role in combatting the laissez-faire approach, reducing the wasteful exploitation of 'national resources' and encouraging conservation efforts (ibid.: 53). Ultimately, the proposed SSNE never came to fruition, as it did not attract sufficient support to justify its establishment. According to Ely (1936, 144), the proposed 'platform' of the SSNE was 'too narrow' to 'enlist the sympathy of a sufficiently large group of American economists.' In particular, Americans were not prepared to digest its support for more state involvement in the economy.

Despite falling short in their attempt to establish the SSNE, James and Patten still believed that it was necessary to have an association that could unite political economists and encourage them to take on a new attitude when it came to the teachings and practices of their discipline. However, it was ultimately Ely who took the initiative to found the AEA, which would retain the fundamental ideas of the SSNE, while also taking steps to 'appeal to all the younger economists' (Ely 1938, 135). Ely (1936, 144) drafted 'a statement of principles' for the AEA and played a major role in its establishment and subsequent success.

On September 8, 1885, Henry Carter Adams, Clark, and Ely held a meeting in Saratoga to discuss the formation of the AEA. Most of the attendees ended up being Americans who studied in Germany, including 'Hon. Andrew D. White, President C. K. Adams,' 'Professor E. J. James, Rev. Washington Gladden, Professor E. Benjamin Andrews, Rev. Samuel W. Dike':

> Mr. V. B. Denslow, Professor Alexander Johnston, Dr. E. R. A. Seligman, Professor H. B. Adams, Mr. F. B. Sanborn, Miss Katharine Comnan, Mr. Davis R. Dewey, Edward W. Bemis, Ph.D., Mr. John A. Porter, Clarence Bowen, Ph.D., Professor Herbert Tuttle, Hon. Eugene Schuyler.
> (Ely 1910, 58)

The following day, on September 9, the AEA was officially founded. Its overarching goal was to 'seek light, to bear light, to diffuse light-ever the highest aim of all true science' (Ely 1886, 6). That is to say, it was designed to encourage independent economic research and the publication of economic monographs, ensure freedom in all economic discussions, and 'disseminate economic knowledge' (Ely 1887, 5). In fact, Ely (1910, 69) stated:

> We felt called upon to fight those who, rightly or wrongly, we believed, stood in the way of intellectual expansion and of social growth ... Some of us felt that men who thought as we did were denied the right to exist scientifically, and this denial we believed to proceed from certain older men able to exercise a very large influence over thought, particularly thought in university circles. Very soon we felt that we had won our battle so far as the right to exist scientifically was concerned.

Like *Verein für Sozialpolitik*, the AEA sought to gather 'like-minded men' to work together and protest 'against the narrow English economists' (Ely 1910, 80). In fact, the AEA was essentially a revolt against classical orthodoxy. Its early members were of the view that classical orthodoxy was outdated and did not belong to the realm of science, which led them to call for a new brand of political economy. The principles of the AEA stated that laissez-faire was 'unsafe in politics and unsound in morals' and provided 'an inadequate explanation of the relations between the state and the citizens' (Ely 1910, 58). The AEA also accepted the state as 'an educational and ethical agency whose positive aid is an indispensable condition of human progress' (ibid.). Much like the theorists of the GHSE, members of the AEA 'would do nothing to weaken individual activity,' but were of the opinion that 'certain spheres of activity which do not belong to the individual' would be best managed by the state (Ely 1887, 16).

With the establishment of the AEA, young American economists or 'the young rebels' were made to feel as though 'economics was not a dead thing of the past, but a live thing of the present, inviting young men to put the best they had into this field' (Ely 1936, 146). There is no doubt that, in the early years of the AEA, its members were highly influenced by the GHSE and widely regarded as the new generation of economists. Meanwhile, the old generation of economists, including Arthur Twining Hadley (1856–1930), Simon Newcomb (1835–1909), Laughlin, Sumner, and Frank William Taussig (1859–1940), refused to join the AEA, accusing it of being a socialistic organization that was influenced by German socialist policies, even though members of the AEA made it abundantly clear that they did not champion any class interests.

Walker, who was president of MIT, became the inaugural president of the AEA when it was founded in 1885 and served in that capacity for the first seven years of its existence, with Ely acting as its secretary during that same period (Ely 1936). That same year, Henry Carter Adams (University of Michigan and Cornell) became the first vice president of the AEA, James (University of Pennsylvania) was appointed second vice president, Clark (Smith College) was made third vice president, and Seligman (Columbia College) became Treasurer (Ely 1887, 40). Ely (1936, 147) stated that members of the AEA looked to Walker as their 'leader and were proud to hail him as chief.' Walker, in turn, was 'thrilled by the thought' that the younger generation were 'giving him support and were to carry on' activities of the AEA 'in the free and scientific spirit which always characterized his writings' (ibid.). However, his election as the first president of the AEA also led people to mistakenly believe that Walker represented the New School, when, in fact, he could 'not be said to have represented any particular school' (Dunbar 1897, 445). In reality, he was 'both theorist and observer, the framer of a theory of distribution, and also an industrious student of past and current history' (ibid.). In 1892, Walker vacated the presidency of the AEA, as he and Ely were fully confident that it was 'thoroughly established and any doubts about its future disappeared from' their minds (Ely 1936, 147). In 1893, Dunbar was appointed as the second president of the AEA, even though 'he was a progressive of the old school' (ibid.). However, Ely (1936, 147) pointed out that this selection did not mean that there was a shift to the left or to the right at the AEA. Shortly thereafter, Ely nominated Edward Alsworth Ross (1866–1951), his former student, to be his successor as secretary of the AEA (ibid.).

In the first few decades after the AEA came into existence, the majority of its presidents studied under theorists of the GHSE or adherents of the New School. For example, Clark, who studied at the University of Heidelberg under Conrad and Karl Knies (1821–1898), was president of the AEA in 1894–1895. Then, Henry Carter Adams, who studied in Heidelberg and Berlin for two years, served in that capacity during 1896–1897. Subsequently, Hadley, who studied political economy at the University of Berlin under Adolph Wagner (1835–1917), was president of the AEA in 1898–1899. In 1900–1901, the presidency was given to Ely, who obtained his PhD from Heidelberg under Knies, followed by Seligman during 1902–1903, who had previously attended the universities of Berlin and Heidelberg. In 1905–1906, the position was given to Taussig, who studied economics at the University of Berlin. Next, Jeremiah Whipple Jenks (1856–1929), who obtained his PhD from the University of Halle under Conrad, was president of the AEA in 1906–1907. In 1908–1909, the presidency was assumed by Patten, another alumnus of the University of Halle (1876–1879) who studied under Conrad. Then, Davis Rich Dewey (1858–1942), who studied at Johns Hopkins University under Ely and Henry Baxter Adams (1850–1901), became president in 1909–1910. He was followed by James, who obtained his doctorate in political economy from the University of Halle in 1877 and served as president of the AEA in 1910–1911. Next was Farnam, who was president in 1911–1912 after previously having his thesis evaluated by Schmoller at the University of Berlin. In 1912–1913, Frank Albert Fetter (1863–1949), who obtained his PhD from the University of Halle, became president of the AEA. Subsequently, David

Kinley (1861–1944), a former graduate student of Ely at Johns Hopkins University, was made president of the AEA in 1913–1914. The following year, the position was given to John Henry Gray (1859–1946), another American economist who obtained his PhD under Conrad at the University of Halle. Then, in 1916–1917, the presidency of the AEA was assumed by Thomas Nixon Carver (1865–1961), who studied under Clark and Ely at Johns Hopkins University. Following Carver, only a few of the subsequent presidents of the AEA were directly influenced by the ideas and methods of the New School.

The AEA stimulated significant progress and improvement in economic and statistical work, while also playing an active part in the establishment of a permanent census bureau (Ely 1938, 158). Additionally, the AEA helped develop 'a growing awareness of collective interests' among political economists (Coats 1985, 1703). Its members extensively discussed and worked on labor rights and 'railway problems,' which led to railway reforms being enacted (Ely 1910, 82). The AEA also played a major role in the implementation of publicly funded social and economic reforms and programs. In fact, Ely (1936, 141) claimed that without the AEA, 'neither the New Deal nor the old could be understood.' He believed that the New Deal was directly influenced by the social and economic reforms that were implemented by Bismarck in Germany during the 1880s. Moreover, Patten was considered to be a forerunner of New Dealers.

In its early years, there is no disputing the fact that the AEA was a key driver of 'thought-forces' within the discipline of economics (Ely 1910, 81). It provided 'a forum for discussion and a medium for the publication and dissemination of ideas' (Ely 1936, 148). It also played a significant role in 'the emergence of a national scholarly elite' (Coats 1985, 1703). During that time, the AEA was mainly shaped by adherents of the New School. Accordingly, its publications focused on positive state actions with respect to public utilities, the achievement of the general welfare of society, and 'the principle of competition, as a regulating factor in the sphere of industry' (Ely 1936, 148). Other topics that were frequently covered included transportation, international trade, public finance, and statistics. It also published a number of monographs on labor and cooperation that were written by some of Ely's former students from Johns Hopkins University who were influenced by theorists of the GHSE (ibid.). Additionally, the AEA offered 'prizes for essays on various economic questions of the day' to inspire 'popular interest in economic questions' and direct 'a few young people in useful careers' as political economists (Ely 1910, 74). The membership of the AEA expanded considerably since it was first established in 1885, due in large part to the fact that 'all the active economic workers' in the US were invited to join and participate (Walker 1889, 17).

Although one cannot precisely measure the contributions that the AEA made to the rapid development and progress of the discipline of economics in the US, Ely (1910, 98) stated that 'the indefinable influence and intangible effects' of this association were 'very great.' Before the AEA gained prominence, theorists of the New School were isolated, even facing a hostile environment perpetrated by adherents of the Old School (Devine 1894). Eventually, the AEA became so important that some supporters of the classical orthodoxy joined 'in spite of objections' about its goals and principles (Walker 1889, 22). Prominent among them was Newcomb, who joined the AEA in 1894 even though he was highly critical of Ely's views, even stating that 'Dr. Ely seems to … be seriously out of place in a university chair' (Barber 1993, 220). Over time, cooperation among American economists from different schools of thought resulted in 'indifference, distrust, antagonism' gradually dissipating (Walker 1889, 22). In other words, the AEA contributed to easing tensions and putting battles between the Old and New Schools behind them, mainly due to compromises 'in tactical matters' made by German-trained economists (Herbst 1965, 149). In essence, the AEA represented 'the wave of the future' for the discipline of economics (Coats 1985, 1701).

According to James, the AEA and American economists in general owed 'a great debt' to Ely for his 'untiring industry and devotion' to reforming the discipline of economics (Ely 1910, 111). He emphasized that without Ely, the AEA would not have been established when it was, nor would it have 'succeeded so well' (ibid.). The AEA 'awakened new interest in economics, has brought kindred minds into fruitful contact, has aided students by advice and counsel' (Ely 1886, 32). As a result, there was an 'increased influence of economists and statisticians in the public life' (Ely 1910, 98). Ely (1910, 98) pointed to 'the aggregate change in the attitude of the American people toward expert knowledge of economic affairs which this Association can claim as its great and significant achievement.' The AEA also exerted:

> an influence on foreign countries. In Glasgow it served as a stimulus for a local University Economic Association. From Oxford, England, came the suggestion made by a well-known English economist of the formation of a local association in alliance with the American Economic Association.
>
> (ibid.: 85)

The AEA was essentially 'a stimulus and a model' for economists in Great Britain, who established the British Economic Association (later renamed The Royal Economic Society) in 1890 (Ely 1936, 148). It also served as a catalyst for the establishment of similar associations in Australia, South Africa, and Japan (ibid.). Although many of the important achievements of the AEA could be attributed to the ideas, methods, and policies that it imported from the GHSE, this school of thought was nonetheless abandoned by AEA members for most of the 20th century.

The American Academy of Political and Social Science

In 1889, the AAPSS was founded in Philadelphia to promote progress in the social sciences (AAPSS 1889). This initiative was started by German-trained political economists James and Patten, in response to concerns expressed by some adherents of the New School that the AEA was increasingly focusing on the profession and discipline of economics while neglecting other branches of social science. Divisions also formed between members of the AEA, because many of them believed that the original goals and purposes of the AEA, which were set by Ely, James, and Patten, were too radical.

The AAPSS sought to bring 'in specialized and professionalized experts to voice and confront the problems collectively' in the different disciplines of the social sciences (ibid.). It basically focused on advancing research on political, economic, social, and policy issues. More specifically, the AAPSS was dedicated to: the 'accumulation of a library of works pertaining to the subjects cultivated by the Academy'; the 'encouragement of investigation by the offering of prizes for specified contributions to science'; the 'publication of valuable papers and reports presented to the Academy either by members or others'; and the 'dissemination of political and economic knowledge throughout the community by the establishment of public lecture courses in political and social science' (AAPSS 1897, 16).

James was elected as the inaugural president of the AAPSS at its first meeting, and remained as such until 1895. Subsequently, Roland P. Falkner (1866–1940), who studied economics at Berlin, Leipzig, and Halle, held the position during 1896–1900. He was followed by Samuel McCune Lindsay (1869–1960), who received his PhD from the University of Halle in 1892 and served as president of the AAPSS from 1900 to 1902. Then, from 1902 to 1929, the position was filled by Leo Stanton Rowe (1871–1946), who received his PhD from the University of Halle in 1893. The AAPSS also included many prominent members that originated from the New School, including Richmond Mayo-Smith (1854–1901), who studied in Berlin during 1875–1877 and then in Heidelberg in 1878; Edward Thomas Devine (1867–1948), who completed his PhD in economics under Patten at the University of Pennsylvania in 1889 and later studied in Germany for one year; Fetter, who obtained his PhD from the University of Halle in Germany in 1894; Kinley, who was significantly influenced by Ely's lectures and views at both Johns Hopkins University and the University of Wisconsin; Clark, who studied at the University of Heidelberg under Conrad and Knies; Henry Rogers Seager (1870–1930), who studied at Johns Hopkins University under Ely and Herbert Baxter Adams, before furthering his education in Halle, Berlin, and Vienna; and Seligman, who graduated from Columbia College and studied at universities in Berlin, Paris, and Heidelberg.

The AAPSS organized annual meetings that 'historically drew crowds that numbered over 1,000 and garnered widespread coverage from periodicals such as the *New York Times, Philadelphia Inquirer,* and *Chicago Tribune*' (AAPSS 1889). Moreover, many 'ambassadors, government officials, politicians, university scholars, and scientific and business organizations' participated in the meetings (ibid.). Even though the original founders and members of the AAPSS were strongly influenced by the GHSE, all of the goals and ideas of this school of thought were abandoned in the 20th century.

The American Political Science Association

Some members of the AEA supported the establishment of a separate association for political science (Ely 1910, 80). They argued that having another association would reduce 'the expense, the additional labor and the danger of weakening existing organizations' (Proceedings of the American Political Science Association 1904, 10). They also believed that the establishment and maintenance of a new association was necessary in order to attract new members and participants from different areas of the social sciences. This would also help strengthen the old associations, because they would only attract new members that were highly specialized in their areas. However, some members of the AEA were opposed to the establishment of an independent association for political scientists, as well as the idea of having a separate section for them within the AEA. They believed that neither option would attract active supporters to the AEA (ibid.).

Despite opposition from some members of the AEA, the APSA was established in 1903, with a focus on advancing 'the scientific study of Politics, Public Law, Administration and Diplomacy' (Herbst 1965, 45). In addition to publishing articles and reports, the APSA aimed to have 'the scientific lead in all matters of a political interest,' encourage 'research, aiding if possible in the collection and publication of valuable material,' and generally advance 'the scientific study of politics' in the US (Proceedings of the American Political Science Association 1904, 11). It sought out support and contributions from political scientists, 'public administrators, lawyers of broader culture, and, in general, all those interested in the scientific study of the great and increasingly important questions of practical and theoretical politics' (ibid.: 10). Despite separating from the AEA, members of the APSA still wanted the two associations to be in harmony with one another. In fact, the APSA ended up being 'affiliated with the American Historical and the American Economic Associations' (ibid.). The APSA has become a very important association in the development of the discipline of political science. Today, it boasts more than 10,000 members from around 100 different countries.

Newly Established Economic Journals in the US

The earliest known economics journal was *Archiv der politischen Okonomie und Polizeiwissenschaften*, which was founded in 1835 by Karl Heinrich Rau (1792–1870), who was a professor of political economy at the University of Heidelberg. Another one of the oldest economics journals was the *Zeitschrift für die gesamte Staatswissenschaft* (1844–1985), which was founded in 1844 by Robert von Mohl (1799–1875), a professor of political science and political economy at the University of Tübingen. Subsequently, the *Jahrbücher für Nationalökonomie und Statistik*, a scientific periodical for economics, was established by Bruno Hildebrand in 1862. Then, in 1871, the *Jahrbuch für Gesetzgebung, Verwaltung und Volkswirtschaft Deutschen Reich* (formally renamed

Schmollers Jahrbuch after 1913) was founded; it was edited by Brentano until his death in 1931, after which Schmoller took over.

There was no established 'American school of writers on political economy' prior to the influence of the GHSE becoming widespread throughout the country (Dunbar 1904, 14). Furthermore, since American economists did not make any notable contributions to the development of political economy at that time, especially when compared to their German counterparts, it should come as no surprise that there were no domestic academic journals where original research could be published. Consequently, American colleges and universities had little choice other than to provide their staff and students with foreign periodicals, particularly from Germany, like the *Jahrbücher für Nationalökonomie und Statistik*, *Jahrbuch fur Gesetzgebung, Verwaltung und Volkswirthschaft*, and *Tübinger Zeitschrift für die Gesammte Staatswissenchaft* (Ely 1895, 69). In addition to German periodicals, they also frequently provided *Journal des Économistes* from France and the *English Economist*, *Bradstreets*, and *Banker's Magazine* from the UK (ibid.).

Before the GHSE attained prominence in the US, American economists focused much of their attention on preparing textbooks for college instruction, because they were 'chiefly interested in bringing principles previously worked out by others within the easy comprehension of under-graduate students' (Dunbar 1904, 13). This approach was not conducive to making discoveries or advances in political economy, as such publications had an 'absolute disregard of the existence of those who hold other views' (Patten 1895, 134). However, the eventual return of American students from Germany significantly changed this scene, as they wanted to establish American journals and periodicals that could publish high-quality scholarly work on economic issues and questions, so that they would be respected and on par with the scientific status of their German counterparts.

The AEA started printing *Publications of the American Economic Association* in 1886. Initially, it published monthly monographs, while its annual conference involved the presentation of many articles. Then, in 1900, this publication became a regular quarterly monograph series, which featured articles discussing the economic issues, concerns and problems of the time, while also providing reports about the annual meeting of the AEA. In 1908, *Publications of the American Economic Association* separated into two different journals: the *Economic Bulletin* and the *American Economic Association Quarterly*. They both published articles separately until 1910. However, in 1911, the *Economic Bulletin* and the *American Economic Association Quarterly* merged back together to form *The American Economic Review*, which went on to become one of the most prestigious academic journals in the field of economics.

A number of economic journals were also established at American universities. For example, the QJE was founded at Harvard University in 1886, making it the first professional journal of economics in the English speaking world (Eliot 1900). The QJE adopted a pluralistic approach in its early volumes, whereby it welcomed articles from American and European scholars belonging to different schools of economic thought, including the Austrian School of Economics, the GHSE, the New School, the Old School, and Classical Economics. Dunbar was appointed as the first editor of the QJE and remained in 'charge from 1886 to 1896' (Taussig 1901, 573). In 1896, he was succeeded by Taussig, who remained editor of the QJE until 1935, though Carver also served in that capacity from 1901 to 1904 and from 1918 to 1922. However, it was the early work of Dunbar that was credited with setting a high standard at the QJE, thereby solidifying 'the position of the Journal in this country and in Europe as a valuable medium for economic discussions and researches' (Eliot 1900, 480). He was successful from 'the outset in making for the Journal a distinguished place in the literature of the subject' (Taussig 1904, XIV). In fact, the QJE became 'a medium of communication for investigators, and took rank at once as one of the leading scholarly repertories on its subject' (Taussig 1901, 574). For internationally renowned academics, having their works published in the QJE 'served as guarantee of a claim to the attention of the learned world' (ibid.). It has even been suggested that Dunbar's contributions led to the QJE playing a major role in 'stimulating the remarkable advance of economic science which took place in the United States in the decade after its establishment' (Taussig 1904, XIV).

In 1886, the same year that the QJE was established, the PSQ was founded by Columbia University Professor John William Burgess (1844–1931), though Seligman also played an instrumental role in launching it. Although its title did not include any references to economics, it actually had 'considerable economic content' (Barber 2001, 228). The PSQ was dedicated to historical studies, statistics, and the comparative study of politics, economics, and public law. It also focused on relevant domestic and international issues of the time.

In 1890, the AAPSS launched the *ANNALS*, a policy and scientific journal covering political and social science, which served 'as a bimonthly journal for the Academy's scholarship' (AAPSS 1889). It published academic articles that mainly focused on the current issues of the time in a broad array of social science disciplines, which included topics like economic theory, banking, education, finance, institutional history, international law, jurisprudence, political institutions, political reforms, taxation, and transportation. The *ANNALS* also featured 'a large number of papers submitted to the Academy' that were read and discussed at its meetings (AAPSS 1897, 7). This resulted in a 'stimulating influence' on the scientific research of scholars in the areas of political and social science (ibid.). Some of the well-known contributing authors to this publication included Ashley, Bemis, J. B. Clark, Ely, Commons, Cunningham, Falkner, Hadley, James, Kinley, Patten, Ross, Schmoller, and Walras.

In 1892, 'to promote the image of Yale political economy,' Farnam relaunched *The Yale Review: A Quarterly Journal of History and Political Science*, which had previously been known as the *New Englander* since 1843 (Barber 1993, 165). Farnam also served as its editor from 1892 until 1911, the year it was transformed into a literary magazine. Originally, Farnam wanted Yale's journal to be competitive in 'the learned journal market with rival institutions, particularly' the QJE of Harvard and the PSQ of Columbia (ibid.). What really distinguished *The Yale Review* from these other two journals was that it was receptive to 'historical materials' (ibid.). It also published articles on the philosophy of economics, the history of economics, and the history of economic thought. However, it did not offer any 'space for articles in mathematical economics' (ibid.). Adherents of the New School regularly published articles in *The Yale Review*, including Clark, Walker, Seligman, and Fetter.

Laughlin, who was an adherent of the Old School, established the *Journal of Political Economy* in 1892. It was published by the University of Chicago Press and focused on highly specialized articles covering a variety of economic issues, as well as economic theory. During the 1890s, the *Journal of Political Economy* of the University of Chicago, the *Annals of the American Academy of Political and Social Science*, and *The Yale Review* were 'in direct competition with the AEA's search for quality materials for its own publishing programme' (Barber 2001, 228). In fact, these 'journal-publishing universities, acting on their perceived self-interest, effectively blocked the creation of a quarterly journal sponsored by the AEA: *The American Economic Review* did not come into existence until' 1911 (ibid.: 229).

In their early days, all these economic journals that were established by adherents of the New School primarily focused on addressing many of the same economic questions and issues being pondered by their counterparts in Germany. Also, many of the articles that American economists published in these journals referred to books and articles written by prominent theorists of the GHSE, including Wagner, Schmoller, Conrad, Roscher, and Knies, among others.

Other Major Contributions of the New School

In addition to establishing economic associations and journals, adherents of the New School also contributed to the development of the discipline of economics in the US in various other ways that helped raise the status of economists in society. For instance, many German-trained economists and their students provided 'expertise for a variety of federal, state, and local bodies and to private businesses' (Coats 1993, 348). They also encouraged 'team work' between 'the universities, the governments, and the various societies and institutions devoted to economic research' (Farnam 1913, 31). An example of this type of collaboration was the American Bureau of Industrial Research, which was founded by Farnam in 1904 and supported by adherents of the New School, including Ely, Clark, and John Rogers Commons (1862–1945). It was essentially a research center that brought together supporters of labor rights and reform-minded academics to collect and organize all available material on the history of the American industrial society, with a focus on understanding the history of the labor movement in the country. With the help of Ely and his students, the American Bureau of Industrial Research ended up publishing 11 volumes of a *Documentary History of American Industrial Society* in 1910 and 1911 (Commons 1918). Then, in 1918, it published the two volumes of the *History of Labour in the United States* that were prepared by Commons and his graduate students (Commons 1963, 97). These volumes were extremely important, because they were the first systematically organized archived collections on the history of labor in the US.

Commons and his students also played instrumental roles in the area of government legislation and policy in the US, including the establishment of labor laws and the development and administration of social security programs and services. For example, they contributed to 'drafting the Civil Service Law of 1906, and the Public Utility Act of 1907' (Yefimov 2009, 39). Edwin E. Witte (1887–1960) and Elizabeth Brandeis Raushenbush (1896–1984) were among Commons's students who were well known for participating in the drafting of laws pertaining to unemployment insurance, social security, and public health insurance in the US (ibid.). Over the course of his career, Witte was Executive Director of President Franklin D. Roosevelt's Committee of Economic Security in 1934, the first president of the Industrial Relations Research Association in 1948, and president of the AEA in 1956–1957 (Cohen 1960). Witte, who was strongly influenced by Commons, was highly critical of 'the power of the large impersonal corporation, the political influence of private insurance companies, the control of "Wall Street," and the influence of professors from eastern universities in government, business, and labor' (ibid.). Like many theorists of the GHSE, he essentially combined economics, history, ethics, and politics with the realities of life in order to improve the living conditions of all citizens. In fact, he came to be known as 'the father of the Social Security Act' in the US, as he played a crucial role in 'the formulating of the social security program' (ibid.). Furthermore, he and other Wisconsin institutionalists defended 'the trade union when such defense was dangerous' (ibid.). Witte also advocated for 'social security and public health insurance,' even though there were strong attacks against any efforts aimed at establishing a 'welfare-state' or 'socialized medicine' at that time (ibid.).

Adherents of the New School also made important contributions to the establishment of the American Association for Labor Legislation (AALL) in 1906.[2] Ely was appointed as the first president of the AALL, while Taussig, Seager, Farnam, and Commons were among its well-known members. The membership of the AALL, which was comprised of 'state and federal officials dealing with labor problems, and of professors and social workers, continually developed plans for labor legislation' (Lafayette 1962, 72). The goal of the AALL was 'to promote uniformity of labor legislation and to encourage the study of labor conditions with a view toward promoting desirable legislation.'[3] It focused on the elimination of child labor and the improvement of working conditions at factories (Gee 2012, 49). It also pushed for minimum wage legislation, compensation for work-related injuries, and unemployment and health insurance. In fact, 'the AALL has been remembered primarily for being the first organization to mount a campaign for compulsory health insurance' (ibid.). Starting in 1911, the AALL published a quarterly journal called the *American Labor Legislation Review*, which welcomed academic articles that supported social, political, and economic reforms. According to Ely, most adherents of the Old School were opposed to labor legislation on principle because it 'seemed to them to be a futile interference with economic laws,' whereas adherents of the New School supported it (Farnam 1913, 82).

In 1920, Ely established the Institute for Research in Land Economics and Public Utilities, which was associated with, but independent from, the University of Wisconsin (Ely and Shine 1924, 315). It was headquartered at the University of Wisconsin until 1925, when it moved to Northwestern University, where it remained until about 1935. The institute also established its own journal entitled the *Journal of Land and Public Utility Economics*, which published research papers from 1925 to 1947. Ely believed that land economics was a field that was neglected by economists. Accordingly, the institute focused on research in the areas of land valuation, conservation, urbanization, and public utilities. It was supported 'entirely by contributions of public-spirited citizens and organizations' that were 'interested in the securing of the truth for its own sake and of others who have private interests that involve land problems' (ibid.). As a result, it was 'entirely free from political influence' (ibid.). Since 'no public money' was 'paid into its treasury, no political power' could intervene in its investigations and its publication (ibid.).

Members of the New School also made important contributions to the development of welfare economics. In fact, their ideas played a major role in the creation of the New Deal. To be more precise, the welfare economics of Patten, who is also known as the 'forerunner of New Dealers,' highly influenced Rexford Tugwell (1891–1979), who was instrumental in the implementation of Roosevelt's New Deal. According to Ely (1936, 141), who trained and influenced many eminent American economists, 'neither the New Deal nor the old could be understood' without the AEA. Moreover, he believed that the New Deal was directly influenced by the social and economic reforms that Bismarck installed in Germany during the 1880s.

Conclusion

Originally, various associations and journals in the US were founded and organized by economists who were influenced by the GHSE, either by having studied under its theorist in Germany or by training with American economists who returned to the US after completing their education in Germany. These newly established American economic journals and associations were modeled after the ones that already existed in Germany. For their founders, these associations and journals constituted a protest against the ahistorical value-free science, the laissez-faire doctrine, and the abstract individualistic and mechanical laws that were being promoted by classical economists. Their intention was to provide a platform that would facilitate cooperation, including with members of the Old School, the church, the state, and scientists. In doing so, they were hoping to give political economy a new direction. They also sought to find remedies to the growing social and economic problems that Americans were facing.

Another goal of the newly established American economic associations, journals, and periodicals was to foster and promote the ideas and scholarly research of the GHSE in the US. Basically, they aimed to encourage creative and independent economic research and the publication of economic monographs, while also providing an environment where fruitful academic and professional discussions could occur among political economists. It has even been suggested that they sought to rectify the backward situation that prevailed within the discipline of economics in the US. Some of these associations and journals ended up becoming very influential, and remain so up to this day; however, their priorities, goals, and roles have changed significantly over time. Unfortunately, contemporary economists are largely unaware of the remarkable contributions that adherents of the New School made to the development of political economy in the US, both as an academic discipline and as a profession, through their efforts to establish influential associations, institutions, and journals that were inspired by the GHSE.

Notes

1 https://archives.yale.edu/repositories/12/resources/3709.
2 Cornell University Library. American Association for Labor Legislation Records on Microfilm: Collection Number: 5001 mf. https://rmc.library.cornell.edu/EAD/htmldocs/KCL05001mf.html.
3 Ibid.

Bibliography

AAPSS. 1889. 'On the Morning of December 14, 1889, Twenty-Two People Met in Philadelphia to form the American Academy of Political and Social Science.' https://www.aapss.org/about-us/history/

AAPSS. 1897. *Handbook of the American Academy of Political and Social Science*. Philadelphia: American Academy of Political and Social Science.

American Social Science Association. 1866. 'Constitution, Address, and List of Members of American Association for the Promotion of Social Science.' Boston: Right & Potter, Printers, No. 4 Spring Lane.

Balabkins, Nicholas W. 1988. *Not by Theory Alone . . . : The Economics of Gustav von Schmoller and Its Legacy to America*. Berlin: Duncker und Humblot.

Barber, William J. 1993. *Economists and Higher Learning in the Nineteenth Century*. New Brunswick: Transaction Publishers.

Barber, William J. 2001. 'Economists and Professional Organisations in Pre-World War I America.' Ed. Augello, Massimo M. and Marco E. L. Guidi. *The Spread of Political Economy and the Professionalisation of Economists: Economic Societies in Europe, America and Japan in the Nineteenth Century*. London: Routledge. 216–232.

Coats, Alfred William. 1985. 'The American Economic Association and the Economics Profession.' *Journal of Economic Literature*. Vol. 23, No. 4: 1697–1727. URL: http://www.jstor.com/stable/2725706

Coats, Alfred William. 1993. 'The Educational Revolution and the Professionalization of American Economics.' Ed. William J. Barber. *Breaking the Academic Mould: Economists and Higher Learning in the Nineteenth Century*. New Brunswick: Transaction Publishers. 340–375.

Cohen, Wilbur J. 1960. 'The Beginnings of Social Security: Edwin E. Witte (1887–1960): Father of the Social Security.' https://www.ssa.gov/history/cohenwitte.html

Commons, John R. 1918. *History of Labour in the United States*. New York: The MacMillan Company.

Commons, John R. 1963 [1934]. *Myself. The Autobiography of John R. Commons*. Madison: The University of Wisconsin Press.

Devine, Edward T. 1894. 'Economic Science in America.' *University Extension Bulletin: A Record of Current University Extension Work*. Vol. 1–2, No. 5: 86–88. https://babel.hathitrust.org/cgi/pt?id=mdp.39015086683797&view=1up&seq=65

Dunbar, Charles F. 1897. 'The Career of Francis Amasa Walker.' *Quarterly Journal of Economics*. July: 436–448.

Dunbar, Charles F. 1904. *Economic Essays*. New York: Macmillan & CO., LTD.

Eliot, Charles W. 1900. 'Charles Franklin Dunbar.' *The Harvard Graduates' Magazine*. Vol. VIII, No. 32: 469–484. The Harvard graduates' magazine. v.8 (1899-1900). - Full View | HathiTrust Digital Library | HathiTrust Digital Library

Ely, Richard T. 1886. 'Report of the Organization of the American Economic Association.' *Publications of the American Economic Association*. Vol. 1, No. 1: 5–32. URL: https://www.jstor.org/stable/2485628

Ely, Richard T. 1887. 'Report of the Organization of the American Economic.' *American Economic Association*. Vol. 1, No. 1: 5–46.

Ely, Richard T. 1895. 'On Methods of Teaching Political Economy.' Ed. G. Stanley Hall. *Vol. I. Methods of Teaching History*. Boston: D. C. Heath & Company. 61–72.

Ely, Richard T. 1910. 'The American Economic Association 1885–1909.' *American Economic Association Quarterly*. Vol. 11, No. 1: 47–111. URL: https://www.jstor.org/stable/3000023Ely, Richard T. 1936 (March). 'The Founding and Early History of the American Economic Association.' *The American Economic Review*. Vol. 26, No. 1: 141–150. URL: https://www.jstor.org/stable/1807774

Ely, Richard T. 1938. *Ground under Our Feet*. New York: Macmillan.

Ely, Richard T. and Mary L. Shine 1924. 'The Institute for Research in Land Economics and Public Utilities.' *The Johns Hopkins University Press*. Vol. 32, No. 3: 313–316. URL: https://www.jstor.org/stable/27533772

Farnam, Henry W. 1913. *The Economic Utilisation of History*. New Haven: Yale University Press.

Gee, John. 2012. 'Twilight of Consensus: The American Association for Labor Legislation and Academic Public Policy Research.' *Penn History Review*. Vol. 19, No. 2: 44–70. https://repository.upenn.edu/phr/vol19/iss2/4

Lafayette, G. Harter Jr. 1962. *John R. Commons: His Assault on Laissez-faire*. Oregon: Oregon State University Press.

Patten, Simon Nelson. 1895. 'The Teaching of Economics in the Secondary Schools.' *American Economic Association*. Vol. 10, No. 3: 119–138. URL: https://www.jstor.org/stable/2485652.

Philippovich, Eugen von. 1891. 'The Verein Für Sozialpolitik.' *The Quarterly Journal of Economics*. Vol. 5, No. 2: 220–237.

Proceedings of the American Political Science Association. 1904. 'The Organization of the American Political Science Association.' https://archive.org/details/jstor-3038312

Taussig, Frank William. 1901. 'Charles Franklin Dunbar.' *Proceedings of the American Academy of Arts and Sciences*. Vol. 36, No. 29: 569–557. URL: https://www.jstor.org/stable/20021619

Taussig, Frank William. 1904. 'Introduction.' Ed. Charles F. Dunbar. *Economic Essays*. New York: Macmillan & CO., LTD. VII–XVII.

Tribe, Keith. 2002. 'Historical Schools of Economics: German and English.' *Keele Economics Research Papers*. No. 2002/02. SSRN: https://ssrn.com/abstract=316689 or http://dx.doi.org/10.2139/ssrn.316689

Walker, Francis A. 1889. 'Recent Progress of Political Economy in the United States.' *Publications of the American Economic Association*. Vol. 4, No. 4: 17–40. URL: https://www.jstor.org/stable/2485572

Yefimov, Vladimir. 2009. 'Comparative Historical Institutional Analysis of German, English and American Economics.' *Munich Personal RePEc Archive*. http://mpra.ub.uni-muenchen.de/48173/

7 The New School on the Conservation of the Natural Environment

Introduction

In European aristocratic societies, lands were often passed down from 'generation to generation without being divided' (Tocqueville 2010V1, 116). It was widely accepted that the 'family spirit' was 'embodied in the land,' which meant it had to be preserved and kept intact across generations (ibid.). That is to say, 'the family represents the land; the land represents the family; the land perpetuates its name, origin, glory, power and virtues' (ibid.). Meanwhile, in democratic America, people's ancestors came from many different parts of the world, which meant 'the family no longer enters the mind except as something vague, indeterminate, and uncertain' (ibid.). Also, contrary to the aristocratic societies of Europe, land in the US was regularly divided, because it was not attached to memory, pride, or ambition; it was simply bought or sold for economic purposes (ibid.). Basically, each person in America focuses on the interests, prosperity, and 'present convenience' of the current generation, in addition to 'the establishment of the generation immediately following, and nothing more' (ibid.). Consequently, natural resources were regarded as mere factors of production to be used and exploited for the acquisition of material gains and profits in the early days of democratic America. At that time, little consideration was given to the notion of protecting, cultivating, or caring for the environment in order to preserve it for future generations.

Theorist of the German Historical School of Economics (GHSE) and their American students recognized the importance of protecting the natural environment and conserving natural resources. In fact, the necessity of addressing environmental problems and preserving natural resources for the sake of humanity was 'first clearly recognized in Germany and has been taught and practiced there' by adherents of the historical school since 1860 (Hess 1917, 113). This chapter explains that early efforts to protect the environment and natural resources in the US originated in the work of the New School, whose members were concerned that destructive business practices that led to deforestation, the erosion of soil, oil and gas pollution, and the depletion of mineral reserves could have detrimental social and economic consequences and possibly lead to climate change. This chapter also explains how they tried

DOI: 10.4324/9781003247715-7

to find remedies to such issues in order to help conserve the environment for current and future generations.

The GHSE and the Protection of the Natural Environment

Richard T. Ely (1854–1943) (1917, 12) was one of the pioneers of the conservation movement in the US, which sought to prevent the waste or destruction of natural resources. In fact, he regarded conservation as one of 'the foundations of national prosperity' (ibid.: V). He explained that Americans who studied in Germany were exposed to the importance and merits of conservation by the theorists of the GHSE, who were already raising awareness about the need to protect the natural environment (ibid.: 12). This is because they were conscious of the fact that any changes to the natural environment and climate could affect all life on earth. For example, Georg Friedrich Roscher (1817–1894) was concerned about climate change and highlighted the importance of striking an ecological balance. In particular, he pointed out that climate change would be destructive for agriculture sectors, as the production of many agriculture products would be impossible at certain temperatures. When Roscher (1878V1, 122) explained the role of the 'climate, and of its heat or moisture' on economic activities, he emphasized the importance of:

> the average temperature of the whole year, but especially with the distribution of heat among the several parts of the day and the different seasons of the year, and the maximum summer heat and winter cold (the isothermal and isocheimenal lines).

In fact, he argued that 'the lines called isothermal, that is, lines of equal annual heat, are, therefore, of greatest importance to public economy, because the "zones of production" depend mainly on them' (ibid.). Roscher also emphasized that human activities could degrade soil quality, which is essential to the yields produced by agriculture sector. Broadly speaking, he argued that since all of the raw materials that the land provides are 'the indispensable foundation of all economy,' it was crucial to protect the natural environment (ibid.: 164).

Ely (1917, 19) also mentioned that the importance of conserving the natural environment was taught 'in the lectures of Professor Karl Knies [1821–1898] on Practical National Applied Economics and Economic Policy.' Knies supported state actions that were favorable to the conservation of the natural environment (ibid.). Additionally, Roscher, Karl Heinrich Rau (1792–1870), and Adolf Wagner (1835–1917) were among the German political economists who played major roles in promoting positive state actions that protected natural environment. They regarded the state as the main institution for conservation, with interventions and regulations being its main tools (ibid.: 13). For example, they supported the state ownership of forests as the best way to protect the natural environment. In fact, the conservation of forestry was 'developed in Germany for a longer time and to a more refined degree than in other countries' (Fernow 1911, XI). As such, it was generally accepted that 'both the science and art of forestry are most thoroughly developed and most intensively applied throughout Germany' (ibid.: 22). According to the adherents of the GHSE, anyone who was opposed to the notion of state forests was 'fit for the lunatic asylum' (ibid.: 143).

Contrary to the GHSE, the conservation of the natural environment did not receive very much attention during the prominence of classical economics, because it was in conflict with the laissez-faire doctrine and methodological individualism (Ely 1917, 12). However, the fact that the GHSE focused on the realities of life and favored a 'look and see' approach 'compelled a careful study' of 'most of what is embraced in conservation' (ibid.: 14). More precisely, the 'look and see' approach allowed the Germans to observe that their nation did not have 'fertile soil' or rich 'mineral deposits' (ibid.: 13). Thus, they realized that they were 'obliged to use with care the natural resources of the land, and to improve the natural heritage in order to provide for a rapidly growing population' (ibid.). As a result, the natural resources in Germany were not 'slaughtered; on the contrary,' they were 'cultivated, so as to yield maximum returns' (ibid.: 14).

Unlike in Germany, where the GHSE supported various measures that were taken to protect the natural environment, adherents of classical economics in the US promoted the capitalist system that allowed for unfettered business practices and wasteful consumption, which were extremely detrimental to the environment. For most of the 19th century, conservation efforts essentially did not exist in the US, and Americans had 'at many points been wasteful in the true sense of that term' (James 1911, 9). At that time, Germans already looked upon the US as 'a nation of butchers,' because they were 'butchering or slaughtering the gifts of nature, wasting' their forests and mineral treasures, and degrading their soil (Ely 1917, 11). Since the early days of the US, its sparse population, abundant land, and seemingly unlimited natural resources were key factors that encouraged wasteful exploitation and consumption and contributed to the lack of interest in protecting the natural environment.

The Exploitation of Natural Resources and the Rise of Conservation Efforts in the US

The political economy department at the University of Wisconsin ended up becoming 'a pioneer in the development of land economics' and 'agriculture economics,' both of which focused on conservation efforts (Ely 1938, 191). This is not overly surprising, given that adherents of the New School played a main role in its establishment (ibid.). To be more precise, it was actually Ely who introduced classes on conservation to the political economy department, which were based on lectures given by Knies in Germany. In 1896, Bernhard

Eduard Fernow (1851–1923), who previously studied and practiced forestry in Germany and was 'the founding president of the Canadian Society of Forest Engineers in 1908 and he served on the federal Commission of Conservation from 1910 to 1923,'[1] gave 'a course of lectures on the economic aspects of forestry under the auspices of the Department of Political Economy in the University of Wisconsin' (Ely 1917, 17–20). This was 'the first course of forestry lectures in the country,' and it predated any similar offerings in England (ibid.: 17). Fernow's class ended up having an 'historical role in the conservation movement' across English-speaking nations (ibid.). Henry Charles Taylor (1873–1969), a former student of Ely, also focused on the conservation of natural environment. He was also known as the 'father of agriculture economics' and worked as director of the Farm Foundation in the US. In 1909, Taylor (1923) was credited with creating the first academic department that was dedicated to agricultural economics in the US at the University of Wisconsin. Its courses often highlighted the importance of conservation efforts to protect the natural environment. Ultimately, many of Ely's former students from Wisconsin obtained important positions at the Bureau of Agricultural Economics which focused on conservation issues.

Many prominent adherents of the New School earn reputations for raising awareness about the importance of conserving the natural environment, including Ely, Henry Carter Adams (1851–1921), Thomas Nixon Carver (1865–1961), John Bates Clark (1874–1938), Henry W. Farnam (1853–1933), Edmund Janes James (1855–1925), Simon Nelson Patten (1852–1922), Edwin Robert Anderson Seligman (1861–1939), Lewis Cecil Gray (1881–1952), and Taylor. These academics were likely exposed to the topics of environmental protection and conservation by their mentors from GHSE or by their German-trained professors at the American universities. They believed that the detrimental outcomes associated with the excessive exploitation of the natural environment were much more serious than many other issues of their time. More precisely, they were critical of the fact that private businesses in the US were exhausting mineral deposits, clear-cutting forests, stripping away natural pastures, and eroding the quality of soil. Theorists of the New School argued that such business practices involved the destructive appropriation of natural resources for the satisfaction of immediate human wants and the desire for rapid accumulation of private wealth. Furthermore, they pointed out that the unmitigated exploitation of natural resources was indifferent to common welfare and the economic prosperity of future generations. For example, Patten (1889, 34) argued that 'the crude and the selfish' exploitation of 'new lands and mines has allowed an agricultural retrogression' to occur. Meanwhile, Clark (1914, 20) claimed that 'natural resources have been wasted in a prodigal way' in the US. He was also concerned about the overexploitation of natural resources, noting that 'natural gas and oil have been burned with no regard for the future' (ibid.). Edwin Francis Gay (1867–1946) (1929, 11), who obtained his PhD from the University of Berlin, having written his dissertation under the supervision of Schmoller, underlined that Americans 'with superabundant natural resources' have 'always been open to the charge of wastefulness' and the overexploitation of natural resources. In the meantime, Seligman (1910) argued that economic life and the natural environment were profoundly affected by overexploitation. Additionally, James (1911, 8) was disappointed that American society 'permitted the national wealth of the country to be exploited in an uneconomical way in many directions, owing to the greed, or short sightedness, or both, of private interests.' In fact, James (1911, 8) stated that:

> We have undoubtedly used at many points wasteful methods in the cutting off of our forests, and have failed to observe that the larger interest of the community as a whole demanded a greater care in the removal of our timber wealth.

According to James, when it came to the importance of forests for rainfalls, the best development of 'national resources demands that a certain proportion of the surface of the country be covered with forests' (Ely 1910, 52). Clark (1914, 20) was also particularly concerned that in the US, 'forests have been recklessly cut, fires been invited and the soil itself has been sacrificed.' Ely (1917, 3) was also worried that the depletion of forests across the US resulted in soil being 'washed by rapidly flowing surface water from mountain sides.' He also pointed out that the excessive cutting of forests raised the risk of fires. Meanwhile, Seligman warned that protecting forests was an immediate concern and necessity, because they played an important role in preventing climate change, which is 'the most difficult to alter' (Seligman 1910, 42). He pointed to 'the history of the Italian Maremma' during Roman times, which was known for its advanced farms before the neglect of drainage and the overexploitation of natural resources led to the ruinous decline of agriculture and, ultimately, the disappearance of the human life from the area (Seligman 1910, 43). According to Seligman (1910, 43), the case of Maremma demonstrated 'the alternate consequences of neglect and intelligent effort on climate and soil.' This led him to emphasize the importance of forests in 'affecting the rainfall,' 'equalizing the flow of the rivers,' and 'obviating the sudden alternations of inundation and drought with their devastating effects on cultivation' (ibid.). Patten (1885, 26) also expressed reservations about forests 'being cleared away so that the ground may be cultivated.' He explained that it was crucial to protect and expand forests because, in order to secure 'a proper rainfall' and eliminate the conditions of a dry climate, 'it is necessary that a large part of the land of a country should be covered with trees' (ibid.: 25, 174). If the trees are cleared away to:

> bring all the land into cultivation, while the owners of the forest lands may profit by it, the owners of the other lands will lose more than the first gain, and on the whole the country will lose, since, the gross production being diminished, a less population than before can be supported.
>
> (ibid.: 25)

Additionally, Gray (1913, 500), who was highly influenced by the views of Ely and Taylor on the topic of conservation during his time at the University of Wisconsin, suggested that 'the conservation of resources such as forests' does not 'involve the more difficult and fundamental phases of conservation,' given that 'a forest destroyed can be restored.' That said, he made it clear that if 'the original stock is exhausted, the problem becomes one of economical production and consumption,' because 'the replacement of forest requires a long period of time' (ibid.).

Economists of the New School were also concerned about the overexploitation of mining and oil and gas resources. According to Gray (1913, 501), 'the most serious phases of the conservation problem grow out of the fact that some of the most important elements, such as coal, petroleum, and iron, are being rapidly and completely used up without hope of replacement.' Meanwhile, James (1911, 10) pointed out that Americans were creating 'great waste in the exploitation' of their 'stores of iron, and such waste ought to be stopped.' James (1911, 8) further stated that:

> We have mined our coal oftentimes in such a way as to destroy forever the value of a large part of it. We have allowed our natural gas in great quantities to escape into the atmosphere or be burned as it came from the bowels of the earth, with no resulting economic gain.

Similarly, Charles Kenneth Leith (1875–1956), who headed the geology department at the University of Wisconsin for 30 years and coauthored *The Foundation of National Prosperity Studies in The Conservation of Permanent National Resources* (1917) with Ely and Carver, was concerned about the exploitation of mining and mineral resources. That is to say, Leith (1917, 187) maintained that 'mineral resources are being wastefully mined and used.' With that in mind, he explained that 'the movement for conservation of mineral resources in the United States has been based' on 'the recognition of the fact that the reserves of the mineral products are not unlimited' (ibid.). In fact, Leith (1917, 187) advocated for the careful conservation of mineral resources, since increasing the exploitation of such 'reserves will exhaust them within a period comparatively short as compared with the future of the race.'

Another environmental problem that was of great concern to adherents of the New School was the degradation of soil quality. Seligman (1910, 36) emphasized that 'man, like all animals, is indissolubly bound to the soil.' With that in mind, he was worried that unsustainable farming practices caused land to rapidly lose its fertility, as even 'the best land can become the poorest through wasteful cultivation' (ibid.: 44). Since man is 'dependent upon nature for what he is and what he has accomplished,' he argued that it was crucial to protect the quality of soil (ibid.). Similarly, Ely (1910, 52) was concerned that even though the US had a great variety of soils and climates, its 'system of land laws' permitted farmers 'to adopt a system of culture' that only took present profits into account. This situation exhausted the quality of soil, making it less fertile (ibid.). Meanwhile, Patten (1889, 34) was very critical of the reckless exploitation of new lands for agricultural purposes. In particular, he believed that the poor usage of the best arable lands was ruining their quality, as 'the rich lands lose most in fertility under improper tillage' (Patten 1885, 27). He warned that if a nation does not:

> change on account of a better adjustment of themselves to nature, they can supply the wants of an increasing population only from soils less fitted than those before in use for the production of the commodities desired by those not conforming to nature.
>
> (ibid.: 70)

In other words, the 'greater the conformity to nature the more will all the qualities in land be brought into use, and the larger will be the ratio of the good land to the poor' (ibid.). Additionally, Patten (1885, 26) was concerned about rivers being 'precipitated so rapidly into the valleys below that they are overflowed, and much of the best land in the country rendered useless for cultivation.' Carver (1949, 270), who was an advisor to the US Department of Agriculture, was also concerned about erosion that carried away 'incalculable tons of topsoil most of which can never be replaced.' In response, he proposed greater efforts to delay 'the rate of further erosion and rebuild a little of it' (ibid.). He also advised future generations to find new frontiers by which to improve the quality of soil. Likewise, Adams (1886, 9) explained that since 'many industrial conditions are determined by the character of the soil,' efforts to improve soil quality needed to be a priority for every nation. As such, he called for the development of environmentally friendly farming techniques that could protect and improve the quality of soil (Adams 1887, 394). He also believed that broader economic activities needed to be adjusted in ways that safeguarded soil.

Seligman (1910, 44) pointed out that people across different places and civilizations worked on improving the character of their soil, because they were fully aware of its importance for the survival and economic development of society. He also noted that if the soil is well taken care of, then even 'the worst land can be converted into the most fruitful' (ibid.). According to him, the improvement of soil requires the use of 'manures, both animal and mineral, and the replacement of an extensive by an intensive cultivation with the proper rotation of crops,' which would alter 'the chemical ingredients of the soil' (ibid.). Basically, Seligman was explaining that properly caring for the soil would change the poor land of today into the fertile land tomorrow. Similarly, Gray (1913, 502) contended that 'through rotation of crops, animal husbandry, and other scientific methods, it is possible to prevent the impairment of soil fertility.' James and Patten also suggested that 'a suitable rotation and variety of crops be observed' if people wanted to develop their resources in the best manner possible and for the best interests of society (Ely 1910, 52).

Seligman (1910, 37) believed that people had the ability to change the natural environment to some extent in ways that could improve the quality of soil and increase the size of forests. At the same time, he cautioned that the economic activities of people could induce climate change, which could lead to significant ecological imbalances that are irreversible (ibid.: 42). Seligman believed that since economic resources are dependent on the ways in which man modifies the environment, people had to be very careful when they engaged in economic activities that could alter the climate. As such, he advised for the development of strategies to mitigate climate change.

Seligman (1910, 40) tried to emphasize the importance of preventing climate change by explaining that the life cycle of 'the vegetable and animal' are 'a result of the climatic and geological conditions.' He also highlighted that the 'rain, sun and chemical ingredients of the soil' were key factors in 'the possibility of raising all the staple crops like hay, wheat, cotton, rice, tobacco, sugar, coffee or tea, or of obtaining the timber, rubber, cork and other products of the forest' (ibid.). An increase in temperature would affect 'the forestry conditions, as well as the size and therefore the economic utility of the rivers' (ibid.: 38). It could also cause many species of plant to die off in large numbers, which would substantially disrupt the food chains that rely on them. Seligman further stressed that since only a portion of the globe was livable and economic life as well as life in general were dependent on the forces of nature, it was necessary to conserve the natural environment in order to prevent climate change. He also noted that 'even in the habitable portions of the globe the climatic conditions are of the first importance. At the very outset the influence of temperature is obvious' (ibid.: 37).

Among adherents of the New School, James (1887, 61) took the damaging effects of pollution on people very seriously, as he believed that it represented a real danger to 'the power of regenerating the moral as well as the physical life of man.' He was particularly concerned that higher levels of pollution would have a disproportionate impact on 'the poorer classes,' because they usually lived 'in the least ventilated and most smoky districts' (ibid.). The poor are also 'less able than other persons to get away to fresher air and purer surroundings' (ibid.: 62). Moreover, he contended that the pollution of the:

> town atmosphere is one of the chief reasons of people living out of town and thus necessarily withdrawing to a great degree their active sympathy and various social influences for good from their poorer brethren who are compelled to remain continually in town.
>
> (ibid.)

Some of the theorists of the New School were highly concerned about overconsumption, because they considered it to be the most immediate obstacle to conservation efforts in the US. In fact, Patten (1885, 59) warned about wasteful consumption as early as 1885, pointing out that fashionable goods and articles generated 'a great waste of labor and material.' According to Gray

(1913, 516), overconsumption was 'neither based on welfare, nor on enjoyment; it is solely dictated by convention.' He pointed to 'the enormous waste of coal required for the electrical advertising' in American cities as being 'illustrative of this exploitative consumption' (ibid.). He specifically stated that 'every great White Way in every American city is nightly one more chemical orgy of waste, a crime of competitive advertising for which some day thousands of individuals must shiver for months' (ibid.).

Ely (1917, 39) suggested that excessive consumption led to Americans spoiling a lot of food, much of which simply ended up in the garbage. He attributed this 'wicked waste' to the fact that 'food was superabundant' in the US (ibid.: 38). Ely (1917, 39) also believed that 'when an excessive amount of food is consumed,' 'intellectual activity' is impaired and 'diseased conditions of the body' are generated. He argued that the prevention of wasteful consumption and behavior necessitated the improvement of 'the human race' through the 'intellectual and moral education' of the people (ibid.). Meanwhile, when it came to preventing the overexploitation of natural resources, Leith (1917, 187) proposed modifications to the 'method of extraction' and a reduction in the use of natural resources. He believed that such changes could be achieved through the education and self-development of the people to some extent (ibid.).

Environmental Protection Measures Proposed by the Adherents of the New School

According to Ely, the dominance of the abstract and deductive approaches of the classical orthodoxy was one of the key reasons behind the lack of effort to develop conservation measures in the US. However, this situation started to change with the return of German-trained American political economists. For example, Ely (1917, 5) pointed out that James and Patten, who were both conservationists, included the 'conservation of natural resources' as one the goals in 'their programme or statement of aims' when they released their proposal to establish the Society for the Study of National Economy (SSNE). They also highlighted the importance of a state role in the conservation of natural resources. Ultimately, the SSNE never came to fruition, because it did not attract sufficient support to justify its establishment. However, the founding members of the American Economic Association (AEA), which was established in 1885 and retained the fundamental ideas of the SSNE, also defended conservation efforts. That said, the founders of the AEA held the view that the 'excessive cultivation of deduction' and the 'narrow view of the scope of economics' shut 'men's eyes to the economic significance of conservation' (ibid.: 14). In fact, 'its statement of principles' stated that the AEA was strongly opposed to 'laissez-faire, which in its very essence is fatal to conservation' (ibid.: 15).

In the US, 'the idea of conservation has developed from a general recognition of rapidly increasing scarcity of natural resources' in the early decades of the 20th century (Gray 1913, 497). At that time, it was already recognized that nearly all natural resources were appropriated and being overexploited. As a result, Americans started to experience 'the greatest inequality in the distribution of wealth the world has ever seen, and the greatest degree of concentration and control of that wealth' (Gray 1914, 19). By excessively exploiting natural resources, powerful and rich business owners were depriving 'others, not only of exploiting in the same manner, but even of the right of attaining a decent living' (ibid.). In response, American economists began to engage in discussions with the conservation movement and participate in the preparation of conservation policies in the early decades of the 20th century. In doing so, they advised that it was necessary to determine 'the proper balance in conservational practice between public and private interests and between the present and the future' (Leith 1917, 188).

Seligman (1910, 21) explained that natural resources allow a nation 'to acquire wealth, just as intelligence or strength enables a man to acquire wealth.' Given his view of natural resources as a 'source of wealth,' Seligman (ibid.) argued that the protection and conservation of the environment are crucial for the well-being and prosperity of the people. Similarly, Adams (1886, 9) emphasized the importance of using natural resources carefully and strategically in order to secure economic progress and development. Meanwhile, Gray (1913, 516) explained that exploitation resulted 'in maximum production under certain conditions, but maximum production does not necessarily mean progress.' As for Ely (1917, 22), he argued that:

> whether fertile lands are turned into deserts, forests into waste places, brooks into torrents, rivers changed from means of power and intercourse into means of destruction and desolation-these are questions which concern the material existence itself of society, and since such changes become often irreversible, the damage irremediable, and at the same time the extent of available resources becomes smaller in proportion to population conservation efforts should be an immediate priority.

When it came to the use of the natural resources of the nation, adherents of the New School thought that economic agents do not always consider the common good of society when they pursue their own self-interests. Generally speaking, they were opposed to the laissez-faire approach and individualism while advocating for positive state actions in the development of conservation measures (Seager 1910, 1, 4). As such, they called on state to protect the natural environment, even though they were conscious that Americans, particularly businessmen and farmers, believed that 'government is best which attempts least' (ibid.: 4). For example, Adams (1887) supported positive state action for the protection and expansion of forests, as he knew that business classes would not invest in such endeavors because they would not see immediate returns. Similarly, Farnam (1913) supported the conservation of natural resources, particularly forests, via positive state action. Seligman also believed that forest conservation required positive state action because it was crucial for the national interest. More specifically, he argued that 'the afforestation of treeless lands and the reforestation of denuded hillsides' should be 'a part of the economic policy of every careful government' (Seligman 1910, 43). Meanwhile, in his own conservation efforts, Gray supported the establishment of a national system of land use planning. He also advocated for positive state action to correct 'the habit of exploitation' as well as the wasteful practices of individuals (Gray 1913, 498).

Ely (1917, 47) was also of the opinion that positive state action was required in order to implement conservation policies that would maintain natural 'resources so far as possible, improve them whenever and wherever possible,' and 'secure as high a degree of justice in distribution.' When it came to the issue of deforestation, Ely (1910, 52) believed that the main problem was the 'system of land laws,' which allowed 'individuals and localities, led by motives of private interest, to reduce the amount of forest land below the proportion which it should bear to arable land.' In response, Ely proposed reforestation efforts and the public ownership and management of forests, with a focus on long-term conservation (Ely 1917, 4). He believed that state ownership was necessary for 'preserving our forests,' because 'the ordinary laws of supply and demand' were not adequate in doing so (Ely 1883, 232). In fact, he argued that in order to protect forests, 'the civilized world now recognizes a large amount of public ownership as necessary; so also with regard to the shores of harbors; so also with regard to mineral treasures' (Ely 1917, 45). According to Ely (1910, 52), the state should:

> insist that in every locality there shall be reserved for forests such a proportion of its area as the public welfare demands, and to change our present laws so as to favor the acquisition of the land by those whose interests in management will coincide with those of the public.

The support of the New School for positive state actions aimed at protecting the natural environment was not limited to forests. For instance, Leith (1917, 269) defended 'the application of public power to further conservation of privately owned mineral sources' in the interests of future generations. In doing so, 'a larger proportion of the mineral resources may be saved for the future than under present methods' (ibid.: 187). He insisted that 'conservation measures may be made really effective only by the application of government power' (ibid.). Basically, he believed that it was possible to have 'an intelligent plan for government control without the difficulties which arise in dealing with private ownership' (ibid.: 209). He primarily supported state interventions in instances where individual and general interests do not harmonize. According to Leith (1917, 269), 'there is no essential conflict between public and private, present and future, welfare' under this kind of arrangement. Furthermore, he believed that the positive state action he proposed was neither oppressive nor authoritarian.

In his own research on conservation, Ralph Henry Hess (1877–1956) (1917, 157), a professor of political economy at the University of Wisconsin, determined that 'private monopoly and true conservation are essentially incompatible.' To be more precise, he was of the opinion that 'in so far as corporations may covet monopoly gains, they will be out of sympathy with the aims and objects of conservation' (ibid.). In particular, Hess (1917, 161) believed that it was impossible to attain adequate and effective conservation 'under the regime of corporation dominance in the development and management of natural resources,' 'unless there is brought about a more effective public control of private property.' Accordingly, he defended positive state actions that facilitated conservation, as he claimed that 'every impulse which moves the individual to conserve natural resources is either inadequate or ineffectual because it originates within the springs of personal interest and its action is primarily confined to the realm of private affairs and individual relations' (ibid.: 162). According to Hess (1917, 175), when the private ownership of a property is 'incompatible with the public use of such property, then private ownership should be displaced by public ownership.' That is to say, an 'incompatibility of public use and private ownership is the imperative justification of eminent domain and of the conversion of private property to public or government ownership' (ibid.). In addition to public ownership, Hess (1917, 167) also supported state regulations on the use of natural resources when:

> there is more or less conflict between the public interests and private interests; and regulative agencies are exercised in behalf of the public, since, otherwise, society is defenseless against the persistent aggression of individuals who are motivated by personal desires and interests.

Essentially, he concluded that 'a definite public policy and positive governmental action' were necessary in order to ensure the conservation of the natural environment that is so crucial to the future safety and prosperity of the nation (ibid.: 162).

In addition to positive state actions, Carver (1917, 275) argued that when it came to conservation, the 'most valuable resource of any country is its fund of human' resources, which led him to focus on facilitating the fullest self-development of individuals via training and education. Meanwhile, Ely wanted to prepare the public mind for the importance of conservation through lectures and books, as he believed that:

> in every part of the country, almost in every village and hamlet, a new economic philosophy, a new way of looking at things, a new attitude towards the State gradually made its way and prepared men for the extension of governmental functions called for by conservation measures.
>
> (Ely 1917, 16)

Ely (1917, 39) also highlighted the importance of ethical and moral values in conservation, as they provided men with 'more self-control and ability to sacrifice within rational limits the present for the future.' Carver (1917) agreed that ethical practices had an important role to play in the conservation of natural resources, as he associated the wasteful consumption and use of natural resources with vices. Additionally, Hess (1917, 167) pointed out that practicing ethical values could contribute to conservation efforts, while Gray (1913, 514) maintained that protecting the natural environment required ethical judgments.

The fact that the New School supported safeguarding the natural environment by providing an ethical education and encouraging ethical practices was in accordance with the principles of the GHSE, which promoted the idea that every human action was not merely an individual decision, it also had ethical implications for society as a whole. The emphasis that the GHSE placed on ethical economics makes this school of thought very relevant at the present time, given that the world is faced with the possibility of ecological collapse and environmental disasters. That would also suggest that many of the questions and concerns raised by GHSE have never really disappeared; they have simply been veiled or obscured.

Conclusion

In recent decades, scientists have been warning people that they need to change their economic activities and lifestyles in order to avoid an impending ecological catastrophe in the foreseeable future. During that time, many environmental movements, nongovernmental organizations, and national and international institutions were established with the intention of monitoring and protecting the environment. However, such efforts to protect and conserve the environment and natural resources are nothing new. In reality, theorists of the GHSE and their American students were already attempting to raise awareness about the importance of protecting the environment in the early 20th century, including from pollution, deforestation, the erosion of soil quality, the overexploitation of natural resources, and climate change. They were opposed to the notion of nature being controlled and dominated by man; instead, they called for harmony and balance so that the natural environment is disturbed as little as possible.

Members of the New School advocated for the proper care and cautious use of natural resources on the basis that humanity could not indefinitely continue to excessively exploit them in order to satisfy the selfish wants and desires of the ideal man of classical economics. In fact, the New School believed that rivers, oceans, seas, mineral reserves, forests, and many other natural resources constituted essential parts of public wealth. As such, they should be placed under the control of the state rather than private investors. That is to say, the New School generally supported positive state action to protect the natural environment. They also believed that providing the population with an ethical education could contribute to protecting the natural environment and avoiding environmental catastrophes.

More than a century ago, members of the New School and the GHSE cultivated the core of environmental economics. They published books and articles that should have been highly valued and widely promoted by economists and anybody else that cared about the conservation of the natural environment. At that time, Ely predicted that students of political economy 'will see that this branch of their science, the economy of natural resources, so important and yet so much neglected, requires on their part a fuller and more careful consideration' (Ely 1917, 23). Unfortunately, the noble efforts of the New School and the GHSE aimed at protecting the environment have been largely unsuccessful, because measures that effectively do so are often directly opposed to the methodological individualism and laissez-faire of classical, neoclassical, and neoliberal economics. That means the fundamental features of the variants of classical economics have been major obstacles to efforts aimed at protecting and conserving the natural environment. Sadly, the immense destruction unleashed upon the natural environment since the rise of neoliberalism is a testament to the fact that the New School was ultimately correct in its prophecy that the dominance of the laissez-faire doctrine and methodological individualism would always hinder conservation efforts.

Note

1 Dictionary of Canadian Biography. 'Bernhard Eduard Fernow.' http://www.biographi.ca/en/bio/fernow_bernhard_eduard_15E.html.

Bibliography

Adams, Henry Carter. 1886. *Outline of Lectures Upon Political Economy.* Ann Arbor: Press of Register Publishing House.

Adams, Henry Carter. 1887. *Public Debts: An Essay in the Science of Finance.* New York: Appleton.

Carver, Thomas Nixon. 1917. 'Conservation of Human Resources.' Ed. Richard T. Ely, Ralph Hess, Charles K. Leith, and Thomas Nixon Carver. *The Foundation of National Prosperity Studies in The Conservation of Permanent National Resources.* New York: The Macmillan Company. 275–361.

Carver, Thomas Nixon. 1949. *Recollections of an Unplanned Life: Autobiography of T.N. Carver.* Los Angeles: The Ward Ritchie Press.

Clark, John Bates. 1914. *Social Justice without Socialism.* New York: Houghton Mifflin Company.

Ely, Richard T. 1883. 'The Past and the Present of Political Economy.' *Overland Monthly.* Vol. 2, No. 9: 225–235. The Overland monthly. ser.2:v.2 (1883). - Full View | HathiTrust Digital Library | HathiTrust Digital Library

Ely, Richard T. 1910. 'The American Economic Association 1885–1909.' *American Economic Association Quarterly, 3rd Series.* Vol. 11, No. 1: 47–111. URL: https://www.jstor.org/stable/3000023

Ely, Richard T. 1917. 'Conservation and Economic Theory.' Ed. Richard T. Ely, Ralph Hess, Charles K. Leith, and Thomas Nixon Carver. *The Foundation of*

National Prosperity Studies in The Conservation of Permanent National Resources. New York: The Macmillan Company. 3–68.
Ely, Richard T. 1938. *Ground under our Feet*. New York: Macmillan.
Farnam, Henry W. 1913. *The Economic Utilisation of History*. New Haven: Yale University Press.
Fernow, Bernhard Eduard. 1911. *A Brief History of Forestry: In Europe, the United States and Other Countries*. Toronto: University Press Toronto.
Filip, Birsen. 2020. *The Rise of Neo-liberalism and the Decline of Freedom*. Cham: Palgrave Macmillan.
Gay, Edwin Francis. 1929. *Recent Economic Changes in the United States, Volumes 1 and 2*. Publisher: NBER. URL: http://www.nber.org/books/comm29-1
Gray, Lewis Cecil. 1913. 'Economic Possibilities of Conservation.' *Quarter Journal of Economics*. Vol. 27: 497–519.
Gray, Lewis Cecil. 1914. 'The Regulation of Public Service Corporations: The Vagaries of Valuation.' *The American Economic Review*. Vol. 4, No. 1: 18–44. URL: https://www.jstor.org/stable/1827702
Hess, Ralph Henry. 1917. 'Conservation and Economic Evolution.' Ed. Richard T. Ely, Ralph Henry Hess, Charles K. Leith, and Thomas Nixon Carver. *The Foundation of National Prosperity Studies in The Conservation of Permanent National Resources*. New York: The Macmillan Company. 95–183.
James, Edmund J. 1887. 'The Relation of the Modern Municipality to the Gas Supply.' *American Economic Association*. Vol. 1, No. 2–3: 53–122.
James, Edmund J. 1911. 'The Economic Significance of a Comprehensive System of National Education: Annual Address of the President.' *The American Economic Review*. Vol. 1, No. 2: 1–25. URL: https://www.jstor.org/stable/1814911
Leith, Charles K. 1917. 'Conservation of Certain Mineral Resources.' Ed. Richard T. Ely, Ralph Henry Hess, Charles K. Leith, and Thomas Nixon Carver. *The Foundation of National Prosperity Studies in The Conservation of Permanent National Resources*. New York: The Macmillan Company. 187–270.
Patten, Simon Nelson. 1885. *The Premises of Political Economy: Being a Re-examination of Certain Fundamental Principles of Economic Science*. Philadelphia: J. B. Lippincott Company.
Patten, Simon Nelson. 1889. 'Malthus and Ricardo.' *Publications of the American Economic Association*. Vol. 4, No. 5: 9–34. URL: https://www.jstor.org/stable/2485684
Roscher, William. 1878V1 [1843]. *Principles of Political Economy V1*. 13th Ed. New York: Henry Holt & CO.
Seager, Henry Rogers. 1910. *Social Insurance: A program of Social Reform*. New York: The MacMillan Company.
Seligman, Edwin R. A. 1910. *Principles of Economics: With Special Reference to American Conditions*. New York: Longmans, Green, and Co.
Taylor, Henry. 1923. *Agricultural Economics*. New York: The Macmillan Company.
Tocqueville, Alexis de. 2010 [1835]. *Democracy in America: Historical-Critical Edition, Vol. 1*. Indianapolis: Liberty Fund.

8 The Decline and Demise of the German Historical School of Economics

Introduction

The global dominance of English classical economics began to rapidly diminish in the 1850s. By around 1870, 'England lost her intellectual leadership in the political and social sphere and became an importer of ideas' (Hayek 2006, 21). Meanwhile, Germany stepped in to serve as 'the centre from which the ideas destined to govern the world' spread from the mid-19th century until the early decades of the 20th century (ibid.). In fact:

> whether it was Hegel or Marx, List or Schmoller, Sombart or Mannheim, whether it was socialism in its more radical form or merely "organisation" or "planning" of a less radical kind, German ideas were everywhere readily imported and German institutions imitated.
>
> (ibid.)

In the case of political economy, the German Historical School of Economics (GHSE) achieved such a level of international prestige and dominance from the second half of the 19th century until the outbreak of WWI that it essentially forestalled the possibility of a rival economic program of research emerging at the same scale of advancement and sophistication. For much of that period, economists and economics students could not even participate in the main debates and discussions within their discipline without possessing an adequate grasp of the German language or being familiar with the goals, principles, and methods of the GHSE. This level of prestige commanded by the GHSE, combined with the lack of viable options at home, made Germany the destination of choice for American political economy students looking to obtain an advanced education in their discipline. However, the emergence of quality graduate economic programs at US colleges and universities began to stem the flow of American students heading to the political economy departments of German universities at the beginning of the 20th century. Interestingly, this was largely the result of efforts on the part of Americans trained by the theorists of the GHSE, as they took the initiative to integrate many of the features they experienced at the political economy departments of German

DOI: 10.4324/9781003247715-8

universities into their domestic institutions of higher learning. Naturally, American students stopped going to Germany when WWI actually broke out. After the fighting concluded, the GHSE had lost its international and domestic influence, as well as its leading status in the discipline of economics.

This chapter presents a number of possible explanations as to why the GHSE declined as it did. It begins by highlighting the role of the Battle of Methods (*Methodenstreit*) between Gustav von Schmoller (1838–1917) and Carl Menger (1840–1921) in damaging the reputation of the GHSE. It also describes how theorists of the Austrian School of Economics (ASE) helped fabricate and spread the view that the GHSE had the 'worst reputation' among all economic research programs in history. Additionally, it briefly explains the significant roles that WWI and the rise of Nazism played in the demise of the GHSE. This chapter then focuses on the decline of the GHSE in the US, where neoclassical economics, and later neoliberalism, became the leading school of economic thought. It argues that the leading theorists of neoclassical and neoliberal economics have turned their discipline into an ahistorical and value-free science, while also intensifying its mathematization and formalization, in order to make it into a branch of the natural sciences. In fact, they elevated mathematics to the point that it became the main purpose of economics, which transformed it into a one-dimensional discipline that essentially discarded its own origins, development, and historical background. Meanwhile, they eliminated many of the fundamental features of the GHSE that were highly prized by adherents of the New School and previously played major roles in revolutionizing the education and profession of economics in the US.

The Role of the Austrian School of Economics in the Decline of the GHSE

In the 19th century, political economy was underdeveloped in Austria, where 'there were practically no native economists' (Hayek 2007, 15). As a result, the Austrian universities that Menger attended were mainly being operated by 'economists imported from Germany,' which was internationally praised as the place to go if one wanted to obtain a higher academic education or advanced training (ibid.). Accordingly, Menger considered himself to be a disciple of the GHSE, though he would go on to become one of the most well-known and influential economists of the ASE, before playing an instrumental role in the decline of the GHSE.

During Menger's formative years, his early ideas and work were shaped by his GHSE professors, particularly Wilhelm Georg Friedrich Roscher (1817–1894), who he accepted as a true authority in the discipline of economics. He had a high opinion of Roscher's views on a variety of issues, such as welfare, the path of economic development to higher levels of well-being, the nature and origin of money, the theory of value, the development of the theory of the good in Germany, and the scientific concept of commodity.

The influence of the GHSE on Menger was obvious, as he frequently cited and complimented its theorists in his book, *Principles of Economics* (*Grundsätze der Volkswirtschaftslehre*) (1871). In particular, Menger's book referred to Roscher's *Grundriss zu Vorlesungen über die Staatswirthschaft* (1843), *Die Grundlagen der Nationalökonomie* (1861), *Ansichten der Volkswirthschaft aus dem geschichtlichen Standpunkte* (1861), and *System der Volkswirthschaft* (1857). Moreover, the first page of *Principles of Economics* states that the book is 'dedicated by the author with respectful esteem to Dr. Wilhem Roscher, Royal Saxonian Councillor Professor of Political and Cameral Sciences at the University of Leipzig.'

In addition to Roscher, the development of Menger's ideas was also influenced by the work of Karl Knies (1821–1898). Menger mainly referred to the writings of Knies when discussing the money character of the good, the principle of value, and the theory of the good. In *Principles of Economics*, he specifically mentioned Knies's *Die nationalökonomische Lehre vom Werth, Zeitschrift für die gesammte Stattswissenschaft*, XI (1855), *Die politische Oekonomie vom Standpunkte der geschichtlichen Methode* (1853), and *Über die Geldentwerthung und die mit ihr in Verbindung gebrachten Erscheinungen, Zeitschrift für die gesammte Staatswissenschaft*, XIV (1858). Another authority in the discipline of economics that Menger referred to was Karl Heinrich Rau (1792–1870), who focused on the development of cameralism in the 19th century and 'influenced Roscher's efforts to transform political economy into a historical science' (Filip 2018, 96). Specifically, Menger made references to Rau's concept of the 'abstract value of goods,' while also examining the 'use value and exchange value' that were discussed in Rau's *Grundsätze der Volkswirthschaftslehre* (1847) (ibid.).

Menger became very influential in Austria following the publication of *Principles of Economics*, with a number of young and talented students becoming his devoted followers. In 1873, he was promoted to the rank of professor 'extraordinarius' at the University of Vienna (Hayek 2007, 21, 22). With his growing influence as a political economist, his lectures and seminars were being attended by 'an increasing number of students, many of whom soon became economists of considerable reputation' (ibid.: 22). Ultimately, Menger's work led to the emergence of the ASE, which adopted his *Principles of Economics* as its founding manuscript, and represented an alternative to the GHSE. Although Eugen Ritter von Böhm-Bawerk (1851–1914) and Friedrich von Wieser (1851–1926) also contributed to the development of the ASE in its early days, its fundamental ideas belonged 'fully and wholly' to Menger (ibid.: 12). Menger was an inspiration for his pupils and other theorists in Austria; however, his works for a 'long time have remained little known' outside of the German-speaking countries (ibid.). This is not particularly surprising, given that Menger's *Principles of Economics* was not translated into English for about 80 years. Consequently, his work was not widely read in English-speaking countries.

Contrary to Austria, 'economists maintained a hostile attitude' toward Menger and his followers in Germany (ibid.: 22). This was to be expected, as Menger criticized the methodological collectivism and inductive approach of the GHSE in *Principles of Economics* despite having been influenced by this school of thought. Furthermore, *Principles of Economics* did not attract the attention of 'reviewers in the German journals,' who did not accept 'the nature of its main contribution' at the time of its publication (ibid.: 21). Menger was genuinely surprised about this unreceptive attitude, because he did not think that *Principles of Economics* represented a rupture between his work and the GHSE (Filip 2018). To the contrary, he believed that his book was part of the German economic tradition. According to him, *Principles of Economics* 'fit perfectly into the continuity of the German school and apparently does not comprise any analytical break with this tradition which has, for many years, been entrenched in a subjectivist perspective of demand' (Gloria-Palermo 1999, 17). In fact, Menger was so convinced of this that he sent a copy of *Principles of Economics* to Schmoller in 1871 along with a letter. Even though Menger dedicated his book to Roscher and referenced his views, in addition to those of Knies and Rau, Schmoller condemned Menger for being a follower of Ricardo and the British classical school. Moreover, Roscher claimed that Menger's work did not have sufficient 'scientific performance' (Giouras 1995, 118).

Menger, who was known for being very irritated with criticisms and having a hard time digesting them, was disappointed that Roscher and Schmoller did not value his book's contribution to political economy (St. Marc 1892, 76). He was particularly tormented by his failure to demonstrate that he was, in fact, contributing to the GHSE. Nonetheless, because theorists of the historical school 'failed to appreciate his contribution to historicist theory,' Menger 'turned from liking to disliking the historical economists' (Alter 1990, 323). This led to the emergence of a debate between Menger and Schmoller, which came to be known as the Battle of Methods and ended up lasting for decades. It has frequently been described as one of the 'most important methodological debates in the history of economics' (Senn 1989, 268). Each considered his own method of investigation to be scientific while criticizing the other's work for not being valuable.

The Battle of Methods

Since Menger was not able to garner the respect that he thought he deserved from his former peers following the publication of *Principles of Economics*, he became more critical of the GHSE. Although it took more than a decade, he eventually outlined his arguments against the GHSE with the publication of his second book, *Investigation into the Methods of the Social Sciences with Special Reference to Economics (Untersuchungen über die Methode der Socialwissenschaften und der politischen Ökonomie insbesondere*) (1883). This manuscript directly attacked the GHSE and was highly critical of the views of Roscher, Hildebrand, Knies, and Schmoller. In response, Schmoller published a critical review of Menger's new book in the *Jahrbuch für Gesetzgebung, Verwaltung und Volkswirtschaft*. Subsequently, in 1884, Menger replied to Schmoller's unfavorable review by publishing *The Errors of Historicism in German Economics* (*Irrthümer des Historismus in der deutschen Nationalokönomie*), which included '16 public letters' addressed to Schmoller that were mainly detailed discussions about the nature of economic science and its proper methods.

Over the course of the Battle of Methods, Menger developed strong attacks against some of the fundamental features of the GHSE. For example, he rejected the GHSE argument that the main task of economics was not to 'explain regularities which somehow emerge from the rational behaviour of individuals,' but 'to analyse the historical development of such "wholes" as nations, economic systems and classes, and to detect their historical laws of development' (Milford 1995, 39). According to Menger, although historical studies could have a complementary role in economics, it was 'not a substitute for, the development of theoretical principles' (Tribe 2002, 13). He also insisted that it was not possible to derive economic laws from historical studies. While acknowledging 'the value of history and statistics,' he rejected the idea that 'they are the only sources of materials' (Ingram 1915, 146, Menger 1984, 29). More precisely, Menger accepted that historical studies and investigations provide 'insights into understanding the general development of economic phenomena; at the same time, he maintained that historical studies could not enhance our understanding of individual decisions and behaviours' (Filip 2018, 96). He argued that economics was the study of individual phenomena, a task for which he believed the historical method was not well suited. Thus, Menger would derive principles of action for an isolated individual and then apply them to more complex economic interactions.

Menger (1985, 27) described GHSE methodology as 'erroneous' and argued that the 'progress of a science is blocked because erroneous methodological principles prevail.' He further claimed that the methodological views of the GHSE were very destructive, because they obstructed solutions to some important economic problems and issues. As such, he argued that economic theory required the abstract deductive method instead of inductive historical method, because 'even the most realistic orientation of theoretical research imaginable must accordingly operate with abstractions' (Menger 1985, 80). Menger (2007, 46–47) maintained that economists could use the abstract deductive method to develop universal theoretical laws that could explain complex economic phenomena by reducing 'the complex phenomena of human economic activity to the simplest elements that can still be subjected to accurate observation.'

Menger (1884, 24–25, 28) was of the opinion that the main mission of economic analysis was to elaborate theory and policy, not to gather historical economic facts. According to him, the fact that adherents of the GHSE confused the theory of economy 'with the historical sciences of economy' meant that 'theoretical investigations in the field of political economy' had not 'progressed' (Menger 1985, 23, 51). More specifically, he accused the GHSE of delaying the progress of economic theory for a full half century. He even went so far as to suggest that the GHSE left people ignorant as to what economic theory actually meant (Menger 1884, 30). Menger believed that economic theory possessed the scientific rigor of the natural sciences while having little to do with historical and ethical foundations (Seager 1893). Conversely, adherents of the GHSE were of the view that matters in economics were far too complex to be accurately described in formulas and theorems. They emphasized that the various societal organizations across history, in addition to contemporary nations and cultures, were so fundamentally different from one another that their actions, progress, and failures could not be understood via a uniform theory. According to the GHSE, studying large-scale historical economic facts was required prior to theoretical formulation in order to avoid any hasty generalizations based on a poor empirical basis. In fact, its adherents believed that statistics and extensive empirical studies were required to form a theory as opposed to relying on a priori abstract assumptions (Nasse 1887). Schmoller pointed out that the historical school represented 'a return to the scientific grasp of reality instead of vague abstractions lacking the desired connection to reality' (Louzek 2011, 450). Meanwhile, he thought that Menger was 'absolutely incapable of understanding the fundamental causes and merits of the historical school because he lacks the authority to do so' (ibid.).

Menger was also strongly opposed to the GHSE view that a society and its institutions were collective organizations that were designed according to the public spirit of the nation, which aims to achieve common welfare. By focusing on the public spirit, adherents of the GHSE aimed to improve the situations of weak and poor members of society, which, in turn, would contribute to achieving the common welfare. According to Menger, if economists aimed to achieve common welfare based on methodological collectivism, then economic decisions and actions would need to be guided by some kind of superior authority or ruler who denies individuals their freedom, which would hinder efforts to resolve economic problems. He insisted that economists needed to focus on individual behavior as opposed coming up with strategies to achieve common welfare (Menger 1884, 30). Contrary to Menger, Schmoller rejected methodological individualism, arguing that the acceptance of self-interest maximization as a universal characteristic of economic agents was far from reality. Instead, he emphasized the importance of achieving common welfare through methodological collectivism.

Schmoller (1894) also underlined the importance of ethical economics in the achievement of common welfare. However, Menger objected to the social reforms advocated by the GHSE that were intended to achieve common welfare based on ethics. While he accepted that some economic decisions could be affected by people's moral and ethical commitments, he emphasized that ethics could not be used in the formation of theoretical models. As such, he believed that Schmoller's acceptance of economics as an ethical science was inhibiting the development of economic theory. Menger (1985, 237) was of the opinion that the 'ethical orientation of political economy' was ingrained 'in a failure to recognize the nature and peculiar problems of the theoretical and the practical sciences of national economy.'

During the *Methodenstreit*, both Menger and Schmoller claimed that the method of investigation employed by their respective schools of economic thought was the only scientific one. However, in addition to featuring dynamic and aggressive arguments put forth by both participants, the *Methodenstreit* did not always remain professional, often including attacks of an 'unnecessarily personal character' (Seager 1893, 237). In fact, their attacks against each other became 'abusive and derogatory' on many occasions (Filip 2018, 101). It is widely accepted that over the course of this dispute, Menger and Schmoller displayed a 'degree of hostility not often equalled in scientific controversy' (Hayek 2007, 24). For example, Schmoller publicly stated that followers and theorists of the ASE were unfit to obtain teaching positions in German universities because they did not understand the importance of historical ethical economics, the inductive approach, the national economy, and methodological collectivism. Meanwhile, in many of his own attacks, Menger claimed that Schmoller was ignorant, inexperienced, incompetent and not scientific. He also maintained that Schmoller did not deserve to be taken seriously (Menger 1884, 73). For example, in *The Errors of Historicism in German Economics*, Menger wrote:

> The future, I hope that not too distant future, will decide whether Schmoller finished me off with his methodological analysis or whether I finished off Schmoller … Yet one thing seems to be certain already today. May the methodologist Schmoller ever so stride across the sand of the river Spree [a Berlin river] in the future, shake his mane, raise his paw, yawn methodologically; only children and fools will in the future take his methodological gestures seriously … I for myself will be remunerated, for the little pains I took, by the knowledge of having done a good deed in the field of German economics in more than one respect.
>
> (Richter 1996, 585)

The methodological battle not 'only created a lot of bad feeling but also set running a stream of literature, both of which took decades to subside' (Schumpeter 2006, 782). Adherents of the ASE were of the view that Menger's publication of *The Errors of Historicism in German Economics* in 1884 'ruthlessly demolished Schmoller's position' and demonstrated 'the best instance of the extraordinary power and brilliance of expression' (Hayek 2007, 24). To the contrary, Schmoller regarded Menger's text as little more than an unprofessional and abusive attack against him that had no academic merit. As such, he thought that it did not warrant a response. From Schmoller's point of view, this marked the end of the *Methodenstreit*.

Ultimately, the *Methodenstreit* between the GHSE and the ASE shaped the direction and development of the discipline of economics. In the end, neither of these schools of economic thought officially achieved a clear and decisive victory, Schmoller and Menger could not reconcile their views, and Menger failed to provide conclusive arguments against the GHSE. Nonetheless, the false belief that Menger won the battle was fairly widespread. This perception irreparably damaged the reputation of the GHSE as the leading school of economic thought while enhancing the standing of the ASE around the world. However, since the *Methodenstreit* concluded without a decisive victory for either the GHSE or the ASE, 'the problem of the adequate methods remained the dominating concern' in the writings of Menger and other members of the ASE (Hayek 2007, 24). Subsequently, Menger continued to dedicate a significant portion of his academic career to refuting the fundamental ideas, principles, and methods of the GHSE. To this day, a number of the issues raised during the *Methodenstreit* have never been fully resolved by Menger, Schmoller, their students, or other economic schools of thought in 20th and 21st centuries.

Unfortunately, one of the main outcomes of the *Methodenstreit* was that it contributed to the discipline of economics while forgetting about the important role that the GHSE played in its development. The end of this battle also played an instrumental role in shaping the direction and development of the discipline of economics, as a majority of economists ended up supporting Menger's defense of methodological individualism, the universality assumption, ahistorical investigation, and the deductive method. Contrary to the experience of the GHSE, Menger's views and ideas persisted and ended up having a significant impact on the development of economics. This is not particularly surprising, given that Menger supported many of the methods, principles, goals, and approaches advocated by the doctrines of classical economists (Neff 1950, 400).

The end of the methodological debate between Schmoller and Menger also marked the separation of political economy from historical ethical economics. This led to adherents of the GHSE being criticized for valuing useless ideas and methods like the historical approach and ethical and moral commitments in economics. They were also accused of being nonscientific and ignorant about economic theory. In fact, the end of the *Methodenstreit* resulted in the proliferation of the opinion that 'among schools of economic thought none has a worse reputation, especially in the English-speaking world, than the German historical school' (Peukert 2001, 71).

Despite the detrimental consequences of the methodological battle for the GHSE, Schmoller was 'able to make a showing of strength upon his side in the *Metkodenstreit* which his position hardly warrants' (Seager 1893, 251). It was widely recognized that if an economist were to read Schmoller's publications, he would realize that 'his comprehension of the modern situation has been rendered wider and more secure' (Mitchell 1949, 200). In fact, it was accepted that Schmoller's *Grundriss der Allgemeinen Volkswirtschaftslehre* would 'impress anyone as a satisfactory illumination on any single problem' (ibid.). It is a 'sad fact' that 'so few American students of economics nowadays' were 'really equipping themselves to make use in the original of this exceedingly valuable contribution' (ibid.).

The Demise of the GHSE: Two World Wars and the Rise of the Nazi Regime

The US and England were openly hostile toward 'Germany and the works of Germans for not only the years of the First and Second World Wars but also several years before and after' them (Senn 1989, 254). During WWI, Americans were concerned that the Germans with 'the greatest navy in the world, would take over Canada, Australia and the islands surrounding … Panama Canal' (Commons 1963, 183). If that were to happen, then the Americans would be obligated to 'fight Germany alone' (Commons 1963, 183). Meanwhile, American scholars were frustrated that German scholars were not critical of the aggressive actions being taken by their country during WWI. For example, German-trained Albion W. Small (1854–1926) (1923, 413) confessed that 'no American was and is more disappointed and disgusted' than himself 'all through the war with the attitude of German scholars.' He further claimed that by not strongly opposing 'the policy of their government,' 'their conduct was disgraceful and humiliating' (ibid.: 413–414). He believed that 'German social scientists have less excuse than the rank and file of citizens for their failure to stand out on principle against war in general, and especially against that particular war and the German methods of fighting it' (ibid.: 414).

The end of WWI brought about an educational and 'cultural withdrawal of the United States' from Germany (Goldschmidt 1992, 19). In the 1920s, only a few Americans went to Germany to receive a higher education in political economy, as the GHSE was no longer a school of thought that American economists looked toward for inspiration. Essentially, 'the influence of those friendly to Germany diminished' in the US, 'while, at the same time, hostility to Germany intensified in many areas to the point where German-Americans were ostracized and even persecuted' (ibid.). For example, 'the umbrella organization of German-Americans, the National German-American Alliance, which had had approximately two million members prior to the war, dissolved itself in 1918' (ibid.).

Germany's aggressive international policies and actions in the early 20th century led to American economists adopting a new orientation. They went from supporting historical ethical economics to becoming critical of it, even going so far as to regard it as a danger that delayed the progress of economics. They also renounced 'collectivistic theories' and once again identified themselves with the ideals of classical economics (Herbst 1965, 163). In fact, many American economists came to believe that the withdrawal of German influence saved the social sciences in the US from becoming a mere matter of collecting large-scale facts (Small 1923). According to Small (1923, 413), after WWI:

> No American can now hear German scholarship mentioned without demanding a reckoning with the charge that German scholars as a class, with German social scientists conspicuous in the class, hopelessly

> discredited themselves by their attitude during the war. I am aware that for a long time it will seem to most Americans like treason to science as well as to country to admit that there can be anything good in German scholarship.

Ely (1918, 4) pointed out that Americans were 'disappointed in the German universities' during WWI for not reacting against the war policies of their government. He also questioned: 'Why were we not told before about Germany's plans? Why did not the men who lived in Germany and who were familiar with Germany tell us about what was going on?' (ibid.: 5). At the end of WWI, Ely (1918, 16) wrote that war was glorified and 'the gospel of war' entered 'into the very life blood of the German nation.' He argued that this was 'a part of their false religion and a part of their worship of their false tribal god' (ibid.: 43). He concluded that the war would essentially erase the German ideas and concepts that had previously conquered the world. Ely's views on such matters were highly respected, because he was regarded as an expert on Germany. In 1880, he completed his PhD in political economy at the University of Heidelberg under the guidance of Knies, and subsequently returned to Germany on many occasions. Ely had many German friends, read 'German newspapers and German literature,' published articles on 'German life and German institutions,' had 'a high appreciation of the excellencies of Germany,' and was inspired by his German professors to revolutionize the discipline of economics in the US (ibid.: 16).

The reputation of the GHSE was clearly damaged by WWI. Unfortunately, things kept getting worse early in the interwar period, as adherents of the historical school were blamed for the deterioration of the German economy. Given that GHSE theorists were 'very intimately connected with the old regime in Germany,' when 'the empire collapsed and a new social order came into being' after WWI, 'this whole group of quasi-official economic advisers suffered loss of prestige with the public at large' (Mitchell 1949, 200). In fact, they were held responsible for the hyperinflation that gripped Germany from 1921 to 1923, with German scholars arguing that the GHSE had so 'perverted the German bureaucracy and that hardly anyone in the Reich's Finance Ministry had any ideas of what inflation was' (Balabkins 1988, 76). Furthermore, it was claimed that 'the huge reparations bill' that Germany was forced to pay after WWI, which greatly contributed to the onset of hyperinflation, 'virtually destroyed the German middle-class and, in many ways, paved the way for Hitler and the Third Reich' (ibid.). Schmoller was particularly targeted for blame, because of 'his supposed neglect of the mechanics of inflation and social consequences' of hyperinflation (ibid.: 77).

The standing of the GHSE was further tarnished by the rise of national socialism and WWII. Austrian economist, Ludwig von Mises (1881–1973) (1978, 44) was among those who claimed that the GHSE was responsible of the rise of national socialism and the two world wars. He argued that 'the war came as a result of an ideology that for hundreds of years' was venerated by 'all

German institutions of learning' (ibid.). According to him, 'the professors of economics' contributed 'diligently to the intellectual preparation for war … No longer did they teach economics; they were preaching the doctrines of war' (ibid.). Mises (1978, 144) further argued that 'Schmoller and his friends and disciples' supported 'state socialism; i.e., a system of socialism-planning-in which the top management would be in the hands of the Junker aristocracy.' He was of the opinion that this was the type of socialism that 'Bismarck and his successors were aiming' for (ibid.). Mises (1978, 144) also made the accusation that supporters of 'the Historical School and Sozialpolitik transferred their loyalty to various splinter groups, out of which the German Nationalist Socialist Workers' Party, the Nazis, eventually emerged.' He further added that, in 1918, most of the members of *Verein für Sozialpolitik* (Association for Social Policy) 'sympathized with the Social Democrats; in 1933 they joined the Nazis' (ibid.: 71). Mises (1978, 72) even went so far as to claim that, based on his acquaintances with adherents of the historical school, he came to 'realize that the German people were no longer salvable,' specifically stating:

> For these characterless simpletons were the select best of the elite of society. At the universities they taught in a field that was the most important one for political education. The masses of the people and the educated classes treated them with highest respect as the intellectual aristocrats in the sciences.

In fact, German professors who were trained by the GHSE were accused of preparing 'the soil, for the most part unwittingly for the subsequent acceptance of the National Socialist creed' (Pribram 1983, 372). According to Mises, the students educated by these professors went on to become adherent of nationalist socialism. He further claimed that there were no longer 'any liberal thinkers left in Germany' at that time because of the teachings and influence of the GHSE (Mises 1978, 144). In the post-WWII period, he suggested that it was not 'worthwhile to dwell upon the stuff that was handed down as a substitute for economics at Berlin, Munich, and other universities of the Reich' by the adherents of the GHSE (ibid.: 143). In his arguments against the GHSE, Mises (1978, 143) stated that:

> nobody cares today about all that Gustav von Schmoller, Adolf Wagner, Lujo Brentano, and their numerous adepts wrote in their voluminous books and magazines. The political significance of the work of the Historical School consisted in the fact that it rendered Germany safe for the ideas, the acceptance of which made popular with the German people all those disastrous policies that resulted in the great catastrophes. The aggressive imperialism that twice ended in war and defeat, the limitless inflation of the early 1920s, the *Zwangswirtschaft* [command economy] and all the horrors of the Nazi regime were achievements of politicians who acted as they had been taught by the champions of the Historical School.

To further damage the reputation of the GHSE, Mises (1978, 70) contended that members of the *Verein für Sozialpolitik* were 'no economists,' because 'they were the pupils of Schmoller, Wagner, Bücher and Brentano.' He also claimed that members of the *Verein für Sozialpolitik* were 'unaware of the basic mathematical problems in the use of statistics. They were laymen in jurisprudence, technology, banking, and trade techniques. With amazing unconcern they published books and essays on things of which they understood nothing' (ibid.: 71). Mises (1978, 70) further stated that members of the *Verein für Sozialpolitik* did not 'know the economic literature, had no conception of economic problems, and suspected every economist as an enemy of the State, as non-German, and as protagonists of business interests and of free trade.'

Max Weber (1864–1920) (1975), who was trained by the GHSE, criticized Roscher and Knies for defending ethical economics. In his publications, Weber advocated for 'neutrality in economic sciences for the sake of scientific objectivity, stating that value judgements cannot be perceived by economic reasoning' (Hansen 2012, 393). In fact, he fought 'against German pseudo-historicism all his life' (Mises 1978, 7). While in Vienna in 1918, Weber, who was a member of the *Verein für Sozialpolitik*, told Mises (1978, 72):

> You do not like the Association for Social Policy; I like it even less. But it is a fact that it is the only Association of men in our discipline. It is useless for us to criticize it from the outside. We must work with the Association and remove its shortcomings. I am trying it in my way, and you must do it in your way.

With that in mind, Mises (1978, 72), who was also a member of the *Verein für Sozialpolitik*, thought that his efforts to reform it would be ineffective due to the fact that 'as an Austrian, as a *Privatdozent* without a chair,[1] as a theorist,' he would always be viewed as 'an outsider in the Association.' He further added that he was 'treated with the utmost courtesy, but the other members always looked upon' him 'as an alien' (ibid.).

Thorstein Bunde Veblen (1857–1929), another well-known scholar outside of Germany who was an adherent of institutional economics, also provided arguments that diminished the reputation of the GHSE. He was very familiar with the writings of GHSE theorists, as well as the *Methodenstreit*, as he had extensively read the works of Schmoller and Sombart. He accused the GHSE of producing 'history,' 'not economics' (Spengler and Allen 1960, 496). He explained that the theorists of the GHSE 'have contented themselves with an enumeration of data and a narrative account of industrial development, and have not presumed to offer a theory of anything' (Veblen 1898, 375). Nevertheless, he had a positive opinion of the work of Schmoller, whom he credited with modernizing the GHSE (Veblen 1901). In particular, Veblen considered the publication of *Grundriss der Allgemeinen Volkswirtschaftslehre* to be 'an event of the first importance' and 'a work of the first magnitude' for the discipline of economics (Balabkins 1988, 69, 70). That said, he argued that Schmoller's support of 'a powerful military state' and his defense of the development of the national economy influenced 'developments in Germany' during the Nazi regime (Mitchell 1949, 193). Furthermore, ordo-liberal Walter Eucken (1891–1950) suggested that Schmoller's work, as well as that of other disciples of the GHSE, represented 'a step backwards, not a thrust forward, in the evolution of economics' (Balabkins 1988, 79). Until recent decades, 'no self-respecting authors on economic thought deal with him and his work, except in passing-maybe in a footnote' (ibid.: 83).

Friedrich von Hayek (1899–1992) (2006, 196) argued that since WWII, 'the road to serfdom' (or the road to unfreedom) was accepted as 'a German Road,' which became associated with 'Nazi totalitarianism.' He, along with Karl Popper (1902–1994), accused the historicist approach of playing a major role in the formation of the doctrine of Nazi Germany, which was an enemy of open societies and entailed the death of liberalism (Filip 2018). Hayek (2006, 196) explained that with few exceptions, German 'scholars and scientists put themselves readily at the service of the new rulers' during the Nazi regime. He considered this to be 'one of the most depressing and shameful spectacles in the whole history of the rise of National-Socialism' (ibid.). Hayek (2006, 173) also suggested that 'the connection between socialism and nationalism in Germany was close from the beginning,' pointing out that Werner Sombart (1863–1941), a member of the Youngest Historical School, was responsible of rise of socialism in Germany. He elaborated that Sombart had done:

> as much as any man to spread socialist ideas and anti-capitalist resentment of varying shades throughout Germany; and if German thought became penetrated with Marxian elements in a way that was true of no other country till the Russian revolution, this was in a large measure due to Sombart.
>
> (ibid.: 174)

Hayek (2006, 175) further added that 'Sombart knew that the Germans were held in contempt by other people because they regard war as sacred.' Nonetheless, Sombart idolized war, believing in 'a life higher than the individual life, the life of the people and the life of the state' and that it was 'the purpose of the individual to sacrifice himself for that higher life' (ibid.). Hayek was convinced that the road toward Fascism and Nazism could always be 'prevented if people realise in time where their efforts may lead' (ibid.: 4).

The conclusion of WWII also saw 'the enormous amount of constructive work' of the GHSE, particularly that of 'the generations following 1870,' become 'distinctly' undervalued (Mitchell 1949, 189). After the war, German journals and reviews published 'many articles' that criticized, in 'very severe language, the work of the historical school' (ibid.). Even Schmoller's *Jahrbuch* occasionally included work by authors who discussed 'the collapse of the historical school,' with some even describing 'Schmoller's great effort as after all fundamentally a failure' (ibid.: 199). There was 'quite a decided tendency to put down Schmoller, for instance, as a man of comparatively minor consequence' (ibid.: 189). Some even went so far as to deem him 'a dead dog' (Kempski 1964, 200). Ultimately, even though Schmoller's contributions to the discipline of economics were being diminished and ignored, he was nonetheless regarded as a 'great scholar very widely read' during his lifetime (Mitchell 1949, 196). He was not 'only a thorough economist, but a thorough historian and fully equipped with the widest philosophical training and knowledge' (Seligman 1889, 543). In particular, his work in the area of history, including mediaeval industry, 'mediaeval commerce,' and 'mediaeval taxation,' which were 'characterized by this broad philosophic spirit,' enabled him to 'more successfully than any economist ... to clearly expound the connection between the economic and the other phases of the world's development and to point out the close interdependence between law, politics, ethics and economics' (ibid.). He was also credited with trying to 'see economic life as a whole and to bring the resources of history and statistics, as well as of analysis, to promote an understanding' of demand and supply factors (Mitchell 1949, 196).

Contrary to accusations that Schmoller's works and teachings resulted in the rise of nationalist socialism, in reality, his goal was to integrate the working classes 'in the most peaceful way possible, into the mainstream of German society' (Balabkins 1988, 54). However, his efforts to create a welfare state and his defense of social justice led to Schmoller gaining a reputation as a socialist. He was actually critical of socialism, as well as capitalism, for failing to understand and care about man's true nature and 'his place in the world and in history,' which are important if one is to 'comprehend the state and society' (Schmoller 2018, 216). According to Schmoller (2018, 218), socialism and capitalism missed a good part of the realistic and 'down-to-earth roots' of the human nature. He also pointed out that 'the main weakness of both individualist and socialist theories was that they feigned and operated with an abstract economic society detached from the state and law' (ibid.). For him, socialism and capitalism remained 'closed systems which directly aim at new ideals of the economy, of social life, of the entirety of economic and legal institutions. In terms of method and content, they do not fully rise to the rank of real science' (ibid.). Schmoller (2018, 218) also emphasized that both ideologies distanced themselves from ethics and 'the theory of the state and administration in order to attain the dignity of their own independent theory.' In fact, he claimed that 'the biggest social and economic challenge of the newly-created German Reich was the threat of the Marxist-inspired communism, which he called nothing but "centralistic despotism"' (Balabkins 1988, 54). Thus, contrary to many of the accusations directed at him, Schmoller was opposed to socialist or Marxist revolutions, despotism, and tyranny, as were many of the disciples of the GHSE.

One of the likely reasons why adherents of the GHSE were accused of motivating and supporting nationalist socialism was that they historically had close relationships with the ruling party in Germany. In other words, the GHSE was subjected to those false accusations due to the fact that many of its members were 'persons of large political influence, people who stood rather close to the center of German policy' prior to the rise of Nazism (Mitchell 1949, 188). For example, Knies and Schmoller, who served in their parliament, played an important role in designing and establishing the social and economic policies of Otto von Bismarck (1815–1898), while Adolph Wagner (1835–1917) and Johannes Ernst Conrad (1839–1915) were both economic advisors to Bismarck.

While there is no doubt that theorists of the GHSE supported positive state actions when it came to implementing ethical social and economic reforms, they did not advocate for the type of state authority that existed in Nazi Germany. In fact, German 'national socialists very early denounced members of the historical school such as Schmoller for their humanitarianism and liberalism' (Peukert 2001, 79). The Nazis also fired 'a good many University professors, and dismissed a good many scientists from research laboratories' (Mitchell 1949, 188). Furthermore, 'the Nazi's policies forced out many great scholars, (for example Adolph Lowe, Gerhard Colm, and Hans Neisser, to name but a few)' (Senn 1989, 276). As it turned out, most of these scholars were 'influenced by Schmoller in several ways, through direct acquaintance with his work' as well as 'via the reexportation' of ideas by their 'teachers who had been influenced by Schmoller' (ibid.). It should also be noted that 'on 19th December 1936,' members of the *Verein für Sozialpolitik* decided 'to dissolve the *Verein für Sozialpolitik* in order to avoid having to bow to the Nazis or being taken over by Nazi economists' (Hagemann 2001, 170).

All of the accusations that the GHSE was the original source of nationalist socialism and responsible for the destructive consequences of WWI and WWII severely damaged the prestigious status that this school of thought enjoyed in the 19th century. Additionally, 'the intellectual emigration' that took place during Nazi rule and in the aftermath of WWII seriously weakened the reputation of German universities (Hagemann 2001, 170). In fact, 'after 1945 the German historical school was little more than a pale afterglow' of its former self (Hodgson 2001, 134). Ultimately, Germany 'never fully recovered' from the departure of thousands of intellectuals and academics (Hagemann 2001, 170). Following the decline of the GHSE, 'the younger generation of German academic teachers of Economics' turned once more to 'Smith, Ricardo and Mill, and giving their support to the marginal theory of value' (Senn 1989, 279).

Despite the many achievements of the disciples of the GHSE, both within and outside Germany, it is likely that accusations that their school of thought contributed to the rise of national socialism and served as an apologist for imperial Germany were among 'the reasons that others, like the Austrians, were translated' into English, whereas a majority of the work attributed to the GHSE was not translated into other languages (ibid.: 275). Meanwhile, the rise of neoclassical economics in the US led to German language requirements being dropped from the curricula of American universities and colleges, which meant students were no longer expected to read and comprehend articles and books that were written in German. As a result, the work and ideas of the GHSE became largely inaccessible for a majority of American economists for most of the 20th century. They could only obtain information about the GHSE from secondary sources, which were often hostile toward this school of thought. Therefore, it is not surprising that current economists are overwhelmingly ignorant of the many truly revolutionary achievements of the GHSE in the discipline of economics during the 19th century.

Unfortunately, many of the publications written by Schmoller and other contributors to the GHSE have also not been read in German-speaking countries since the end of the WWII. In fact, 'no self-respecting West German academic economist would touch Schmoller's writings' during the Cold War era (Balabkins 1988, 62). It is important to point out that, even though WWI damaged the reputation of the GHSE, American academics who previously studied under the disciples of the GHSE, such as Seligman, Ely, and Patten, did not 'give up what they had learned' during the interwar period (Senn 1995, 70). Additionally, German and Austrian immigrants, who previously studied under the theorists of the GHSE, kept some of their ideas 'alive' in the US (ibid.).

There were other significant factors that diminished the important role that the GHSE played in the development of economics. For example, the success of Keynesian economics resulted in a considerable downgrade in the role of the history of economic thought within the discipline of economics, because John Maynard Keynes (1883–1946), who was a key figure in the revival of economics at Cambridge University and on the world stage, was not familiar with the work of the GHSE. The discipline of economics and economic policy underwent dramatic changes on account of the rise of Keynesian economics following the publication of Keynes's highly influential book *The General Theory of Employment, Interest and Money* (1936). However, Keynes made no mention of the leading economists of the GHSE in this book, as they did not play a significant role in his theoretical and intellectual development. Accordingly, his followers did not familiarize themselves with the work of the GHSE.

After the neoclassical, and subsequently neoliberal, school of economic thought achieved dominance within the discipline of economics, the GHSE became largely forgotten. This was even true among German economists, who no longer valued the distinguished heritage of the GHSE. Today, the significant contributions that the GHSE made to the discipline of economics are only known to scholars that are specialized in the history of economic thought and the history of economics. In fact, many academics likely do not realize that their work was 'building upon foundations' established by theorists of the GHSE that they have never heard of (Senn 1989, 284). That means the work of the GHSE is 'now part' of a complex 'web of economic knowledge' (ibid.). Therefore, any criticisms of the GHSE are not 'on sound ground if they imply that the German historical school has made no contributions to our understanding of economic life' (Mitchell 1949, 200).

The Discipline of Economics in the United States in the Aftermath of the Decline of the GHSE

When the GHSE was the leading school of economic thought, it was accepted that the discipline of economics was 'most assiduously and most fruitfully cultivated' (Seager 1893, 239). At that time, German universities were like 'magnets, attracting to themselves economic students from all countries,' who were fully aware that studying in Germany would boost their prestige back home (ibid.). Many Americans were among the foreign students that came to Germany to study and obtain a higher education under its theorists in those fruitful days. As a result, the GHSE played a major role in revolutionizing the discipline of economic in the US from the 1870s until WWI. However, following the outbreak of WWI, the importance and influence of the GHSE waned considerably, whereas the economics departments at American universities were on their way to surpassing their German models.[2] That said, the improvements taking place at US colleges and universities were mainly due to the effort and work of German-trained American political economists. The raising of standards at American institutions of higher learning, in combination with the inability to travel to Germany during WWI, severely stemmed the flow of Americans going to Germany to further their education. In the early 1930s, Americans saw little reason to measure 'the excellence of their own educational system against European systems,' as 'the American university system began to establish its worldwide pre-eminence' (Goldschmidt 1992, 19, Senn 1995, 59). In fact, 'German academic economists have been the most thorough emulators of the American academic economic theorists' since the end of WWII (Balabkins 1988, 62).

In the 1920s, the decline in the influence of the GHSE led to 'the relationships between the economists and the business community' becoming 'noticeably more harmonious' in the US (Coats 1985, 1710). Instead of focusing their attention on the destructive outcomes associated with the accumulation of wealth in the hands of a few large businesses and elite individuals, economists prioritized 'their responsibilities as advisers to government,' private businesses and various other organizations (ibid.). Furthermore, they worked on fewer research projects aimed at protecting the weaker segments of the population from strong and greedy private businesses, based on 'the acceptance of continuing research grants or retainers from private sources and vested interest groups' (ibid.).

After the downfall of the GHSE, American economists essentially turned their discipline into an ahistorical and value-free science while also intensifying its mathematization and formalization. They also neglected to familiarize themselves with other fields of the social sciences, as they became obsessed with achieving a high degree of specialization as opposed to engaging in multidisciplinary studies and research. Even though adherents of the New School originally supported the premise of increasing the number of courses and specializations being offered at economics departments, Ely (1938, 192) subsequently became concerned that specialization in economics had gone too far in the 1930s, arguing that 'an ever-increasing number of economists know more and more of less and less.' He pointed out that many economists had become so highly specialized in their narrow areas of research that they were effectively incapable of expressing any opinions on other subjects when they got together with their colleagues. This combination of excessive specialization and ignorance exhibited by the new generation of economists led Ely (1938, 192) to opine that their contributions 'to the enlightenment and to prosperity' of Americans suffered 'deterioration.'

The Rise of Mathematical Economics

The principles, approaches, methods, and goals of classical economics reemerged within the discipline of economics after the influence of the GHSE faded away in the US. The return of classical economics, under the umbrella of neoclassical economics, led to a renaissance of American individualism and the laissez-faire approach. At the same time, neoclassical economists enthusiastically integrated mathematical and statistical methods into economics, while systematically purging ethics, the historical inductive approach, methodological collectivism, and positive state action, all of which were advocated by the GHSE. That said, it should be noted that a few of the important features of neoclassical economics were originally developed by the GHSE. For example, a number of prominent German political economists worked on public choice theory, including 'Adolf Wagner, Friedrich von Wieser, Lorenz von Stein, Hans Ritschl, Edgar Salin, etc.' (Frey and Frey 1973, 81). As a matter of fact, 'in their meeting, several study groups of the *Verein für Sozialpolitik*' dealt with 'problems of public choice' (Frey and Frey 1973, 82). However, while the GHSE contributed to the original development of public choice theory, 'the increasing interest in questions of public choice' around the world found its 'roots in the works of Downs, Arrow, Buchanan, Tullock, Olson, and a few other American scholars' (ibid.: 81). Additionally, the origins of marginal utility theory were found in the works of Knies, who focused on 'the individual consumer to draw more general inferences about economic behavior' and on 'the individual with regard to the satisfaction of his own human needs' (Papadopoulos and Bateman 2011, 31). Knies provided 'great insights regarding utility theory that were later to become part of the foundations of neoclassical economics' (ibid.).

Since the 1950s, neoclassical economists were obsessed with integrating mathematics into economics, to the point where they elevated mathematical economics to become the main purpose of their discipline. However, the use of mathematics in economics was not something new in the US, as adherents of the New School had already accepted that mathematics had a complementary role in their discipline at the end of the 19th century. In doing so, they 'greatly' modified 'economics and made it more empirical' and 'more statistical' (Spengler and Allen 1960, 493). Although mathematics was 'accepted as a desirable tool' in economics by the New School, 'even those professors who were competent in its use, specifically Allyn A. Young, did not consider it essential in economics' (Carlson 1968, 105). Fellow New School member Henry Walcott Farnam (1853–1933) (1913, 32) also supported the use of mathematics in economics, while cautioning against the extensive application of highly sophisticated mathematical modeling to economics. Similarly, Simon Nelson Patten (1852–1922) (1891, 100) also opposed the widespread use of mathematics in economics. He explained that political economy was 'in many respects fitted to become a substitute for mathematics as a means of cultivating the reasoning powers' (ibid.). That said, Patten (1891, 102) also underlined that 'teaching political economy as a compact whole as mathematics' was a mistake, because many of the problems and issues in economics needed to be investigated separately from mathematics. He insisted that since political economy was an inductive and historical science, it needed to focus on statistics to the fullest extent possible instead of mathematical economics.

After WWI, the Rockefeller Foundation played a crucial role in the rise of mathematical economics in the US. It financed fellowships, university programs, and research in order to present 'Schmoller's inductivism in updated pragmatist American dress' (Craver and Leijonhufvud 1987, 179). Subsequently, after WWII, 'economics refashioned itself as economic science' (Weintraub 2007, 272). At the same time, the Rockefeller Foundation continued to finance projects and research that focused on sophisticated mathematical modeling and statistical economics, which largely centered on the works of 'about fifty of Europe's leading scholars in the field' who moved to the US (Craver and Leijonhufvud 1987, 180–181).

In the early 20th century, Wesley Clair Mitchell (1874–1948) and Irving Fisher (1867–1947) played key roles in the development of statistical techniques and the use of mathematical methods in economics. Both of them were familiar with the works of the GHSE. In fact, Fisher, who was broadly accepted as 'America's first mathematical economist' and 'the greatest economist America has produced,' went to Berlin during 1893–1894 in order to improve his German so that he could read books written by theorists of the GHSE (Tobin 1987). Other key contributors to the development of mathematical economics during the 20th century included Paul Samuelson (1915–2009), Milton Friedman (1912–2006), James Tobin (1918–2002), John Hicks (1904–1989), Kenneth Arrow (1921–2017), Oskar Ryszard Lange (1904–1965), and many others. The contributions of all these prominent scholars led to the extensive incorporation of techniques of the natural sciences into the discipline of economics, especially mathematical formulas (Filip 2020). This increasing importance being attributed to the methods of the natural sciences has meant that studying and conducting research in the discipline of economics required a strong understanding of both econometrics and mathematics. As a result, proficiency with mathematical formulas has become more important than understanding economic issues and realities. Meanwhile, an inability to master mathematical economics has come to be regarded as a sign of weakness and incompetence. In fact, mainstream economists have defended mathematical economics while urging against literary economics. It could even be argued that the language of mathematics has almost replaced spoken and written languages in the teaching, studying, and publication of economics. Unfortunately, supporters of mathematical economics have neglected the fact that everything that happens in the social and economic realms do not have an equivalent mathematical expression or symbol.

The acceptance of economics as a branch of the natural sciences resulted in previous theories, methodologies, procedures, explanations, preoccupations, and goals that were attributed to other economic schools of thought being largely abandoned. In fact, with the rise of mathematical economics, 'doing the history and methodology of economics came to be seen as doing no economics at all' at most American universities (Weintraub 2007, 277). Moreover, economists who continued 'doing history and methodology of economics were generally seen as critics, often hostile critics, of mainstream economics' (ibid.). Consequently, already 'after WWII, economics departments around the world started to significantly reduce the resources and funding allocated for the research and teaching of the history of economic thought' (Filip 2020, 289). Furthermore, neither private foundations nor governments were 'at all interested in intellectual history' of economics (Stigler 1965, V). Meanwhile, mathematical economists managed to obtain 'large funding to finance their research from both the public and private sectors' (Filip 2020, 289).

In the 1970s, 'the history of economic thought began to officially be abandoned as a mandatory class in most graduate economic programs' in the US and elsewhere around the world (Filip 2020, 290). That led to the 'involuntary removal of historians and philosophers of economics from the Economics Department,' to be replaced by mathematical economists (Weintraub 2007, 278). It also became extremely difficult for historians of economics and specialists in the history of economic thought to obtain a 'post at universities or publish their work in leading economics journals' (Filip 2020, 289). In the 1980s, 'anyone with historicist sympathies … would have been barred even from a junior university post in any leading department of economics' (Hodgson 2001, 99). The dominance of mathematical economics has meant that 'page after page of professional economic journals are filled with mathematical formulas leading the reader from sets of more or less plausible but entirely arbitrary assumptions to precisely stated but irrelevant theoretical conclusions' (Leontief 1982, 104). As a result, economists have become largely unfamiliar with the origins or development of their own discipline. In fact, a large majority of economists have come to regard 'the study of the history of economic thought as a mere hobby that is of little practical use' (Filip 2020, 290). Moreover, they believe that 'since mainstream economics is the latest and best program of research, there is no reason to study the history of economic thought or any of the other failed economic programs of research that came before neo-liberalism' (ibid.). Since training in the field of economics no longer required any familiarity with the history of economics and the history of economic thought or fluency in any foreign languages, mainstream economists ended up with a very limited knowledge and understanding of society, social phenomena, and economics in general. According to John Kenneth Galbraith (1908–2006), modern economics departments have been 'graduating a generation of idiot savants, brilliant at esoteric mathematics yet innocent of actual economic life,' in addition to being ignorant about the history of economic thought (Balabkins 1988, 27).

Mathematical economists rely on 'unrealistic assumptions and hypotheses that grossly over-simplify the real world, ignore human content, and do not account for intangible value' (Filip 2020, 313). By making mathematics into the essence of economics, they have come to believe that anything stated in mathematical terms must not only be correct, but also universal. As a result, they have ignored the changing conditions of society, while also becoming disconnected from the realities of social and economic life. They are blinded to the fact that economics deals with highly complex situations formed by social interrelationships between human beings, which cannot be fully understood through mathematical formulas and expressions. To be more precise, mathematical economists have failed to recognize that human decisions and actions are shaped by a multitude of factors, including culture, social solidarity, social responsibility, traditions, religion, and moral and ethical values, 'none of which can be effectively translated into numbers and formulas or interpreted through mathematical modelling' (ibid.).

Given that advanced mathematical modeling is disconnected from the complex realities of life, the extensive representation of the economic world through the methods, presentations, and language of mathematics meant that economists were unable to gain a proper understanding of social and economic phenomena. Consequently, the overreliance on mathematical techniques and formulas that has characterized economics since the Reagan-Thatcher era has given economists a distorted perspective of real economic matters and issues. Contrary to the opinions of neoliberals, the discipline of economics has actually been weakened, not strengthened, by the extensive use of complex mathematical modeling, which ultimately became an end in itself as opposed to a useful tool of analysis. Economics has also been weakened by its adherents neglecting the importance of historical investigation in economics, and ethical values in the choice of human action.

The Demise of Ethical Economics

Neoclassicals and neoliberals accepted economics as a branch of the natural sciences that is free of moral and ethical values. In other words, they considered economics to be an abstract and value-free science, where the behaviors of individuals are mechanistic. The elimination of ethics from political economy facilitated the widespread acceptance of the unrestrained pursuit of self-interests on the part of economic agents as though it was a fundamental and universal principle of human behavior. In the US, the rise of the neoclassical economics led many American economists to believe that economics should not involve moral and ethical norms and standards; rather, it should focus on the individual and his decisions and actions, which are guided by the pursuit of his self-interests. Consequently, mainstream economics has created a generation of economists that do not comprehend or appreciate moral and ethical values, because they consider them to be matters of individual choice and parts of the individual realm, as opposed to issues that concern society or the state (Filip 2020).

Contrary to the view that economics is a value-free science, which was defended by classical, neoclassical, and neoliberal economists, adherents of the New School and the GHSE applied ethical standards to economic relationships and economic institutions. That is to say, they adopted 'an ethical ideal' and encouraged 'people to strive for it' (Ely 1886, 530). The ethical ideal was to achieve 'the most perfect development of all human faculties in each individual' in order to attain common welfare (ibid.: 531). The origins of this ethical ideal can be traced back to the Ancient Greek philosophers. Like them, adherents of the GHSE and the New School wanted to have a society and an economic system where people practiced virtue ethics, which, in turn, contributed to the achievement of common welfare (Ely 1886).

Ethical economics is a departure from individualism. It places society 'above the individual, because the whole is more than any of its parts' (Ely 1886, 532). The application of moral and ethical values to economics would help resist selfish and egoistic temptations. According to adherents of the New School, if temptations were not restricted and simply allowed to be fully realized, then people would enjoy 'intense present pleasures at the expense of future welfare' (Patten 1896, 103). This would not only result in the destruction of common welfare in the present and future, but also in the decline of progress and civilization. In fact, much like the GHSE, adherents of the New School associated the existence of higher moral obligations with superior civilizations and advancement. That is to say, they believed that ethical and moral 'ideals which raise men's thoughts above temptation would become the great social forces' (ibid.: 107). Consequently, integrating ethics into economics would lead people toward higher civilization.

In the last few decades of the 19th century, no economist of repute 'would attempt to ignore the ethical aspects' of economics (Hadley 1896, 23). As such, political economists had to consider the ethical implications of the decisions and actions taken by economic agents. There was almost unanimous agreement among political economists that 'nothing could be economically beneficial which was ethically bad' (ibid.). Consequently, they advocated for moral and ethical values to limit the destructive outcomes of free trade and competitive markets. They also believed that the growing complexity of social and economic life meant that there was a greater need for moral and ethical values. As such, they were hopeful that ethical economics would eliminate the evils of economic decisions in all types of societal organization, particularly capitalist societies.

For most of the 20th century, mainstream economists have persistently argued that economics is a value-free science and advised for economic principles and reasoning to be integrated into every aspect of life. That is to say, they have been encouraging all economic agents to adopt 'self-interested, rational, impersonal, and individualistic behaviors in their daily actions and decisions' (Filip 2020, 261). In essence, these economists became 'ideologues whose principles replaced religion and moral philosophy as the sources of people's core beliefs, views, practices, and values' (Filip 2020, 262). Ultimately, 'the widespread adoption of neo-liberal economic views and values around the world has led to the disengagement of moral and ethical judgements from people's decisions and actions' (ibid.: 262).

Conclusion

Even though the methodological battle between Menger and Schmoller concluded without a decisive victor, it ended up causing significant damage to the reputation of the GHSE. The status and prestige of the GHSE were also seriously downgraded by accusations that its adherents provided the theoretical foundations that led to WWI, the rise of Nazism, and WWII. As such, the GHSE was blamed for many of the devastating outcomes associated with these events, including the destruction and horrors of both wars, the rise of authoritarianism and tyranny, and various economic problems. Subsequently, the important contributions made by the GHSE to the discipline of economics were largely forgotten by neoclassical and neoliberal economists, including its role in establishing political economy as an independent academic discipline, as well as its influence on the development of economic thought and education in the US.

After WWI, American economists, who were once so impressed with the GHSE that they integrated many of its fundamental features into the curricula of their own universities, gradually emancipated themselves from any European influence on their system of education. The GHSE was no longer a school of thought that they looked toward for inspiration. To the contrary, they became critical of the historical method, the collectivist approach, and positive state action, while dismissing the notion of a relationship between ethics and economics. In fact, they actually purged these features of the GHSE from the discipline of economics. However, doing so deprived mainstream economists of important sources of enlightenment, creativity, critical thinking, and social and economic progress.

Contrary to the totalitarian regimes of the 20th century, the GHSE was opposed to dictating the actions of individuals in their private spheres. Since its adherents often argued that universal laws of development did not exist, they did not make any attempts to design the future for individuals based on unrealistic abstract assumptions. In fact, the GHSE represented an alternative to all forms of centralization and authoritarianism, socialist and communist revolutions, as well as the unrestricted and destructive activities of the capitalist system. Its adherents wanted to facilitate the conditions that would provide people with the freedom of self-determination, while simultaneously protecting them from coercion. Accordingly, they supported the limitation of state action, the protection of labor rights, the public ownership or management of strategic industries, and the public provision of various social services and programs. They also accepted the state and all other economic agents as moral and ethical entities that aimed to achieve the common welfare. However, following the demise of the GHSE, ethical economics disappeared from the discipline of economics. More specifically, since the rise of neoliberalism, people have been progressively conditioned to adopt the view that economics should not involve moral and ethical standards, which have been depicted as purely arbitrary and subjective judgments. In recent decades, it has become impossible to hide the fact that economic decisions and actions that are free from ethical and moral judgments have caused enormous damage to societies and the world, including unprecedented social and economic inequality, misery, extreme poverty, unemployment, health problems, pollution, and environmental degradation. Unfortunately, the leading economists who are currently advising governments, international organizations, and institutions on how to address these pressing matters belong to the same school of thought that brought us to this point through its strict commitment to the neoliberal agenda and extensive application of mathematics to economics. In reality, their ignorance of the history of their own discipline, along with their lack of interest in other areas of the social sciences and their outright dismissal of ethical economics, will likely continue to undo more of the human progress that has been achieved since the times of Ancient Greece.

Notes

1 For many years, 'pupils' of the theorists of the ASE, including Menger, von Wieser, and Böhm-Bawerk, were 'excluded from German chairs' (Mitchell 1949, 188). However, this situation changed in the 1920s, as adherents of the ASE, such as Hayek and Mises, as well as some of the disciples of ordo-liberalism, including Wilhelm Röpke (1899–1966), Alfred Müller-Armack, Walter Eucken, and Franz Böhm, played important roles in the discipline of economics, mainly at the universities of Austria and Germany.

2 The emigration of thousands of highly trained German academics who were fleeing Nazi rule after 1933 significantly contributed to the progress and development of almost every single discipline at institutions of higher learning in the US. In fact, this situation played an important role in helping American education and culture attain internationally leading status.

Bibliography

Alter, Max. 1990. 'What Do We Know About Menger.' Ed. Bruce J. Caldwell. *Carl Menger and His Legacy in Economics, Annual Supplement to volume 22, History of Political Economy*. Durham: Duke University Press. 313–348.

Balabkins, Nicholas W. 1988. *Not by Theory Alone . . . : The Economics of Gustav von Schmoller and Its Legacy to America*. Berlin: Duncker und Humblot.

Carlson, Valdemar. 1968. 'The Education of an Economist before the Great Depression: Harvard's Economics Department in the 1920's.' *The American Journal of Economics and Sociology*. Vol. 27, No. 1: 101–112.

Coats, Alfred William. 1985. 'The American Economic Association and the Economics Profession.' *Journal of Economic Literature*. Vol. 23, No. 4: 1697–1727. URL: http://www.jstor.com/stable/2725706Commons, John Rogers. 1963 [1934]. *Myself. The Autobiography of John R. Commons*. Madison: The University of Wisconsin Press.

Craver, Earleen and Axel Leijohnufvud. 1987. 'Economics in America: The Continental Influence.' *History of Political Economy*. Vol. 19, No. 2: 173–182.

Ely, Richard T. 1886. 'Ethics and Economics.' *Science*. Vol. 7, No. 175: 529–533. URL: http://www.jstor.com/stable/1761803

Ely, Richard Theodore. 1918. *The World War and Leadership in a Democracy*. New York: The Macmillan Company.

Ely, Richard T. 1938. *Ground under our Feet*. New York: Macmillan.

Farnam, Henry W. 1913. *The Economic Utilisation of History*. New Haven: Yale University Press.

Filip, Birsen. 2018. 'The German Historical School of Economics and the Foundations and Development of the Austrian School of Economics.' Ed. Robert Leeson. *Hayek: A Collaborative Biography: Part XIII: 'Fascism' and Liberalism in the (Austrian) Classical Tradition*. Cham: Palgrave Macmillan. 79–128.

Filip, Birsen. 2020. *The Rise of Neo-liberalism and the Decline of Freedom*. Cham: Palgrave Macmillan.

Frey, Bruno S. and Rene L. Frey. 1973. 'The Economic Theory of Politics: A Survey of German Contributions.' *Public Choice*. Vol. 16: 81–89.

Giouras, Thanasis. 1995. 'Wilhelm Roscher: The "Historical Method" in the Social Sciences Critical Observations for a Contemporary Evaluation.' *Journal of Economic Studies*. Vol. 22, No. 3/4/5: 106–126.

Gloria-Palermo, Sandye. 1999. *The Evolution of Austrian Economics from Menger to Lachmann*. London: Routledge.

Goldschmidt, Dietrich. 1992. 'Historical Interaction Between Higher Education in Germany and in the United States.' Ed. Ulrich Teichler and Henry Wasser. *German and American Universities: Mutual Influences Past and Present*. Kassel: Wissenschaftliches antrum far Berufs- and Hochschulforschung, ler Gesamthochschule. 12–34.

Hadley, Arthur T. 1886. 'Economic Laws and Methods.' Ed. Henry C. Adams. *Science Economic Discussion*. New York: The Science Company. 92–97.

Hagemann, Harald. 2001. 'The Verein für Sozialpolitik from its foundation (1872) until World War I.' Ed. Augello, Massimo M. and Marco E. L. Guidi. *The Spread of Political Economy and the Professionalisation of Economists: Economic societies in Europe, America and Japan in the nineteenth Century*. London: Routledge. 152–175.

Hansen, Reginald. 2012. 'Gustav Schmoller As a Scientist of Political Economy.' Ed. Jürgen Georg Georg Backhaus. *Handbook of the History of Economic Thought*. New York: Springer. 389–413.

Hayek, Friedrich A. 2006 [1944]. *The Road to Serfdom*. New York: Routledge.

Hayek, Friedrich A. 2007 [1976]. 'Introduction.' Ed. Carl Menger. *Principles of Economics*. Auburn: Ludwig von Mises Institute. 11–36.

Herbst, Jurgen. 1965. *The German Historical School in American Scholarship: A Study in the Transfer of Culture*. New York: Cornell University Press.

Hodgson, Geoffrey M. 2001. *How Economics Forgot History: The Problem of Historical Specificity in Social Science*. New York: Routledge.

Ingram, John Kells. 1915 [1888]. *A History of Political Economy*. London: A. and C. Black.

Kempski, Jürgen von. 1964. 'Stein, Schmoller, Weber und die Einheit der Sozialwissenschaften.' Ed. N. Kloten et al. *Systeme und Methoden in den Wirtschafts und Sozialwissenschaften*. Tübingen: J. C. B. Mohr. 191–206.

Leontief, Wassily. 1982. 'Academic Economics.' *Science*. Vol. 217: 104–107.

Louzek, Marek. 2011. 'The Battle of Methods in Economics: The Classical Methodenstreit: Menger vs. Schmoller.' *American Journal of Economics and Sociology*. Vol. 70, No. 2: 439–463.

Mitchell, Wesley Clair. 1949. *Lecture Notes on Types of Economic Theory: Vol. II*. New York: Kelley.

Menger, Carl. 1884. *Die Irrthümer des Historismus in der Deutschen Nationalökonomie*. Vienna: Alfred Hölder.

Menger, Carl. 1985 [1883]. *Investigations into the Method of the Social Sciences*. New York: New York University Press.

Menger, Carl. 2007 [1976]. *Principles of Economics*. Auburn: Ludwig von Mises Institute.

Milford, Karl. 1995. 'Roscher's Epistemological and Methodological Position Its Importance for the Methodenstreit.' *Journal of Economic Studies*. Vol. 22, No. 3/4/5: 26–52.

Mises, Ludwig von. 1978. *Notes and Recollections with the Historical Setting of the Austrian School of Economics*. Indianapolis: Liberty Fund.

Nasse, Erwin. 1887. 'The Economic Movement in Germany.' *The Quarterly Journal of Economics*. Vol. 1, No. 4: 498–506. URL: https://www.jstor.org/stable/1879345

Neff, Frank Amandus. 1950. *Economic Doctrines*. New York: McGraw-Hill. https://archive.org/details/economic-doctrines-frank-neff

Papadopoulos, Kosmas and Bradley W. Bateman. 2011. 'Karl Knies and the Prehistory of Neoclassical Economics: Understanding the Importance of "Die Nationaloekonomische Lehre vom Werth" (1855).' *Journal of the History of Economic Thought*. Vol. 33, No. 1: 19–35. doi:10.1017/S105383721000061

Patten, Simon Nelson. 1891. 'The Educational Value of Political Economy.' *Publications of the American Economic Association*. Vol. V, No. 6: 100–115.

Patten, Simon N. 1896. 'The Theory of Social Forces.' *The Annals of the American Academy of Political and Social Science*. Vol. 7: 1–151. Stable URL: https://www.jstor.org/stable/1009418

Peukert, Helge. 2001. 'The Schmoller Renaissance.' *History of Political Economy*. Vol. 33. No. 1: 71–116. Duke University Press.

Pribram, Karl. 1983. *A History of Economic Reasoning*. Baltimore: The Johns Hopkins University Press.

Richter, Rudolf. 1996. 'Bridging Old and New Institutional Economics: Gustav Schmoller, the Leader of the Younger German Historical School, Seen with Neoinstitutionalists' Eyes.' *Journal of Institutional and Theoretical Economics*. Vol. 152, No. 4: 567–592. URL: http://www.jstor.org/stable/40751932

Small, Albion W. 1923. 'Some Contributions to The History of Sociology. Section I. Introduction.' *American Journal of Sociology*. Vol. 28, No. 4: 385–418. URL: https://www.jstor.org/stable/2764909

Schmoller, Gustav. 1894 [1881]. 'The Idea of Justice in Political Economy.' *Annals of the American Academy: Political and Social Science*. Vol. 4: 697–737.

Schmoller, Gustav. 2018 [1897]. 'Changing Theories and Fixed Truths in the Field of State and Social Sciences and Contemporary German Political Economy.' *Journal of Contextual Economics*. Vol. 138: 213–232. Berlin: Duncker & Humblot.

Schumpeter, Joseph A. 2006 [1954]. *History of Economic Analysis*. The Taylor & Francis e-Library. ISBN 0–203–98391-2 Master e-book ISBN

Seager, Henry Rogers. 1893. 'Economics at Berlin and Vienna.' *Journal of Political Economy*. Vol. 1, No. 2: 236–262. Economics at Berlin and Vienna: Seager, H. R.: Free Download, Borrow, and Streaming: Internet Archive.

Seligman, Edwin R. A. 1889. 'Reviewed Work(s): Zur Litteraturgeschichte der Staats und Sozialwissenschaften. by Gustav Schmoller.' *Political Science Quarterly*. Vol. 4, No. 3: 543–545. URL: https://www.jstor.org/stable/2139153

Senn, Peter R. 1989. 'What Has Happened to Gustav von Schmoller In English?' *HES Bulletin*. Vol. 11, No. 2: 252–295.

Senn, Peter R. 1995. 'Why had Roscher so much Influence in the USA Compared with the UK.' *Journal of Economic Studies*. Vol. 22. No. 3/4/5: 53–105.

Spengler, Joseph J. and Allen, William Richard. 1960. *Essays in Economic Thought: Aristotle to Marshall*. Chicago: Rand McNally & Company.

St. Marc, Henri. 1892. *Étude sur L'Enseignement de L'Économie Politique dans les Université D'Allemagne et D'Autriche*. Paris: Armand Colin et C.

Stigler, George J. 1965. *Essays in the History of Economics*. Chicago: University of Chicago Press.

Tobin, James. 1987. 'Irving Fisher.' *The New Palgrave: A Dictionary of Economics*. Vol. 2. Ed. John Eatwell, Murray Milgate, and Peter Newman. New York: Stockton Press. 369–376.

Tribe, Keith. 2002. 'Historical Schools of Economics: German and English.' *Keele Economics Research Papers* (KERP). No.02. ISSN 1352–8955.

Veblen, Thornstein. 1898. 'Why Is Economics Not an Evolutionary Science?' *Quarterly Journal of Economics*. Vol. 12, No. 2: 41–69.

Veblen, Thornstein. 1901. 'Gustav Schmoller's Economics.' *The Quarterly Journal of Economics*. Vol. 16, No. 1: 69–93.

Weber, Max. 1975. *Roscher and Knies: The Logical Problems of Historical Economics*. New York: The Free Press.

Weintraub, E. Roy. 2007. 'Economic Science Wars.' *Journal of the History of Economic Thought*. Vol. 29, No. 3: 267–282.

Conclusion

The Demise of the New School and the Abolishment of Freedom and Human Progress via the Coercive Powers of the State and Corporations

In the second half of the 19th century, the German Historical School of Economics (GHSE) became known for raising the standard of education and encouraging advanced scientific research in political economy. This reputation led to students from around the world going to Germany to study under its theorists and obtain a higher education in political economy. At that time, Germany was the main destination of choice for Americans looking to pursue an advanced education, ahead of both the UK and France. After they returned home following the completion of their studies, American disciples of the GHSE, who became known as adherents of the New School, managed to eventually reverse the backward situation that prevailed within the academic discipline and profession of political economy in the US. They did this by essentially importing their experiences at German universities to change the way political economy was being taught and studied in the US in the hopes of advancing economic knowledge, critical thinking and creativity, and encouraging the production of original research. More tangibly, these German-trained Americans helped establish the first dedicated political economy departments, graduate programs, and chairs at American universities and colleges. In doing so, they integrated many of the features from the curriculums of the German universities they attended into those of the political economy departments that they contributed to founding in the US. They also opened new libraries and improved upon existing ones based on the German model. Furthermore, adherents of the New School created prominent economic associations and journals, many of which remain influential up to this day. By implementing such changes, the New School revolutionized the content and improved the quality of education being offered at the political economy departments of universities in the US. Subsequently, their efforts contributed to American political economy departments gaining international respect and recognition in the first decade of the 20th century.

Like the GHSE, adherents of the New School opposed the laissez-faire system, because they believed that unrestricted economic actions would produce great evils. They were also against methodological individualism, arguing that the pursuit of individual interests was too powerful, destructive, and unethical to promote the common welfare. These views contradicted those held by classical economists, who believed that all gains in the wealth and progress of civilizations were outcomes of the pursuit of individual interests in a laissez-faire system. Instead, adherents of the New School argued that the progress of society was a result of ethical economics, which contrasted with the classical economist argument that economics is a value-free science. These German-trained Americans maintained that ethical standards regulated the actions of individuals, private businesses, and governments, so that they would be united in terms of achieving the common welfare, which is directly correlated with the progress of society. They also claimed that societal progress, which is mainly based on the self-development of individuals, eventually led to social and economic relationships becoming more complex, which required a greater reliance on ethical values and positive state actions in order to achieve common welfare. The New School was of the view that the state could contribute to the attainment of common welfare by implementing ethical state reforms and regulations, providing various social services and programs, including health care and education, and engaging in the public ownership and management of natural monopolies like railways, gas, electricity, water, telephone services, and bridges. Additionally, adherents of the New School advocated for protective labor laws and measures, which included setting limits on excessive work hours, prohibiting child workers, improving wage rates, strengthening factory safety regulations, and implementing compulsory state insurance against accidents, sickness, old age, and unemployment.

From the last quarter of the 19th century until the outbreak of WWI, the GHSE was the main inspiration that motivated adherents of the New School to revolutionize the discipline and profession of economics in the US. In fact, it could be argued that theorists from the GHSE and the New School made more contributions to the development of economics than any other economic school of thought that preceded or followed them, as they radically transformed their discipline by broadening the horizons, ideas, methods, and knowledge of political economists. Adherents of both schools also published a number of unparalleled masterpieces in their areas. Nevertheless, the GHSE and the New School are rarely mentioned in standard university textbooks or books discussing the history of economic thought, and their contributions to the development of economics have been largely neglected and obscured in modern times.

The prestigious status held by the GHSE, both domestically and internationally, was irreparably damaged by the Battle of Methods (*Methodenstreit*) between Gustav von Schmoller (1838–1917) and Carl Menger (1840–1921) as well as accusations that its principles and ideas significantly contributed to the outbreaks of both world wars and the rise of nationalist socialism in Germany. Following WWI, American economists, who were once deeply influenced by the GHSE, gradually distanced themselves from this school of thought. Subsequently, the important contributions of the GHSE to the discipline of economics were largely forgotten in the aftermath of WWII, both in the US and around the world. It is also very likely that the influence of the GHSE was short-lived in the US on account of fundamental differences between American and German societies.

Many of the factors that significantly affected the social, political, and economic thoughts of the German people had little to no effect in America, including a shared common history, the inequalities of aristocratic society, a lack of rich natural resources and poor soil quality, a relatively high population density, customs, and religion. In particular, the history of the German people, including those that inhabited the region before it became a country, includes many violent wars and conflicts that brought destruction, misery, and extreme poverty. Given this history of volatility in security that constantly threatened the basic needs of people, it is not surprising that the GHSE defended positive state actions over the laissez-faire doctrine, realistic economics over abstract economics, and common interests over individual self-interests. All these factors played important roles in the development of cameralism, the philosophy of German idealism, socialist ideology, and the historical school of jurisprudence, all of which contributed, in varying degrees, to the emergence and success of the GHSE.

Contrary to Germany, the existence of America was never seriously threatened by an external adversary during its relatively short history, due in large part to the fact that it was separated from its enemies by two oceans. The US was also not subjected to the ambitions of kings and princes or the pious worship of religious beliefs, which caused so many wars across the history of Europe. As a result, Americans were not 'bound down by the necessities of the military rule' to the same extent as their German counterparts (Patten 2003, 7). Given that the US did not endure centuries of devastating and violent wars and conflicts on its territories, which spared its population from the destruction, misery, and extreme poverty that they bring, it is understandable that Americans are inclined to defend the laissez-faire system and object to positive states actions designed to achieve common welfare.

Unlike in Germany, 'the aristocratic element' was 'always feeble' in America 'since its birth,' which prevented it having any real influence 'in the course of public affairs' (Tocqueville 2010V1, 119). Thus, while Germans were divided based on their inherited social status under an aristocratic society for centuries, Americans were similar and equal; they did not have hereditary privilege, wealth, or social status like in 'a caste system' or 'the feudal system' (Farnam 1913, 78). It follows that Americans did not have a 'habit and custom that force in keeping the people in their old lines of occupation' (Patten 2003, 7). All of these factors meant that Americans did not experience the extreme social and economic inequalities associated with aristocratic societies and class struggles, as 'there were neither large fortunes, nor abject poverty' (Bryce 1887, 9). Accordingly, they did not demand positive state actions in order to reduce pervasive social and economic inequalities. In fact, they were of the view that the 'government is best which attempts least' (Seager 1910, 4). In other words, the lack of extreme social and economic inequalities associated with aristocratic societies was another reason why Americans objected to positive state actions in favor of the laissez-faire system.

In older civilizations, history occupied a central place in people's lives, with the chain of history being particularly highly valued. For example, each generation in Germany typically had a great deal of knowledge about and respect for their ancestors and family heritage. The reverence that Germans had for their history is apparent in the emphasis that they placed on great events, illustrious personages, heroic narratives, and warriors. Meanwhile, it could be said that democratic America 'breaks the chain and sets each link apart' (Tocqueville 2010V3, 93). History held little importance in 'a new country' like the US, which was dominated by a love for the present and a distaste for the past (Walker 1889, 19). In fact, Americans barely cared about their own ancestors, let alone 'what happened in Rome and in Athens' (Tocqueville 2010V3, 75). This was to be expected, as 'the inhabitants arrived but yesterday on the soil they occupy. They scarcely know each other, and each one is unaware of the history of his closest neighbor' (Tocqueville 2010V1, 118). Given the lack of importance attributed to history in the US, it is not surprising that historical economics and the history of economic thought were eliminated as requirements for obtaining a higher degree in the discipline of economics when neoclassical economics and later neoliberalism became the leading school of economic thought in the 20th century.

Originally, inhabitants of the US were 'practically all of foreign' to and isolated from each other (Seager 1910, 3). They expected nothing from their countrymen, as they were 'always accustomed to consider themselves in isolation' in the pursuit of their individual goals (Tocqueville 2010V3, 93). That is to say, they wanted to be 'let alone in their quest for prosperity' (Seligman 1910, 38). The availability of vast natural resources, including abundant fertile land and highly productive mines, meant that Americans had 'the freest social and commercial movement' when it came to advancing their wealth and interests (Walker 1889, 19). In essence, the diverse and plentiful supply of land and natural resources provided them with 'unrivaled opportunities for individual achievement,' while blinding them to the need for 'common interests' (Seager 1910, 3). That is to say, Americans were not tied together by a common interest; rather, they were united in their commitment to the pursuit of their individual self-interests in the present (Tocqueville 2010V3, 11). In fact, at the end of the 19th century, Richard Theodore Ely (1854–1943) (1899, 167) stated that 'even up to the present day, we, in the United States, are accustomed to regard projects and measures simply from the standpoint of the immediate interests of a few' as opposed to the common interests of the society (Ely 1899, 167).

The availability of rich natural resources, and a lifestyle that was unencumbered by customs, traditions, hereditary titles, or political limitations, played significant roles in keeping Americans 'crude and selfish' (Patten 1889, 33). In other words, individualism was 'a natural result of the economic,' historical, geographic, and 'the climatic' conditions in the US (Seligman 1910, 39). Furthermore, 'the twenty-seven odd million immigrants who have come to this country since it was discovered by Europeans have thus left a strong individualistic impress on their descendants' (Seager 1910, 3). With that in mind, Henry Rogers Seager (1870–1830, 1910, 3) stated:

> As though it were not enough that heredity and environment combined to make us individualists, our forefathers wrote their individualistic creed into our federal and state constitutions ... As interpreted by the courts, a significance has been given to these constitutional rights that has seemed at times to make a fetish of the merely formal freedom of the individual. Thus it is not too much to say that Americans are born individualists in a country peculiarly favorable to the realization of individual ambitions and under a legal system which discourages and opposes resort to any but individualistic remedies for social evils.

This was really the first time in human history that individualism was integrated into the lives of the entire population of a country (Patten 1889). Since the doctrine of laissez-faire and individualism were integral parts of American society, it should come as little surprise that the variants of classical economics have been so successful in the US.

In the US, the 'business spirit,' which was guided by the pursuit of individual self-interests, was applied to every aspect of life (Tocqueville 2010V3, 57). This should have been expected, as 'business is actually held in greater honor here than else where,' because Americans were blind to 'its defects' and evil outcomes (Clark 1886, 163). This high level of importance attributed to the business spirit meant that Americans devoted little time to leisure, education, enlightenment, establishing close relationships with one another, and formulating new opinions and ideas (Tocqueville 2010V3). As a result, 'literary men (other than journalists) were rare, the universities few and unimportant, science scarcely pursued, philosophy absorbed in theology and theology dryly dogmatic' (Bryce 1887, 9). The love that Americans had for business, combined with their disregard for intellectual activities, was evident in the development of many aspects of their lives (Tocqueville 2010V3, 63). For example, business terminology invaded their vocabularies and displaced the language that originated from philosophical or literary sources, like Greek or Latin (Tocqueville 2010V3, 359–360). Given that Americans did not particularly care about learning other languages, it should not be surprising that economists did not object to the elimination of the German language as a requirement for obtaining a degree at US universities in the 20th century. At that time, the 'only new language that American economists' needed to learn aside from English was mathematics (Balabkins 1988, 111). Unfortunately, this 'deplorable linguistic deficiency among American economists' for most of the 20th century has hindered their 'ability to learn' from the brilliant theorists of the GHSE (Balabkins 1988, 107).

Americans preferred to develop their own language by relying on 'generic terms and abstract words' that avoided details and complex knowledge (Tocqueville 2010V3, 61, 64). That is to say, they liked 'general ideas, because they exempt them from studying particular cases' (Tocqueville 2010V3, 20). However, while generalizations allow 'the human mind to make rapid judgements about a great number of matters,' in the end, 'they never provide it with anything other than incomplete notions' (Tocqueville 2010V3, 17). For instance, 'after an inattentive and short examination,' American researchers would often come to believe that they noticed 'among certain matters a common relationship,' which would lead them to push 'their research no further, and, without examining in detail how these diverse matters are similar or different,' they would rush to 'arrange them according to the same formula, in order to move on' (Tocqueville 2010V3, 20). Given that Americans were prone to treating their singular cases or situations as though they were universal (or general) laws and principles, it makes sense that the abstract deductive approach of classical economics was embraced in the US. In other words, individuals in the US believed that 'all the truths that are applicable to himself seem to him to apply equally or in the same way to each one of his fellow citizens and of his fellow men' (Tocqueville 2010V3, 18). Furthermore, the fact that deduction was an essential feature of the way that people thought in the US, it also makes sense that the inductive approach of the GHSE was short-lived among American economists.

Ethical economics was another feature of the GHSE that was short-lived among American economists. Like the GHSE, the New School had realistic views about society, the nature of human beings, and the reasons behind their actions, which led them to believe that ethical state actions were needed in order to achieve common welfare. They did not regard the state as a violator of freedom; rather, they believed that ethical state action could be used to effectively promote and safeguard freedom. In fact, adherents of the GHSE and the New School thought that ethical state actions and ethical public institutions were indispensable to achieving the conditions of freedom. At the same time, they were fully conscious of the dangers that unrestricted state actions posed to freedom. In particular, they acknowledged that an oppressive authoritarian state cannot provide shelter for freedom, which is a necessary condition for the achievement of common welfare.

Freedom was 'strongly cherished and very precious' for adherents of the New School (Ely 1910, 69). In fact, they believed that freedom is 'the foundation stone of all human progress' (James 1918, 3). Therefore, the progress of society and humanity are measured by 'the growth in freedom' (Ely 1902, 63). The specific conceptions of freedom defended by the New School included: negative freedom (freedom from) or freedom from coercion; positive freedom (freedom to) or freedom of self-determination; economic freedom; and civil liberties (e.g., the freedom of assembly, expression, the press, speech, thought, and religion, as well as the right to security and liberty, the right to equal treatment under the law, the right to own property, the right to bodily autonomy, etc.).

According to theorists of the New School, based on the concept of negative freedom, nobody should be deprived of freedom by being coerced into obeying a person or an entity with authority, including the state, individuals, and corporations, without their consent (Commons 1918). Furthermore, nobody should be coerced into providing consent, because they lack power or are not provided with a reasonable choice. Meanwhile, positive freedom requires the highest self-development of individuality. It basically refers to developing the capacities and faculties of individuals to the highest level possible. Positive freedom also means having 'a positive power or capacity of doing or enjoying something worth doing or enjoying' (Ely 1902, 63). German-trained American political economists were impressed by the opportunities that were afforded to Germans when it came to achieving their highest self-development, as they felt that 'there was room for growth and encouragement of the development of individuality, which was something new' to them (Ely 1910, 69). They had especially high praise for the fact that the German government exercised its power to 'secure to each individual the highest development of all his faculties' (Ely 1910, 50, Haney 1915, 517).

Like the GHSE, members of the New School believed that the achievement of self-development would be supported by a state that provides the public with education and training, safeguards public health and safety, and improves working conditions and labor rights (James 1918). According to them, individuals do not only benefit themselves when they use all available opportunities to achieve their highest self-development, they also benefit society as a whole. Theorists of the New School also maintained that it would not be possible to achieve positive freedom without economic freedom, which refers to the right to earn one's living and the ability to freely spend, invest, and save one's earnings with the greatest possible number of opportunities in the marketplace.

Adherents of the New School believed that freedom could only be fully realized when people are free to pursue their inclinations and goals based on their own free wills and ideas. However, they also thought that freedom required legal restraints if social progress was to be achieved, while also avoiding social dissolution. That is to say, according to the New School, the law was required in order to protect people from the oppressive and coercive powers of the state, corporations, and other individuals. They were aware that without a legal framework to ensure the conditions of freedom, the wills of poor and weak people would be subjugated to the wills of their wealthy and strong counterparts. They also realized that in societies where self-interest maximization, individualism, and the laissez-faire doctrine are highly valued, influential individuals, elite groups, and the business classes could acquire large-scale authoritative power and use it to control the social, economic, and political lives of the majority of citizens. In this case, only those with the authoritative power could enjoy freedom at the expense of the freedom of the masses.

According to Henry Carter Adams (1851–1921) (1887, 393), Americans 'deceive themselves in assuming to think their liberties are endangered only by the encroachments of government.' In fact, Adams and other adherents of the New School believed that the greatest threat to the freedom of the masses came from the growing power to control and coerce that was being accumulated by the corporate world under the laissez-faire system. For instance, Ely (1899, 262) stated that 'the most serious menace to freedom at the present time comes from private monopoly which invades even our churches and institutions of learning.' Meanwhile, David Kinley (1861–1944) (1914, 5) explained that competition degenerated from 'a struggle between equals to an exploitation of the weak by the strong,' whereby industry was 'swallowed up by industry until in many lines' only a monopoly existed, to the point 'that prices, wages, terms of employment, and the welfare of large numbers of people, are in the control' of a few large corporations. He was particularly concerned that corporations had been given 'the attributes of a natural person, without imposing upon it the consequences of personal responsibility' (Kinley 1914, 6).

Adams (1887, 532) was concerned that the rise of corporate power menaced 'the stability of society, by controlling in their favor legislation' (Adams 1887, 532). That is to say, the laissez-faire system turned the government into a 'weak and inefficient' entity that became obedient to the dictates of powerful corporations (Adams 1887, 502). He explained that:

> a weak government placed in the midst of a society controlled by the commercial spirit will quickly become a corrupt government; this in its turn reacts upon commercial society by encouraging private corporations to adopt bold measures for gaining control of government machinery.
> (ibid.)

According to Adams (ibid.: 475–476), the goal of political economy should not be to deliberately make the government 'weaker, or more corrupt and more inefficient, by continuing to preach the illogical doctrine of laissez-faire.' Adherents of the New School advocated for measures that effectively restrained the activities of corporations and ensured the conditions that would facilitate the achievement of the highest development of individuality. They believed that failure to do so would lead to the tyranny of corporations destroying freedom and undoing all of the progress achieved by humanity.

The concept of freedom that characterizes most progressive societies is actually the product of contributions made by countless thinkers across history. Those thinkers realized that over the course of human history, 'the world has passed through many stages of civilization, and each of them has a lesson for the present' (Kinley 1893, 31). They believed that since similar ideas, methods, and systems have appeared and reappeared under different conditions, people needed to be very vigilant when it came to preventing states, elite groups, and business classes from acquiring coercive powers that would allow them to engage in large-scale central and authoritarian planning that might lead to the decay and demise of civilization. Contributors to the development of the concept of freedom were cognizant that anyone with coercive powers would end up abolishing freedom, destroying human progress, and bringing misery to the masses, even if their true intention was to achieve noble ends. To the contrary, when the coercive powers of states, elite groups, and business classes are effectively obstructed, civilization can reach 'its highest development' and 'the irresistible power of public opinion' can be 'governed by the ideas of the universal brotherhood of man and of democratic equality' (Roscher 1878V1, 223). Unfortunately, recent years have demonstrated that despite historical evidence and the many warnings of countless thinkers since the times of Ancient Greece, the masses were poorly equipped and disarmed when it came to dealing with the coercive powers of the state and large and powerful corporations.

Bibliography

Adams, Henry Carter. 1887. *Public Debts: An Essay in the Science of Finance*. New York: Appleton.

Balabkins, Nicholas W. 1988. *Not by Theory Alone . . . : The Economics of Gustav von Schmoller and Its Legacy to America*. Berlin: Duncker und Humblot.

Bryce, James. 1887. *The Predictions of Hamilton and De Tocqueville*. Baltimore: Johns Hopkins University.

Clark, John Bates. 1886. *The Philosophy of Wealth: Economic Principles Newly Formulated*. Boston: Gin & Company.

Commons, John R. 1918. 'Economic Reconstruction: Foreign and Domestic Investments: Annual Address of the President.' *The American Economic Review*. Vol. 8, No. 1: 5–17. URL: https://www.jstor.org/stable/1814627

Ely, Richard T. 1895. *The Strength and Weakness of Socialism*. Cleveland: Chautauqua Press.

Ely, Richard T. 1902. 'Industrial Liberty.' *Publications of the American Economic Association*. Vol. 3, No. 1: 59–79. URL: https://www.jstor.org/stable/2485757

Ely Richard T. 1910. 'The American Economic Association 1885–1909.' *American Economic Association Quarterly, 3rd Series*. Vol. 11, No. 1: 47–111. URL: https://www.jstor.org/stable/3000023

Farnam, Henry W. 1913. *The Economic Utilisation of History*. New Haven: Yale University Press.

Haney, Lewis T. 1915. *History of Economic Thought*. New York: The Macmillan Company.

James, Edmund Janes. 1918. 'What the United States Has Achieved in War Activities and Moral Leadership.' *University of Illinois Bulletin*. https://hdl.handle.net/2027/loc.ark:/13960/t2r50352b

Kinley, David. 1893. *The Ethical Basis of Labor Legislation*. Boston: Christian Social Union. https://babel.hathitrust.org/cgi/pt?id=uiug.30112062843617&view=1up&seq=7&skin=2021

Kinley, David. 1914. 'The Renewed Extension off Government Control of Economic Life: Annual Address of the President.' *The American Economic Review*. Vol. 4, No. 1: 3–17. URL: https://www.jstor.org/stable/1827701

Patten, Simon Nelson. 1889. 'President Walker's Theory of Distribution.' *The Quarterly Journal of Economics*. Vol. 4, No. 1: 34–49. URL: https://www.jstor.org/stable/188300.

Patten, Simon Nelson. 2003 [1890]. *The Economic Basis of Protection.* Kitchener: Batoche Books.

Roscher, William. 1878V1 [1843]. *Principles of Political Economy Vol. 1.* 13th Ed. New York: Henry Holt & CO.

Seager, Henry Rogers. 1910. *Social Insurance, a Program of Social Reform.* New York: The Macmillan Company. https://hdl.handle.net/2027/coo1.ark:/13960/t4cn7pr71

Seligman, Edwin R. A. 1910. *Principles of Economics: With Special Reference to American Conditions.* New York: Longmans, Green, and Co.

Tocqueville, Alexis de. 2010 [1835]. *Democracy in America: Historical-Critical Edition, Vol. 1.* Indianapolis: Liberty Fund.

Tocqueville, Alexis de. 2010 [1835]. *Democracy in America: Historical-Critical Edition, Vol. 3.* Indianapolis: Liberty Fund.

Walker, Francis A. 1889B. 'Recent Progress of Political Economy in the United States.' *Publications of the American Economic Association.* Vol. 4, No. 4: 17–40. URL: https://www.jstor.org/stable/2485572

Index